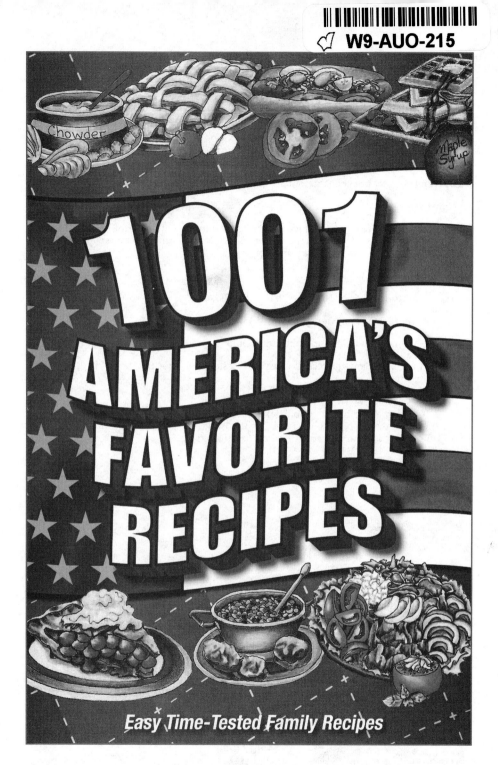

1001

AMERICA'S

FAVORITE

RECIPES

Easy Time-Tested Family Recipes

Cookbook Resources, LLC
Highland Village, Texas

1001 America's Favorite Recipes
Easy Time-Tested Family Recipes

Printed April 2011

International Standard Book Number: 978-1-59769-075-1

Library of Congress Control Number: 2010053574

Library of Congress Cataloging-in-Publication Data:

    1001 America's favorite recipes : easy time-tested family recipes.
      p. cm.
    Includes bibliographical references and index.
    ISBN 978-1-59769-075-1
    1. Cooking, American. 2. Cookbooks. I. Cookbook Resources, LLC. II. Title:
America's favorite recipes. III. Title: One thousand one America's favorite recipes. IV.
Title: One thousand and one America's favorite recipes.
    TX715.A11435 2011
    641.5973--dc22

                    2010053574

Cover by Razer Designs

Illustrations by Nancy Griffith and Nancy Bohanan

Edited, Designed, Published and Manufactured in the United States of America by
Cookbook Resources, LLC
541 Doubletree Drive
Highland Village, Texas 75077

Toll free 866-229-2665

www.cookbookresources.com

cookbook
resources LLC
Bringing Family and Friends to the Table

1001 America's Favorite Recipes

For many of us these recipes bring back great family memories now and in our past. Some of our best memories start in the kitchen.

The importance of family meals cannot be underestimated. The simple ritual of sitting down at the kitchen table and having a meal with moms and dads, brothers and sisters strengthens our homes and our country.

In 1994 Lou Harris stated in a *Reader's Digest* national poll that high school seniors who ate with their families scored higher on tests than those who didn't have family meals. They also appeared to be happier with themselves and their prospects for the future.

Harvard University's "Archives of Family Medicine" in March 2000 reported that families who ate together each week or almost every night got more nutrients and vitamins than those who did not eat with their families. Children got more calcium, iron, fiber, vitamin B6, vitamin C, vitamin E and ate less fat.

The University of Minnesota reported in their "The Archives of Pediatrics and Adolescent Medicine" in August 2004 that frequent family meals are directly related to better nutrition and to decreased risk of obesity and substance abuse.

When you have meals at home, you can teach children about good nutrition and social skills while helping create a home that feels nurturing and secure.

The meals don't have to be time-consuming; they can be very simple. The benefits from eating at home are amazing.

We hope this cookbook helps you have simple meals and brings your family and friends to the table.

There are nine regional cuisines that are distinctively different in the United States. They are Southern, Tex-Mex, Southwest, Cajun-Creole, Pacific Rim, Midwest, New England, Pennsylvania Dutch and Floribbean.

Contents

Appetizers and Snacks

Original Buffalo Wings

*In 1964 the Anchor Bar in Buffalo, New York created buffalo wings
and, in 2003, was awarded the James Beard Foundation America's
Classics Award for restaurants that reflect the history and
character of the community. This is almost like the original recipe.*

4 - 5 pounds chicken wings
4 cups oil
¼ cup (½ stick) butter, melted
5 tablespoons Frank's® RedHot® Buffalo Wings Sauce
1 tablespoon wine vinegar

★ Season with a little salt and freshly ground black pepper. Heat oil
in large saucepan or deep fryer. When oil starts to pop and bubble,
carefully drop wings into hot oil. Cook 3 to 5 minutes or until juices run
clear. Drain on paper towel and stack on platter. Combine butter, sauce
and vinegar and pour over wings. Serves 8 to 10.

Honey Wings

1½ cups flour
¼ cup (½ stick) butter
18 - 20 chicken wings
¾ cup honey
⅔ cup chili sauce

★ Preheat oven to 325°. Combine flour and a little salt in shallow bowl and
dredge chicken in flour. Melt butter in large skillet and brown wings a
few at a time on medium heat. Place in sprayed 9 x 13-inch baking pan.

★ In small bowl, combine honey and chili sauce, mix well and pour over
each wing. Cover and bake for 45 minutes. Serves 4.

Party Sausages

1 cup ketchup
1 cup plum jelly
1 tablespoon lemon juice
2 tablespoons mustard
2 (5 ounce) packages tiny smoked sausages

★ In saucepan, combine all ingredients except sausages, heat and mix
well. Add sausages and simmer for 10 minutes. Serve with cocktail
toothpicks. Serves 4 to 6.

Pigs in a Blanket

1 (10 count) package wieners
3 (10 count) cans biscuits
Dijon-style mustard

★ Preheat oven to 400°. Cut each wiener into thirds. Flatten each biscuit slightly and spread with mustard. Wrap each wiener piece in biscuit and pinch to seal. Bake for 10 to 12 minutes. Serves 10 to 12.

Variations:

1. Add jalapeno slices and nacho cheese sauce.

2. Add fresh tomatoes, basil and thin mozzarella cheese slices.

3. Add guacamole on top of blankets after cooking.

4. Add cheddar or gorgonzola cheese.

5. Add narrow pickle slices and onion slices.

Crab Bites

This recipe is a scrumptious dish.
Serve as hors d'oeuvres or luncheon sandwich.

1 (7 ounce) can crabmeat
1 cup (2 sticks) butter, softened
1 (5 ounce) jar sharp Old English cheese
½ teaspoon garlic salt or seasoned salt
2 tablespoons mayonnaise
2 dashes Worcestershire sauce
6 English muffins, split

★ Preheat oven to 400°. Combine crab, butter, cheese, seasoning, mayonnaise and Worcestershire sauce into paste in bowl. Spread on muffins. Bake thawed for 10 to 15 minutes or until brown. Each muffin may be cut into 8 bite-size pieces or left whole and frozen. Serves 6 to 8.

Garlic Shrimp

1 clove garlic, minced
⅔ cup chili sauce
½ pound thin bacon strips
1 pound medium shrimp, cooked

★ Add garlic to chili sauce and set aside for several hours. Broil bacon on 1 side only. Cut in half.

★ Dip shrimp in chili sauce and wrap with ½ bacon strip on uncooked side out; fasten with toothpicks. Refrigerate. Just before serving, broil shrimp until bacon is crisp. Serves 6 to 8.

Everyday Fried Clams

1 pint fresh, shelled clams
Canola oil
1 cup club soda or beer
¾ cup flour

★ Cut large clams into 1 to 1½-inch pieces. Heat oil in deep fryer or heavy
pot to 375°. Mix club soda or beer with flour in bowl to make batter.
(Add more liquid if needed to get smooth consistency that will stick
to clams.)

★ Dredge clams through batter and coat well. Carefully drop clams into
hot oil and fry for 2 to 3 minutes. Drain on paper towels and keep warm
in oven at 250° until ready to serve. Serves 3 to 4.

Angels on Horseback

12 slices bacon
1 pint oysters, well drained
Toothpicks
Paprika
Fresh parsley

★ Preheat oven to 350°. Cut bacon into same number of pieces as oysters
and wrap bacon around each oyster. Secure with toothpicks.

★ Sprinkle each oyster with salt, pepper and paprika. Place on rack in
shallow baking pan and bake for 15 to 20 minutes or until brown. Serve
on bed of parsley. Serves 6 to 8.

Oysters-on-the-Half Shell
with Red Wine Vinegar Sauce

6 shallots
¾ cup red wine vinegar
34 - 38 fresh oysters

★ Peel and slice shallots. Place shallots in blender and puree with red wine
vinegar until mixture is smooth. Shuck oysters. (Oysters, covered with
a wet towel, may be kept in the refrigerator for 1 hour, if necessary.)
To serve, spoon about 1 teaspoon sauce over each oyster and serve
immediately. Serves 4.

 Clam Capital of the World   Chincoteague, Virginia

Mussels with White Wine

⅓ cup olive oil
1 tablespoon garlic, minced
2 pounds fresh mussels, scrubbed cleaned
4 tomatoes, chopped
½ cup dry white wine
¼ cup chopped fresh basil

★ Heat oil in large saucepan and saute garlic about 2 minutes. Add mussels, tomatoes, wine and ¼ teaspoon salt. Cover and cook, stirring occasionally, over medium heat for 7 to 8 minutes or until mussels open.

★ Discard mussels that do not open. Serve in 4 large bowls and sprinkle with fresh basil. Serves 4.

Tuna-Stuffed Peppers

6 - 8 large Anaheim chilies or banana peppers
1 (3 ounce) package cream cheese, softened
¼ cup mayonnaise
1 (7 ounce) can white tuna in water, drained
2 tablespoons lemon juice
¼ cup chopped walnuts
Olive oil

★ Slice whole chilies in half, remove seeds, drain and soak in ice water. Beat cream cheese, mayonnaise, tuna, lemon juice and walnuts in bowl and mix well. Rub each chile half with a little oil and stuff each half with cream cheese filling. Serves 6 to 8.

Baked Asparagus Rolls

¾ cup (1 ½ sticks) butter, softened, divided
½ cup gorgonzola cheese, crumbled
14 slices bread, thin-sliced
1 (15 ounce) can asparagus spears
Grated parmesan cheese

★ Preheat oven to 350°. Cream ½ cup butter and gorgonzola cheese in bowl. Remove crusts from bread slices and roll each slice flat with rolling pin. Spread cheese mixture on bread.

★ Drain asparagus on paper towels. Place 1 spear on bread and roll in jellyroll fashion. Place rolls side by side on baking sheet with seam-side down. Melt remaining butter in saucepan and drizzle over rolls.

★ Sprinkle generously with parmesan cheese and bake for 15 to 20 minutes or until crisp and brown. Cut in thirds and serve hot. Serves 8.

TIP: *Make the day before but do not bake. Refrigerate. Wait until baking time before sprinkling remaining butter and parmesan cheese.*

Jalapeno Squares

1 - 2 (4 ounce) cans jalapeno peppers, seeded, chopped
1 (1 pound) package bacon, fried, crumbled
1 (12 ounce) package shredded Mexican 4-cheese blend
1 (4 ounce) can sliced mushroom stems and pieces, drained
10 eggs, well beaten

★ Preheat oven to 325°. Line bottom of sprayed 9 x 13-inch baking dish
   with jalapenos. Sprinkle bacon pieces, cheese and mushrooms in layers.
   Pour beaten eggs over top.

★ Cook for about 25 to 30 minutes or until center is firm. Let stand
   for 15 minutes before slicing. Cut into squares and serve hot.
   Serves 10 to 12.

Stuffed Jalapenos

12 - 15 medium jalapeno chilies with stems
1 (8 ounce) package cream cheese, softened, whipped
¾ cup finely shredded Monterey Jack cheese
1 tablespoon lime juice
1 tablespoon garlic powder

★ Preheat oven to 325°. Cut each jalapeno lengthwise through stem and
   remove ribs and seeds. (Use rubber gloves.)

★ In bowl, combine remaining ingredients and mix well. Fill each
   jalapeno half with cheese mixture. Place on sprayed baking sheet and
   bake for 15 minutes. Cool slightly before serving. Serves 10 to 12.

Variations Before Baking:

1. Wrap ⅓ to ½ slice bacon around jalapeno halves and secure
   with toothpick.

2. Use imitation crab meat mixed with whipped cream cheese instead of
   cheese mixture above.

3. Use 1 large uncooked shrimp chopped and mixed with whipped cream
   cheese seasoned with garlic powder.

4. Use bacon bits mixed with whipped cream cheese and shredded
   Mexican 4-cheese blend.

5. Use cooked sausage mixed with whipped cream cheese or Mexican
   4-cheese blend.

6. Stuff with pimento cheese.

7. Use pecans in any of the combinations above.

8. Try grilling instead of baking.

Grilled Tomato-Basil Flatbread

Extra-virgin olive oil
1 (11 ounce) package flatbread
2 large tomatoes, seeded, diced, drained
1 bunch green onions with tops
¼ cup snipped basil leaves
1 cup shredded mozzarella cheese

★ Spread light coating of olive oil on both sides of flatbread. Spread tomatoes, onions and basil on top of each flatbread. Cover with cheese.

★ Place over low heat on charcoal or gas grill and cook until cheese melts. Break into smaller pieces or serve whole. Serves 4 to 6.

Baked Brie with Roasted Garlic and Sun-Dried Tomatoes

1 large whole head garlic, peeled
Extra-virgin olive oil
1 (12 ounce) round brie cheese
¾ - 1 cup sun-dried tomatoes in oil, drained, chopped
⅓ cup pine nuts
½ cup snipped fresh basil leaves
Crostini

★ Preheat oven to 350°. Cut about ¼ inch from pointed end of garlic head to expose cloves inside. Place cut end up in foil bowl formed around garlic head.

★ Drizzle a little olive oil on top of garlic. Close foil package loosely. Bake for 45 minutes or until cloves of garlic are tender.

★ When garlic cools enough to touch, squeeze garlic out of cloves into small bowl. Stir and spread over round of brie. Arrange tomatoes and pine nuts on top.

★ Bake brie for about 15 minutes or until creamy on the inside. Cover top with foil if it begins to brown too much. Sprinkle top with basil and serve immediately with crostini or crackers. Serves 8 to 12.

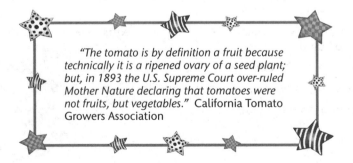

"The tomato is by definition a fruit because technically it is a ripened ovary of a seed plant; but, in 1893 the U.S. Supreme Court over-ruled Mother Nature declaring that tomatoes were not fruits, but vegetables." California Tomato Growers Association

Baked Garlic

2 large heads elephant garlic or 4 - 6 regular heads garlic, peeled
½ cup chicken stock or broth
½ cup white wine
2 tablespoons unsalted butter, melted
Italian bread, sliced

★ Preheat oven to 300°. Cut off top of garlic heads and discard. Place
in small baking dish and pour chicken stock and wine to almost
cover garlic.

★ Pour melted butter into heads and sprinkle with a little salt and pepper.
Bake for 3 hours. Remove garlic, break into cloves and squeeze garlic
from outer skin. Spread on Italian bread and serve with sauce from
baking dish for dipping. Yields 1 cup.

Garlic-Stuffed Mushrooms

1 tablespoon extra-virgin olive oil
2 tablespoons butter
¾ cup Italian breadcrumbs
3 cloves garlic, peeled, minced
¼ teaspoon oregano
Seasoned salt
Cracked black pepper
18 large mushrooms, stems removed

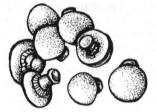

★ Preheat oven to 400°. Heat olive oil and butter in skillet over medium
heat. Add breadcrumbs, stir to coat and cook for about 5 minutes.

★ Add garlic, oregano, seasoned salt and fresh ground black pepper and
saute until garlic is translucent.

★ Stuff each mushroom with breadcrumb mixture and place in sprayed
9 x 13-inch baking pan. Bake for 20 minutes or until mushrooms are
tender. Serve hot or at room temperature. Serves 10 to 12.

Variations Before Baking:

1. Mix ¾ cup breadcrumbs with 1¼ to 1½ shredded parmesan cheese and
a little garlic powder.

2. Mix ¾ cup gorgonzola cheese with ¼ cup whipped cream cheese and stir
in chopped pecans.

3. Cook and drain completely (blot with paper towels) 1 (10 ounce) carton
frozen spinach. Saute with diced mushroom stems, 2 cloves garlic,
minced, and ¼ cup whipped cream cheese.

Easy Baked Mozzarella Sticks

1 (12 ounce) package mozzarella string cheese
1 egg
½ cup Italian-seasoned breadcrumbs
Marinara sauce

★ Preheat oven to 350°. Beat egg until foamy in small bowl. In small skillet, cook breadcrumbs over medium heat until light brown, about 5 minutes.

★ Dip cheese in egg, then coat completely with breadcrumbs. Place on sprayed, foil-lined baking sheet. Lightly spray tops of cheese sticks. Bake for 5 to 6 minutes or until hot. Serve with warmed marinara sauce. Yields 10 to 12.

Cheese Strips

1 loaf thin-sliced bread
1 (8 ounce) package shredded cheddar cheese
6 slices bacon, fried, drained, coarsely broken
½ cup chopped onion
1 cup mayonnaise

★ Preheat oven to 400°. Remove crust from bread. Combine cheese, bacon, onion and mayonnaise and spread mixture on slices. Cut into 3 strips and place on cookie sheet.

★ Bake for 10 minutes. Serves 10 to 12.

TIP: For a special touch, add ⅓ cup slivered almonds, toasted.

Party Cheese Ball

2 (8 ounce) packages cream cheese, softened
2 (8 ounce) packages shredded sharp cheddar cheese
1 tablespoon pimento
1 tablespoon minced onion
2 teaspoon Worcestershire sauce
1 teaspoon lemon juice
Cayenne
Ground pecans

★ Combine cream cheese and cheddar cheese until they blend. Add pimento, onion, Worcestershire, lemon juice, a dash of cayenne and salt and mix well. Shape into ball and refrigerate. Roll in ground pecans and serve.

Cheese Stik

2 cups baking mix
⅔ cup milk
⅔ cup grated sharp cheddar cheese
¼ cup (½ stick) butter, melted

★ Preheat oven to 400°. Mix baking mix, milk and cheese. Drop 1 heaping tablespoon dough for each biscuit onto sprayed baking sheet.

★ Bake for 10 minutes or until slightly brown. While warm, brush tops of biscuits with melted butter. Serve hot.

Fried Cheese Grits Party Bites

1 cup quick-cooking grits
1½ cups shredded extra sharp American cheese
1 egg, slightly beaten
Dash cayenne red pepper
Flour
Shortening

★ Cook grits according to package directions. Remove from burner when done and stir in cheese and egg. Continue to stir until cheese melts. Add a dash of cayenne pepper.

★ Pour grits into large, shallow dish. Grits should not be more than ½ inch thick in dish. When completely cool, refrigerate for several hours or overnight.

★ When ready to serve, slice grits into bite-size pieces. Place in paper bag containing enough flour to coat grits when shaken. Deep fry in hot shortening until golden brown. Drain well and serve immediately. Serves 8.

Southerner's Favorite Crab Dip

2 (8 ounce) packages cream cheese, softened
2 tablespoons milk
1 tablespoon horseradish
2 (6 ounce) cans crabmeat, drained
1 bunch fresh green onions, minced, divided
1 teaspoon garlic salt
⅓ cup slivered almonds, toasted
Wheat crackers

★ Preheat oven to 350°. Beat cream cheese, milk and horseradish in bowl. Fold in crabmeat, half green onions and garlic salt.

★ Pour mixture into shallow 9 x 9-inch baking dish and top with remaining green onions and almonds. Bake for 20 minutes and serve with wheat crackers. Serves 8 to 10.

Quickie Clam Dip

1 (8 ounce) package cream cheese, softened
½ cup sour cream
4 green onions with tops, chopped
2 tablespoons ketchup
1 teaspoon Worcestershire sauce
1 teaspoon seasoned salt
1 (6 ounce) can minced clams

★ Combine all ingredients except clams in bowl. Drain clams, but do not wash. Mix clams into cream cheese mixture. Serves 6.

Creamy Onion Dip

2 (8 ounce) packages cream cheese, softened
3 tablespoons lemon juice
1 (1 ounce) packet dry onion soup mix
1 (8 ounce) carton sour cream

★ Beat cream cheese in mixing bowl until smooth. Blend in lemon juice and onion soup mix.

★ Gradually fold in sour cream until it blends well. Chill. Serve with chips, crackers or fresh vegetables.

Three-Cheese Fondue

¾ pound gruyere, very cold
¾ pound emmental, very cold
½ pound brie, rind removed, very cold
1 cup dry white wine
1 tablespoon cornstarch
1 tablespoon kirsch
Ground nutmeg, optional
1 loaf French bread, cubed

★ Grate gruyere, Emmental and brie. Bring cheeses, wine and cornstarch almost to boil over medium heat and stir constantly. When fondue is smooth and thick, remove from heat.

★ Add kirsch and season to taste with salt, pepper and nutmeg. Pour into fondue pot and keep warm over low heat. Serve with French bread. Serves 6 to 8.

Watermelon Capital of the World   Weatherford, Texas
Hope, Arkansas   Rush Springs, Oklahoma

Easy Cheese Fondue

Adding soup keeps this from getting stringy.

1 cup dry white wine
2 cloves garlic, minced
1 (1 pound) package shredded natural Swiss cheese
¼ cup flour
1 (10 ounce) can cheddar cheese soup
French bread, cubed

★ In fondue pot mix wine and garlic and cook over medium heat until garlic is tender. Cook cheese and melt, stirring constantly. Add flour and condensed soup, continue stirring and cooking until cheese melts and blends with other ingredients. Yields about 4 cups.

Koch Käse

(Quick-Cook Cheese)

6 tablespoons butter
1 (16 ounce) carton cottage cheese
1 tablespoon flour
1 teaspoon baking soda
½ teaspoon caraway seeds

★ Stir butter into cottage cheese in double boiler. Stir in flour and baking soda and cook, while stirring, until ingredients become creamy. Add caraway seeds and stir. Serve warm or cold with crackers or toast points. Serves 4 to 6.

Hot Cheese Dip

Arkansas claims to be the birthplace of the original cheese dip when a man from a Texas border town moved to Arkansas and started serving hot cheese to customers. Cheez Whiz® says they started the original cheese dip and Ro-Tel® added its version with tomatoes and green chilies.

1 onion, finely chopped
¼ cup (½ stick) butter
1 (10 ounce) can diced tomatoes and green chilies
1 (4 ounce) can diced green chilies
1 (2 pound) box Velveeta® cheese
Chips

★ Combine onion and butter in large saucepan. Cook slowly until onion is clear. Add tomatoes and green chilies and green chilies and stir well.

★ Cut cheese in chunks and add to onion-tomato mixture. Heat mixture on low until cheese melts, stirring constantly. Serve hot or at room temperature with chips. Yields 1½ pints.

Hot Chili-Cheese Dip

1½ cups milk
1 (1 pound) box Velveeta® cheese, cubed
2 (4 ounce) cans diced green chilies, drained
1 (15 ounce) can chili without beans
Chips

★ In double boiler or microwave melt cheese in saucepan over medium-high heat. Stir constantly so cheese won't burn on bottom of pan. Remove from heat, add milk, green chilies and chili and mix well. Refrigerate overnight. Before serving, heat so cheese melts and is easy to dip with chips. Yields 2 pints.

Hot Artichoke Dip

1 (14 ounce) can artichoke hearts, drained, chopped
1 cup mayonnaise
1 cup grated parmesan cheese

★ Preheat oven to 350°. Combine all ingredients and place in sprayed 8-inch pie pan. Bake for 25 minutes.

Roasted Garlic Dip

4 - 5 whole garlic cloves with peels
Olive oil
2 (8 ounce) packages cream cheese, softened
¾ cup mayonnaise
1 (7 - 9 ounce) jar sweet roasted red peppers, drained, coarsely chopped
1 bunch fresh green onions with tops, chopped
Chips

★ Preheat oven to 400°. Lightly brush outside of garlic cloves with a little oil and place in shallow baking pan. Heat for about 10 minutes and cool. Press roasted garlic out of cloves.

★ Beat cream cheese and mayonnaise in bowl until creamy. Add roasted garlic, roasted pepper and green onions and mix well. (Roasted peppers are great in this recipe, but if you want it a little spicy, add several drops of hot sauce.) Serve with chips. Yields 3½ cups.

 Artichoke Capital of the World   Castroville, California

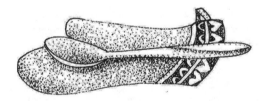

Classic Guacamole

Traditional guacamole is mashed with a fork to get the right chunky texture. It is simple, fresh and unbelievably good.

4 - 5 ripe avocados
1 lemon
1 tomato, peeled, seeded, diced, drained
2 green onions with tops, minced
½ - 1 teaspoon minced garlic

★ Peel, remove seeds and mash avocados in bowl with fork. Squeeze juice of lemon over avocados and mix well.

★ Add tomato, green onions and garlic and mix thoroughly. Serve on bed of lettuce as individual salads or with chips as an appetizer. Yields 1 to 1½ cups.

California Growers' Guacamole

4 - 5 ripe California avocados
4 - 5 cloves garlic, minced
1 cup crumbled gorgonzola or goat cheese
½ cup minced cilantro
¼ cup minced pistachios, toasted
½ teaspoon crushed peppercorns

★ Peel and coarsely mash avocados in bowl, but leave some bite-sized pieces. Add remaining ingredients and serve immediately. Yields about 1 pint.

Easy Cheesy Bean Dip

1 (15 ounce) can refried beans
1 teaspoon minced garlic
1 cup milk
1 (16 ounce) package shredded Mexican Velveeta® cheese
Chips

★ Combine beans, garlic and milk in large saucepan and stir on low heat until smooth. Cut cheese in chunks and add to bean mixture. Stir on low heat until cheese melts. Serve warm with chips. Yields 2 pints.

TIP: Use this dip for soft, bean tacos or burritos. Spread bean dip on flour tortillas, add chopped tomatoes, chopped jalapenos and shredded cheese, roll and pig out.

Research shows that chilies can boost your metabolism rate causing your body to burn calories faster.

Chicken Liver Dip

This recipe was a party favorite in the 1960's.

2 tablespoons butter
1 clove garlic, minced
½ pound chicken livers
3 tablespoons dark rum
1 (8 ounce) cream cheese, softened
¼ cup plain yogurt

★ Melt butter in skillet and sauté garlic until translucent. Add chicken livers and cook through. Remove from heat, drain and cut into pieces.

★ Add chicken livers, garlic, rum, cream cheese, yogurt and a little salt and pepper to blender and process until smooth. Form into ball or loaf and refrigerate before serving. Yields about 1⅓ cups.

Homemade Salsa

3 large tomatoes, peeled, seeded, chopped
3 - 4 fresh green chilies, roasted, seeded, minced
2 cloves garlic, minced
1 jalapeno chile, seeded, minced
1 bunch green onions with tops, minced
1 bunch fresh cilantro, snipped
½ teaspoon cumin

★ Mix all ingredients and a little salt and pepper in large bowl and refrigerate for several hours for flavors to blend. Serve in small bowls with chips or over fish or vegetables.

Salsa Picante

1 bunch green onions with tops, diced
2 cloves garlic, minced
1 - 2 jalapeno peppers, stemmed, seeded, diced*
1 tablespoon corn oil
1 (7 ounce) can diced green chilies
1 teaspoon vinegar
1 (4 ounce) can tomato sauce

★ Cook onions, garlic and jalapenos in oil in skillet until onions are translucent. Remove from heat and add green chilies, vinegar, tomato sauce, a little salt and pepper and serve. Yields 1½ cups.

TIP: Wear rubber gloves when removing seeds from jalapenos.

Green Chile Salsa

1 (15 ounce) can Mexican-stewed tomatoes
2 (4 ounce) cans diced green chilies, drained
½ cup chopped green onion with tops
1 clove garlic, minced
2 tablespoons chopped cilantro
1 fresh serrano chile, minced
1 tablespoon lime juice
1 teaspoon olive oil

★ Drain tomatoes, set aside liquid and chop tomatoes into small pieces.
Combine tomatoes, remaining ingredients plus ½ teaspoon salt and ¼
cup set aside tomato liquid in medium bowl and refrigerate.

Fresh Tomato Salsa

4 medium tomatoes
2 - 4 green onions with tops
1 - 2 jalapeno peppers*
½ cup snipped cilantro leaves
Juice of 1 small lime
1 teaspoon sugar

★ Dice tomatoes and onions in large bowl to save juices. Wash jalapenos,
remove stems and seeds and dry with paper towels. Dice jalapenos and
add to tomatoes.

★ Combine with remaining ingredients and 1 teaspoon salt and refrigerate
for about 15 to 20 minutes. Remove from refrigerator and taste.

★ If tomatoes are too tart, add a little sugar to cut tartness. Refrigerate for
about 30 minutes more to blend flavors and serve. Yields 1½ cups.

TIP: Wear rubber gloves when removing seeds from jalapenos.

Pico de Gallo

*The 1015 SuperSweet Onion or Vidalia® sweet onion is
the star in this terrific salsa. It's great over quesadillas,
fajitas, tacos, black-eyed peas or grilled entrees.*

2 cups diced tomatoes
1½ cups diced Texas 1015 SuperSweet Onions or Vidalia® Sweet Onions
2 cups diced ripe avocado
⅓ cup snipped fresh cilantro

★ Mix all ingredients with ½ teaspoon each of salt and pepper in bowl and
refrigerate for several hours before serving. Serve as an appetizer with
chips or as a side dish. Yields 4½ cups.

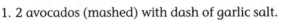

Classic Nachos

36 corn tortilla chips
5 pickled jalapeno peppers, sliced
1 cup diced tomatoes, drained
1 (12 ounce) package shredded sharp cheddar cheese
1 (8 ounce) package shredded Monterey Jack cheese
4 green onions with tops, chopped
Bean dip, optional

★ Preheat oven to 450°. Arrange chips on baking sheet evenly. Sprinkle
   with jalapenos, tomatoes and cheeses. Bake for about 5 minutes or
   until cheese melts. Sprinkle with green onions and serve. Serves 6 to 8.

Fresh Tortilla Chips

1 (12 count) package corn tortillas
Canola oil
Salsa

★ Cut corn tortillas like pizza in pie-shaped triangles. In heavy skillet or
   griddle with hot oil, drop tortilla triangles, turn once and fry until crispy.

★ Remove from oil, drain on paper towel and sprinkle a little salt on top.
   Serve immediately with salsas and dips.

Simple Salmon Spread

3 ounces smoked salmon
1 (3 ounce) package cream cheese, softened
1 lemon
Garlic salt
Seasoned salt

★ Beat salmon, cream cheese and a little lemon juice with seasoning to
   taste in bowl. Serve with crackers. Yields about 1 cup.

Basic Sour Cream Dip

1 (8 ounce) carton sour cream
1 (8 ounce) package cream cheese, softened

★ Beat together until creamy. Mix with one of the following variations.
   Yields 2 cups.

Variations:

1. 2 avocados (mashed) with dash of garlic salt.

2. 1 tomato, chopped; 1 cucumber, peeled and diced; and 1 small onion, diced.

3. 2 to 3 hard-boiled eggs, diced, and cracked black pepper.

4. 3 to 4 slices bacon, crumbled, blue cheese and chopped celery.

Cheesy Pecan Spread

1 (8 ounce) package cream cheese
2 tablespoons milk
1 (2.5 ounce) jar dried beef, shredded
2 tablespoons dried onion flakes
¼ teaspoon garlic powder
¼ cup finely chopped red bell pepper
½ cup sour cream
½ cup chopped pecans
2 tablespoons butter
Crackers or melba toast rounds

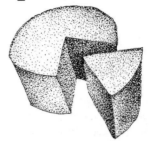

★ Preheat oven to 325°. Combine cream cheese milk in bowl and blend until smooth. Add beef, onion flakes, ¼ teaspoon pepper, garlic powder and bell pepper. Fold in sour cream. Spread mixture in shallow baking dish.

★ Heat pecans with butter in saucepan over low heat. Remove from heat, sprinkle over cheese mixture and bake for 30 minutes. Spread on crackers or melba toast rounds. Yields 2 cups.

Southern Pimento Cheese

Everyone has their favorite variation, but this is a basic pimento cheese. If you want to add minced onions, pickles, jalapenos, cream cheese or other cheeses, go right ahead. It's all good.

1 (1 pound) package shredded sharp cheddar cheese
3 tablespoons mayonnaise
1 (4 ounce) jar diced pimentos, drained well

★ Place cheese in large bowl and add mayonnaise and pimentos (make sure pimentos are well drained). If you want it drier, don't use as much mayonnaise. If you want it creamier, add a little more mayonnaise. Serves 4 for sandwiches.

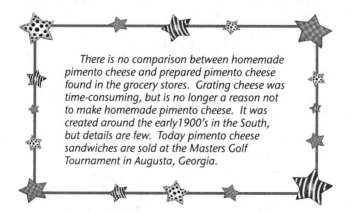

There is no comparison between homemade pimento cheese and prepared pimento cheese found in the grocery stores. Grating cheese was time-consuming, but is no longer a reason not to make homemade pimento cheese. It was created around the early1900's in the South, but details are few. Today pimento cheese sandwiches are sold at the Masters Golf Tournament in Augusta, Georgia.

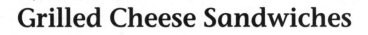

Grilled Cheese Sandwiches

Butter
Bread
American, cheddar or Velveeta® cheese slices

★ Butter 1 side of bread slice and put in hot skillet over medium-high heat. Add cheese over bread and put another bread slice, buttered on 1 side, on top. Cook 2 to 3 minutes for cheese to melt and bread to brown. Flatten sandwich slightly with spatula. If bread slices stick together, turn sandwich with spatula and brown other side. When second side is brown, serve immediately.

Variations:

★ Add some of the following ingredients for a change: ham slice, lunch meat slice, cooked, crispy slices of bacon, thin slices of tomato, jalapenos, thin slices of onion, mozzarella cheese, parmesan cheese, sharp cheddar cheese, Monterey Jack cheese and Swiss cheese.

Po' Boy Orleans

These delicious sandwiches start with fresh French bread, halved horizontally and loaded with just about anything and everything you want to put on them. It was one of the least expensive meals using the least expensive ingredients, hence the name "poor boy".

★ The most popular fillings are roast beef and shrimp. Other fillings include oysters, catfish, chicken breasts, duck, just about everything. Many of the sandwiches are enhanced with gravies and some are "dressed". "Dressed" means accompaniments to meats on the sandwiches including gravy, Creole mustard, ketchup, butter, lettuce, tomatoes, pickles and onions.

★ Other sandwiches made on loaf-style bread are regional specialties known as submarines, grinders, hoagies, heroes, rockets, torpedoes, Dagwoods and Italian sandwiches.

Muffuletta

(muff uh LET uh)

★ Muffulettas are large sandwiches made with provolone cheese, ham, salami and olive salad on round Italian bread and made famous in New Orleans. Family-owned Central Grocery in New Orleans is credited with introducing the muffuletta in the early 1900's. Today having a muffuletta is a true New Orleans experience.

Original 1960's TV Snacks

1 (12 ounce) box Corn Chex®
1 (12 ounce) box Wheat Chex®
1 (12 ounce) box Rice Chex®
2 - 3 cups thin pretzel sticks
2 (12 ounce) cans mixed nuts
2 (12 ounce) cans peanuts
1 - 1¼ cups (2 - 2½ sticks) butter
2 tablespoons seasoned salt
1 tablespoon garlic powder
2 tablespoons hot sauce
2 tablespoons Worcestershire sauce
1 - 2 teaspoons cayenne pepper

★ Preheat oven to 225°. Mix Corn Chex®, Wheat Chex®, Rice Chex®, pretzels, mixed nuts and peanuts in large roasting pan.

★ Melt butter in saucepan and stir in seasoned salt, garlic powder, hot sauce, Worcestershire and cayenne pepper. Pour over cereal mixture and mix well.

★ Bake for about 2 hours, stirring every 30 minutes. Cool and store in airtight containers. Serves 10 to 20.

Club Sandwich

3 slices whole grain bread
Mayonnaise
1 slice sharp cheddar cheese
2 slices bacon, cooked crisp
2 thin slices tomato
4 lettuce leaves
2 thin slices deli chicken or turkey
2 thin slices deli ham
1 slice pepper Jack cheese

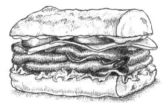

★ Toast bread in toaster or under the broiler. Spread mayonnaise on 1 slice bread and stack 1 slice cheddar cheese, bacon, 1 slice tomato and 2 leaves lettuce. Spread mayonnaise on both sides of second slice of bread and lay it on top of lettuce.

★ Stack chicken breast and remaining tomato slice and lettuce leaves. On last layer stack ham and pepper Jack cheese. Top with remaining slice of bread. Yields 1 sandwich.

TIP: Use 4 hors d'oeuvres picks to hold sandwich together by piercing it in a diamond pattern and then cutting it into four triangles.

Old-Fashioned Popcorn Balls

1 cup sugar
⅓ cup light corn syrup
1 teaspoon vinegar
Green or red food coloring, optional
½ teaspoon vanilla
3 quarts popped popcorn

★ Boil sugar, ½ cup water, corn syrup, ½ teaspoon salt and vinegar until hardball stage. Add desired food coloring and vanilla and stir well. Pour over popcorn. Butter hands lightly and shape into balls. Wrap each in plastic wrap. Yields 10.

Barney's Boiled Peanuts

Usually only true Southerners go for these authentic, traditional boiled peanuts. That's right...boiled.

Raw peanuts

★ Pour enough water into large saucepan to cover peanuts. Add a little salt and boil for about 30 minutes. Taste to see if peanuts are done. They should have consistency of cooked dried bean. Add a little more salt, if needed.

★ If peanuts are not done, keep boiling and taste every 5 to 10 minutes. Drain peanuts and serve hot or chilled. Store in refrigerator.

Beverages

Victorian Iced Tea

4 individual tea bags
¼ cup sugar
1 (11 ounce) can frozen cranberry-raspberry juice concentrate, thawed

★ Place tea bags in teapot and add 4 cups boiling water. Cover and steep for 5 minutes. Remove and discard tea bags. Add sugar and stir until it dissolves. Refrigerate.

★ Just before serving, combine cranberry-raspberry concentrate and 4 cups cold water in 2½-quart pitcher. Stir in tea and serve with ice cubes. Serves 24.

Southerner's Sweet Tea

*In the South you have a choice between sweet tea and
unsweetened tea. As the popularity of sweet tea spreads,
sweet tea is appearing in more places across America.*

4 teaspoons bulk tea or 2 tea bags
1 - 1½ cups sugar
Mint sprigs

★ Boil 4 cups water in pot, add tea and remove from heat. Cover and let
steep for 10 to 15 minutes.

★ Pour 4 cups cold water into pitcher and add sugar. Pour tea through
strainer into pitcher and serve over lots of ice. Garnish with sprig of
mint. Serves 8.

Summertime Iced Tea

1 cup sugar
6 - 8 small tea bags
6 sprigs fresh mint
½ cup orange juice
¼ cup lemon juice

★ Bring 6 cups water to boil in saucepan. Add sugar, tea bags and mint and
steep for 5 minutes. Remove tea bags and mint and let cool. Add orange
and lemon juices and stir well. Refrigerate before serving. Serves 6.

Green Tea Wake-Up

3 cups sparkling ginger ale
¾ cup green tea and honey concentrate
1½ teaspoons honey
4 fresh mint leaves

★ Pour ginger ale, green tea and honey concentrate, honey and mint into
pitcher and mix. Pour over ice and serve cold. Serves 4 to 6.

Weinsaft
(Grape Juice)

5 pounds ripe Concord grapes, washed
1 pound sugar

★ Heat grapes and 1 quart water in large saucepan over medium-high
heat for about 5 minutes; strain through cheesecloth into separate
saucepan.

★ Add half sugar to juice and cook for about 15 minutes. Check sweetness
about halfway through cooking process and add sugar if needed. Fill
bottles and seal. Serves 4 to 6.

Fresh Lemonade

1 cup fresh lemon juice (about 6 - 8 lemons)
1 cup sugar

★ In large pitcher combine lemon juice with 3 cups cold water. Add sugar and stir well. Serve over cracked ice. Store in refrigerator. Serves 2 to 3.

Variations:

1. Use equal parts lemonade and peach nectar.

2. Use twice as much lemonade as 7UP® or ginger ale.

3. Blend about a dozen strawberries, add to lemonade and garnish with strawberry on rim of glass.

Hot Dr Pepper

Cold or hot, it's a Texas favorite.

1 Dr Pepper®
1 slice lemon

★ Pour Dr Pepper® in cup and zap in microwave or heat it in saucepan on stove. Serve piping hot with slice of lemon. Serves 1.

Spiced Mulled Cider

¼ cup packed brown sugar
2 quarts apple cider
1 teaspoon whole allspice
1 teaspoon whole cloves
1 (3 inch) stick cinnamon
Whole nutmeg

★ Mix brown sugar, apple cider and ¼ teaspoon salt in saucepan. Put spices in tea ball or cheesecloth sack and add to cider.

★ Bring to a boil, reduce heat and simmer for about 15 to 20 minutes. Remove spices and serve hot. Serves about 10.

Wassail

English immigrants brought their tradition of toasting to health, wealth and good fortune during the holidays. After toasting, they joined together to sing "Here We Go A-Wassailing" which probably led to our tradition of singing Christmas carols and going from door to door.

4 (1 quart) jars apple cider
4 (6 ounce) cans frozen lemonade concentrate
1 tablespoon ground cloves
4 sticks cinnamon
½ teaspoon ground allspice

★ Heat ingredients in saucepan and boil for 10 to 15 minutes. Serve hot. Serves 32 to 36.

Old-Fashioned Hot Chocolate

½ cup sugar
¼ cup chocolate syrup
4 cups milk
1 teaspoon vanilla

★ Mix sugar and cocoa with ⅓ cup water in saucepan over medium heat until sugar and cocoa dissolve and mixture begins to boil.

★ Add milk, stirring constantly, and simmer until hot. (Do not boil.) Remove from heat, add vanilla and stir briskly with whisk until frothy. Serve immediately. Serves 4.

Instant Cocoa Mix

1 (8 quart) box dry milk powder
1 (12 ounce) jar non-dairy creamer
1 (16 ounce) can instant chocolate-flavored drink mix
1¼ cups powdered sugar

★ Combine all ingredients and store in airtight container. To serve, use ¼ cup cocoa mix for each cup of hot water. Serves 48.

Original Hot Chocolate

1 (6 - 8 ounce) chocolate bar
¼ cup water
3 cups hot milk

★ Melt chocolate bar in double boiler to keep from burning. Stir into hot milk. Serves 2 to 3.

Instant Chai Tea Mix

2½ cups sugar
2 cups powdered non-dairy creamer
1½ cups unsweetened instant tea
1 cup nonfat dry milk powder
2 teaspoons ground cinnamon
2 teaspoons ground ginger
1 teaspoon ground cardamom
1 teaspoon ground cloves
Vanilla

★ Combine all ingredients except vanilla in blender or food processor and process until all ingredients mix evenly. Store in airtight jar.

★ When ready to serve, pour boiling water into mugs and add ½ to 1 teaspoon vanilla plus 2 heaping tablespoons of chai tea mix for each mug. Serve hot. Yields 3 cups of mix.

Praline Coffee

3 cups hot brewed coffee
¾ cup half-and-half cream
¾ cup packed light brown sugar
2 tablespoons butter
¾ cup praline liqueur
1 tablespoon sugar
Whipped cream

★ Cook coffee, half-and-half cream, brown sugar and butter in large saucepan over medium heat, stirring constantly. Do not boil. Stir in liqueur and add sugar to whipped cream and serve. Serves 5 to 6.

Icy Caramel Coffee

1½ cups brewed coffee, room temperature
½ cup milk
½ cup sugar
2 tablespoons caramel syrup
1 teaspoon chocolate syrup
A few drops vanilla

★ Mix coffee, milk sugar, caramel syrup, chocolate syrup, vanilla and a pinch of salt in blender container. Add about 2 to 3 cups ice cubes and blend until creamy. Serves 2 to 3.

Cafe Latte

1 - 2 ounces ground espresso coffee
8 - 10 ounces milk

★ Add 1 to 2 ounces water to espresso machine. Add 1 to 2 ounces of ground espresso coffee into coffee basket. Place cup under spout, turn machine on and wait for machine to force coffee out under pressure.

★ Steam 8 to 10 ounces milk and spray into cup about ¾ full. Pour espresso into steamed milk. Sprinkle nutmeg or cinnamon on top. Serves 1.

Instant Cafe Latte

1 (12 ounce) can evaporated low-fat milk
2 cups strong, hot, freshly brewed coffee
1 tablespoon sugar

★ Pour evaporated milk over coffee in 4-cup measure. Add sugar and microwave on HIGH for 90 seconds. Stir and serve hot or over crushed ice. Serves 2.

Smooth Mocha Mudslide

2 cups cafe mocha liquid coffee creamer
2 tablespoons French roast instant coffee granules
2 cups vanilla ice cream or frozen yogurt

★ Mix creamer and coffee in blender. Add ice cream and about 3 to 4 cups ice and blend until smooth. Serve cold. Serves 3 to 4.

Cappuccino Punch

¼ cup instant coffee granules
¾ cup sugar
3 pints milk
1 (1 pint) carton half-and-half cream
1 quart chocolate ice cream, softened
1 quart vanilla ice cream, softened

★ Combine coffee granules and sugar in bowl and stir in 1 cup boiling water. Cover and refrigerate. When ready to serve, pour chilled coffee mixture into 1-gallon punch bowl.

★ Stir in milk and half-and-half cream. Add scoops of both ice creams and stir until most of ice cream melts. Serves 16 to 22.

Almond-Tea Punch

½ cup lemon juice
1¼ cups sugar
2 tablespoons almond extract
1 tablespoon vanilla
1¼ cups strong tea
1 quart ginger ale, chilled
1 lemon, thinly sliced

★ Combine lemon juice, sugar, almond extract, vanilla and tea in saucepan. Bring to a boil, remove from heat and pour into large pitcher.

★ Add 2 cups chilled water and ginger ale. Serve over crushed ice with lemon slices for garnish. Yields 1½ quarts.

Good Ol' Summertime Punch

1 (3 ounce) package lime gelatin
1 (6 ounce) can frozen limeade, thawed
1 (6 ounce) can frozen lemonade, thawed
1 quart orange juice
1 quart pineapple juice
1 tablespoon almond extract
2 - 3 drops green food coloring
1 liter ginger ale, chilled

★ Dissolve lime gelatin in 1 cup boiling water in bowl and stir well. Combine dissolved gelatin, limeade, lemonade, orange juice, pineapple juice, almond extract and food coloring in large pitcher or 1-gallon bottle and refrigerate.

★ When ready to serve, place juice mixture in punch bowl and add ginger ale. Yields 4 quarts.

Quick Strawberry Punch

2 (10 ounce) boxes frozen strawberries, thawed
2 (6 ounce) cans frozen pink lemonade concentrate
2 (2 liter) bottles ginger ale, chilled

★ Process strawberries through blender. Pour lemonade into punch bowl and stir in strawberries. Add chilled ginger ale and stir well. (It would be nice to make an ice ring out of another bottle of ginger ale.) Serves 24.

Frosty Lime Cooler

1½ pints lime sherbet, divided
1 (6 ounce) can frozen limeade concentrate
3 cups milk
Lime slices

★ Beat 1 pint lime sherbet in bowl and add limeade concentrate and milk.
  Stir until they blend well. Pour into 5 glasses and top each with small
  scoop of lime sherbet. Garnish with lime slices. Serve immediately.
  Serves 5.

Mary Opal's Reception Punch

4 cups sugar
5 ripe bananas, mashed
Juice of 2 lemons
1 (46 ounce) can pineapple juice
1 (6 ounce) can frozen orange juice concentrate
2 quarts ginger ale

★ Boil sugar and 6 cups water in saucepan over low heat for 3 minutes.
  Cool. Combine bananas with lemon juice in bowl and add pineapple
  and orange juice.

★ Combine all ingredients except ginger ale in large container and freeze.
  To serve, thaw for 1 hour 30 minutes, then add ginger ale. Punch will be
  slushy. Serves 32 to 36.

Citrus Grove Punch

3 cups sugar
6 cups orange juice, chilled
6 cups grapefruit juice, chilled
1½ cups lime juice, chilled
1 (1 liter) bottle ginger ale, chilled

★ Bring sugar and 2 cups water in saucepan to a boil and cook for
  5 minutes. Cover and refrigerate until cool.

★ Combine juices and sugar mixture in bowl and mix well. Just before
  serving, stir in ginger ale. Serve over ice. Serves 18 to 22.

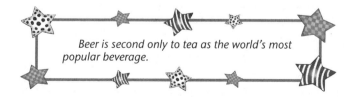

*Beer is second only to tea as the world's most
popular beverage.*

Pink Cranberry Punch

2 (28 ounce) bottles ginger ale
1 (46 ounce) can pineapple juice
1 (1 quart) jar cranberry juice
1 (1 quart) carton pineapple sherbet, softened

★ Refrigerate all ingredients. Mix in punch bowl. Serves 30 to 36.

Lime Punch

2 (2 liter) bottles 7UP®, chilled
1 (2 liter) bottle ginger ale, chilled L
½ gallon lime sherbet

★ Combine 7UP® and ginger ale.

★ When ready to serve, add lime sherbet and stir until it mixes well.

★ Serve in punch cups. Serves about 30.

Betsy Ross Dandelion Wine

Dandelion wine was a traditional May Day and midsummer celebration punch.

1 quart dandelion flower blossoms
2½ pounds sugar
½ yeast cake

★ Boil dandelion blossoms in 1 gallon water for about 10 minutes and set
   aside to cool. Squeeze blossoms into juice and discard.

★ Pour sugar and yeast cake into cooled juice. Let ferment until it stops.
   Strain slowly and pour into jars. Serves 2 to 4.

TIP: *Cut 1 orange and ½ lemon into very thin slices and add to juice with sugar.*
   Remove slices before pouring into jars.

You cannot help the poor by destroying the rich.
You cannot strengthen the weak by weakening
the strong. You cannot bring about prosperity by
discouraging thrift. You cannot lift the wage earner
up by pulling the wage payer down. You cannot further
the brotherhood of man by inciting class hatred. You
cannot build character and courage by taking away
people's initiative and independence. You cannot
help people permanently by doing for them what they
could and should do for themselves.
–Abraham Lincoln

Kentucky Tea

Bourbon (corn whiskey) originated in Bourbon County, Kentucky. The U.S. government recognized it as uniquely American in 1964 and it is now protected by law.

3 tea bags
1¼ cups sugar
1 (6 ounce) can frozen orange juice concentrate
½ (6 ounce) can frozen lemon juice concentrate
¾ cup bourbon

★ Add tea bags to 1½ cups water in saucepan, bring to boil and steep for 5 minutes. Remove tea bags, add 3½ cups water and remaining ingredients and stir until sugar dissolves.

★ Place in freezer for about 30 minutes to 1 hour. Scoop slushy drink into tall glasses and garnish with lemon slices. Serves 6 to 8.

Sangria

1 quart (4 cups) red table wine
1 quart (1 liter) club soda
2 oranges, divided
2 lemons
2 limes
1 cup sugar

★ Combine red wine, club soda, 1 cup water, juice of 1 orange, and juice of lemons and limes in large pitcher and stir well. Cut remaining orange into ¼ inch slices and put several slices into pitcher.

★ Add sugar and crushed ice and stir well. Pour into glasses and put 1 slice orange on rim of each glass before serving.

Creamy Strawberry Punch

1 (10 ounce) package frozen strawberries, thawed
½ gallon strawberry ice cream, softened
2 (2 liter) bottles ginger ale, chilled

★ Process strawberries through blender. Combine strawberries, chunks of ice cream and ginger ale in punch bowl. Stir and serve immediately. Serves 24.

Kentucky Mint Julep

Official drink of the Kentucky Derby

2 cups sugar
¼ cup fresh mint leaves
¼ cup Kentucky bourbon

★ Cook 2 cups water and sugar in saucepan over medium-high heat for several minutes and stir constantly. Remove from heat and drop mint leaves in pan. Cover and steam for 30 minutes. Set aside and cool.

★ Place cracked ice in glasses and pour in Kentucky bourbon and ½ cup sugar-syrup mixture. Stir well and garnish with mint leaves and serve with straw. Serves 4.

Homemade Kahlua

1 cup instant coffee granules
4 cups sugar
1 quart vodka
3 tablespoons Mexican vanilla

★ Combine 3 cups hot water and coffee in large saucepan and mix well. Add sugar and boil for 2 minutes. Turn off heat and cool.

★ Add vodka and vanilla. Pour into bottle or jar and store in refrigerator. Shake occasionally. Yields 2 quarts.

Homemade Amaretto

3 cups sugar
1 pint vodka
3 tablespoons almond extract
1 tablespoon vanilla

★ Combine sugar and 2¼ cups water in large saucepan. Bring mixture to a boil and reduce heat. Simmer for 5 minutes, stirring occasionally and remove from stove.

★ Add vodka, almond extract and vanilla. Stir to mix well. Store in airtight jars. Yields 1½ pints.

An excellent health tip: Throw Something Away That You Haven't Used or Seen in the Past Year.

Easy Frozen Strawberry Margarita

1 (10 ounce) can frozen strawberries
1 (6 ounce) can frozen limeade
1 (6 ounce) can tequila

★ Pour strawberries, limeade, tequila and ice into blender and process until smooth.

★ Add enough ice to fill blender. Pour into margarita glasses. Serves 6.

Create-Your-Own Smoothies

*Here's a basic formula. You choose the ingredients
and make your favorite concoctions.*

Ingredients:	**Choices:**
2 cups liquid:	apple juice, orange juice, milk
½ - 1 cup fresh fruit slices:	peach, apricot, pears, strawberries, raspberries, blueberries
Creamy ingredient:	1 banana
Sweetener:	1 teaspoon honey
Calcium source:	¼ cup yogurt, frozen yogurt
Flavorings:	Vanilla, almond extract, cinnamon, nutmeg

★ Combine selected ingredients in blender and process until smooth. Pour into tall glass with ice or plain. For an icy texture, add ice to the blender while processing. Serves 2.

Banana Split Float Smoothie

2 ripe bananas, mashed
3 cups milk
1 (10 ounce) package frozen sweetened strawberries, thawed
1½ pints chocolate ice cream, divided

★ Place bananas in blender and add milk, strawberries and ½ pint chocolate ice cream. Process just until they blend. Pour into tall, chilled glasses and top each with scoop of chocolate ice cream. Serves 3.

An excellent health tip: Read More Books Than You Did Last Year.

Strawberry Smoothie

2 bananas, peeled, sliced
1 pint fresh strawberries, washed, quartered
1 (8 ounce) container strawberry yogurt
¼ cup orange juice

★ Place all ingredients in blender. Process until smooth. Serves 2.

Chocolate-Banana Smoothie

1 cup milk
1 banana
1 tablespoon chocolate syrup

★ Combine all ingredients in blender and process with crushed ice until slushy. Serves 1.

TIP: For a creamier texture, substitute ice cream or frozen yogurt for milk.

Breakfast and Brunch

Basic Pancakes

2 cups flour
1 tablespoon sugar
1 tablespoon baking powder
2 eggs
1½ - 2 cups milk, divided
Vegetable oil
Maple syrup
½ cup melted butter

★ Combine flour, sugar, baking powder and ¼ teaspoon salt in large mixing bowl. In separate bowl, beat eggs and 1½ cups milk. Pour eggs mixture into flour mixture and stir until smooth. If batter is too thick, add a little milk. There will be a few lumps in batter.

★ Heat griddle and coat lightly with oil. Slowly pour circle of batter on griddle to equal desired size of pancake. After bubbles form on top and edges brown, gently flip pancake to cook other side. Cook and serve immediately with warm syrup and melted butter.

Continued next page...

 Avocado Capital of the World   Fallbrook, California

Continued from previous page...

Blueberry Pancakes:

★ Wash and drain thoroughly about 1 cup fresh or frozen blueberries. (If blueberries are frozen, do not thaw before adding to pancake batter.) Stir into pancake batter gently and pour onto griddle or skillet.

Buttermilk Pancakes:

★ Substitute buttermilk instead of milk. If batter is too thick, add just a little milk. (To make buttermilk, add 1 tablespoon lemon juice or vinegar to 8 ounces milk and let stand for 10 minutes.)

Banana Pancakes:

★ Slice 1 or 2 ripe bananas about ¼-inch thick. When batter is poured onto griddle, place as many slices as desired on batter and lightly push bananas into batter. Cook slowly to make sure inside is firm.

TIP: Other variations include ½ cup diced apples, 1 cup cranberries, ½ cup coconut, 6 slices cooked bacon (crumbled), ½ cup diced ham or 1 cup chopped pecans.

Jumbo German Pancake

½ cup flour
3 eggs, slightly beaten
½ cup milk
2 tablespoons butter, melted
Powdered sugar
Maple syrup

★ Preheat oven to 425°. Beat flour and eggs in bowl. Stir in remaining ingredients and ¼ teaspoon salt. Pour into sprayed 9-inch pie pan. Bake for 20 minutes.

★ Pancake will puff into big bubbles while baking. Cut into wedges and dust with powdered sugar. Serve with melted butter and maple syrup. Serves 3 to 4.

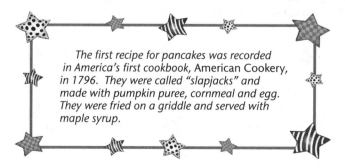

The first recipe for pancakes was recorded in America's first cookbook, American Cookery, in 1796. They were called "slapjacks" and made with pumpkin puree, cornmeal and egg. They were fried on a griddle and served with maple syrup.

Puffy Pancakes

These are a little like a crepe and real fun to bake in the oven.

2 eggs
½ cup milk
½ cup flour
Pinch freshly grated nutmeg
2 tablespoons butter

★ Preheat oven to 400°. Lightly beat eggs in bowl and whisk in milk. Pour in flour, pinch of nutmeg and salt and mix well.

★ Melt butter in cast-iron skillet or oven-proof crepe pan over medium-high heat. Pour batter into skillet and place in oven.

★ Bake for about 8 minutes or until pancake is golden brown and puffy. Remove from oven and serve immediately. Dust with powdered sugar. Serves 2.

Light and Crispy Waffles

2 cups biscuit mix
1 egg
½ cup oil
1⅓ cups club soda

★ Preheat waffle iron. Combine all ingredients in mixing bowl and stir by hand. Pour just enough batter to cover waffle iron, but not run over.

TIP: To have waffles for a "company weekend", make all waffles in advance. Freeze separately on baking sheet and place in large resealable plastic bags. To heat, warm at 350° for about 10 minutes.

Pecan Waffles

2 cups self-rising flour
½ cup oil
½ cup milk
⅔ cup finely chopped pecans

★ Preheat waffle iron. In bowl, combine flour, oil and milk. Beat until they mix well. Stir in chopped pecans. Pour approximately ¾ cup batter into hot waffle iron and bake until brown and crispy.

Vermont produces more maple syrup than any other state in the U.S. All the maple syrup in the world is produced in North America.

Buttermilk Waffles

2 eggs, separated
2 tablespoons oil
2 (1 pint) cups buttermilk
2¼ cups flour
1½ teaspoons baking powder
½ teaspoon baking soda
½ teaspoon salt

★ Beat egg yolks with oil and add buttermilk. Combine dry ingredients and add to buttermilk mixture.

★ In separate bowl beat egg whites until stiff peaks form. Slowly fold into batter. Bake in preheated waffle iron until crispy brown.

Easy Brunch Biscuits

½ cup (1 stick) butter, melted
2 cups self-rising flour
1 (8 ounce) carton sour cream

★ Preheat oven to 350°. Combine all ingredients in bowl and mix well. Spoon in sprayed miniature muffin cups (or cups with paper liners). Bake for 15 minutes or until light brown. Yields 8 biscuits.

TIP: These biscuits are so rich they do not need butter.

Biscuits and Sausage Gravy

*This is about as down-home as you can get and
it is every bit as good as you can imagine.*

3 cups biscuit mix
4 cups milk, divided
½ pound pork sausage
2 tablespoons butter
⅓ cup flour

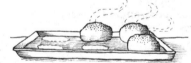

★ Preheat oven to 400°. Combine biscuit mix and ¾ cup milk in bowl and stir. Roll dough on floured wax paper to ¾ inch thickness and cut with biscuit cutter. Place on sprayed baking sheet. Bake for 12 to 15 minutes or until golden.

★ For gravy, brown sausage in skillet, drain and reserve pan drippings in skillet. Set sausage aside. Add butter to drippings and melt. Add flour and cook 1 minute, stirring constantly.

★ Gradually add 3¼ cups milk, cook over medium heat, stirring constantly until mixture thickens. Stir in ½ teaspoon each of salt and pepper and sausage. Cook until heated, stirring constantly. Serve sausage gravy over cooked biscuits. Serves 8.

French Toast

2 eggs
1 cup milk
1 tablespoon sugar
1 teaspoon vanilla or ground cinnamon
1 tablespoon butter
6 - 8 slices white bread
Powdered sugar
Maple syrup

★ Beat eggs, milk, sugar and vanilla or ground cinnamon. Heat griddle until butter melts. Dip both sides of bread into milk-egg mixture. Cook on both sides until brown. Remove from griddle and sprinkle with powdered sugar or maple syrup. Serves 4 to 6.

Crispy French Toast:

★ Crispy French Toast has a crust or coating on outside that makes it crispy. Use ½ cup flour in batter to make crust. Cook until crispy.

Breads:

★ Many kinds of breads may be used for French Toast. Texas toast or challah, about one-inch thick bread, French bread cut in thick slices are just a few of the possibilities.

Orange French Toast

1 egg, beaten
¼ cup orange juice
5 slices raisin bread
1 cup crushed graham crackers
2 tablespoons margarine

★ Combine egg and orange juice. Dip bread in mixture than in crumbs. Brown on buttered griddle until golden brown. Serves 3 to 4.

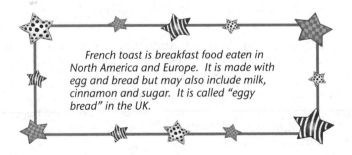

French toast is breakfast food eaten in North America and Europe. It is made with egg and bread but may also include milk, cinnamon and sugar. It is called "eggy bread" in the UK.

Banana-Nut Bread

½ cup (1 stick) butter, softened
1 cup sugar
2 eggs
4 very ripe bananas
1 teaspoon baking soda
1 teaspoon vanilla
2 cups flour
1 cup chopped pecans

★ Preheat oven to 350°.

★ Cream butter and sugar. Stir in eggs and bananas. Dissolve baking soda in 3 tablespoons cold water and add to sugar mixture. Add remaining ingredients and 1 teaspoon salt and mix well.

★ Pour into sprayed 9-inch loaf pan. Bake for 40 to 45 minutes or until toothpick inserted in center comes out clean. Makes 1 loaf.

Strawberry Bread

3 cups flour
1 teaspoon baking soda
1 tablespoon cinnamon
2 cups sugar
4 eggs
1¼ cups oil
2 (10 ounce) packages frozen strawberries
1 cup chopped pecans

★ Preheat oven to 350°.

★ Mix flour, baking soda, cinnamon, sugar and 1 teaspoon salt. Add eggs and oil and mix well. Drain ½ cup juice from thawed strawberries and set aside.

★ Add strawberries and pecans. Mix well. Pour batter into 2 sprayed, floured loaf pans and bake 1 hour. Makes 2 loaves.

TIP: Blend reserved strawberry juice with 1 (8 ounce) package cream cheese and use as a spread for bread. Bread is great toasted.

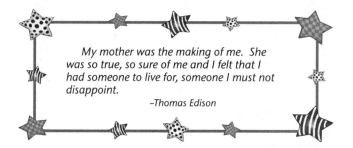

My mother was the making of me. She was so true, so sure of me and I felt that I had someone to live for, someone I must not disappoint.
–Thomas Edison

Monkey Bread

½ cup sugar
2 tablespoons cinnamon
4 (10 biscuit) cans refrigerated biscuits
¾ cup (1½ sticks) butter
1 cup packed brown sugar
½ cup chopped pecans or raisins
1¼ cups packed brown sugar

★ Preheat oven to 350°.

★ Combine sugar and cinnamon in plastic bag. Cut each biscuits into quarters, place 6 to 7 pieces at a time in sugar-cinnamon mixture and shake well.

★ Layer these pieces in well-sprayed 10-inch tube pan. Repeat steps to continue layering all pieces in pan. Spread pecans or raisins among biscuit pieces as you are layering.

★ In saucepan, melt butter with brown sugar over medium heat and bring to a boil. Stirring constantly, boil for 1 minute and pour over layered biscuits.

★ Bake for 35 to 40 minutes. Let bread cool in pan for 10 to 15 minutes; turn out onto round platter. This is a "pull apart" bread. Serves 8.

Icing:

½ pound cream cheese, softened
½ pound (2 sticks) butter, softened
1 pound powdered sugar
1 teaspoon vanilla extract
1 teaspoon lemon juice

★ Beat butter and cream cheese together in large bowl with a mixer. Slowly add in pound of powdered sugar.

★ After powdered sugar is added, mix for 12 minutes (do not mix less than that). When almost done, add extract and lemon juice.

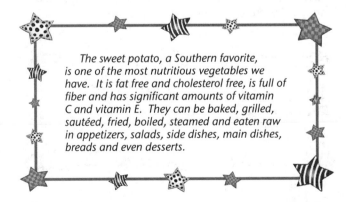

The sweet potato, a Southern favorite, is one of the most nutritious vegetables we have. It is fat free and cholesterol free, is full of fiber and has significant amounts of vitamin C and vitamin E. They can be baked, grilled, sautéed, fried, boiled, steamed and eaten raw in appetizers, salads, side dishes, main dishes, breads and even desserts.

Sticky Buns

*Try these for brunch or a morning get-together. Soft
and fluffy, topped with caramel-coated pecans, they
look and taste like they came straight from the bakery!*

2 (.25 ounce) packages dry yeast
1 (18 ounce) box yellow cake mix
4 cups flour
½ cup butter, divided
2 tablespoons sugar
1 teaspoon ground cinnamon
¼ cup light corn syrup
¼ cup packed brown sugar
2 cups pecan halves

★ Dissolve yeast in 2½ cups warm water and let stand for 10 minutes.
Combine cake mix and flour in large bowl. Stir in yeast mixture and
blend well. Cover bowl and let rise in warm place until doubled in size,
about 1 hour.

★ Roll dough on floured work surface into rectangle about ¼-inch thick
(about 12 x 24 inch). Melt ¼ cup butter and spread over dough using
pastry brush or back of spoon. Combine sugar and cinnamon in small
bowl and sprinkle evenly over dough. Starting with longest side, roll
dough into log.

★ Combine corn syrup, brown sugar and remaining ¼ cup butter in small
saucepan. Cook over low heat, stirring frequently, until butter melts and
mixture is smooth. Pour evenly into sprayed 10 x 15-inch baking pan.
Sprinkle pecans evenly.

★ Slice dough into 1½ to 2-inch pieces and place close together (flat-side
down) over pecans in pan. Cover with plastic wrap and let rise again
until doubled in size, about 30 minutes.

★ When ready to bake, preheat oven to 350°. Bake for 25 minutes or until
toothpick inserted halfway in center comes out clean. Remove from
oven, let stand for 2 to 3 minutes, then unmold onto serving tray. Cool
slightly and serve warm or cold. Yields about 20 rolls.

*I totally take back all those times I
didn't want to take a nap when I was
younger.*

Jingle Bread

Yes, the sausage is right in the bread! A slice or
two, warmed or toasted makes a great breakfast!

1 pound hot ground sausage
1½ cups packed light brown sugar
1½ cups sugar
2 eggs
1 cup chopped pecans
3 cups flour
1 teaspoon ground allspice
1 teaspoon ground cinnamon
1 teaspoon baking powder
1 teaspoon baking soda
1 cup cold brewed coffee

★ Preheat oven to 350°. Combine uncooked sausage, brown sugar, sugar
  and eggs in bowl and stir in pecans. In separate bowl, combine flour,
  allspice, cinnamon and baking powder.

★ In separate bowl, stir baking soda into coffee, blend coffee into flour
  mixture and stir all into sausage mixture. (This is when you have fun
  mixing with your hands.)

★ Pour into 2 sprayed, floured loaf pans. Bake for 1 hour 10 minutes or
  until toothpick inserted in center comes out clean. Serves 20.

New England Doughnuts

1 pound shortening
1 cup sugar
1 egg, well beaten
1 cup milk
½ teaspoon nutmeg
2 cups flour
2 teaspoons baking powder
Oil for frying

★ Cream shortening and sugar with mixer. Stir in egg, milk, ½ teaspoon
  salt, and nutmeg. Sift flour with baking powder. Stir into sugar-
  egg mixture and only use enough flour to make a soft roll of dough.
  Refrigerate thoroughly.

★ Place dough onto lightly floured board and roll out to ⅓ inch thickness.
  Cut with a floured doughnut cutter. Heat oil (365 degrees) in deep
  saucepan and fry several doughnuts at a time. Drain on paper towels
  and enjoy. Yields 12 to 14 doughnuts.

Cranberry Crown Coffee Cake

½ cup butter, softened
1 cup plus 2 tablespoons sugar
2 eggs
2 cups flour
1 teaspoon baking powder
1 teaspoon baking soda
1 (8 ounce) carton sour cream
1 teaspoon almond extract
1 (16 ounce) can whole cranberry sauce
¾ cup chopped slivered almonds, divided

★ Preheat oven to 350°. Combine butter and sugar and beat well. Beat in eggs one at a time. In separate bowl, combine flour, baking powder and baking soda and add alternately with sour cream. Stir in almond extract. Spoon one-half of batter in sprayed, floured bundt or tube pan.

★ Stir cranberry sauce in small bowl so it can be spread easily. Spread three-fourths of cranberry sauce over batter and sprinkle ½ cup almonds.

★ Pour remaining batter on top, spoon remaining cranberry sauce over batter and sprinkle almonds on top. Insert long knife into batter and swirl batter and cranberries. Bake for 60 minutes. Cool for about 20 minutes before removing cake from pan.

Glaze:

¾ cup powdered sugar
1 teaspoon almond extract

★ When cake is cool, mix glaze ingredients plus 1 teaspoon water in bowl until smooth. Drizzle on cake. Serves 10 to 12.

Short-Cut Blueberry Coffee Cake

1 (16 ounce) package blueberry muffin mix
⅓ cup sour cream
1 egg
⅔ cup powdered sugar

★ Preheat oven to 400°. Combine muffin mix, sour cream, egg and ½ cup water in bowl. Rinse blueberries from muffin mix and gently fold into batter. Pour into sprayed, floured 7 x 11-inch baking dish.

★ Bake for about 25 minutes and cool. Mix powdered sugar and 1 tablespoon water in bowl and drizzle over coffee cake. Serves 12.

Coffee Lover's Coffee Cake

2 cups flour
2 teaspoons instant coffee granules
2 cups packed brown sugar
1 teaspoon ground cinnamon
½ cup (1 stick) butter
1 (8 ounce) carton sour cream
1 teaspoon baking soda
1 egg
¾ cup chopped pecans

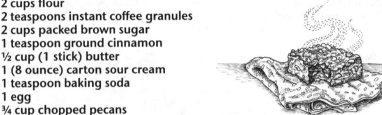

★ Preheat oven to 350°. Combine flour, instant coffee, brown sugar, ½ teaspoon salt and cinnamon in bowl and stir well. Cut in butter until crumbly. Press half of mixture into sprayed 9-inch square pan.

★ In separate bowl, combine sour cream, baking soda and egg and mix well. Add to remaining crumb mixture and stir until dry ingredients are moist.

★ Pour mixture over crumb crust in pan. Sprinkle with pecans. Bake for 45 to 60 minutes. Serves 16.

Graham-Streusel Coffee Cake

2 cups graham cracker crumbs
¾ cup chopped pecans
¾ cup firmly packed brown sugar
1½ teaspoons ground cinnamon
¾ cup (1½ sticks) butter
1 (18 ounce) box yellow cake mix
½ cup canola oil
3 eggs

★ Preheat oven to 350°. Mix graham cracker crumbs, pecans, brown sugar, cinnamon and butter in bowl and set aside.

★ In separate bowl, blend cake mix, 1 cup water, oil and eggs on medium speed for 3 minutes. Pour half batter in sprayed, floured 9 x 13-inch baking pan.

★ Sprinkle with half crumb mixture. Spread remaining batter evenly over crumb mixture. Sprinkle remaining crumb mixture over top. Bake for 45 to 50 minutes.

Glaze:

1½ cups powdered sugar

★ Mix powdered sugar and 2 tablespoons water in bowl and drizzle over cake while still hot. Serves 8 to 10.

Pineapple Coffee Cake

1 (18 ounce) box butter cake mix
½ cup canola oil
4 eggs, slightly beaten
1 (20 ounce) can pineapple pie filling

★ Preheat oven to 350°. Combine mix, oil and eggs in bowl and beat well.
   Pour batter into sprayed, floured 9 x 13-inch baking pan.

★ Bake for 45 to 50 minutes. Cake is done when toothpick inserted in
   center comes out clean. Punch holes in cake about 2 inches apart with
   knife. Spread pineapple pie filling over cake while it is still hot. Serves
   12 to 14.

Fresh Blueberry Muffins

1¼ cups sugar
2 cups flour
1½ teaspoons baking powder
½ cup (1 stick) butter, softened
1 egg, beaten
1 cup milk
1½ cups fresh blueberries
½ cup chopped pecans

★ Preheat oven to 375°. Combine sugar, flour, baking powder and ½
   teaspoon salt in large bowl. Cut in softened butter until mixture is
   coarse.

★ Stir in egg and milk and beat well. Gently fold in blueberries and
   pecans, but do not beat. Spoon into sprayed, floured muffin cups (or
   cups with paper liners) and bake for 35 minutes or until light brown.
   Yields 12 muffins.

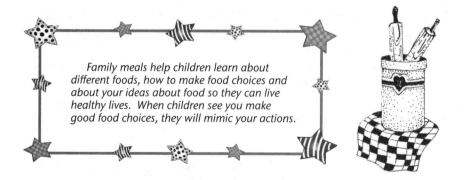

*Family meals help children learn about
different foods, how to make food choices and
about your ideas about food so they can live
healthy lives. When children see you make
good food choices, they will mimic your actions.*

Ginger-Raisin Muffins

1 (18 ounce) box gingerbread mix
1 egg
2 (1.5 ounce) boxes seedless raisins

★ Preheat oven to 350°. Combine gingerbread mix, 1¼ cups lukewarm water and egg in bowl and mix well. Stir in raisins.

★ Pour into sprayed, floured muffin cups (or cups with paper liners) until filled half full. Bake for 20 minutes or until toothpick inserted in center comes out clean. Yields 12 muffins.

Hidden Secret Muffins

Filling:

1 (8 ounce) package cream cheese, softened
1 egg
⅓ cup sugar
1 tablespoon grated orange peel

Batter:

1 cup (2 sticks) butter, softened
1¾ cups sugar
3 eggs
3 cups flour
2 teaspoons baking powder
1 cup milk
1 teaspoon almond extract
1 cup chopped almonds, toasted

★ Preheat oven to 375°. To prepare filling, beat cream cheese, eggs, sugar and orange peel in bowl and set aside.

★ To prepare batter, cream butter and sugar in bowl until light and fluffy. Add eggs one at a time and beat after each addition.

★ In separate bowl, combine flour and baking powder and add alternately with milk to butter-sugar mixture. Begin and end with flour. Add almond extract and fold in almonds.

★ Fill 26 lightly sprayed muffin cups half full with batter. Spoon 1 heaping tablespoon filling in each muffin cup and top with remaining batter.

★ Bake muffins for 20 to 25 minutes or until muffin bounces back when pressed or until they are light brown. Yields 12 muffins.

Maple-Spice Muffins

1¼ cups flour
1½ cups whole wheat flour
½ cup quick-cooking oats
1 teaspoon baking soda
2 teaspoons baking powder
2 teaspoons ground cinnamon
½ teaspoon ground cloves
2 eggs
1 (8 ounce) carton sour cream
1 cup maple syrup
1 cup packed brown sugar
½ cup canola oil
½ teaspoon maple flavoring, optional
1 banana, mashed
1 cup chopped walnuts

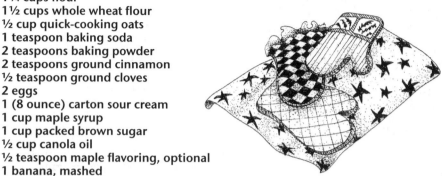

★ Preheat oven to 375°. Combine both flours, oats, baking soda, baking powder, cinnamon and cloves in bowl and mix well.

★ Add eggs, sour cream, maple syrup, brown sugar, oil, maple flavoring and mashed banana and stir well with spoon.

★ Add walnuts and pour into 24 paper-lined muffin cups. Bake for 18 to 20 minutes. Yields 24 muffins.

Pear Muffins

1 cup flour
1 cup whole wheat flour
⅓ cup packed brown sugar
2½ teaspoons baking powder
½ teaspoon baking soda
½ teaspoon ground ginger
¼ teaspoon ground allspice
¾ cup buttermilk*
⅓ cup canola oil
1 egg, beaten
1 large pear

★ Preheat oven to 400°. Mix flour, whole wheat flour, brown sugar, baking powder, baking soda, ginger, allspice and ¼ teaspoon salt in large bowl.

★ In separate bowl, mix buttermilk, oil and egg. Gradually pour into flour mixture and fold gently. Peel, core and shred pear and add to batter. Pour into sprayed muffin pan and bake for about 20 minutes. Yields 12 muffins.

TIP: To make buttermilk, mix 1 cup milk with 1 tablespoon lemon juice or vinegar and let milk stand for about 10 minutes.

Apple-Spice Muffins

1 cup (2 sticks) butter, softened
1 cup packed brown sugar
1 cup sugar
2 eggs
1¾ cups applesauce
2 teaspoons ground cinnamon
1 teaspoon ground allspice
½ teaspoon ground cloves
2 teaspoons baking soda
3½ cups flour
1½ cups chopped pecans

★ Preheat oven to 375°. Cream butter, brown sugar and sugar in bowl. Add eggs, applesauce, cinnamon, allspice, cloves, ½ teaspoon salt, baking soda and flour and mix well. Add pecans and stir well.

★ Pour into 28 sprayed, floured muffin cups or pans with paper liners. Bake for 16 minutes or until toothpick inserted in center comes out clean. Serves 28.

Banana Bran Muffins

1 cup flour
½ teaspoon baking soda
1 teaspoon baking powder
2 tablespoons butter, softened
¼ cup sugar
1 egg, well beaten
1 cup shredded bran
2 tablespoons milk
2 cups bananas, smashed

★ Preheat oven to 375°. Sift flour with ½ teaspoon salt, baking soda and baking powder in bowl. In separate bowl, cream butter. Add sugar and cream gradually. Add egg, bran and milk. Mix and allow to stand while mashing bananas.

★ Add bananas and mix well. Add sifted dry ingredients, stirring as little as possible. Bake in sprayed muffin cups for 20 to 30 minutes. Yields 12 muffins.

 Broccoli Capital of the World   Greenfield, California

Kids' Corn Dog Muffins

2 (6 ounce) packages cornbread muffin mix
2 tablespoons brown sugar
2 eggs
1 cup milk
1 (8 ounce) can whole kernel corn, drained
5 hot dogs, chopped

★ Preheat oven to 400°.

★ Combine cornbread mix and brown sugar in bowl. In separate bowl, combine eggs and milk and stir into dry ingredients.

★ Stir in corn and hot dogs. (Batter will be thin.) Fill sprayed muffin cups three-fourths full. Bake for 16 to 18 minutes or until golden brown. Serves 8.

Ranch Sausage and Grits

1 cup quick-cooking grits
1 pound pork sausage, cooked, drained
1 onion, chopped, cooked
1 cup salsa
1 (8 ounce) package shredded cheddar cheese, divided

★ Preheat oven to 350°.

★ Cook grits according to package directions. Combine grits, sausage, onion, salsa and half cheese in bowl. Spoon into sprayed 2-quart baking dish.

★ Bake for 15 minutes. Remove from oven and add remaining cheese on top of casserole. Bake for additional 10 minutes and serve hot. Serves 8.

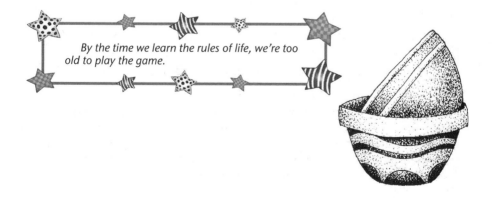

By the time we learn the rules of life, we're too old to play the game.

Smoked Salmon Breakfast Tacos

1 medium onion, chopped
1 teaspoon canola oil
3 eggs
2 (6 ounce) cans red salmon, drained, flaked
½ teaspoon hot sauce
12 flour tortillas
1 (8 ounce) package shredded cheese
2 cups shredded cabbage

★ Saute onions in oil in skillet until onions are translucent. Beat eggs in
bowl and add to onions. Scramble eggs and cook over medium heat.
Add salmon and hot sauce and cook until eggs are firm. Stir often.

★ Heat tortillas in oven or microwave wrapped in slightly damp paper
towels. Spread egg mixture equally on tortillas. Add cheese and
cabbage, roll and serve immediately. Serves 4.

Veggie Breakfast Tacos

6 - 8 flour tortillas
1 cup frozen hash-brown potatoes, thawed
1 onion, chopped
1 bell pepper, seeded, chopped
1 (4 ounce) can diced green chilies, drained
4 eggs
2 - 3 tablespoons milk
Salsa

★ Wrap flour tortillas in foil and warm in oven at 200°. Cook hash browns
on griddle or large skillet. Brown onions, bell peppers and green chilies.

★ Beat eggs with milk in bowl. Move potato mixture to one side, pour in
beaten eggs and scramble.

★ Mix hash-browns, onions, bell peppers, green chilies and eggs and spoon
into flour tortilla. Roll tortilla and serve hot with salsa. Serves 6 to 8.

Variations:

1. Cook chorizo sausage, drain and mix with scrambled eggs instead of
hash browns.

2. Cook bacon, drain and mix with scrambled eggs instead of hash browns.

3. Add refried beans to any variation above.

4. When you have company, try serving "make-your-own" breakfast
tacos with separate bowls of these ingredients: scrambled eggs,
sausage, bacon, shredded cheese, chopped onions, bell pepper, green
chilies, tomatoes, hash browns, refried beans, salsa, hot pepper sauce,
corn chips, chili, pinto beans, etc., along with warmed tortillas and
taco shells.

Breakfast Burritos

6 large flour tortillas
½ pound ground sausage
2 fresh green onions, chopped
5 large eggs, slightly beaten
2 tablespoons milk
⅔ cup shredded cheddar cheese
Salsa

★ Wrap tortillas tightly in foil and heat in oven at 250° for about
   15 minutes. Brown sausage and onions in skillet, drain and set aside.

★ Combine eggs, milk and a little salt and pepper in bowl. Pour into
   separate skillet and cook, stirring constantly. When eggs are still slightly
   moist, remove from heat. Add sausage-onion to eggs.

★ Spoon sausage-egg mixture into middle of tortillas. Top with cheese and
   about 1 tablespoon salsa, roll and tuck ends inside the rolls. Serves 6.

Bacon and Egg Burrito

2 slices bacon, cooked, chopped
2 eggs, scrambled
¼ cup shredded cheddar cheese
1 flour tortilla

★ Sprinkle bacon, eggs and cheese in middle of tortilla. (Add salsa, if you
   like.) Fold tortilla sides over and place seam-side down on dinner plate.
   Microwave for 30 seconds or just until it is hot. Serves 1.

Avocado-Stuffed Omelet

8 large eggs
½ cup milk
1 avocado, seeded, peeled, diced
¾ cup shredded Monterey Jack cheese
¾ cup seeded, diced, drained tomatoes
½ cup minced green onions with tops

★ Beat eggs with milk in bowl vigorously. Pour into large, sprayed skillet.
   Cook over low heat until eggs begin to firm up. Slide eggs around in
   skillet while cooking.

★ Mix avocado, cheese, tomatoes and onions in bowl and spread over one-
   half of eggs. Use spatula to lift other half of eggs onto cheese mixture.
   Cook until firm on the inside and cheese melts. Serves 4 to 6.

Asparagus Capital of the World   Sacramento, California

Bacon-Cheese Omelet

2 strips bacon
2 eggs
1 tablespoon milk
2 green onions with tops, chopped
1 tablespoon butter
¼ cup grated cheddar cheese

★ Fry bacon crispy, drain, cool and crumble. Saute onion in remaining bacon drippings and drain. Beat eggs with milk. Over medium heat melt butter in omelet pan and pour in egg mixture. Tilt pan or use spoon to move liquid of eggs around pan to cook evenly. Cook until eggs are almost firm in center.

★ Sprinkle bacon, onions and cheese evenly over half of eggs. Fold one half of omelet over to cover cheese and continue cooking 1 or 2 minutes until cheese melts. Serve immediately. Serves 1.

Western Omelet

6 eggs
6 tablespoons milk
½ cup grated cheddar cheese
½ cup diced cooked ham
¼ cup finely chopped onion
¼ cup finely chopped green peppers or diced green chilies, drained
¼ cup chopped tomatoes
Salsa

★ Beat eggs with milk. Over medium heat melt butter in omelet pan or skillet and pour one half eggs into pan. Tilt pan or use spoon to move liquid of eggs around pan to cook evenly.

★ Cook until eggs are almost firm in the middle. Sprinkle cheese, ham, onion, green peppers and tomatoes over one half the eggs.

★ Fold other half of omelet over to cover cheese mixture and continue cooking 1 or 2 minutes longer or until eggs are firm and cheese melts. Slide out of pan, pour salsa over top and serve immediately. Serves 3 to 4.

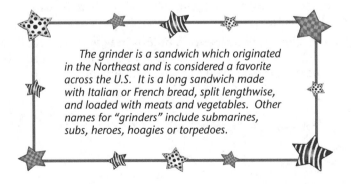

The grinder is a sandwich which originated in the Northeast and is considered a favorite across the U.S. It is a long sandwich made with Italian or French bread, split lengthwise, and loaded with meats and vegetables. Other names for "grinders" include submarines, subs, heroes, hoagies or torpedoes.

Ham and Cheese Omelet

6 large eggs
½ cup half-and-half cream
½ cup chopped ham
¼ cup chopped onion
1 cup shredded cheddar cheese

★ Beat eggs and cream until they blend. Cook diced ham and onions until onion is tender. Pour egg mixture over ham and onions. Cool on low in covered pan until eggs are set, 6 to 8 minutes. Sprinkle with cheddar cheese and serve. Serves 3 to 4.

Omelet a la Spam

6 eggs
⅓ cup milk
¼ cup chopped onion
½ cup diced Spam®
¼ cup green peppers
Dash hot pepper sauce
2 slices American cheese

★ Beat eggs with milk until they blend. Combine chopped onion, diced Spam®, green peppers, and hot pepper sauce in lightly buttered skillet. Simmer until desired consistency. Pour egg mixture over skillet ingredients, top with cheese and cook on low until set. Serves 2.

Baggie Omelet for One

This is so easy, it's funny.

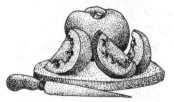

2 eggs
Shredded cheese
Chopped bell peppers
Chopped tomatoes
Chopped onions
Chopped mushrooms
Crumbled bacon
Chopped ham

★ Crack eggs in 7-inch resealable plastic bag. Choose favorite ingredients and place in resealable plastic bag. Seal and shake to mix ingredients and "scramble" eggs.

★ Place in boiling water for 13 minutes. Pick up bag with tongs and let cool for several minutes before opening. Roll omelet out of bag onto plate and serve. Serves 1.

Breakfast Frittata

2 medium zucchini, diced, drained
1 cup finely diced fresh mushrooms
Oil
2 ripe avocados, peeled, cubed
5 eggs
1½ cups shredded Swiss cheese

★ Cook zucchini and mushrooms in large skillet with a little oil over medium heat for 4 to 5 minutes or just until tender. Remove from heat and sprinkle with a little salt and pepper.

★ Place cubed avocado over top of vegetable mixture. Beat eggs and about 1 cup water or milk in bowl until frothy and pour over ingredients in skillet.

★ Return skillet to medium heat, cover and cook for 5 minutes or until eggs set. Top with cheese, cover and cook for an additional 1 minute or just until cheese melts. Cut in wedges to serve. Serves 8.

Southwestern Huevos Rancheros

The traditional version of Huevos Rancheros in the Southwest uses poached eggs and the basic Red Chile Sauce used on so many Southwestern dishes.

8 - 10 New Mexico dried red chilies
1 onion, chopped
1 teaspoon minced garlic
1 tomato, finely chopped, drained
6 corn tortillas
Canola oil
6 eggs

★ Preheat oven to 250°. Place dried chilies on baking pan and cook in oven until chilies blister, but do not burn. Remove stems and seeds. Crush or crumble chilies in saucepan with 2 cups water and add onion, garlic and tomato.

★ Bring to a boil, reduce heat and simmer for about 30 minutes or until desired thickness. Pour into blender and puree mixture.

★ Fry each tortilla in a little hot oil in skillet until soft. Pour sauce in large skillet with lid on low heat. Crack eggs in sauce and cover with lid. Poach eggs until yolks are partially done.

★ To serve, place tortilla on serving plate or individual plates, spoon about ⅓ cup sauce over each tortilla and gently slip eggs onto tortilla. Serve hot. Serves 3 to 4.

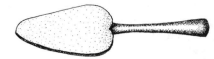

Crabmeat Quiche

3 eggs, beaten
1 (8 ounce) carton sour cream
1 (6 ounce) can crabmeat, rinsed
½ cup shredded Swiss cheese
Garlic salt
1 (9 inch) piecrust

★ Preheat oven to 350°. Combine eggs and sour cream in bowl. Blend in crabmeat and cheese and add a little garlic salt and pepper. Pour into piecrust and bake for 35 minutes. Serves 6.

Home-Style Asparagus Quiche

1 (9 inch) frozen piecrust
¼ cup (½ stick) butter
3 tablespoons flour
1½ cups milk
4 eggs
1 pound fresh asparagus, trimmed, chopped
½ cup shredded Swiss cheese
¼ cup breadcrumbs

★ Preheat oven to 450°. Place several sheets of heavy-duty foil in piecrust and over edge. Bake for about 5 minutes. Remove from oven, discard foil and bake for additional 5 minutes.

★ Melt butter in saucepan and stir in flour and a little salt. Stir to dissolve all lumps. Cook over medium heat and gradually pour in milk. Continue to stir until mixture thickens.

★ Add remaining ingredients except breadcrumbs and beat. Pour into piecrust and sprinkle breadcrumbs over quiche. Bake for about 30 minutes or until knife inserted in center comes out clean. Cool slightly, slice into wedges and serve warm. Serves 6.

Easy Breakfast Casserole

6 eggs
2 cups milk
1 pound sausage, cooked, browned
¾ cup shredded Velveeta® cheese
6 slices white bread, trimmed, cubed

★ Preheat oven to 350°. Beat eggs in bowl, add milk, sausage and cheese and pour over bread. Mix well. Pour into sprayed 9 x 13-inch baking pan.

★ Cover and bake for 20 minutes. Uncover, turn oven to 375° and bake for additional 10 minutes. Serves 6.

Bandit Sausage Ring

This is a pretty impressive presentation. The sausage has a doughnut shape and the scrambled eggs are in the middle.

1 pound mild sausage
1 pound hot sausage
1½ cups crushed cracker crumbs
2 eggs, slightly beaten
½ cup milk
½ cup finely chopped onion
1 cup finely chopped apple
12 eggs, beaten

★ Preheat oven to 350°. Combine sausage, cracker crumbs, eggs, milk, onion and apple in bowl. Press tightly into sprayed ring mold and turn out onto shallow baking pan with sides.

★ Bake for 50 minutes. Drain well before placing on serving platter. Fill center with scrambled eggs and serve immediately. Serves 8 to 10.

TIP: *This recipe may be made in advance, baked partially for 30 minutes, drained and refrigerated until ready to serve. Continue baking for 20 to 30 minutes until it is hot.*

Quesadilla Pie

1 (4 ounce) can diced green chilies, drained
½ pound ground sausage, cooked
1 (12 ounce) package shredded cheddar cheese
3 eggs, well beaten
1½ cups milk
¾ cup biscuit mix
Hot salsa

★ Preheat oven to 350°. Sprinkle green chilies, cooked sausage and cheddar cheese in sprayed 9-inch pie pan.

★ Mix eggs, milk and biscuit mix in bowl and pour over green chilies, sausage and cheese. Bake for 30 minutes. To serve top each slice with salsa. Serves 6.

Nine out of every ten tomatoes grown in the U.S. are grown in California. In addition, over 85% of all home gardeners in the U.S. grow tomatoes.

Glazed Bacon

1 (1 pound) package bacon
⅓ cup packed brown sugar
1 teaspoon flour
½ cup finely chopped pecans

★ Preheat oven to 350°. Arrange bacon slices close together, but not overlapping, on wire rack over drip pan.

★ In bowl, combine brown sugar, flour and pecans and sprinkle evenly over bacon. Bake for about 20 to 30 minutes. Drain on paper towels. Serves 4 to 6.

Variations:

1. Dip fried bacon in maple syrup, lay on baking sheet and bake at 350° for about 10 to 15 minutes or until maple syrup is no longer runny.

2. Mix brown sugar, maple syrup and Dijon-style mustard and spread on bacon slices. Bake at 350° for 20 to 30 minutes.

3. Brush honey on bacon and bake at 350° for 20 to 30 minutes or until bacon is crispy.

4. Bake bacon on baking sheet at 350° for about 20 minutes. Mix ¼ cup packed brown sugar and ¼ cup dark beer. Brush on bacon and cook additional 10 minutes or until crispy.

Red Flannel Hash

Traditional Red Flannel Hash was the breakfast served after a New England Boiled Dinner. It had all the vegetables and corned beef from the Boiled Dinner stirred together in a skillet, cooked until there's a crusty bottom and served with a poached egg on top.

6 red new potatoes, boiled, cubed
4 beets, peeled, boiled, cubed
1 carrot, boiled, sliced
½ head cabbage, boiled, chopped
1 cup cooked corned beef, chopped, optional
½ cup beef broth, divided
2 - 3 tablespoons bacon drippings or shortening
4 eggs, poached, optional

★ Stir potatoes, beets, carrot, cabbage and corned beef together carefully in large bowl. Heat bacon drippings in large skillet. Add mixed vegetables to skillet and pat down evenly.

★ Pour a little beef broth over top and cook over medium heat for about 15 minutes. (Do not turn or stir. Add more beef broth if needed.)

★ Turn heat to high and brown bottom of hash. Cut into 4 pieces and place on dinner plates. Poach eggs and place on top of hash. Serve immediately. Serves 4.

Old-Fashioned Blueberry Buckle

Excellent for brunch!

2 cups flour
3 cups sugar
2 teaspoons baking powder
1 egg
½ cup milk
¼ cup (½ stick) butter, softened
2 cups blueberries

★ Preheat oven to 375°. Combine flour, sugar, baking powder, egg,
   ½ teaspoon salt, milk and butter in large bowl. Fold in blueberries
   carefully. Spread in sprayed, floured 9-inch square pan and set aside.

Topping:

¼ cup (½ stick) butter, softened
⅓ cup flour
½ cup sugar
½ teaspoon ground cinnamon

★ Combine butter, flour, sugar and cinnamon in bowl and sprinkle over
   blueberry mixture. Bake for 30 to 35 minutes. Serve warm. Serves 8 to 10.

Yummy Cooked Apples

⅓ cup butter
⅓ cup packed brown sugar
2 tablespoons lemon juice
6 red delicious apples, peeled, cored, sliced

★ Mix butter, brown sugar, lemon juice and ¼ cup water in large
   saucepan. Add apple slices, cover and cook over medium heat until
   tender. Stir frequently to prevent sticking. Do not burn. Remove from
   heat and set aside for about 10 minutes before serving. Serves 6.

Fruit Dip

1 (8 ounce) package cream cheese, softened
½ cup sour cream
½ cup packed brown sugar
2 tablespoons maple syrup
Fruit

★ Beat cream cheese and sour cream in bowl until smooth and stir in
   brown sugar and maple syrup. Serve with strawberries, apple slices or
   fresh pineapple chunks. Yields 1 pint.

Breakfast Fruit Bowl

1 cup flavored or plain yogurt
1 tablespoon honey
½ cup granola cereal
2 cups fresh pear, peach and/or apricot slices

★ Mix yogurt and honey with granola in bowl and top with fruit slices. Make as individual servings in bowls or mix together and serve. Serves 4.

Happy Trails Granola

6 cups old-fashioned oats
1½ cups unsweetened coconut
1 cup sliced almonds or pistachios
½ cup crushed wheat germ
½ cup sunflower seeds
½ cup sesame seeds
⅔ cup honey
½ cup canola oil
1 tablespoon vanilla
2 teaspoons ground cinnamon
1 teaspoon ground nutmeg

★ Preheat oven to 350°. Mix oats, coconut, almonds, wheat germ, sunflower seeds and sesame seeds in 9 x 13-inch baking pan.

★ Mix honey, oil, vanilla, cinnamon and nutmeg in bowl and pour over granola mix. Stir well to coat all pieces with honey mixture. Bake for about 30 minutes. Cool mixture. Serves 8 to 10.

Easy Homemade Granola

2 cups dry oatmeal
1 cup chopped pecans
1 cup chopped walnuts
½ cup packed brown sugar
½ cup honey
2 teaspoons vanilla

★ Preheat oven to 350°. Combine all ingredients in large bowl. Pour into 8 x 12-inch baking dish and bake for about 15 minutes or until crispy. Yields about 4 cups.

Variation:

★ Add one or all of the following: dried cranberries, Craisins®, raisins, shredded coconut and/or dried fruits.

Devil's Canyon Cooked-Up Granola

2 cups old-fashioned oats
1 tablespoon canola oil
⅓ cup packed brown sugar
⅓ cup butter
2 tablespoons honey
⅓ cup dried cranberries
½ cup sliced almonds

★ Place oats in skillet with hot oil and cook over medium heat until oats begin to brown and crisp. Drain and transfer oats to baking sheet.

★ Mix brown sugar, butter and honey in same skillet and cook over medium heat, stirring constantly, until bubbly. Remove from heat and pour in oats.

★ Mix well and return all ingredients to baking sheet to cool. Add cranberries and almonds to mixture and store in airtight container. Serves 8.

TIP: Add your favorite dried fruits and nuts to the mixture for your own special blend of flavors.

Easy Apple Butter

6 apples, peeled, finely chopped
½ cup apple cider
2 cups packed brown sugar
1½ teaspoons ground cinnamon
1 teaspoon ground nutmeg
½ teaspoon ground cloves

★ Place apples and apple cider in 1½-quart microwaveable bowl. Cover tightly with plastic wrap. Microwave on HIGH for 15 minutes. Stir in brown sugar and spices.

★ Microwave uncovered on HIGH for 10 minutes and stir every 2 to 3 minutes. Process mixture in blender or food processor until smooth. Refrigerate. Yields 1 quart.

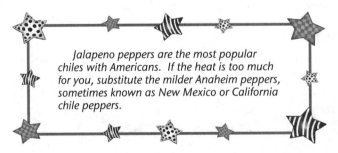

Jalapeno peppers are the most popular chiles with Americans. If the heat is too much for you, substitute the milder Anaheim peppers, sometimes known as New Mexico or California chile peppers.

Pickled Peaches

1½ cups plus 2 tablespoons vinegar, divided
4 pounds peaches
4 cups sugar
1 teaspoon whole ginger
1 tablespoon whole cloves
3 (3 inch) cinnamon sticks

★ Mix vinegar with 2 quarts water. Peel peaches and drop in water-vinegar solution to prevent peaches from turning dark.

★ Make syrup of sugar, 1½ cups vinegar and ¾ cup water. Tie ginger, cloves and cinnamon into cheesecloth bag and drop into syrup; bring to a boil. Drop in peaches, a few at a time and cook until thoroughly hot.

★ Remove peaches and pack in jars. When all peaches are cooked and packed in jars, remove spice bag, pour remaining syrup over peaches and seal. Be sure peaches are completely covered by syrup.

Homemade Plum Jelly

5 - 6 pounds tart plums
(5½ cups plum juice)
1 (1.75 ounce) package fruit pectin
6½ cups sugar

★ Wash and place plums in very large roasting pan or pot and cover with water. Boil until plums are soft and mushy and stir often. Watch carefully to keep pan from boiling over.

★ Pour plums and juice into large colander with large pan to catch juice. You should have 5½ cups juice. Add up to ½ cup water, if necessary to have exactly 5½ cups juice.

★ Place juice and fruit pectin in large roasting pan and bring to a boil (again watch for spillage). Add sugar, return to a full rolling boil (a boil that doesn't stop bubbling when stirred), and stir constantly. Boil for exactly 1 minute.

★ Remove from heat and skim off any foam with metal spoon. Ladle quickly into sterilized jars, filling to within ⅛-inch top of jars.

★ Cover with two-piece lids and screw bands on tightly. Let stand at room temperature for at least 24 hours. Refrigerate after jars are opened. Yields 6 half-pint jars.

Plums, peaches and apricots are all members of the rose family.

Jalapeno Jelly

1 green bell pepper, seeded, finely ground
¼ cup fresh jalapeno peppers, ground
1 cup cider vinegar
5 cups sugar
1 (6 ounce) box liquid fruit pectin
Green food coloring
Cream cheese
Crackers

★ Combine bell pepper, jalapeno peppers, vinegar and sugar in large saucepan. Boil for about 4 minutes.

★ Cool for 1 minute and stir in fruit pectin and a few drops of green coloring. Pour into 5 (6 ounce) sterilized, hot jelly jars and seal. Serve over cream cheese with crackers. Yields 5 half pint jars.

Old-Fashioned Watermelon Preserves

2 pounds watermelon rind, peeled, cubed
¼ cup pickling salt, not iodized
1 teaspoon powdered alum
2 cups white vinegar
4 cups sugar
1 lemon, thinly sliced
1 stick cinnamon
12 whole cloves
1 teaspoon whole allspice

★ When peeling watermelon rind be sure to leave some of pink meat on. Make brine with pickling salt, 4 cups water and alum in large bowl. Soak rind in mixture overnight. Drain, rinse and cook slowly in fresh water in large pot until barely tender. Do not overcook or preserves will be too soft. Drain.

★ Combine 2 cups water, vinegar, sugar, lemon and spices tied in cloth bag in large saucepan and bring to a boil. Remove spice bag and pour hot syrup over rind. Let stand overnight.

★ Drain and reheat syrup for 3 mornings and pour over rind. On fourth morning, drain and reheat syrup and pour over rind packed in sterilized pint or half-pint jars. Seal. Yields 6 to 8 half-pint jars.

Southern Mint Jelly

1½ cups packed mint leaves
Green food coloring
1 (1.7 ounce) box fruit pectin
4 cups sugar
¼ cup lemon juice

★ Pick out and wash fresh mint leaves. Place in saucepan with 3¼ cups water and heat to boil. Cover and steep for 10 minutes.

★ Strain leaves and measure 3 cups liquid. Add few drops of green food coloring and pectin and bring to a boil. Add sugar and lemon juice and bring to a hard-rolling boil for 1 minute. Stir constantly.

★ Remove from heat and skim foam off top. Pour immediately into hot, sterilized jars and seal. Yields 3 to 4 (8 ounce) jars.

Breads

Everyday Butter Rolls

2 cups biscuit mix
1 (8 ounce) carton sour cream
½ cup (1 stick) butter, melted

★ Preheat oven to 400°. Combine all ingredients in bowl and mix well. Spoon into sprayed muffin cups (or cups with paper liners) and fill only half full. Bake for 12 to 14 minutes or light brown. Serves 6 to 8.

No Need to Knead Rolls

2 packages dry yeast
1 egg
¼ cup shortening
6½ cups flour

★ Combine 2 cups lukewarm water, 1½ teaspoons salt and remaining ingredients in bowl, mix well and shape into rolls. Place rolls in sprayed round cake pans. Cover and let rise for 1 hour 30 minutes to 2 hours.

★ When ready to bake, preheat oven to 400°. Bake for 15 to 20 minutes. Yields 30 rolls.

Rich Dinner Rolls

1 cup milk
¼ cup sugar
¼ cup (½ stick) butter, softened
2 packages yeast or yeast cakes
2 eggs, beaten
5¼ cups flour, divided
Melted butter

★ Scald milk in saucepan over low heat. Stir in sugar, 1 teaspoon salt and butter. Remove from heat and cool to lukewarm. Measure ½ cup warm water into large warm bowl, sprinkle or crumble in yeast and stir until it dissolves. Add lukewarm milk mixture, eggs and 2 cups flour. Beat until smooth.

★ Stir in enough remaining flour to make soft dough and turn out onto lightly floured board. Knead for 8 to 10 minutes or until smooth and elastic. Place in greased bowl and turn to grease top. Cover and let rise in warm place (free from draft) for 30 minutes or until doubled in bulk.

★ Punch down and divide dough into 3 equal pieces. Form each piece into 9-inch roll. Cut into 9 equal pieces and form into smooth balls. Place in 3 sprayed round cake pans. Cover and let rise for 30 minutes or until doubled in bulk.

★ When ready to bake, preheat oven to 375°. Brush lightly with melted butter and bake for 15 to 20 minutes. Yields 27 rolls.

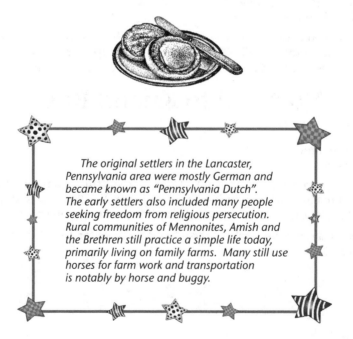

The original settlers in the Lancaster, Pennsylvania area were mostly German and became known as "Pennsylvania Dutch". The early settlers also included many people seeking freedom from religious persecution. Rural communities of Mennonites, Amish and the Brethren still practice a simple life today, primarily living on family farms. Many still use horses for farm work and transportation is notably by horse and buggy.

Buttermilk Refrigerator Rolls

3 packages dry yeast
5 cups flour
¼ cup sugar
¾ cup shortening, melted
2 cups buttermilk*

★ Dissolve yeast in ¼ cup warm water in bowl and set aside. In separate
   bowl, combine flour, sugar and shortening. Add buttermilk and yeast
   mixture and mix thoroughly by hand. Add more flour, if needed. Cover
   and refrigerate.

★ About 1 hour 30 minutes before baking, shape dough pieces into 1-inch
   balls and place in muffin cups, three to a cup. Prepare as many rolls as
   needed and refrigerate remaining dough.

★ Cover rolls and let rise in warm place for 1 hour before baking. When
   ready to bake, preheat oven to 425°.

★ Bake for 12 minutes or until brown. Dough will last 10 days in plastic
   container in refrigerator. Yields 24 to 30 rolls.

*TIP: To make buttermilk, mix 1 cup milk with 1 tablespoon lemon juice or
    vinegar and let milk stand for about 10 minutes.*

Easy Drop Biscuits

1⅓ cups self-rising flour
1 (8 ounce) carton whipping cream
2 tablespoons sugar
Butter

★ Preheat oven to 400°. Combine all ingredients and stir until they blend.
   Drop biscuits by teaspoon onto greased baking sheet. Bake for about
   10 minutes or until light brown. Serve with butter. Yields about 10 to
   12 biscuits.

Sour Cream Biscuits

2 cups plus 1 tablespoon flour
3 teaspoons baking powder
½ teaspoon baking soda
½ cup shortening
1 (8 ounce) carton sour cream

★ Preheat oven to 400°. Combine dry ingredients and add pinch of salt.
   Cut in shortening. Gradually add sour cream and mix lightly.

★ Turn on lightly floured board and knead a few times. Roll to ½-inch
   thick. Cut with biscuit cutter and place on sprayed baking sheet. Bake
   15 minutes or until light brown.

Angel Biscuits

3 packages yeast
5 cups flour
⅓ cup sugar
1 cup shortening
2 cups buttermilk*

★ Dissolve yeast in ⅓ cup warm water in bowl and set aside. In separate bowl, combine flour and sugar and cut in shortening. Add buttermilk and yeast and stir. Refrigerate.

★ On floured board or wax paper, pat out dough. Cut out biscuits with biscuit cutter and place on sprayed baking pan. Let rise in warm place for 2 to 3 hours.

★ When ready to bake, preheat oven to 425°. Bake for 12 minutes or until brown. Dough should last about 10 days in plastic container in refrigerator. Yields 24 to 30 biscuits.

TIP: To make buttermilk, mix 1 cup milk with 1 tablespoon lemon juice or vinegar and let milk stand for about 10 minutes.

Quick and Easy Luncheon Muffins

1 cup (2 sticks) butter, softened
2 cups flour
1 (8 ounce) carton sour cream

★ Preheat oven to 350°. Combine all ingredients in bowl and mix well. Pour mixture into sprayed muffin cups and bake for 20 to 25 minutes. Serves 8.

Knepp

This is a well-known dish in Pennsylvania Dutch cooking.

2 cups flour
1 tablespoon baking powder
2 tablespoons butter, softened
1½ cups milk
Juices from freshly baked ham

★ Mix flour, baking powder and ¼ teaspoon salt in bowl. Cut in butter until it is coarsely mixed. Place dough in blender and slowly pour in milk. Process just until lumps are gone and mixture is smooth.

★ Pour juices from freshly baked ham into saucepan. Add a little water if necessary and bring to a boil. Drop tablespoonfuls of dough in boiling juices, cover and cook on low for about 10 to 12 minutes. Do not open lid while cooking. Remove with slotted spoon, drain and serve hot. Serves 4 to 6.

Cornbread

When the native Indians taught settlers about corn, they also taught them how to make cornbread. Today, it varies from state to state, but some of the more popular versions are listed here. Cornbread is considered a "soul food" in the South and is a little denser than the cornbread popular in the northern U.S.

Cornbread can be baked, fried or cooked over an open fire. Corn pone is found mainly in the Appalachia area and is cooked in a skillet. Johnny Cakes are similar to hot water cornbread that is fried in a skillet, but it is thinner, more like a pancake. And hush puppies are usually golf-ball size rounds of cornmeal that are crispy on the outside and moist in the middle.

Cook's Best Cornbread

This is moist, much like spoonbread. It's also very good reheated and great with maple syrup.

2 eggs
1 (8 ounce) carton sour cream
½ cup vegetable oil
1 (8 ounce) can cream-style corn
1 cup cornmeal
3 teaspoons baking powder

★ Preheat oven to 375°. Beat eggs, sour cream, oil and corn in bowl. Blend in cornmeal, baking powder and 1½ teaspoons salt. Pour in sprayed 9 x 9-inch pan. Bake for 30 to 50 minutes. Serves 8 to 9.

Hot Water Cornbread

1½ cups cornmeal
1 egg, beaten
¼ cup (½ stick) butter, melted
Canola oil
Butter

★ Pour 1¼ cups boiling water over cornmeal and 1 teaspoon salt in bowl, stir very well and cool. Stir in egg and butter.

★ Drop tablespoonfuls of mixture into skillet with a little oil and flatten into small patty shapes with spatula. Brown on both sides and drain on paper towels. Serve hot with butter. Serves 6.

Tex-Mex Cornbread

This is a meal by itself – very good.

2 eggs, beaten
1 cup sour cream
1 (15 ounce) can cream-style corn
½ cup canola oil
1 (8 ounce) package shredded cheddar cheese
1 (4 ounce) can diced green chilies
3 tablespoons diced onion
3 tablespoons chopped bell pepper
1½ cups cornmeal
2½ teaspoons baking powder

★ Preheat oven to 350°. Mix eggs, sour cream, creamed corn, oil, cheese, green chilies, onion and bell pepper in bowl.

★ In separate bowl, mix cornmeal, baking powder and 1 teaspoon salt and quickly add to sour cream mixture. Pour in sprayed 9 x 13-inch baking pan and bake for 45 minutes. Serves 8.

Easy Cheddar Cornbread

2 (8.5 ounce) packages cornbread-muffin mix
2 eggs, beaten
1 cup plain yogurt
1 (14 ounce) can cream-style corn
½ cup shredded cheddar cheese

★ Preheat oven to 400°. Combine cornbread mix, eggs and yogurt in bowl and blend well. Stir in corn and cheese.

★ Pour into sprayed 9 x 13-inch baking dish. Bake for 18 to 20 minutes or until slightly brown. Serves 8 to 10.

Mama's Corn Fritters

3 teaspoons baking powder
1½ cups flour
½ teaspoon sugar
1 egg, beaten
1 (8 ounce) can whole kernel corn, drained
Milk
Canola oil

★ Sift dry ingredients plus ½ teaspoon salt in bowl and add egg, corn and only enough milk to make batter consistency.

★ Mix well and drop tablespoonfuls of batter in hot oil and fry until golden brown. Yields about 2 dozen fritters.

Down-Home Sweet Potato Fritters

1 cup grated sweet potatoes
1 cup sifted flour
2 tablespoons sugar
1 egg, beaten
½ cup milk
Canola oil

★ Combine all ingredients and ¼ teaspoon salt except oil in bowl. Mix well to form batter. Drop tablespoonfuls of mixture into pot of hot oil. When brown, drain, sprinkle with sugar and serve. Serves 4 to 6.

Hush Puppies

Hush puppies are standard fare with fried catfish.

2 cups yellow cornmeal
1 cup flour
2 teaspoons baking powder
2 tablespoons sugar
1 cup corn, drained
1 small onion, very finely minced
2 eggs
1 cup milk
2 tablespoons bacon drippings
Canola oil

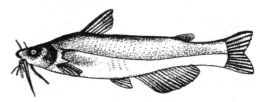

★ Combine cornmeal, flour, 2 teaspoons salt, baking powder and sugar in bowl and mix well. Add corn, onion, eggs, milk and bacon drippings and mix until they blend well.

★ Heat oil in deep fryer and drop batter about the size of golf balls in oil. Cook until golden brown and drain on paper towels. Serves 8.

Cornmeal Pone

2 cups cornmeal
¼ cup vegetable oil

★ Combine cornmeal, 2 cups cold water and 1 teaspoon salt in bowl and stir well. Set aside for 2 minutes.

★ Heat oil in flat-bottomed skillet. Drop tablespoonfuls of mixture into hot oil and fry until brown on both sides. Serve with ham slices or vegetable meal. Serves 4 to 6.

 Potato Capital of the World   Blackfoot, Idaho

Johnnycake

1 cup cornmeal
2 tablespoons whole wheat flour
1 tablespoon sugar
1½ tablespoons butter, melted
1 cup boiling milk
1 egg, separated

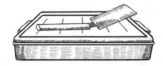

★ Preheat oven to 400°. Sift cornmeal, wheat flour, ½ teaspoon salt and sugar in bowl. Add butter and quickly stir in milk. Beat egg white until stiff. Beat yolk and fold into egg white. Fold into cornmeal.

★ Drop spoonfuls of batter in rectangular shape onto sprayed baking sheet, leaving ½ inch between each biscuit. Bake for 30 minutes. Yields 12 johnnycakes.

Corn Sticks

2 cups biscuit mix
2 tablespoons minced green onions
1 (8 ounce) can cream-style corn
Melted butter

★ Preheat oven to 400°. Combine biscuit mix, green onions and cream-style corn. Place dough on floured surface and cut into 3 x 1-inch strips. Roll in melted butter. Bake for 15 to 16 minutes. Serves 4.

Spicy Cornbread Twists

3 tablespoons butter
½ cup cornmeal
¼ teaspoon cayenne pepper
1 (11 ounce) can refrigerated soft breadsticks

★ Preheat oven to 350°. Melt butter in pie pan in oven. Remove from oven as soon as butter melts. Mix cornmeal and cayenne pepper on wax paper.

★ Roll breadsticks in butter and in cornmeal mixture. Twist breadsticks according to label directions and place on large baking sheet. Bake for 15 to 18 minutes. Serves 6.

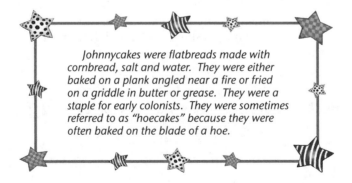

Johnnycakes were flatbreads made with cornbread, salt and water. They were either baked on a plank angled near a fire or fried on a griddle in butter or grease. They were a staple for early colonists. They were sometimes referred to as "hoecakes" because they were often baked on the blade of a hoe.

Crunchy Bread Sticks

Try these for lunch or dinner. You'll be surprised.

1 (8 count) package hot dog buns
1 cup (2 sticks) butter, melted
Garlic powder
Paprika

★ Preheat oven to 225°. Slice each bun in half lengthwise. Use pastry
brush to butter all breadsticks and sprinkle a little garlic powder and a
couple sprinkles of paprika on each. Place on baking sheet and bake for
45 minutes. Serves 8.

Garlic Toast

1 loaf thick-sliced bread
1 tablespoon garlic powder
¼ cup finely chopped parsley
1 teaspoon marjoram leaves
½ cup (1 stick) butter, melted
1 cup grated parmesan cheese

★ Preheat oven to 225°. Slice bread in 1 inch slices diagonally. Combine
garlic powder, parsley, marjoram leaves and butter in small bowl and
mix well.

★ Use brush to spread mixture on bread slices and sprinkle with parmesan
cheese. Place on baking sheet and bake for about 1 hour. Yields 14 to
16 slices.

Soft Pretzels

The first pretzel bakery was founded in Lititz, Pennsylvania in 1861.

1 (.75 ounce) packet yeast
1½ cups plus 1 tablespoon lukewarm water
1 tablespoon sugar
2 teaspoons salt
4 cups flour
1 egg yolk
Coarse salt

★ Dissolve yeast in 1½ cups lukewarm water. Add sugar and salt and
stir until they dissolve. Stir in flour until all ingredients mix well. Turn
dough onto floured board and knead for about 5 minutes.

★ Roll dough into thin strips and shape into pretzels. Place pretzels on well
greased baking sheet. Beat egg yolk with 1 tablespoon water and brush
on pretzels. Sprinkle generously with coarse salt. Bake at 425° for 15 to
20 minutes. Yields about 14 pretzels.

Boston Brown Bread

Boston Brown Bread originates with early settlers who used rye, cornmeal, wheat flour and molasses because that's all they had. Today many people use a two-pound coffee can to steam the bread. This bread is often served with Boston Baked Beans (recipe on page 125).

1 cup cornmeal
1 cup whole wheat flour
1 cup rye flour
1½ teaspoons baking soda
¾ cup raisins
¼ cup walnuts, chopped
2 cups buttermilk, room temperature*
¾ cup molasses

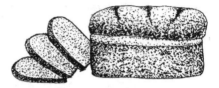

★ Preheat oven to 325°. Combine cornmeal, wheat flour, rye flour, baking soda and 1 teaspoon salt in large bowl. Stir in raisins and walnuts and toss to separate and to coat with flour mixture.

★ Combine buttermilk and molasses in mixing bowl. Pour into flour mixture gradually and stir until dry ingredients are moist. Spoon into 2 (3 x 8 inch) sprayed, floured loaf pans or well-greased 2-pound coffee cans.

★ Place pans on rack on top of large kettle, filled half way with boiling water. Steam bread for 2½ to 3 hours or until wooden toothpick inserted in center comes out clean. (Add more boiling water to kettle, if needed.)

★ Cool on wire rack 5 to 10 minutes; carefully remove bread from the pans. Cool completely before slicing. Yields 2 small loaves.

Apricot Brown Bread:

★ To make a delicious Apricot Brown Bread, substitute 1 cup finely chopped apricots for the raisins and walnuts.

TIP: For baked brown bread, pour batter into sprayed, floured 9 x 5 loaf pan. Bake 1 hour or until a wooden toothpick inserted in center comes out clean.

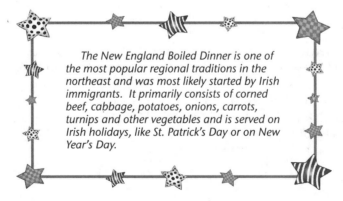

The New England Boiled Dinner is one of the most popular regional traditions in the northeast and was most likely started by Irish immigrants. It primarily consists of corned beef, cabbage, potatoes, onions, carrots, turnips and other vegetables and is served on Irish holidays, like St. Patrick's Day or on New Year's Day.

Sourdough Starter and Bread

Starter:

1 package yeast
2 cups flour

★ Dissolve yeast in 2 cups warm water in glass bowl. Add flour and mix well. (Use only glass bowl for mixing and do NOT leave metal utensils in starter.)

★ Place starter in warm place overnight. Next morning, cover container and refrigerate. Use only glass container to store starter. Refrigerate starter when not in use and keep covered. Every 5 days add and stir into starter:

> 1 cup milk
> ¼ cup sugar
> 1 cup flour

★ Do not use starter on day it is "fed." Always keep at least 2 cups mixture in container. Starter may be fed more frequently than every 5 days.

Sourdough Bread:

2 cups flour
1 tablespoon baking powder
2 tablespoons sugar
1 egg
2 cups Sourdough Starter

★ Preheat oven to 350°.

★ Mix flour, baking powder, 1 teaspoon salt and sugar in bowl, add egg and starter and mix well. Pour into loaf pan and place in warm place. Allow to double in bulk.

★ When ready to bake, preheat oven to 350°. Bake for 30 to 35 minutes. Yields 1 loaf.

> *While chuck wagon cooks were making sourdough bread at every stop along the cattle trails from Texas and Oklahoma to markets in Kansas, Gold Rush prospectors or "49'ers" were making the same sourdough bread daily. San Francisco is famous for sourdough bread today primarily because it continues with this culinary tradition traced back to the Gold Rush days in 1849.*

Mom's Quick Never-Fail Bread

This whole process takes less than 5 hours, which is good when you're talking about yeast breads.

1½ yeast cakes
½ cup milk, room temperature
1 tablespoon sugar
2 tablespoons butter, melted
5 - 6 cups flour

★ Dissolve yeast in 1½ cups warm water and warm milk in large bowl. Mix in sugar, 1½ teaspoons salt and butter until it blends well.

★ Slowly pour flour into mixture and stir after each addition. Add flour until dough is stiff enough to knead. Place on lightly floured board and knead until dough is smooth and springs back when touched.

★ Cover and set aside in warm place until dough doubles in size. Punch down lightly and divide into 2 equal parts. Place in sprayed, floured loaf pans, cover and let stand in warm place until dough doubles in size again.

★ When ready to bake, preheat oven to 450°. Bake for 15 minutes. Reduce heat to 350° and bake for 30 minutes or until golden brown on top. Yields 2 loaves.

Williamsburg Sally Lunn Bread

1 package yeast or yeast cake
1 cup warm milk
½ cup (1 stick) butter, softened
⅓ cup sugar
3 eggs, beaten
4 cups flour

★ Put yeast in warm milk. Cream butter, sugar and eggs in bowl. Add yeast-milk mixture. Sift flour into mixture and mix well. Let rise in warm place.

★ Punch down and place into sprayed mold or 3-quart ring mold. Let rise again. When ready to bake, preheat oven to 350°. Bake for 45 minutes or until done. Serve hot. Serves 6 to 8.

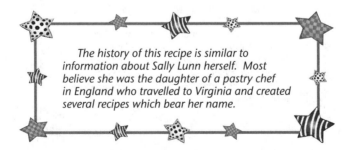

The history of this recipe is similar to information about Sally Lunn herself. Most believe she was the daughter of a pastry chef in England who travelled to Virginia and created several recipes which bear her name.

Irish Soda Bread

The Society for the Preservation of Irish Soda Bread states that traditional Irish soda bread was made with basic ingredients of flour, baking soda, salt and buttermilk and it was often the only bread a family might afford.

3 cups flour
1 tablespoon baking powder
1 teaspoon baking soda
⅓ cup sugar
1 egg, beaten
2 cups buttermilk, room temperature*
¼ cup (½ stick) butter, melted

★ Preheat oven to 325°. Combine flour, baking powder, baking soda, sugar and 1 teaspoon salt in mixing bowl. Mix egg and buttermilk and stir just enough into dry mixture until flour is moist. Stir in butter and pour into sprayed, floured 9 x 5-inch loaf pan.

★ Bake for 60 minutes or until wooden toothpick inserted in center comes out clean. Cool loaf on wire rack and wrap in foil. Bread is best if made the day before or at least several hours before slicing. Yields 1 loaf.

TIP: You can make buttermilk by adding 1 tablespoon lemon juice or vinegar to an 8-ounce glass of milk. Give it about 10 minutes to work.

Navajo Fry Bread

Navajo made bread from meager provisions given to them in the 1860's. This is a derivation of that bread.

2 cups flour
2 teaspoons baking powder
⅓ cup powdered milk
2 tablespoons lard or shortening
Canola oil

★ Combine flour, baking powder, 1 teaspoon salt and powdered milk in large bowl. Slowly pour in ¾ cup warm water and stir well. Stir and knead with hands for about 5 minutes.

★ Divide into 10 to 12 balls. Melt lard and brush on outside of dough balls. Let stand for about 30 minutes. On lightly floured surface, spread each ball to about 7 to 8 inches in diameter.

★ Poke hole in center and fry in 350° oil in heavy skillet until it browns lightly. Turn once and drain. Serve with butter or jam.

Shredded Wheat Bread

This recipe originated in the 1950's and is a found in many New England community cookbooks.

¼ cup sugar
3 full-size shredded wheat biscuits, broken
1 (¼ ounce) package active dry yeast
2 egg yolks
⅓ cup oil
1 cup dry milk powder
4 cups bread flour

★ Place 1½ cups warm water in large bowl. Stir in sugar and shredded wheat and mix well. Sprinkle yeast over mixture and let stand for 10 minutes.

★ Stir in egg yolks, oil and dry milk powder and mix with fork. Add flour, 1 cup at a time, to egg yolk mixture and blend after each addition. Dough will appear lumpy and dry. Cover and place in warm area for 30 minutes.

★ Knead dough, cover and let dough double in size. Shape dough into 2 loaves and place in two (8 x 4-inch) loaf pans. Let loaves rise up to pan rim and place in cold oven with shallow pan of hot water on bottom shelf. Bake at 350° for 45 minutes. Turn out onto wire rack to cool. Yield: 2 small loaves.

Easy Bran Bread

1 cup bran flour
1 yeast cake
1 teaspoon sugar
6 tablespoons shortening
8 cups flour

★ Boil 2 cups water and pour over bran. Mix yeast and sugar in 1 cup warm water and let stand until it bubbles. Combine all ingredients plus 1 cup water in large bowl. If dough isn't stiff enough to knead and punch down, add a little more flour.

★ Knead dough for about 3 or 4 minutes and let stand in warm place until it doubles in size. Divide into 2 large balls and place in sprayed, floured loaf pans. Let stand until it doubles in size again.

★ When ready to bake, preheat oven to 350°. Bake for 45 minutes or until it browns on top. Yields 2 loaves.

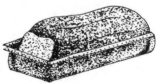

Virginia Spoonbread

1 cup cornmeal
1 tablespoon sugar
¼ cup (½ stick) butter
3 eggs
2 teaspoons baking powder
1⅓ cups milk

★ Preheat oven to 350°. Combine cornmeal, sugar and 1 teaspoon salt in bowl. Add 1⅓ cups boiling water and butter to mixture. Stir constantly and set aside to cool.

★ In separate bowl, beat eggs until light. Stir eggs, baking powder and milk into batter and mix well. Pour into sprayed 2-quart baking dish and place dish in baking pan with about ½ inch water. Bake for about 30 to 35 minutes or until set. Serves 8 to 10.

Beer Bread

3 cups self-rising flour
¼ cup sugar
1 (12 ounce) can beer, room temperature
1 egg, beaten
2 tablespoons butter, melted

★ Preheat oven to 350°. Combine flour, sugar and beer in bowl; mix until blended well. Spoon into 9 x 3-inch loaf pan.

★ To give bread a nice glaze, combine egg and 1 tablespoon water in bowl; brush top of loaf with mixture. Bake for 40 to 45 minutes; when removing loaf from oven, brush top with melted butter. Serves 8.

Zucchini Bread

3 eggs
2 cups sugar
1 cup oil
2 cups grated zucchini with peels
3 cups flour
1 teaspoon cinnamon
1 teaspoon baking powder
1 teaspoon baking soda
1 cup chopped nuts
1 teaspoon vanilla

★ Preheat oven to 350°.

★ Mix all ingredients and 1 teaspoon salt and pour into 2 sprayed, floured 9 x 5-inch loaf pans. Bake for 1 hour or until golden brown. Yields 2 loaves.

Christmas Cranberry Bread

2 cups flour
1 cup sugar
1½ teaspoons baking powder
½ teaspoon baking soda
¼ cup shortening
¾ cup orange juice
1 tablespoon grated orange peel
1 egg, well beaten
½ cup chopped nuts
1 (16 ounce) can whole cranberry sauce

★ Preheat oven to 350°. Sift flour, sugar, baking powder, baking soda and 1 teaspoon salt in bowl. Cut in shortening until mixture resembles coarse cornmeal.

★ In separate bowl, combine orange juice, orange peel and egg and pour into dry ingredients. Mix just enough to dampen and fold in nuts and cranberry sauce. Spoon mixture into sprayed loaf pan and spread corners and sides slightly higher than center.

★ Bake for 1 hour until crust is brown and center is done. Remove, cool and store overnight for easy slicing. Serves 6 to 8.

Nut Bread

1 cup milk
2 tablespoons butter
¼ cup sugar
1 cake yeast
2 cups white flour
⅔ cup chopped walnuts
1½ - 2 cups whole wheat flour

★ Heat milk in saucepan and add butter, sugar and 1 teaspoon salt. Dissolve yeast in 2 tablespoons lukewarm water. When milk mixture cools, add yeast. Add white flour and walnuts and beat until smooth. Cover and set in warm plate to rise for about 1 hour.

★ Add whole wheat flour and knead or mix in stand mixer until it is elastic to touch and does not stick to unfloured board. Cover and set in warm place to rise until double in bulk.

★ Knead or mix again until free from air bubbles. Place in sprayed loaf pan. Cover and set in warm place to rise until doubled in bulk. Bake at 350° for 50 to 60 minutes. Yields 1 loaf.

Pilgrim Pumpkin Bread

*This is fabulous served with lots of butter or
for sandwiches with cream cheese filling.*

1 cup canola oil
3 cups sugar
4 eggs
1 teaspoon vanilla
1 (15 ounce) can pumpkin
2 teaspoons baking soda
2 teaspoons ground cinnamon
¼ teaspoon ground allspice
3 cups flour
1½ - 2 cups chopped pecans

★ Preheat oven to 350°. Combine oil and sugar in bowl; add eggs one at a time and beat well after each addition. Add vanilla and pumpkin and mix well.

★ In separate bowl, sift 1 teaspoon salt, baking soda, cinnamon, allspice and flour. Add to sugar-pumpkin mixture and beat well. Stir in pecans.

★ Pour into 2 large sprayed, floured 9 x 5-inch loaf pans. Bake for 1 hour 10 minutes to 1 hour 15 minutes. Bread is done when toothpick inserted in center comes out clean. Serves 12 to 16.

Quick Pumpkin Bread

1 (16 ounce) package pound cake mix
1 cup canned pumpkin
2 eggs
⅓ cup milk
1 teaspoon allspice

★ Preheat oven to 350°. Beat all ingredients in bowl and blend well. Pour into sprayed, floured 9 x 5-inch loaf pan.

★ Bake for 1 hour. Bread is done when toothpick inserted in center comes out clean. Cool and turn out onto cooling rack. Serves 15.

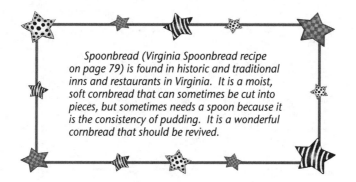

Spoonbread (Virginia Spoonbread recipe on page 79) is found in historic and traditional inns and restaurants in Virginia. It is a moist, soft cornbread that can sometimes be cut into pieces, but sometimes needs a spoon because it is the consistency of pudding. It is a wonderful cornbread that should be revived.

Very Berry Strawberry Bread

3 cups sifted flour
2 cups sugar
1 teaspoon baking soda
1 tablespoon ground cinnamon
3 large eggs, beaten
1 cup canola oil
1¼ cups chopped walnuts
2 (10 ounce) packages frozen sweetened strawberries with juice, thawed
1 (8 ounce) package light cream cheese, softened

★ Preheat oven to 350°. Combine flour, sugar, 1 teaspoon salt, baking soda and cinnamon in large bowl. Add remaining ingredients except cream cheese.

★ Pour in 2 sprayed, floured 9 x 5-inch loaf pans. Bake for 1 hour or when toothpick inserted in center comes out clean. Cool for several minutes before removing from pan.

★ To serve, slice bread and spread cream cheese between 2 slices. For finger sandwiches, cut in smaller pieces. Serves 12 to 16.

Salads

Waldorf Salad

⅓ cup mayonnaise
¼ cup sour cream
1 tablespoon lemon juice
1 teaspoon honey
2 cups cored and diced red apples
1 cup chopped celery
1 cup raisins
½ cup walnuts

★ Combine mayonnaise, sour cream, lemon juice, honey and ¼ teaspoon salt in large bowl. Add apples, celery, raisins and nuts. Toss until coated well. Refrigerate until ready to serve. Serves 6.

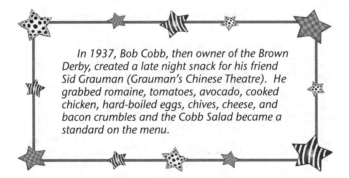

In 1937, Bob Cobb, then owner of the Brown Derby, created a late night snack for his friend Sid Grauman (Grauman's Chinese Theatre). He grabbed romaine, tomatoes, avocado, cooked chicken, hard-boiled eggs, chives, cheese, and bacon crumbles and the Cobb Salad became a standard on the menu.

Quick Caesar Salad

1 (1 ounce) package Caesar salad dressing
½ head romaine lettuce
¼ cup shredded parmesan cheese
Croutons

★ Tear lettuce in small pieces. Pour on Caesar salad dressing and toss.
   Add shredded parmesan cheese and croutons. Refrigerate before
   serving.

Classic Spinach Salad

Dressing:

½ cup olive oil
½ cup red wine vinegar
3 tablespoons ketchup
¼ cup sugar
½ teaspoon garlic powder
½ teaspoon dry mustard

★ Combine oil, vinegar, ketchup, sugar, 1 teaspoon salt, garlic powder, dry
   mustard and a little pepper in bowl to make dressing. Refrigerate for at
   least 6 hours before serving.

Salad:

1 (10 ounce) package fresh spinach
4 eggs, hard-boiled, sliced
8 slices bacon, crisply cooked, crumbled
1 cup sliced fresh mushrooms
1 small red onion, sliced
1 (8 ounce) can sliced water chestnuts, drained
Croutons

★ Wash, drain and tear spinach in bite-size pieces. When ready to serve,
   toss spinach with eggs, bacon, mushrooms, onion and dressing. Top
   with croutons and serve. Serves 6.

Spinach-Strawberry Salad

2 (10 ounce) packages fresh spinach
1 quart fresh strawberries, halved
½ cup slivered almonds, toasted
Poppy seed dressing

★ Wash and remove stems from spinach leaves. Tear leaves into smaller
   pieces and add strawberries and almonds in bowl. Refrigerate until
   ready to serve. Serve with Poppy Seed Dressing. Serves 6 to 8.

Spinach Salad Mold

1 (10 ounce) package frozen chopped spinach, thawed
1 (3 ounce) package lemon or lime gelatin
1 cup mayonnaise
1 cup cottage cheese, drained
⅓ cup diced celery
⅓ cup diced onion

★ Squeeze spinach between paper towels to completely remove excess moisture. Do not cook. Dissolve gelatin in ¾ cup boiling water in bowl and set aside to cool.

★ Combine spinach and remaining ingredients with gelatin and mix well. Pour mixture into ring mold and refrigerate until firm. Unmold and garnish as desired to serve. Serves 8.

Avocado-Spinach Salad

2 ripe avocados
1 (5 ounce) package baby spinach
½ carton grape tomatoes, halved
1 (4 ounce) package crumbled feta cheese
1 small red onion, chopped
⅓ cup coarsely chopped pistachios
Freshly ground peppercorns

★ Just before serving, peel, slice and cube avocados. Mix with remaining ingredients in bowl except dressing. Serve your favorite dressing on the side. Serves 4.

Texas 1015 or Georgia's Sweet Vidalia Onion Salad

No tears when you peel these onions.

2 large Texas 1015 or Vidalia® onions, sliced
1 (11 ounce) can mandarin oranges, drained, divided
½ cup walnuts, toasted
½ cup crumbled blue cheese
Assorted salad greens
Light vinaigrette dressing

★ Combine onion and half mandarin oranges in bowl. Toss with remaining ingredients. Add remaining oranges, if needed. Serves 6.

 Spinach Capital of the World   Alma, Arkansas

Fiesta Taco Salad

Meat:

1 pound ground beef
1 (8 ounce) jar hot salsa, divided
1 (1 ounce) packet taco seasoning

★ Crumble meat into large skillet, stir over medium heat until meat browns and drain. Add ½ cup salsa, taco seasoning and ½ teaspoon salt and cook for 2 minutes, stirring constantly.

Dressing:

½ cup sour cream
½ cup French or ranch dressing

★ To make dressing, whisk sour cream, French dressing and ½ cup salsa in small bowl until it blends well.

Salad:

1 medium head romaine lettuce, shredded
2 tomatoes, diced
½ red onion, chopped
1 (8 ounce) package shredded cheddar cheese
1 avocado, sliced
1 (16 ounce) bag tortilla chips

★ When ready to serve, place meat on plate with chips around it. Layer lettuce, tomatoes, onion and cheese on top of meat. Top with avocado slices and dressing. Serve immediately with tortilla chips. Serves 4.

Chile or Chili?

The controversy over the spelling of chile and chili is a matter of record between the people of Texas and New Mexico. Texans believe that chili spelled with an "i" is a dish. New Mexicans believe that chile with an "e" refers to the plant and to the dish. Texans claim to know how to spell the dish they invented and that the dictionary agrees with them.

Senator Pete Dominici of New Mexico officially stated the case for all New Mexicans in the Congressional Record in 1983. He said, "Knowing that criticizing the dictionary is akin to criticizing the Bible, I nevertheless stand here before the full Senate of the United States and with the backing of my New Mexican constituents state unequivocally, that the dictionary is wrong."

To signify the support of Dominici's constituents, the Albuquerque Journal reported "The I's of Texas are no longer on us. 'Chili' is dead. The only time we will use "i" will be when we quote the written word of some Texan."

Savory Layer Salad

Make this salad the day before you need it. Flavors will
strengthen and the layers will even look better.

Dressing:

2½ cups mayonnaise
1 (16 ounce) carton sour cream
1 teaspoon Worcestershire sauce
Hot sauce
¼ cup lemon juice

★ Combine mayonnaise, sour cream, Worcestershire sauce, hot sauce,
    lemon juice, and a little salt and pepper in bowl and mix well.

Salad:

1 package fresh spinach, torn in pieces
1 head iceberg lettuce, torn in pieces
1 cup (or less) sliced green onions
1 pound bacon, cooked, crumbled
6 eggs, hard-boiled, sliced
1 (10 ounce) package frozen green peas, thawed
1½ cups shredded Swiss cheese

★ Combine salad greens, onion and crumbled bacon. Pour salad mixture
    into 9 x 13-inch baking dish or large glass bowl and spread mayonnaise
    mixture over salad. Layer eggs and peas. Top with Swiss cheese. Cover
    and refrigerate for 24 hours. Serves 12 to 16.

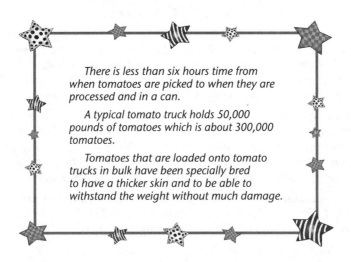

There is less than six hours time from
when tomatoes are picked to when they are
processed and in a can.

A typical tomato truck holds 50,000
pounds of tomatoes which is about 300,000
tomatoes.

Tomatoes that are loaded onto tomato
trucks in bulk have been specially bred
to have a thicker skin and to be able to
withstand the weight without much damage.

Cobb Salad

2 - 3 boneless, skinless chicken breast halves
6 slices bacon
½ head iceberg lettuce
½ head romaine lettuce
2 avocados, peeled, pitted, diced
2 hard-boiled eggs, diced
4 green onions with tops, chopped
2 tomatoes, peeled, diced
1 cup shredded sharp cheddar cheese
2 ounces crumbled roquefort cheese
Favorite salad dressing

★ In large saucepan boil chicken breast halves in enough water to cover
  for 30 to 40 minutes. Cool and dice. Fry bacon crispy, drain, cool and
  crumble. Tear iceberg and romaine lettuce in small pieces and toss
  together in salad bowl.

★ Arrange each ingredient in its own area on top of lettuce: one area for
  chicken, one for bacon, one for avocado, one for eggs, one for onion and
  one for tomatoes. Sprinkle with both cheeses or arrange them in their own
  areas. Refrigerate before serving. Serve with favorite dressing. Serves 4.

Chicken Salad

6 - 8 boneless, skinless chicken breast halves
½ cup chopped celery
½ cup chopped onion
2 eggs, hard-boiled, diced
6 tablespoons mayonnaise

★ In large saucepan boil chicken breast halves in enough water to cover for
  30 to 40 minutes. Cool, dice chicken and place in large bowl.

★ Add onion, celery, eggs and mayonnaise and mix well. Salt and pepper
  to taste. Spread on favorite bread, mound on lettuce leaves or stuff in
  hollowed out tomato. Serves 6 to 8.

Chicken, U.S.A. – Four cities in the United States have the word "chicken" in their names: Chicken, Alaska; Chicken Bristle, Illinois; Chicken Bristle, Kentucky; and Chicken Town, Pennsylvania. According to lore, Chicken, Alaska got its name because the locals wanted to honor the state bird, the ptarmigan, by naming their town Ptarmigan, Alaska. But they couldn't spell ptarmigan but they could spell chicken.

Hot Chicken Salad

4 cups cooked, diced cold chicken
2 cups chopped celery
4 eggs, hard-boiled, diced
2 tablespoons finely minced onions
2 tablespoons lemon juice
¾ cup mayonnaise
¾ cup cream of chicken soup
1 cup shredded cheese
1½ cups crushed potato chips
⅔ cup toasted, finely chopped almonds

★ Combine chicken, celery, eggs, onion, 1 teaspoon salt, lemon juice, mayonnaise and soup in bowl and mix well. Pour into 9 x 13-inch baking dish.

★ In separate bowl, combine cheese, potato chips and almonds and spread over top. Cover and refrigerate overnight. When ready to bake, preheat oven to 400°. Bake for 20 to 25 minutes. Serves 8.

Harbor Lobster Salad

2 pounds cooked lobster meat, flaked
2 tablespoons lemon juice
2 ribs celery, sliced
2 tomatoes, chopped
1 onion, minced
4 eggs, hard-boiled, diced
½ cucumber, peeled, diced
1 - 1¼ cups mayonnaise
Fresh parsley

★ Combine lobster, lemon juice, celery, tomatoes, onion, eggs and cucumber in bowl. Toss with 1 cup mayonnaise. (Add more if needed.) Refrigerate 3 to 4 hours before serving. Garnish with fresh parsley. Serves 4 to 6.

Maine is responsible for about 90% (about 40 million pounds) of the nation's lobster supply and about 25% of all the blueberries grown in North America. Maine is the largest producer of wild blueberries in the world.

Lobster Capital of the World   Rockland, Maine

Cape Cod Summer Salad

1 pound Atlantic cod fillets
4 cups chopped lettuce
3 medium cucumbers, peeled, seeded
2 medium tomatoes, cut into wedges
½ small red onion, sliced
½ cup chopped Greek olives
½ cup feta cheese

★ Cut cod into 1-inch pieces and place in shallow, microwave-safe dish. Cover loosely with wax paper or plastic wrap. Microwave on HIGH for 2 minutes, rotate dish and microwave for another 1 to 2 minutes or until fish flakes with fork. Set aside to cool.

★ Cut cucumbers into bite-size pieces and place in large bowl. Add tomatoes, onion and Greek olives, sprinkle on a little salt and pepper and toss lightly. Toss with just enough vinaigrette dressing to coat all ingredients. Add feta and cod and gently toss. Just before serving, sprinkle with a little salt and pepper to taste. Serves 4

Tuna Fish Salad

1 (12 ounce) can tuna fish, drained
½ cup chopped celery
¼ cup chopped pecans
2 eggs, hard-boiled, finely chopped
¼ teaspoon onion salt
Mayonnaise

★ Drain tuna and put in medium bowl. Add celery, pecans, eggs, onion salt and enough mayonnaise to moisten mixture. Refrigerate and serve. Serves 4.

TIP: You don't have to use chopped pecans or onion salt to make it good.

Simply Scrumptious Shrimp Salad

3 cups cooked, chopped shrimp
1 cup chopped celery
4 eggs, hard-boiled, chopped
¼ cup sliced green onions
1 cup mayonnaise
2 tablespoons chili sauce
1 tablespoon horseradish

★ Combine all ingredients in bowl, toss lightly with a little salt and pepper or seasoned salt and seasoned pepper. Refrigerate before serving. Serves 6 to 8.

 Tuna Capital of the World   Galilee, Rhode Island

Shrimp and English Pea Salad

2 cups small shrimp, cooked, cleaned
1 (10 ounce) package frozen green peas, thawed, drained
2 ribs celery, chopped
1 cup mayonnaise
⅓ cup sweet relish, drained
1 tablespoon lemon juice
1 (3 ounce) can chow mein noodles
1 cup chopped cashews
Lettuce leaves

★ Pat dry shrimp with paper towel to remove all liquid and place in large bowl. Add peas celery and toss lightly. Mix mayonnaise, relish, lemon juice and a little salt and pepper in small bowl and gently toss it with shrimp, peas and celery to mix well.

★ Cover and refrigerate for at least 1 hour. Just before serving, add noodles and cashews and toss. Serve on lettuce leaves. Serves 8.

Egg Salad

4 eggs, hard-boiled
⅓ cup mayonnaise
1 tablespoon dijon-style mustard
1 rib celery, minced
Bread

★ Mash eggs with fork and stir in mayonnaise, mustard and celery. Add salt and pepper to taste. Spread on bread and serve as sandwiches. Serves 2.

Deviled Eggs

6 eggs, hard-boiled
3 tablespoons mayonnaise
½ teaspoon mustard
Paprika

★ Peel eggs and cut in half lengthwise. Mash yolks with fork in bowl. Add mayonnaise and mustard to yolks. Place yolk mixture into egg white halves. Sprinkle with paprika. Serves 6 to 8.

Variations:

1. Add 1 (6 ounce) can crabmeat, drained and flaked, to yolk mixture.

2. Add 2 teaspoons pickle relish, 1 tablespoon minced onion and ¼ teaspoon cayenne.

3. Substitute dijon-style mustard for prepared mustard. Add chopped chives and 1 teaspoon chopped jalapenos (remove seeds).

Pear and Goat Cheese Salad

1 (10 ounce) package baby salad greens
¾ cup crumbled goat cheese
2 pears, peeled, sliced
½ cup balsamic vinaigrette salad dressing
½ cup coarsely chopped walnuts

★ In salad bowl, combine salad greens, cheese and pear slices and toss with salad dressing. Sprinkle walnuts over top of salad to serve. Serves 4.

Frozen Holiday Salad

2 (3 ounce) packages cream cheese, softened
2 tablespoons mayonnaise
2 tablespoons sugar
1 (16 ounce) can whole cranberry sauce
1 (8 ounce) can crushed pineapple, drained
½ cup chopped pecans
1 cup miniature marshmallows
1 (8 ounce) carton frozen whipped topping, thawed

★ Beat cream cheese, mayonnaise and sugar in bowl to smooth consistency. Add fruit, pecans and marshmallows and fold in whipped topping.

★ Pour in sprayed 9 x 13-inch shallow glass dish and freeze. When ready to serve, take salad out of freezer a few minutes before cutting in squares. Serves 8 to 10.

Chilled Cranberry Salad

1 (8 ounce) package cream cheese, softened
½ cup powdered sugar
1 tablespoon lemon juice
½ cup mayonnaise
1 (16 ounce) can whole cranberry sauce
1 cup frozen whipped topping, thawed

★ Beat cream cheese, powdered sugar, lemon juice and mayonnaise in bowl and blend well. Add cranberry sauce and whipped topping to cream cheese mixture and turn into 8 x 8-inch pan. Refrigerate. Cut into squares before serving. Serves 9.

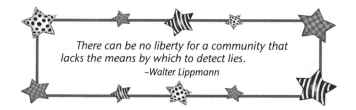

There can be no liberty for a community that lacks the means by which to detect lies.
–Walter Lippmann

Cherry-Cranberry Salad

1 (6 ounce) package cherry gelatin
1 (20 ounce) can cherry pie filling
1 (16 ounce) can whole cranberry sauce

★ In mixing bowl, combine cherry gelatin and 1 cup boiling water and mix until gelatin dissolves.

★ Mix pie filling and cranberry sauce into gelatin. Pour into 7 x 11-inch dish and refrigerate. Serves 4 to 6.

Harvest Berry Salad

A grand accompaniment with turkey or chicken salad.

1 (1 ounce) packet unflavored gelatin
1 (6 ounce) package raspberry or cherry gelatin
1 (15 ounce) can crushed pineapple with juice
1 (14 ounce) jar cranberry-orange relish
1 cup chopped pecans

★ Dissolve unflavored gelatin in ¼ cup cold water in bowl. In separate bowl, dissolve flavored gelatin in 1¼ cups boiling water.

★ Mix remaining ingredients and gelatin mixture and pour into 9 x 13-inch pan or 2-quart mold. Refrigerate until set. Serves 8 to 10.

Fantastic Fruit Salad

2 (11 ounce) cans mandarin oranges, drained
2 (15 ounce) cans pineapple chunks, drained
1 (16 ounce) carton frozen strawberries, drained
1 (20 ounce) can peach pie filling
1 (20 ounce) can apricot pie filling
2 bananas, sliced

★ Combine all ingredients in bowl, fold gently and refrigerate. Serves 12 to 16.

TIP: *If you want to make a day early, mix oranges, pineapple and pie fillings and add drained strawberries and bananas at the last minute.*

Two cannibals are eating a clown. One says to the other, "Does this taste funny to you?"

Stained-Glass Fruit Salad

2 (20 ounce) cans peach pie filling
3 bananas, sliced
1 (16 ounce) package frozen unsweetened strawberries, drained
1 (20 ounce) can pineapple tidbits, drained

★ Mix fruits, refrigerate and place in pretty crystal bowl. Refrigerate overnight. Serves 8.

Strawberry Salad

2 (3 ounce) packages strawberry gelatin
2 (10 ounce) packages frozen strawberries, thawed
1 cup crushed pineapple with juice
1 cup chopped nuts
2 bananas, sliced
1 (16 ounce) carton sour cream

★ Dissolve gelatin in 1⅔ cups boiling water in saucepan. Add frozen strawberries, remove from heat and stir occasionally until strawberries thaw.

★ Add crushed pineapple, nuts and bananas. Pour half mixture into 8 x 8-inch or 9 x 9-inch pan and refrigerate for 1 hour 30 minutes or until firm. Spread sour cream over firm mixture and pour remaining mixture over top. Refrigerate until set. Serves 12.

Dreamy Blueberry Salad

1 (8 ounce) can crushed pineapple with juice
2 (3 ounce) packages raspberry gelatin
1 (16 ounce) can blueberries, drained

★ Drain pineapple and add enough water to pineapple juice to make 2 cups. Pour into saucepan and bring to a boil. Pour hot liquid over gelatin and dissolve.

★ Refrigerate until mixture is consistency of egg whites. Mix blueberries and pineapple into gelatin and pour into a 9 x 9-inch pan. Refrigerate until firm.

Topping:

1 (8 ounce) package cream cheese
1 (8 ounce) carton sour cream
½ cup sugar
½ cup chopped pecans

★ Beat cream cheese, sour cream and sugar in bowl. Stir in pecans. Spread over congealed salad. Serves 9.

Grilled Grapefruit Cups

3 pink or ruby red grapefruits
4 oranges
2 limes
½ cup sherry
¼ cup plus 1 tablespoon packed light brown sugar
3 tablespoons butter

★ Cut grapefruit in half, remove interior flesh over large bowl and divide fruit into sections. Save juices in bowl with fruit and set grapefruit shells aside.

★ Cut top and bottom from oranges and limes over same bowl and discard them. Cut between pulp and inside peel and remove fruit. Remove any white portions on outside of fruit. Divide into sections and mix with grapefruit in bowl. Discard peels.

★ Drain juices from fruit bowl and set aside. Pour sherry over fruit, cover and marinate for 1 hour in refrigerator.

★ Place mixed fruit in grapefruit shells and sprinkle brown sugar over fruit. Divide butter equally among fruit in grapefruit shells. Place in 9 x 13-inch baking dish and broil in oven until butter melts and sugar crystallizes.

★ Pour remaining juices over top and serve immediately. Serves 6.

Divinity Salad

1 (6 ounce) package lemon gelatin
1 (8 ounce) package cream cheese
¾ cup chopped pecans
1 (15 ounce) can crushed pineapple with juice
1 (8 ounce) carton frozen whipped topping, thawed

★ With mixer, mix gelatin with 1 cup boiling water until dissolved.

★ Add cream cheese, beat slowly to start with, beat until smooth. Add pecans and pineapple. Cool in refrigerator until nearly set.

★ Fold in whipped topping. Pour into 9 x 13-inch dish. Refrigerate. Serves 4 to 6.

French fries refer to the French way of deep frying potatoes in a deep pan with oil. In 1802 Thomas Jefferson served "potatoes served in the French way" in the White House. The English and French refer to thick-sliced potatoes as chips and thin-sliced potatoes as crisps.

Cornbread Salad

2 (6 ounce) packages Mexican cornbread mix
2 eggs
1⅓ cups milk
2 ribs celery, sliced
1 bunch green onion with tops, chopped
2 tomatoes, chopped, drained
8 slices bacon, cooked, crumbled
1 (8 ounce) package shredded cheddar cheese
1 (8 ounce) can whole kernel corn, drained
2½ cups mayonnaise

★ Prepare cornbread according to package directions with egg and milk. Cook, cool and crumble cornbread in large bowl.

★ Add celery, green onions, tomatoes, bacon, cheese, corn and mayonnaise and toss. Refrigerate for several hours and serve. Serves 8.

Nutty Slaw

1 (16 ounce) package shredded carrots
3 cups shredded cabbage
2 red delicious apples, diced
¾ cup raisins
¾ cup chopped walnuts
1 (8 ounce) bottle coleslaw dressing

★ In plastic bowl with lid, combine shredded carrots, shredded cabbage, apples, raisins and walnuts. Pour about three-fourths bottle of dressing over mixture and increase dressing as needed. Cover and refrigerate several hours before serving. Serves 4.

Traditional Coleslaw

½ cup sugar
½ cup vinegar
¼ cup milk
1 - 2 cups mayonnaise
1 large head cabbage
1 - 2 carrots, grated, optional

★ Combine sugar, vinegar, milk and just enough mayonnaise to make dressing consistency in bowl. Add a little salt and pepper.

★ Discard outside leaves of cabbage, wash remaining leaves and chop finely in food processor or on grater. Grate carrots and mix with cabbage. Mix dressing and cabbage well, cover and refrigerate. Serves 8 to 10.

Broccoli-Noodle Salad

This is a really good, quick salad that you will make more than once.

1 cup slivered almonds, toasted
1 cup sunflower seeds, toasted
2 (3 ounce) packages chicken-flavored ramen noodles
1 (16 ounce) package broccoli slaw
1 (8 ounce) bottle Italian salad dressing

★ Preheat oven to 255°. Toast almonds and sunflower seeds on baking
sheet for about 10 minutes. Break up ramen noodles and mix with slaw,
almonds and sunflower seeds in bowl. Toss with Italian salad dressing
and refrigerate overnight. Serves 12 to 16.

Broccoli Salad

5 cups cut broccoli florets
1 red bell pepper, julienned
1 cup chopped celery
8 - 12 ounces Monterey Jack cheese, cubed
Italian salad dressing or other favorite dressing

★ Combine all ingredients except dressing and mix well. Toss with Italian
or your favorite dressing and refrigerate. Serves 4 to 6.

Carrot Salad Supreme

2 (3 ounce) packages lemon gelatin
1 tablespoon vinegar or lemon juice
1 (20 ounce) can crushed pineapple with juice
1 cup shredded sharp cheddar cheese
1 cup grated carrots
¾ cup chopped pecans

★ Dissolve gelatin in 2 cups boiling water in bowl and add vinegar and ½
teaspoon salt. Refrigerate slightly. Drain pineapple and add enough
water to juice to equal 2 cups.

★ Fold in cheese, carrots, pineapple, juice and water, and pecans. Pour
into mold rinsed in cold water and refrigerate until firm. Unmold on
platter and serve plain or use dressing consisting of 2 parts mayonnaise
and 1 part sour cream. Serves 8.

Ham Capital of the World　Smithfield, Virginia

Crunchy Cauliflower-Broccoli Salad

1 head cauliflower, cut into florets
1 bunch broccoli, cut into florets
1 cup mayonnaise
¾ cup sour cream
1 tablespoon white wine vinegar
1 tablespoon sugar
1 onion, chopped

★ Wash and pat dry cauliflower and broccoli. Allow vegetables to stand so they will completely drain. Mix mayonnaise, sour cream, vinegar, sugar, onion, 1 teaspoon salt and ½ teaspoon pepper in bowl. Pour dressing over vegetables and toss. Refrigerate for several hours before serving. Serves 8 to 10.

Garlic Green Bean Salad

3 (15 ounce) cans whole green beans, drained
⅔ cup olive oil
½ cup vinegar
½ cup sugar
5 cloves garlic, minced
Cayenne pepper

★ Place green beans in container with lid. Mix oil, vinegar, sugar and garlic in bowl and pour over beans. Sprinkle with a little salt and cayenne pepper. Refrigerate overnight. Serves 8 to 10.

Colorful English Pea Salad

2 (16 ounce) packages frozen green peas, thawed, drained
1 (12 ounce) package cubed mozzarella or cheddar cheese
1 red and 1 orange bell pepper, chopped
1 onion, chopped
1¼ cups mayonnaise

★ In large salad bowl, combine uncooked peas, cubed cheese, bell peppers and onion and toss to mix. Stir in mayonnaise and a little salt and pepper. Refrigerate before serving. Serves 8.

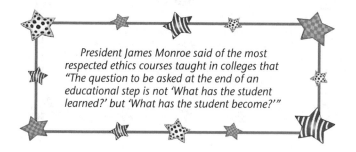

President James Monroe said of the most respected ethics courses taught in colleges that "The question to be asked at the end of an educational step is not 'What has the student learned?' but 'What has the student become?'"

Carrot-Raisin Salad

*This recipe has stood the test of time and is a
great combination of fruits and vegetables.*

3 large carrots, peeled, shredded
½ cup dark raisins
⅓ cup crushed drained pineapple
½ cup reduced-fat mayonnaise
1 teaspoon fresh lemon juice

★ Combine all ingredients. Serve or cover and refrigerate. Serves 5.

Chilled Baby Lima Bean Salad

2 (10 ounce) packages frozen baby lima beans
1 (15 ounce) can shoe-peg corn (or white corn), drained
1 bunch green onions with tops, chopped
1 cup mayonnaise
2 teaspoons ranch salad dressing seasoning

★ Cook beans according to package directions and drain. Add corn,
onions, mayonnaise and seasoning, mix well and refrigerate. Serves 8.

Sweet Onion Stack

2 large Vidalia® or Texas 1015 Sweet Onions
2 large garden tomatoes
Olive oil
Fresh lime juice
Chopped basil
Crumbled blue cheese

★ Cut onions and tomatoes into thick slices and arrange on plate. Sprinkle
with ½ teaspoon salt and let stand for about 30 minutes.

★ Drizzle with olive oil and fresh lime juice. Add chopped basil and
crumbled blue cheese, if desired. Serves 4.

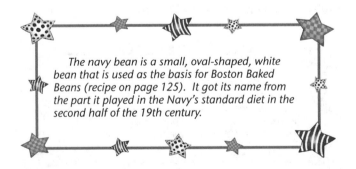

*The navy bean is a small, oval-shaped, white
bean that is used as the basis for Boston Baked
Beans (recipe on page 125). It got its name from
the part it played in the Navy's standard diet in the
second half of the 19th century.*

Mozzarella Cheese with Hot House Tomatoes

8 hot house tomatoes
8 slices fresh mozzarella cheese
1 sweet onion, sliced
3 tablespoons extra-virgin olive oil
8 - 10 leaves fresh basil

★ Slice tomatoes and mozzarella into ½-inch thick, round pieces. Arrange tomatoes and mozzarella slices in overlapping, alternating pattern on serving dish. Drizzle olive oil over arrangement and sprinkle with salt and pepper. Place fresh basil leaves on top of mozzarella slices. Serves 4.

TIP: *Slices of Texas 1015 or Vidalia® sweet onions are a great addition to this popular salad.*

Potato Salad

6 large potatoes
1 egg, hard-boiled, chopped
1 onion, chopped
2 ribs celery, chopped
¼ cup chopped dill pickle
1½ teaspoons mustard
½ cup mayonnaise

★ Peel and wash potatoes, cut each potato in 4 to 6 pieces and put in large saucepan. Cover with water and boil until potatoes are tender. Cool and cut potatoes into bite-size pieces. Stir together cubed potatoes, egg, onion, celery, pickle, mustard, mayonnaise, and salt and pepper to taste. Mix well and refrigerate. Serves 8 to 10.

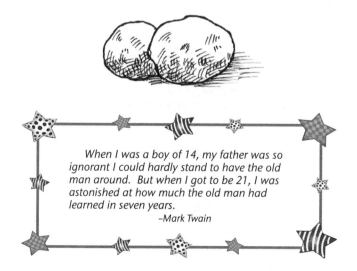

When I was a boy of 14, my father was so ignorant I could hardly stand to have the old man around. But when I got to be 21, I was astonished at how much the old man had learned in seven years.

–Mark Twain

Hot German Potato Salad

8 slices bacon, cooked, crumbled with drippings
1 - 2 pounds red potatoes
1 teaspoon flour
¼ cup cider vinegar
1½ - 2 tablespoons sugar
⅓ cup chopped celery
⅓ cup chopped onion
1 - 2 eggs, hard-boiled

★ Cook bacon in skillet, crumble and set aside. Save bacon drippings. Gently cook potatoes in boiling water in saucepan until just tender. Drain and set aside.

★ Return ¼ cup bacon drippings to skillet over low heat, add flour and stir until flour dissolves. Add vinegar and ¼ cup water, stir constantly and simmer for about 1 minute or until it thickens. Turn heat off and add sugar and stir until it dissolves.

★ When potatoes are just cool enough to handle, slice one-third into large baking dish and add one-third each of celery, onion and bacon.

★ Sprinkle lightly with a little salt and pepper and drizzle several spoonfuls of dressing over top. Repeat this process 1 more time, but reserve 2 spoonfuls of dressing. Slice eggs over top and drizzle remaining dressing over eggs. Serve warm. Serves 4 to 6.

Sour Cream Potato Salad

12 medium red potatoes, unpeeled
¼ cup vinegar
4 eggs, hard-boiled
2 cups sour cream
2 tablespoons mustard
1 clove garlic, minced
1 small onion, diced

★ Boil red potatoes until tender about 20 minutes. Cube potatoes and refrigerate. Combine vinegar, eggs, sour cream and mustard.

★ Add garlic, onion, and 2 teaspoons each of salt and pepper. When potatoes are cool toss with sour cream mixture. Serves 4 to 6.

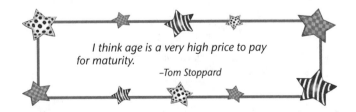

I think age is a very high price to pay for maturity.
–Tom Stoppard

Easy Parslied Potato Salad

2 pounds red potatoes, quartered
¾ - 1 cup Caesar dressing
½ cup grated parmesan cheese
¼ cup chopped fresh parsley
½ cup chopped roasted red peppers

★ Cook potatoes in saucepan in boiling water until fork-tender and drain.
  Cut potatoes in half or thirds, place in large bowl and pour dressing over
  potatoes. Add cheese, parsley and red peppers and toss lightly. Serve
  warm or chilled. Serves 6 to 8.

Sweet Potato Salad

4 medium sweet potatoes
8 slices bacon, fried, drained, crumbled
½ cup minced onion
Canola oil
Sugar
Vinegar

★ Boil sweet potatoes in saucepan until tender and drain. When cool peel
  potatoes and cube. Place cubed potatoes in large bowl.

★ Add a little oil to bacon drippings, add onion and cook over low heat for
  several minutes. Cool slightly and add sugar and vinegar to taste.

★ Pour dressing over sweet potatoes and gently toss. Let stand at room
  temperature for about 15 minutes. Stir again and sprinkle bacon over
  top. Serves 5 to 6.

Soups, Stews and Chowders

Quick Chicken-Noodle Soup

2 (14 ounce) cans chicken broth
2 boneless, skinless chicken breast halves, cubed
1 (8 ounce) can sliced carrots, drained
2 ribs celery, sliced
½ (8 ounce) package medium egg noodles

★ Combine broth, chicken, carrots, celery and generous dash of pepper in
  large saucepan. Boil and cook for 3 minutes.

★ Stir in noodles, reduce heat and cook for 10 minutes or until noodles are
  done; stir often. Serves 4 to 6.

Chicken-Noodle Soup

1 (3 - 4 pound) whole chicken
1 carrot, chopped
2 ribs celery with leaves, chopped
½ - ¾ cups cooked egg noodles, cooked

★ Wash whole chicken and giblets and put in large soup pot. Add 7 to
8 cups water, carrot and celery and bring to boil. Reduce heat and
simmer, partially covered, for 30 minutes to 1 hour or until meat is
tender.

★ Remove chicken from soup pot and cool. Continue simmering and
spoon off fat from top of liquid when needed. Bone chicken and put all
bones and skin back into soup pot.

★ Continue to simmer for 3 to 4 hours. Turn heat off and strain chicken
stock in large bowl. Add chopped chicken and cooked egg noodles. Salt
and pepper to taste. Serves 8 to 10.

15-Minute Turkey Soup

1 (14 ounce) can chicken broth
3 (15 ounce) cans navy beans, rinsed, drained
1 (28 ounce) can diced tomatoes with liquid
2 - 3 cups small chunks white turkey meat
2 teaspoons minced garlic
Freshly grated parmesan cheese

★ Mix all ingredients except cheese in saucepan and heat. Garnish with
parmesan cheese before serving. Serves 6.

TIP: A little cayenne pepper gives this a nice kick.

Turkey-Mushroom Soup

Here's another great way to use leftover chicken or turkey.

2 cups sliced mushrooms
2 ribs celery, chopped
1 small onion, chopped
2 tablespoons butter
1 (15 ounce) can sliced carrots, drained
2 (14 ounce) cans chicken broth
2 cups cooked, chopped turkey

★ Saute mushrooms, celery and onion in butter in skillet. Transfer to slow
cooker and add carrots, broth and turkey. (Do not use smoked turkey.)
Cover and cook on LOW for 2 to 3 hours or on HIGH for 1 to 2 hours.
Serves 6.

Ham and Fresh Okra Soup

1 ham hock
1 cup frozen butter beans or lima beans
1½ pounds cooked, cubed ham or chicken
1 (15 ounce) can chopped stewed tomatoes
3 cups small whole okra
2 large onions, diced
Rice, cooked

★ Boil ham hock in 1½ quarts water in soup pot for about 1 hour 30 minutes. Add remaining ingredients and slow-boil for additional 1 hour. Season with a little salt and pepper and serve over rice. Serves 6 to 8.

Bacon-Potato Soup

2 (14 ounce) cans chicken broth seasoned with garlic
2 potatoes, peeled, cubed
1 onion, finely chopped
6 slices bacon, cooked, crumbled

★ In large saucepan, combine broth, potatoes and onion. Bring to a boil, reduce heat to medium-high and boil about 10 minutes or until potatoes are tender. Season with pepper. Ladle into bowls and sprinkle with crumbled bacon. Serves 3 to 4.

Chorizo-Bean Soup

1 cup dried great northern beans
1 ham hock
2 chorizo sausages
1 onion, chopped
½ teaspoon cayenne
1 large potato, cubed
1 bunch turnip greens, finely shredded

★ Boil beans in 2½ quarts water in large saucepan for 2 minutes. Remove from heat and soak for 1 hour. Add ham hock and bring to a boil. Lower heat and simmer for 1 hour 30 minutes.

★ Prick sausages with fork and add onion, 2 teaspoons salt, cayenne pepper, potato and sausages. Simmer for 30 minutes. About 15 minutes before serving, remove sausages and discard. Add turnip greens and cook on low for remaining 15 minutes. Serves 6.

 Pinto Bean Capital of the World   Dove Creek, Colorado

Easy Crab Soup

3 cups milk
¼ teaspoon mace
1 teaspoon grated lemon peel
1 pound fresh crabmeat, flaked
1 (1 pint) carton whipping cream
¼ cup (½ stick) butter
½ cup cracker crumbs
2 tablespoons sherry

★ Pour milk, mace and lemon peel in double boiler and simmer on low to medium heat for 5 minutes. Add crabmeat, cream and butter and cook over simmer for 15 minutes.

★ Stir in cracker crumbs, a little at a time, to get desired consistency and season soup with a little salt and pepper. Cover, remove from heat and set aside for 5 to 10 minutes so flavors blend. Add sherry before serving. Serves 6.

Oyster Soup

2 (14 ounce) cans chicken broth
1 large onion, chopped
3 ribs celery, sliced
1 red bell pepper, seeded, chopped
2 teaspoons minced garlic
2 (1 pint) cartons fresh oysters, rinsed, drained
½ cup (1 stick) butter
¼ cup flour
2 cups milk
1 tablespoon dried parsley

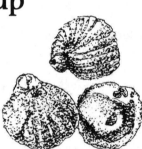

★ Combine broth, onion, celery, bell pepper and garlic in soup pot. Bring to boil, reduce heat and simmer, stirring occasionally for 30 minutes. Boil oysters in 2 cups water in saucepan for 2 minutes or until edges of oysters begin to curl; stir often. Remove oysters with slotted spoon, coarsely chop half and set aside. Pour oyster stock into soup pot with vegetables.

★ Melt butter in saucepan over medium heat, gradually whisk in flour and cook for 1 minute. Add flour mixture to soup pot and simmer, stirring occasionally, over medium heat for 3 minutes.

★ Stir in chopped oysters, milk, parsley and a little salt and pepper. Cook and stir occasionally over medium heat for 8 minutes or until mixture thickens. Stir in remaining whole oysters. Serves 6 to 8.

 Oyster Capital of the World   Port Norris, New Jersey

Spicy Bean Soup

1 (15 ounce) can refried beans
1 (14 ounce) can chicken broth
2 (4 ounce) cans diced green chilies
2 cloves garlic, minced
1 - 3 jalapeno chilies, seeded, chopped*
1 teaspoon chili powder
6 slices bacon
5 ribs celery, chopped
1 bell pepper, seeded, chopped
1 bunch green onions with tops, chopped, divided
1 (8 ounce) package shredded cheddar cheese

★ Heat refried beans and chicken broth in large saucepan and whisk beans and broth together. Add green chilies, garlic, jalapenos, ¼ teaspoon black pepper and chili powder and stir well. Reduce heat to low and stir occasionally.

★ Fry bacon in skillet until crisp and drain. In pan drippings saute celery, bell pepper, and about three-fourths of onions until onions are translucent.

★ Crumble bacon and put into bean soup. Add onions, celery, bell pepper and pan drippings and stir well. Bring to a boil, reduce heat to low and serve immediately. Garnish with remaining onions and cheese. Serves 4.

TIP: Wear rubber gloves when removing seeds from jalapenos.

Slow-Cook Navy Bean and Ham Soup

1½ cups dry navy beans
1 carrot, finely chopped
¼ cup finely chopped celery
1 small onion, finely chopped
1 (¾ pound) ham hock

★ Soak beans for 8 to 12 hours and drain. Place all ingredients, 5 cups water, ½ teaspoon salt and a dash of pepper in 2-quart slow cooker. Cook for 8 to 10 hours on LOW setting.

★ Remove ham hock and discard skin, fat and bone. Cut meat in small pieces and place in soup. Serves 6 to 8.

Jay: Did you hear the joke about the broken egg?

Alfred: Yes, it cracked me up!

Quick Navy Bean Soup

3 (16 ounce) cans navy beans with juice
1 (14 ounce) can chicken broth
1 cup chopped ham
1 large onion, chopped
½ teaspoon garlic powder

★ In large saucepan, combine all ingredients with 1 cup water and bring
to a boil. Simmer until onion is tender-crisp and serve hot with cheese
muffins or cornbread. Serves 4 to 6.

Rainy Day Lentil Soup

¼ cup apple juice
1 cup chopped onions
½ cup diced celery
2 (14 ounce) cans chicken broth
1 cup shredded carrots
½ cup shredded sweet potatoes
1 cup dry lentils, sorted, rinsed
1 - 2 tablespoons minced garlic
½ teaspoon cumin

★ Bring apple juice to a boil in large saucepan. Add onions and celery and
return to boil. Add chicken broth, carrots, sweet potatoes, lentils and
garlic and bring to a boil.

★ Reduce heat to medium, add cumin and cover. Cook for about
30 minutes or until flavors mix. Add a little salt and pepper. Serves 4.

Basic Bean Soup

1 pound dry beans
½ pound ham slice or bacon slices
1 - 2 onions, chopped
6 - 8 baby carrots, chopped
¼ cup tomato sauce or ketchup

★ Soak beans overnight, drain and rinse thoroughly. Place beans in large
saucepan and pour water in about 2 inches above beans. Bring to a boil
and reduce heat to medium. Add onions, carrots and tomato sauce.

★ Cover and cook for about 30 minutes. Reduce heat and cook, covered,
on low for about 1 hour or until beans are slightly tender. Add salt and
pepper to taste and simmer another 20 minutes. Serves 8 to 10.

Incredible Broccoli-Cheese Soup

1 (10 ounce) package frozen chopped broccoli
3 tablespoons butter
¼ onion, finely chopped
¼ cup flour
1 (16 ounce) carton half-and-half cream
1 (14 ounce) can chicken broth
⅛ teaspoon cayenne pepper
1 (8 ounce) package cubed mild Mexican Velveeta® cheese

★ Punch several holes in broccoli package and microwave for 5 minutes. Turn package in microwave and cook for additional 4 minutes. Leave in microwave for 3 minutes.

★ Melt butter in large saucepan over low heat and saute onion but do not brown. Add flour, stir and gradually add half-and-half cream, chicken broth, ½ teaspoon salt, ¼ teaspoon pepper and cayenne pepper.

★ Stir constantly and heat until mixture is slightly thick. Do NOT let mixture come to a boil. Add cheese, stir and heat until cheese melts. Add cooked broccoli. Serve piping hot. Serves 4 to 6.

Cheesy Cauliflower Soup

1 (16 ounce) package frozen cauliflower florets
2 ribs celery, sliced
1 carrot, peeled, cut into chunks
1 onion, chopped
1 tablespoon instant chicken bouillon granules
½ teaspoon lemon pepper
1 (8 ounce) carton whipping cream
1 (8 ounce) package shredded Monterey Jack cheese, divided

★ Combine 2 cups water, cauliflower, celery, carrot, onion, chicken bouillon, ½ teaspoon salt and lemon pepper in large, heavy soup pot. Cover and cook for 1 hour or until vegetables are very tender. Pour half mixture into food processor and blend until smooth.

★ Repeat with remaining soup mixture. Return to soup pot and stir in cream and about three-fourths of cheese. Cook over medium heat, stirring constantly, until cheese melts and mixture is thoroughly hot. Ladle into individual serving bowls and sprinkle remaining cheese over each serving. Serves 6 to 8.

Cream of Carrot Soup

1 small onion, chopped
2 tablespoons butter
6 carrots, chopped
2 tablespoons dry white wine
2 (14 ounce) cans chicken broth
1/8 teaspoon ground nutmeg
1 (8 ounce) carton whipping cream, whipped

★ Saute onion in butter and add carrots, wine, chicken broth, nutmeg, 1/2 teaspoon pepper and a little salt in large saucepan. Boil, reduce heat and simmer for 30 minutes or until carrots are tender.

★ Pour half of carrot mixture into blender, cover and blend on medium speed until mixture is smooth. Repeat with remaining mixture. Return to saucepan and heat just until hot. Stir in cream and serve. Serves 6.

Roasted Garlic Soup

4 - 6 cloves garlic
1 tablespoon olive oil, divided
1 onion, finely chopped
2 (14 ounce) cans chicken broth
4 russet potatoes, peeled, diced
2 teaspoons fresh lemon thyme or 1/2 teaspoon dried thyme
1/2 cup low-fat yogurt
1/2 cup shredded gruyere or jarlsberg cheese
Chives or flat-leaf parsley, chopped

★ Preheat oven to 375°. Remove loose skins and cut pointed end and papery skin from garlic. Rub with 1 teaspoon olive oil. Wrap in foil and place in baking dish. Bake for 35 to 40 minutes or until soft; let cool.

★ Squeeze garlic from outer skin into bowl and set aside. Heat remaining oil in large saucepan over medium heat and saute onion until tender. Add garlic and saute for 1 minute.

★ Add broth, potatoes and thyme. Cover and simmer until potatoes are very tender, about 25 minutes. Puree with yogurt in batches in blender. Serve warm in bowls and top with cheese and chopped chives or parsley. Serves 4.

The press must grow day in and day out – it is our Party's sharpest and most powerful weapon.
–Joseph Stalinn

Easy Potato Soup

1 (16 ounce) package frozen hash-brown potatoes
1 cup chopped onion
1 (14 ounce) can chicken broth
1 (10 ounce) can fiesta-nacho soup
1 (10 ounce) can cream of chicken soup
2 cups milk

★ Combine potatoes, onion and 2 cups water in large saucepan and bring to a boil. Cover, reduce heat and simmer for 30 minutes. Stir in broth, soups and milk and heat thoroughly. Serves 6 to 8.

Creamy Baked Potato Soup

4 slices bacon
1 bunch green onions with tops, chopped
1 - 2 cloves garlic, minced
¼ cup flour
1 (15 ounce) can chicken broth
2 large baking potatoes, baked, peeled, cubed
1 cup half-and-half cream
Shredded cheddar cheese

★ Fry bacon crispy and set aside. Saute onions and garlic in bacon grease until onions are translucent. Stir flour into skillet until lumps are gone. Add chicken broth and a little salt and pepper. Cook on low for about 10 minutes.

★ Add baked potato cubes and cream and stir well. Break up some of the potatoes to blend in with cream. (Do not boil.) Serve hot and garnish with bacon crumbles and cheese. Serves 4.

Pumpkin Soup

1 (8 ounce) package fresh mushrooms, sliced
¼ cup (½ stick) butter
¼ cup flour
2 (14 ounce) cans vegetable broth
1 (15 ounce) can cooked pumpkin
1 (1 pint) carton half-and-half cream
2 tablespoons honey
2 tablespoons sugar
½ teaspoon curry powder
¼ teaspoon ground nutmeg
Sour cream

★ Saute mushrooms in butter in large saucepan. Add flour, stir well and gradually add broth. Boil and cook for 2 minutes or until mixture thickens.

★ Stir in pumpkin, half-and-half cream, honey, sugar, curry powder and nutmeg. Stir constantly until soup is thoroughly hot. Serve with a dollop of sour cream on top of soup. Serves 6.

Old-Fashioned Tomato Soup

2½ pounds fresh tomatoes, peeled, seeded, chopped
    or 4 cups canned stewed, chopped tomatoes
3 - 4 cups chicken stock
2 ribs celery, minced
1 carrot, minced
1 onion, minced
2 tablespoons basil

★ In large soup pot, combine tomatoes, chicken stock, celery, carrot, onion and basil on high heat. After soup begins to boil, reduce heat to low and simmer for 15 to 30 minutes. Add basil, salt and pepper to taste. Serves 4 to 6.

Cream of Tomato Soup:

★ Omit chicken stock and onion and substitute 2 to 3 cups half-and-half cream. Bring to almost boiling and reduce heat to simmer.

Quick and Easy Peanut Soup

¼ cup (½ stick) butter
1 onion, finely chopped
2 ribs celery, chopped
2 (10 ounce) cans cream of chicken soup
2 soup cans milk
1¼ cups crunchy peanut butter

★ Melt butter in saucepan and saute onion and celery over low heat. Blend in soup and milk and stir. Add peanut butter and continue to heat until mixture blends well. Serves 4 to 6.

Edna Earle's Cold Peach Soup

2 pounds peaches
1 tablespoon lemon juice
3 tablespoons quick-cooking tapioca
3 tablespoons sugar
1 (6 ounce) can frozen orange juice concentrate

★ Puree peaches with lemon juice in blender and set aside. Combine tapioca, sugar, dash of salt and 1 cup water in saucepan. Heat to full boil and stir constantly.

★ Transfer to medium-sized bowl. Stir in orange juice until it melts. Add 1½ cups water and stir until smooth. Mix in pureed peaches, cover and refrigerate. Serve cold. Serves 8.

 Peach Capital of the World   Johnston, South Carolina

Sunny Strawberry Soup

1 ½ cups fresh strawberries
1 cup orange juice
¼ cup honey
½ cup sour cream
½ cup white wine

★ Combine all ingredients in blender and puree. Refrigerate thoroughly. Stir before serving. Serves 2.

One-Alarm Chili

Jerry Jeff Walker probably said it best, "If you know beans about chili, you know chili has no beans."

2 pounds beef chuck, cubed
2 tablespoons oil
1 onion, chopped
3 cloves garlic, chopped
1 (8 ounce) can tomato sauce
1 cup beef broth
3 - 5 tablespoons chili powder
2 teaspoons ground cumin

★ Brown beef in hot oil in large, heavy saucepan. Stir in onion, garlic, tomato sauce and beef broth. Stir to mix well. Add chili powder, cumin, ½ teaspoon each of salt and pepper and stir to mix.

★ Cover and simmer for 1 to 2 hours and stir occasionally. If liquid is too thin, remove cover and continue simmering. Note: To make chili hotter, add more chili powder or slices of seeded jalapenos. Add additional seasonings a little at a time, cook 10 minutes and taste. Serves 6 to 8.

Beefy Veggie Soup

1 pound lean ground beef
2 teaspoons minced garlic
2 (15 ounce) cans Italian stewed tomatoes
2 (14 ounce) cans beef broth
2 teaspoons Italian seasoning
1 (16 ounce) package frozen mixed vegetables
⅓ cup shell macaroni
Shredded mozzarella cheese

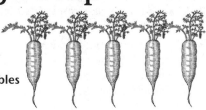

★ Cook beef and garlic in large soup pot for 5 minutes. Stir in tomatoes, broth, 1 cup water, seasoning, mixed vegetables, macaroni and a little salt and pepper.

★ Bring to a boil, reduce heat and simmer for 10 to 15 minutes or until macaroni is tender. Ladle into individual serving bowls and sprinkle several tablespoons cheese over top of soup. Serves 8.

Blue Ribbon Beef Stew

1 (2½ pound) boneless beef chuck roast, cubed
⅓ cup flour
2 (14 ounce) cans beef broth
2 teaspoons minced garlic
1 pound red potatoes with peel, sliced
2 large carrots, chopped
3 ribs celery, chopped
2 onions, finely chopped
1 (10 ounce) package frozen green peas

★ Dredge beef in flour mixed with 1 teaspoon salt; reserve leftover flour. Brown half beef in a little oil in stew pot over medium heat for about 10 minutes and transfer to plate. Repeat with remaining beef.

★ Add a little of reserved flour to stew pot and cook, stir constantly, for 1 minute. Stir in beef broth, ½ cup water, thyme and garlic and boil. Reduce heat, simmer for 50 minutes and stir occasionally.

★ Add potatoes, carrots, celery and onion and cook for 30 minutes. Stir in green peas, a little salt and pepper just before serving; heat to boiling. Serve immediately. Serves 6.

Blue Norther Stew

*When cold weather comes from the north to
the south, Southerners call it a "norther".*

1½ pounds lean ground beef
1 onion, chopped
1 (1 ounce) packet taco seasoning
1 (1 ounce) packet ranch dressing mix
1 (15 ounce) can whole kernel corn, drained
1 (15 ounce) can kidney beans with liquid
2 (15 ounce) cans pinto beans
2 (15 ounce) cans Mexican stewed tomatoes
1 (10 ounce) can diced tomatoes and green chilies

★ Brown ground beef and onion in large roasting pan. Add both packets of seasonings and mix well. Add corn, kidney beans, pinto beans, stewed tomatoes, tomatoes and green chilies, and 1 cup water, mix well and simmer for about 30 minutes. Serves 8.

Meat and Potato Stew

2 pounds beef stew meat
2 (15 ounce) cans new potatoes, drained
1 (15 ounce) can sliced carrots, drained
2 (10 ounce) cans French onion soup

★ Season meat with a little salt and pepper and cook with 2 cups water in
  large pot for 1 hour. Add potatoes, carrots and onion soup and mix well.
  Bring to a boil, reduce heat and simmer for 30 minutes. Serves 6 to 8.

Low Country Frogmore Stew

*Frogmore Stew originated in South Carolina's Low Country and
dates back many years. Here's one version of the famous dish.*

¼ cup Old Bay seafood seasoning
3 pounds smoked link sausage, sliced
3 onions, peeled, chopped
1 lemon, sliced, seeded
½ cup (1 stick) butter
6 ears corn, broken in half
3 pounds large shrimp with peel
Cocktail sauce

★ Add about 2 gallons water, seasoning, sausage, onions, lemon, and a
  little salt and pepper in large stew pot. Bring to a boil. Simmer for
  45 minutes.

★ Add butter and corn and cook for 10 minutes. Add shrimp and cook
  for additional 5 minutes. Drain. Remove with slotted spoon to serving
  platter. Serve with cocktail sauce. Serves 8 to 12.

Easy Basic Stews

Meat
Liquid
Vegetables
Seasonings

★ Meat: Use an inexpensive cut of beef such as chuck roast or London
  broil. Place in roasting pan, almost cover with water and put lid on.
  Bake at 350° for several hours or until tender. Add more water if needed.
  Cut meat into bite-size pieces and return to liquid.

★ Vegetables: Add canned or fresh vegetables (potatoes, carrots, onions,
  tomatoes, corn, etc) to roast and cook until potatoes are tender. Just
  warm up canned vegetables, but cook fresh vegetables about 30 to
  60 minutes with meat and liquid.

★ Seasonings: The best seasonings are salt and pepper. Others you might
  consider include garlic powder, lemon pepper, seasoned salt, oregano,
  bay leaf, thyme, rosemary, etc. Choose your favorites or just what you
  have on hand.

Sister's Brunswick Stew

*This signature southern dish originated in Virginia or Georgia,
both claim its origin. It was first cooked with whatever was
available, squirrel, rabbit, chicken, ham or beef and vegetables.*

1 whole chicken or 3 pounds boneless chicken breasts
½ pound cooked, chopped pork roast or ham
1½ cups peeled, chopped red potatoes
1 (15 ounce) can tomato sauce
2 cups frozen corn
1½ cups frozen lima beans
1 cup chopped onion
2 tablespoons butter
2 tablespoons Worcestershire sauce
¼ teaspoon cayenne pepper
1 teaspoon sugar

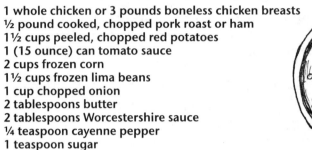

★ Cook chicken in enough water to cover; bring to a boil, reduce heat,
  cover and simmer for 1½ to 2 hours or until done. Reserve stock. Bone
  chicken and cut into bite-size pieces.

★ Skim fat off top of chicken stock and bring to boil. Reduce heat to
  medium and cook until stock reduces to about 2 cups. Add meat,
  vegetables and seasonings and 1 teaspoon each of salt and pepper.
  Serves 8 to 10.

TIP: Some people like to put barbecue sauce or chili sauce into this stew.

Chili

*Authentic chili has no beans. This simple fact is based on
standards adopted by international chili cook-offs in an effort to
capture the true flavors of chiles and meats. It is also supported
by history and the origins of the dish itself. Texans claim chili
originated in their state and cite the "Chili Queens of San
Antonio" who sold chili on street corners before the Civil War
as well as chuck wagon cooks as probable originators.*

*New Mexicans and Arizonans, however, believe that chili
was first made by Indians after the Spanish brought chile
peppers to their territories from Mexico City. The best approach
for most normal people is to never get in a discussion about chile
(the peppers) or chili (the dish) with a Texan, New Mexican or Arizonan.*

Kentucky Burgoo Stew

1 fryer chicken or 2 pounds boneless chicken breasts
1 ½ pounds beef stew meat, browned
1 (15 ounce) can beef broth
2 (14 ounce) cans diced stewed tomatoes
2 (6 ounce) cans tomato sauce
8 - 10 peeled, chopped red potatoes
1 medium head cabbage, shredded
2 (10 ounce) cans corn, drained
1 - 1½ cups frozen lima beans
2 medium onions, diced
2 tablespoons butter
¼ cup Worcestershire sauce
½ teaspoon cayenne pepper

★ Cook chicken in enough water to cover; bring to a boil, reduce heat, cover and simmer for 1½ to 2 hours or until done. Reserve stock. Bone chicken and cut into bite-size pieces.

★ Skim fat off top of chicken stock and bring to boil. Reduce heat to medium and cook until stock reduces by about half. Cook stew meat over medium heat in beef broth until tender, about 45 minutes. Add water if needed.

★ Add tomato sauces, vegetables and seasonings and 1 teaspoon each of salt and pepper. Add both meats with liquid to pot and bring to a boil; reduce heat and simmer, covered, for 2 to 3 hours. If stew is too thin, uncover and continue to cook down liquid. Serves 10 to 12.

TIP: The original dish used mutton in addition to chicken. Many people add carrots and okra as well.

Favorite Fish Stew

1 cup chopped celery
½ cup chopped onion
2 tablespoons butter
1 (15 ounce) can whole kernel corn, drained
1 (15 ounce) can stewed tomatoes, drained
¼ cup minced parsley
1 (1 pound) skinless, boneless cod fillet

★ Saute celery and onion in butter in large soup pot until translucent. Add 2 cups water. Add corn, tomatoes and parsley and cook over medium heat until it is steaming hot, about 10 minutes.

★ Cut fish into bite-size pieces and add to soup pot. Cook for about 5 minutes or until fish cooks. Add a little salt and pepper to taste. Serve hot. Serves 4.

Fresh Oyster Stew

2 (1 pint) cartons fresh oysters with liquor
3 slices bacon
1 small onion, chopped
2 ribs celery, chopped
1 (4 ounce) can sliced mushrooms
1 (10 ounce) can cream of potato soup
3 cups half-and-half cream

★ Drain oysters and save liquor. Fry bacon in skillet until crisp, drain bacon and crumble. Set aside. Cook onion and celery in bacon fat in large skillet on medium heat until tender. Add mushrooms, soup, oyster liquor, half-and-half cream and a little salt and pepper.

★ Heat over medium heat, stirring occasionally, until mixture is thoroughly hot. Stir in bacon and oysters and heat for additional 4 to 5 minutes or until edges of oysters begin to curl. Sprinkle with parsley. Serves 6 to 8.

Ham-Vegetable Chowder

This is a great recipe for leftover ham.

1 medium potato
2 (10 ounce) cans cream of celery soup
1 (14 ounce) can chicken broth
2 cups cooked, finely diced ham
1 (15 ounce) can whole kernel corn
2 carrots, sliced
1 onion, coarsely chopped
1 teaspoon dried basil
1 (10 ounce) package frozen broccoli florets

★ Cut potato into 1-inch pieces. Combine all ingredients except broccoli florets in large slow cooker.

★ Cover and cook on LOW for 5 to 6 hours. Add broccoli and about ½ teaspoon each of salt and pepper and cook for additional 1 hour. Serves 4.

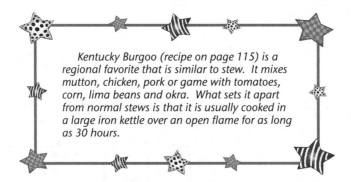

Kentucky Burgoo (recipe on page 115) is a regional favorite that is similar to stew. It mixes mutton, chicken, pork or game with tomatoes, corn, lima beans and okra. What sets it apart from normal stews is that it is usually cooked in a large iron kettle over an open flame for as long as 30 hours.

Sausage-Bean Chowder

2 pounds pork sausage
1 (15 ounce) can pinto beans with liquid
1 (15 ounce) can navy beans with liquid
1 (15 ounce) can kidney beans, drained
2 (15 ounce) cans Mexican stewed tomatoes
2 (14 ounce) cans chicken broth
1 - 2 teaspoons minced garlic

★ Brown and cook sausage in soup pot and stir until sausage crumbles.
Add all beans, tomatoes, broth and garlic. Bring to a boil, reduce heat to
low and simmer for 20 minutes. Serves 6.

Corn-Cod Chowder

8 slices bacon
1 pound cod, cut into bite-size pieces
2 large baking potatoes, peeled, thinly sliced
3 ribs celery, sliced
1 onion, chopped
1 (15 ounce) can whole kernel corn
1 (8 ounce) carton whipping cream

★ Fry bacon in large, heavy soup pot or skillet, remove bacon and drain.
Crumble bacon and set aside. Drain fat from soup pot and stir in
2½ cups water, cod, potatoes, celery, onion, corn and a little salt
and pepper.

★ Boil, reduce heat, cover and simmer for about 20 minutes or until fish
and potatoes are done. Stir in cream and heat just until chowder is
thoroughly hot. To serve, sprinkle crumbled bacon over each serving.
Serves 6.

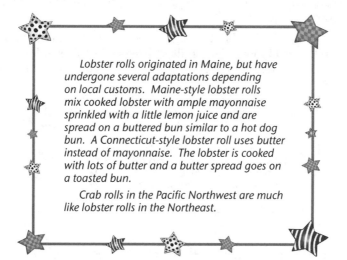

Lobster rolls originated in Maine, but have undergone several adaptations depending on local customs. Maine-style lobster rolls mix cooked lobster with ample mayonnaise sprinkled with a little lemon juice and are spread on a buttered bun similar to a hot dog bun. A Connecticut-style lobster roll uses butter instead of mayonnaise. The lobster is cooked with lots of butter and a butter spread goes on a toasted bun.

Crab rolls in the Pacific Northwest are much like lobster rolls in the Northeast.

Harbor-Town Fish Chowder

3 tablespoons butter
2 medium onions, diced
1 (1 pint) carton fresh, shucked oysters with liquor
3 large potatoes, peeled, diced
2 cups milk
1 cup half-and-half cream
1½ pounds boneless, skinless fish fillets, cubed
1 bay leaf
Hot sauce
Oyster crackers

★ Melt butter in large saucepan and saute onions until they are translucent. Pour oysters with liquor and ¾ cup water into saucepan and mix.

★ Add potatoes, cover and cook over low heat until potatoes are slightly tender, about 10 to 15 minutes. (Do not cook too fast.)

★ Pour in milk, half-and-half cream, fish, bay leaf and a dash of hot sauce. Cover and cook over low heat for about 20 minutes. Season with salt and pepper. Serve hot with oyster crackers. Serves 4.

Yankee Lobster Chowder

1 small onion, diced
2 tablespoons butter, divided
2 large potatoes, peeled, diced
1½ pounds cooked, chopped lobster
1 (8 ounce) can evaporated milk
1½ - 2 cups milk

★ Cook onions with 1 tablespoon butter in large saucepan over low heat until onions are translucent. Add potatoes and just enough water to almost cover potatoes.

★ Cover and cook over low heat until potatoes are just tender, about 10 to 15 minutes. Add lobster and milk. Cover and cook over low heat for about 20 minutes. (Do not boil.) Season with a little salt and white pepper. Serves 4.

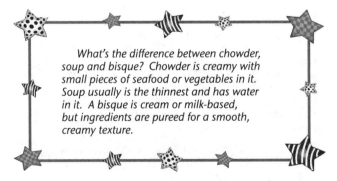

What's the difference between chowder, soup and bisque? Chowder is creamy with small pieces of seafood or vegetables in it. Soup usually is the thinnest and has water in it. A bisque is cream or milk-based, but ingredients are pureed for a smooth, creamy texture.

Manhattan Clam Chowder

3 large potatoes
1 (15 ounce) can Italian-style diced tomatoes
1 cup clam and tomato juice cocktail
1 cup chopped green bell pepper
¼ cup chopped green onions with tops
1 tablespoon Worcestershire sauce
1 pint shucked clams

★ Dice potatoes and onions, place in pot with enough water to cover and cook until barely tender. Add diced tomatoes, clam juice cocktail, bell pepper, onions, Worcestershire and ¼ teaspoon pepper.

★ Bring mixture to a boil, reduce heat and simmer for 15 to 20 minutes. Drain clams into separate cup. Chop clams and add to pot mixture. Strain remaining clam juice to remove shells and add to clams. Heat through. Serves 4.

New England Clam Chowder

¾ pound bacon, chopped
2 cups minced onions
1 cup chopped carrots
1 cup chopped celery
6 bay leaves
¾ cup flour
8 cups clam juice
1½ pounds potatoes, peeled, cubed
1 cup whipping half-and-half cream or whipping cream
1 pint carton littleneck clams with liquor
Oyster crackers

★ Fry chopped bacon until crisp in large soup pot over medium heat. Add onions, carrots and celery and saute until translucent. Season with a little salt and pepper and add bay leaves.

★ Add flour, stir to remove lumps and cook for 10 minutes. Add clam juice and potatoes, season with salt and pepper and reduce heat to medium-low. Simmer until potatoes are fork-tender, about 15 minutes.

★ Add cream and clams with its liquor and simmer for 5 to 10 minutes. Remove bay leaves. Ladle into soup bowls and serve hot with oyster crackers. Serves 6 to 8.

Carrot Capital of the World   Holtville, California

Seafood Chowder

3 onions, chopped
2 bell peppers, seeded, chopped
2 ribs celery, sliced
¼ cup olive oil
3 tablespoons flour
3 (15 ounce) cans stewed tomatoes
1 teaspoon minced garlic
½ - 1 teaspoon hot sauce, optional
2 pounds medium fresh shrimp, peeled, chopped
1 pound fresh lump crabmeat, flaked
1 (12 ounce) carton oysters, chopped, drained

★ Saute onions, bell peppers and celery in hot oil in soup pot. Add flour and cook for 1 minute, stirring constantly. Stir in tomatoes, garlic, hot sauce and a little salt and pepper. Boil, reduce heat and simmer for 15 minutes. Add shrimp, crabmeat and oysters to soup. Cover and simmer for additional 15 minutes. Serves 8.

Cheesy Corn Chowder

2 baking potatoes, peeled, diced
½ cup shredded carrots
½ cup finely chopped onion
1 (15 ounce) can cream-style corn
1 (8 ounce) can whole kernel corn
1 (10 ounce) can cream of celery soup
1 cup milk
1 (8 ounce) package cubed Velveeta® cheese

★ Cook potatoes, carrots and onion in 1½ cups water in large saucepan for about 15 minutes or until potatoes are tender; do not drain.

★ Stir in cream-style corn, whole kernel corn, soup, milk and a little salt and pepper. Heat and stir constantly until mixture is thoroughly hot; stir in cheese and serve. Serves 6.

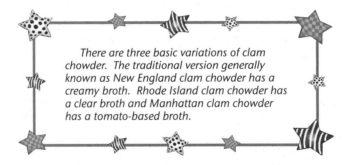

There are three basic variations of clam chowder. The traditional version generally known as New England clam chowder has a creamy broth. Rhode Island clam chowder has a clear broth and Manhattan clam chowder has a tomato-based broth.

Corn Chowder

1 (14 ounce) can chicken broth
1 cup milk
1 (10 ounce) can cream of celery soup
1 (15 ounce) can cream-style corn
1 (15 ounce) can whole kernel corn
½ cup dry potato flakes
1 onion, chopped
2 - 3 cups cooked, chopped ham

★ Combine all ingredients in sprayed 6-quart slow cooker. Cover and cook on LOW for 4 to 5 hours. When ready to serve, season with a little salt and pepper. Serves 6.

Country Chicken Chowder

1½ pounds boneless, skinless chicken breast halves
2 tablespoons butter
2 (10 ounce) cans cream of potato soup
1 (14 ounce) can chicken broth
1 (8 ounce) package frozen whole kernel corn
1 onion, sliced
2 ribs celery, sliced
1 (10 ounce) package frozen peas and carrots, thawed
½ teaspoon dried thyme
½ cup half-and-half cream

★ Cut chicken into 1-inch strips. Brown chicken strips in butter in skillet and transfer to large slow cooker. Add soup, broth, corn, onion, celery, peas and carrots, and thyme and stir.

★ Cover and cook on LOW for 3 to 4 hours or until vegetables are tender. Turn off heat, stir in half-and-half cream and set aside for about 10 minutes before serving. Serves 6.

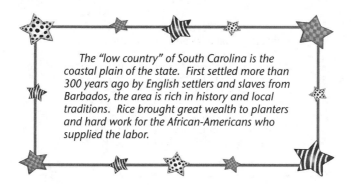

The "low country" of South Carolina is the coastal plain of the state. First settled more than 300 years ago by English settlers and slaves from Barbados, the area is rich in history and local traditions. Rice brought great wealth to planters and hard work for the African-Americans who supplied the labor.

Seafood Bisque

¼ cup (½ stick) butter
1 (8 ounce) package frozen salad shrimp, thawed
1 (6 ounce) can crab, drained, flaked
1 (15 ounce) can whole new potatoes, drained, sliced
1 teaspoon minced garlic
½ cup flour
2 (14 ounce) cans chicken broth, divided
1 cup half-and-half cream

★ Melt butter in large saucepan on medium heat. Add shrimp, crab, new potatoes and garlic and cook for 10 minutes. Stir in flour and cook, stirring constantly for 3 minutes.

★ Gradually add chicken broth, cook and stir until mixture thickens. Stir in half-and-half cream and a little salt and pepper, stirring constantly and cook just until mixture is thoroughly hot; do not boil. Serves 6.

Gulf Coast Oyster Bisque

1 quart oysters, cut up
1 bunch shallots, minced
½ teaspoon minced garlic
½ cup (1 stick) butter
3 tablespoons flour
2 (1 pint) cartons half-and-half cream
¼ cup dry sherry

★ Cook oysters, shallots and garlic with butter in skillet until oysters curl. Stir in flour. Heat half-and-half cream in double boiler, but do not boil and add oyster mixture with a little salt and pepper and sherry. Serves 4.

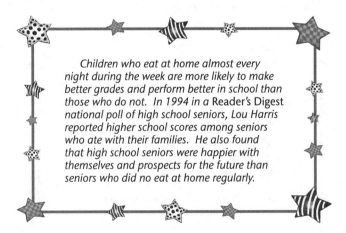

Children who eat at home almost every night during the week are more likely to make better grades and perform better in school than those who do not. In 1994 in a Reader's Digest *national poll of high school seniors, Lou Harris reported higher school scores among seniors who ate with their families. He also found that high school seniors were happier with themselves and prospects for the future than seniors who did no eat at home regularly.*

Shrimp and Sausage Jambalaya

1 pound cooked, smoked sausage links
1 onion, chopped
1 green bell pepper, chopped
2 teaspoons minced garlic
1 (28 ounce) can diced tomatoes
1 tablespoon parsley flakes
½ teaspoon dried thyme leaves
2 teaspoons Cajun seasoning
½ teaspoon cayenne pepper
1 pound peeled, veined shrimp
Rice, cooked

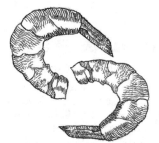

★ Combine all ingredients except shrimp and rice in sprayed slow cooker.
   Cover and cook on LOW for 6 to 8 hours or on HIGH for 3 to 4 hours.
   Stir in shrimp and cook on LOW for additional 1 hour. Serve over rice.
   Serves 4 to 6.

Mama's Seafood Gumbo

¼ cup (½ stick) butter
¼ cup flour
1½ - 2 pounds okra, sliced
6 firm tomatoes
½ cup minced onion
2 pounds shrimp
1 pound crabmeat
1 pound fish fillets
Cayenne pepper
1 pint fresh oysters with liquor
Rice, cooked

★ Melt butter in heavy skillet and add flour. Stir well over medium heat to
   make smooth, paste-like roux. Add 2 quarts water, okra, tomatoes and
   onion and cook on low for 45 minutes.

★ Wash, clean and peel shrimp. Flake crabmeat and remove any pieces of
   shell. Remove all bones and skin from fish.

★ When roux is rich brown color, add a little salt, pepper and cayenne
   pepper and mix well. Add all seafood and cook on medium-low heat for
   30 minutes or until desired consistency. Serve over rice. Serves 6 to 8.

*There are nine regional cuisines that are
distinctively different in the United States.
They are Southern, Tex-Mex, Southwest,
Cajun-Creole, Pacific Rim, Midwest, New
England, Pennsylvania Dutch and Floribbean.*

Vegetables

Favorite Almond-Asparagus Bake

This is a great substitute for Thanksgiving green bean casserole.

5 (10 ounce) cans asparagus, drained, divided
1½ cups cracker crumbs, divided
4 eggs, hard-boiled, sliced, divided
1 (12 ounce) package shredded cheddar cheese, divided
½ cup (1 stick) butter, melted
½ cup milk
1 (2.3 ounce) package sliced almonds

★ Preheat oven to 350°. Arrange half asparagus in sprayed 9 x 13-inch baking dish. Cover with ¾ cup cracker crumbs and half sliced eggs and sprinkle with half cheese.

★ Layer remaining asparagus, remaining eggs and ¾ cup cracker crumbs. Drizzle butter and milk over casserole and top with almonds and remaining cheese. Bake for 30 minutes. Serves 8.

Easy Garlic Asparagus

3 - 4 cloves garlic, peeled, minced
¼ cup butter
1 bunch fresh asparagus

★ Saute garlic with butter in small saucepan over medium heat. Arrange asparagus spears in large saucepan and pour butter mixture over spears.

★ Cover and cook over medium heat for about 10 minutes or until tender. Stir occasionally to coat spears with butter mixture. Asparagus should be slightly crunchy. Serve hot. Serves 4.

Better Butter Beans

1 cup sliced celery
1 onion, chopped
¼ cup (½ stick) butter
1 (10 ounce) can diced tomatoes and green chilies
½ teaspoon sugar
2 (15 ounce) cans butter beans

★ Saute celery and onion in butter in skillet for about 3 minutes. Add tomatoes and green chilies, several sprinkles of salt, and sugar. Add butter beans, cover and simmer for about 20 minutes. Serve hot. Serves 8.

Boston Baked Beans

*Navy beans are called "navy" because they were a staple on all
naval vessels in colonial days. Boston is known as "Bean Town".*

1 pound dried navy beans
½ teaspoon baking soda
½ pound salt pork, cut into 1-inch chunks
1 onion, chopped
¼ cup packed brown sugar
⅓ cup molasses
1 teaspoon dry mustard

★ Place beans in bowl, cover in water and soak overnight.

★ Place baking soda in large saucepan and fill half way with water. Bring
to a boil, add beans and boil for 10 minutes. Drain beans in colander
and run cold water through beans.

★ Place half salt pork chunks on bottom of soup pot or casserole. Top with
beans and whole onion and place remaining salt pork on top.

★ Combine sugar, molasses, mustard and 3 cups hot water in large bowl
and stir to mix. Cover pot, place in oven and bake for 6 hours. Check
pot periodically and add water only if needed. Serves 6 to 7.

*TIP: Great Northern Beans can be substituted for navy beans. They are both
white beans. Navy beans are pea-size and great northern refers to all other
sizes. Some people like to add ⅓ cup ketchup to their baked beans.*

Barbecued Baked Beans

These are not your ordinary beans and they are great with barbecued pork!

1 (15 ounce) can pork and beans
1 (15 ounce) can kidney beans, drained
1 (15 ounce) can green lima beans, drained
1 large onion, chopped
1 clove garlic, minced
1 tablespoon Worcestershire sauce
1 teaspoon ground cumin
2 - 3 tablespoons strong cold brewed coffee
¼ cup packed brown sugar
½ cup ketchup
3 bacon slices

★ Preheat oven to 350°. Combine all ingredients except bacon in
9 x 13-inch baking dish. Place bacon slices on top. Cover and bake
for 1 hour. Uncover and continue baking for additional 15 minutes.
Serves 8 to 10.

Short-Cut Baked Beans

1 (1 pound) can pork and beans
4 tablespoons brown sugar
¼ teaspoon dry mustard
¼ cup ketchup
¼ cup chopped green pepper
¼ cup chopped onion
3 - 4 slices bacon, halved

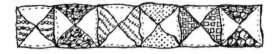

★ Preheat oven to 350°. Combine beans, sugar, ketchup, onion, green pepper and mustard and mix well. Pour into sprayed, casserole dish and top with bacon. Bake for 1 hour. Serve immediately. Serves 4 to 6.

Best Pinto Beans

Pinto beans are traditional to all Southwest cooking.
Here is basic way of cooking a pot of beans.

3 cups dried pinto beans
½ pound salt pork or ham hock
2 - 3 jalapeno peppers, seeded, chopped, optional
1 onion, chopped
2 tablespoons chili powder
1 teaspoon garlic powder
1 teaspoon oregano

★ Wash beans, cover with water in saucepan and soak overnight. Drain beans and cover again with water. Add all ingredients in saucepan and bring to a boil. Reduce heat, cover and simmer for about 3 hours or until beans are tender. (Add water, if needed.) Serves 8.

Frijoles Refritos

Refried beans are just recycled pinto beans and may be used as a
side dish, with tacos, burritos, on tostadas and in a million other ways.

Leftover cooked pinto beans
Bacon drippings
Shredded cheddar cheese

★ Cook leftover beans in saucepan until most or all of liquid is gone. Drain any excess liquid and mash remaining beans.

★ Fry mashed beans in bacon drippings in large heavy skillet until they are thoroughly hot and mixed with bacon drippings. Serve immediately with cheese on top.

TIP: If you want to add more seasonings, try chopped onion, minced garlic, chili powder, cumin and oregano.

Black-Eyed Peas

1 cup dried black-eyed peas
2 slices salt pork
1 medium onion, chopped
¼ teaspoon garlic powder

★ Wash peas and place in large pot with 6 cups hot water. Add pork,
onion, 2 teaspoons salt and garlic powder. Cover, bring to a slow boil
and simmer over low heat for 2 hours 30 minutes or until tender. Drain
before serving. Serves 6.

Hoppin' John

*This recipe for field peas over rice is a southern dish and traditional on New
Year's Eve and New Year's Day. The tradition is to eat field peas (black-eyed
peas) for luck and collard greens for money in the coming New Year.*

2 small onions, chopped
¼ cup (½ stick) butter
8 slices bacon, cut into pieces
1 cup cooked, cubed ham
1 cup rice
3 (15 ounce) cans black-eyed peas with liquid
Cayenne pepper

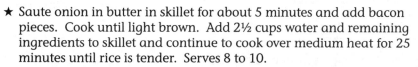

★ Saute onion in butter in skillet for about 5 minutes and add bacon
pieces. Cook until light brown. Add 2½ cups water and remaining
ingredients to skillet and continue to cook over medium heat for 25
minutes until rice is tender. Serves 8 to 10.

Home-Style Broccoli Casserole

2 (16 ounce) packages frozen broccoli spears, thawed
2 (10 ounce) cans cream of chicken soup
1 cup mayonnaise
4 teaspoons lemon juice
1 cup crushed herb dressing mix
¼ cup (½ stick) butter
1 (8 ounce) package shredded sharp cheddar cheese

★ Preheat oven to 350°. Cook broccoli according to package directions.
Cut cooked broccoli into bite-size pieces and arrange in 9 x 13-inch glass
baking dish.

★ Combine soup with mayonnaise and lemon juice in bowl and pour over
broccoli. Brown crushed herb dressing in butter and layer over top of
casserole. Sprinkle cheese on top and bake for 20 to 30 minutes until
bubbly. Serves 12.

Broccoli-Cauliflower Casserole

1 (10 ounce) package frozen broccoli spears
1 (10 ounce) package frozen cauliflower
1 egg
⅔ cup mayonnaise
1 (10 ounce) can cream of chicken soup
1 cup shredded Swiss cheese
1 onion, chopped
1 cup seasoned breadcrumbs
2 tablespoons butter, melted

★ Cook broccoli and cauliflower according to package directions. Drain well and place in large bowl.

★ Combine egg, mayonnaise, soup, cheese and onion in saucepan and heat well. Pour mixture over vegetable-cheese mixture and mix well. Pour into sprayed 9 x 13-inch baking dish.

★ Combine breadcrumbs and butter in bowl and sprinkle over casserole. Sprinkle paprika over top. Bake at 350° for 30 to 35 minutes. Serves 8 to 10.

Creamy Brussels Sprouts

2 pints fresh brussels sprouts
1 onion, chopped
¼ cup (½ stick) butter
1 (1 pint) carton sour cream

★ Take each brussels sprout and cut crisscross mark on bottom of each so tougher ends cook as quickly as tops. Steam or boil sprouts in saucepan with just enough water to cover or microwave until just tender.

★ Saute onion in skillet with butter, add sour cream and brussels sprouts and cook over low heat, stirring constantly. Serve immediately. Serves 8.

Boston Baked Beans (recipe on page 125) became a staple for Saturday nights in Massachusetts because of the Puritans. Their Sabbath rules did not allow for baking from sunset Saturday to sunset Sunday. A hearty dish like baked beans was prepared early for Saturday night's meal and left overnight in the brick oven for the family to eat after church on Sunday.

Irish Cabbage and Apples

1 head red cabbage, cored, shredded
2 tablespoons apple cider vinegar
¼ cup sugar
1 teaspoon cinnamon
1 teaspoon ground cloves
1 teaspoon sea salt
1 pound McIntosh apples, peeled, cored, quartered

★ Combine cabbage, vinegar, sugar, cinnamon, cloves, ½ teaspoon salt and ½ cup water in heavy skillet. Bring to boil and place apples on top of cabbage mixture. Cover and cook on medium heat about 20 minutes or until cabbage is tender and apples are soft.

★ Partially uncover skillet and cook on high heat just until liquid evaporates. Before serving, toss cabbage and apple mixture; serve immediately. Serves 6 to 8.

Creamy Baked Cabbage

1 head cabbage
½ red bell pepper, seeded, chopped
1 (10 ounce) can cream of celery soup
1 (8 ounce) package shredded 4-cheese blend

★ Cut cabbage in chunks and layer in sprayed 7 x 11-inch baking dish with bell pepper, soup and cheese. Cover and bake for 45 minutes. Serves 8.

Fried Cabbage Skillet

5 cups chopped cabbage
2 large onions, sliced
1 green bell pepper, chopped
2 tomatoes, chopped
1 tablespoon sugar
⅓ cup vegetable oil

★ Combine all ingredients, 1 teaspoon salt and ½ teaspoon pepper in heavy skillet and cook over medium heat for 5 to 7 minutes or until tender. Serves 4 to 6.

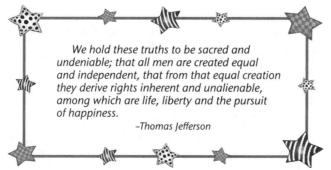

We hold these truths to be sacred and undeniable; that all men are created equal and independent, that from that equal creation they derive rights inherent and unalienable, among which are life, liberty and the pursuit of happiness.

–Thomas Jefferson

Easy Red Cabbage

1 head red cabbage, sliced
2 tablespoons butter
1 tablespoon minced onion
¼ teaspoon cayenne pepper
2 tablespoons vinegar
1 tablespoon sugar

★ Soak cabbage in cold water for 30 to 45 minutes. Drain and place in large saucepan. Add butter, onion, cayenne pepper and a little salt. Add enough water to almost cover and cook over medium-high heat until just tender. Add vinegar and sugar and cook for additional 5 minutes. Serve immediately. Serves 4.

Orange-Glazed Carrots

1 (16 ounce) package pound baby carrots
¼ cup (½ stick) butter
2 tablespoons honey
2 tablespoons orange marmalade
1 tablespoon fresh cilantro, chopped

★ Slice carrots lengthwise. Place carrots in boiling water and cook uncovered for 5 minutes. Remove from heat and drain; place in medium bowl.

★ Melt butter in small saucepan. Stir in honey, marmalade and 3 tablespoons water to make a glaze. Season with salt and pepper to taste.

★ Boil, while stirring for 1 minute, to reduce glaze, pour over the cooked carrots and toss to coat. Sprinkle carrots with cilantro, toss and serve warm. Serves 4.

Brown Sugar Carrots

¼ cup (½ stick) butter
¾ cup packed brown sugar
½ teaspoon cinnamon
2 (16 ounce) packages peeled baby carrots

★ In skillet, combine butter, brown sugar, cinnamon and ½ cup water; cook on medium heat until bubbly. Stir in carrots, cover and cook on medium heat until carrots are glazed and tender. Serves 4 to 6.

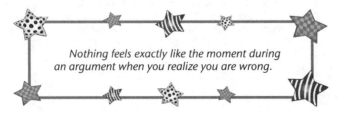

Nothing feels exactly like the moment during an argument when you realize you are wrong.

Creamed Carrots

¼ cup (½ stick) butter
3 tablespoons flour
1½ cups milk
2 (15 ounce) cans sliced carrots

★ Melt butter in saucepan and add flour plus ½ teaspoon salt and mix well. Cook milk with butter-flour mixture over medium heat and stir constantly. Cook until mixture thickens.

★ In smaller saucepan, heat carrots and drain. Add carrots to milk mixture and serve hot. Serves 6 to 8.

Old-Fashioned Henny-Penny Carrots

3 (15 ounce) cans cooked, sliced carrots, drained
1 onion, sliced
1 bell pepper, seeded, sliced

★ Combine carrots, onion and bell pepper in bowl with lid.

Dressing:

1 (10 ounce) can tomato soup
1 teaspoon mustard
1 tablespoon Worcestershire sauce
¾ cup sugar
¼ cup olive oil
¾ cup vinegar

★ Mix dressing ingredients plus ½ teaspoon salt in bowl and pour over vegetables. Cover and refrigerate for at least 24 hours before serving. Serves 8 to 10.

Corn Pudding

2 tablespoons flour
1 teaspoon sugar
3 eggs, well beaten
1 (15 ounce) and 1 (8 ounce) can whole kernel corn, drained
¼ cup (½ stick) butter, melted
1 (16 ounce) carton half-and-half cream

★ Preheat oven to 325°. Combine flour, sugar and ½ teaspoon each of salt and pepper in small bowl and set aside.

★ In separate bowl, combine flour mixture, eggs, corn, butter (slightly cooled) and half-and-half cream. Mix well and pour into sprayed 2-quart baking dish. Cover and bake for 1 hour. Uncover and continue baking until top is delicate brown. Serves 8.

Festive Shoe-Peg Corn

1 (8 ounce) package cream cheese, softened
½ cup (1 stick) butter, softened
3 (15 ounce) cans shoe-peg or white corn
1 (4 ounce) can diced green chilies

★ Preheat oven to 350°. Beat cream cheese and butter in bowl. Add corn
and green chilies and mix well. Spoon into sprayed 9 x 13-inch baking
dish. Cover and bake for 30 minutes. Serves 12.

Parmesan Hominy

*Hominy was a great gift from Native Americans to colonists in the
New World. Today it continues to be a side dish in the South.*

2 slices bacon, diced
2 tablespoons chopped onion
2 tablespoons chopped green bell pepper
1 (15 ounce) can hominy, drained
Seasoned salt
Grated parmesan cheese

★ Fry bacon in skillet and cook just until still transparent. Add onion and
bell pepper and cook until tender. Pour in hominy and add seasoned
salt. Heat thoroughly and top with parmesan cheese before serving.
Serves 4.

Fresh String Beans

2 - 3 pounds fresh green beans
3 tablespoons bacon drippings
2 teaspoons dried basil, optional

★ Snap ends of green beans, wash and place in large saucepan. Pour
about 1 inch water in pan and add bacon drippings, ½ teaspoon salt
and basil. Bring to a boil, reduce heat and cover. Cook over low heat for
15 to 20 minutes. Serves 6 to 8.

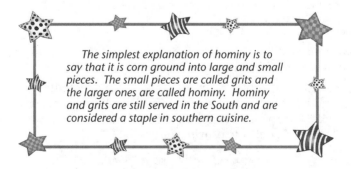

*The simplest explanation of hominy is to
say that it is corn ground into large and small
pieces. The small pieces are called grits and
the larger ones are called hominy. Hominy
and grits are still served in the South and are
considered a staple in southern cuisine.*

Thanksgiving Green Bean Casserole

1 (10 ounce) can cream of mushroom soup
½ cup milk
1 teaspoon soy sauce
4 cups cooked green beans
1⅓ cups french-fried onions

★ Mix soup, milk and soy sauce in 1½-quart baking dish. Pour green beans in and mix. Cover with half of fried onions. Bake at 350° for 25 minutes. Remove from oven, stir beans and add remaining french-fried onions to top of casserole. Return to oven for 5 minutes to brown slightly. Serves 10 to 12.

Variations:

1. Add ½ cup slivered almonds to topping.

2. Cook 4 slices bacon crispy, drain and crumble into bean mixture.

3. Add ½ cup chopped red bell pepper to bean mixture.

4. Delete soy sauce. Add 1 cup shredded cheddar cheese to bean mixture. Add ½ cup shredded cheddar cheese to topping when remaining french-fried onion rings are sprinkled on top.

5. Substitute Campbell's® golden mushroom soup for cream of mushroom.

Green Beans with Pine Nuts

1 (16 ounce) package frozen green beans, thawed
¼ cup (½ stick) butter
¾ cup pine nuts
½ teaspoon garlic powder
½ teaspoon celery salt

★ Cook beans in ½ cup water in 3-quart saucepan, covered, for 10 to 15 minutes or until beans are tender-crisp and drain. Melt butter in skillet over medium heat and add pine nuts.

★ Cook, stirring frequently, until golden. Add pine nuts to green beans and season with garlic powder, ½ teaspoon salt, ½ teaspoon pepper and celery salt. Serves 6.

An Excellent Health Tip: Spend time with people over the age of 70 and under the age of 6.

Green Beans Supreme

2 (15 ounce) cans French-style green beans, drained
1 (8 ounce) can sliced water chestnuts, drained
1 onion, chopped finely
2 tablespoons butter
2 teaspoons soy sauce
⅛ teaspoon hot sauce
2 tablespoons Worcestershire sauce
1 (10 ounce) can cream of mushroom soup
1 (8 ounce) package shredded sharp cheddar cheese
1 (3 ounce) can french-fried onions

★ Preheat oven to 350°. Place green beans and water chestnuts in sprayed 2½-quart baking dish. Saute onion in butter in skillet and add 1 teaspoon salt, soy sauce, hot sauce, Worcestershire sauce, soup and cheese.

★ Spoon mixture over green beans, cover and bake for 30 minutes. Sprinkle french-fried onions over top and bake uncovered for 10 to 15 minutes. Serves 8.

Almond Green Beans

⅓ cup slivered almonds
¼ cup (½ stick) butter
¾ teaspoon garlic salt
3 tablespoons lemon juice
2 (16 ounce) cans French-style green beans

★ In saucepan, cook almonds in butter, garlic salt and lemon juice until slightly golden brown. Add drained green beans to almonds and heat. Serves 4.

Scalloped Okra and Corn

1 (15 ounce) can cut okra, drained
¼ cup (½ stick) butter, divided
1 (15 ounce) can whole kernel corn, drained
1 (10 ounce) can cream of celery soup
1 (8 ounce) package shredded sharp cheddar cheese
1 cup seasoned breadcrumbs

★ Preheat oven to 350°. Stir-fry okra with 2 tablespoons butter in skillet for 10 minutes. Place okra in sprayed 7 x 11-inch baking dish and alternate with layers of corn.

★ Heat soup in saucepan, stir in cheese and pour over vegetables. Cover with breadcrumbs and dot with remaining butter. Bake for 35 minutes or until breadcrumbs brown. Serves 6 to 8.

Okra Lovers' Fried Okra

2 eggs, lightly beaten
2 tablespoons milk
¾ cup cornmeal
¼ cup flour
22 - 28 fresh okra pods, thinly sliced
¼ cup vegetable oil

★ Combine eggs and milk in shallow bowl and mix well. In separate bowl, combine cornmeal, flour and 1 teaspoon salt. Dip okra slices in egg-milk mixture and then in cornmeal mixture.

★ Place okra in heavy skillet with hot oil and cook on medium-high heat until okra browns. Stir occasionally. Drain on paper towels. Serves 8 to 10.

Pickled Okra

1 quart young tender pods fresh okra
4 cups white vinegar
1 clove garlic
1 jalapeno pepper, seeded, diced*

★ Pack okra in sterilized jars. Combine vinegar, 1 cup water, ⅓ cup salt, garlic and jalapeno pepper in saucepan and bring to a boil. Reduce heat and simmer for about 10 minutes. Pour over okra and seal jars. Store for 2 to 3 weeks before serving. Serves 6 to 10.

*TIP: Wear rubber gloves when removing seeds from jalapenos.

Creamed Onions and Peas

1 (10 ounce) can cream of celery soup
½ cup milk
3 (15 ounce) jars tiny white onions, drained
1 (10 ounce) package frozen peas
½ cup slivered almonds
3 tablespoons grated parmesan cheese

★ Preheat oven to 350°. In large saucepan, combine soup and milk, heat and stir until bubbly. Gently stir in onions, peas and almonds and mix well.

★ Spoon into sprayed 2-quart baking dish. Sprinkle with parmesan cheese. Cover and bake for 30 minutes. Serves 4 to 6.

Southern-Style Onion Rings

1 cup beer (not light beer)
1 cup flour
2 large Texas 1015 or Vidalia® sweet onions
Vegetable oil

★ Combine beer and flour in bowl, mix well and set aside for 3 to 4 hours (this is an important step). Slice onions into rings of desired width and dip in batter.

★ Fry in hot oil deep enough to cover rings. Remove, drain on paper towels and place them on shallow baking pan. Keep hot in 200° oven. Serves 6 to 8.

Baked Texas 1015 or Vidalia Sweet Onions

1 large 1015 or Vidalia® onion per person
1 tablespoon butter per onion
1 (8 ounce) package shredded sharp cheddar cheese, divided

★ Preheat oven to 350°. Remove outer skin of onions. With sharp knife, remove very thin slice from bottom or root end of onion to allow onion to sit flat. Quarter onions, almost cutting down to core but not all the way.

★ Insert butter into center slit of each onion. Add ½ teaspoon salt and ¼ teaspoon pepper to each onion and sprinkle heaping tablespoon cheese. Wrap onions individually in foil and bake for about 1 hour. Serves 1 onion per person.

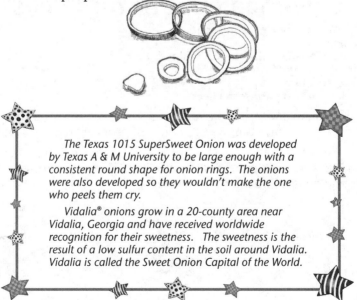

The Texas 1015 SuperSweet Onion was developed by Texas A & M University to be large enough with a consistent round shape for onion rings. The onions were also developed so they wouldn't make the one who peels them cry.

Vidalia® onions grow in a 20-county area near Vidalia, Georgia and have received worldwide recognition for their sweetness. The sweetness is the result of a low sulfur content in the soil around Vidalia. Vidalia is called the Sweet Onion Capital of the World.

Sweet Onion Casserole

This is a great substitute for potatoes or rice.

3 cups cracker crumbs
½ cup (1 stick) butter, melted, divided
4 cups coarsely chopped sweet onions

★ Preheat oven to 300°. Combine and mix cracker crumbs and ¼ cup butter in bowl. Place mixture in 9 x 13-inch baking dish and pat down. Saute onions in remaining butter and spread over crust.

Sauce:

1 cup milk
2 eggs, slightly beaten
1 teaspoon seasoned salt
1½ cups shredded cheddar cheese

★ Combine milk, eggs, seasoned salt, ¼ teaspoon pepper and cheese in saucepan. Cook over low heat until cheese melts.

★ Pour over onions on crust and bake for 45 minutes or until knife inserted in center comes out clean. Serves 6.

Scalloped Onions

6 yellow onions
¾ cup shredded cheddar cheese
½ teaspoon dried thyme
1 cup (2 sticks) butter, sliced
1 (8 ounce) carton whipping cream
1 cup seasoned breadcrumbs
⅓ cup grated parmesan cheese

★ Preheat oven to 350°. Slice onions about 1 inch thick. Place in heavy pot with 1 inch or more of water to cover onions. Add 1 teaspoon salt and bring to a boil.

★ Reduce heat, cover and simmer for 15 minutes. (Add a little more water if necessary to cover onions.) Drain onions and place half in sprayed baking dish. Sprinkle ½ teaspoon salt, ¼ teaspoon pepper, cheddar cheese and thyme.

★ Place butter slices over onions, add last layer of onions and pour cream over top. Sprinkle with breadcrumbs and parmesan cheese and bake uncovered for 35 minutes or until breadcrumbs are light brown. Serves 8 to 12.

 Tomato Capital of the World   Dania Beach, Florida
Jacksonville, Texas

Creamed Peas and Mushrooms

4 slices bacon
¼ cup finely chopped onion
2 tablespoons flour
1 cup milk
1 (15 ounce) can green peas, drained
1 (4 ounce) can sliced mushrooms, drained
1 (2 ounce) jar diced pimentos
1 tablespoon butter
6 small, individual-size frozen piecrusts, baked

★ Fry bacon in skillet until crisp. Remove, drain and crumble. Add
  onion to drippings in skillet and saute until tender. Pour off all but
  1 tablespoon drippings.

★ Blend in flour and add milk, ¼ teaspoon salt and a dash of pepper.
  Cook and stir until thick. Stir in peas. Saute mushrooms and pimentos
  in butter in saucepan and add to peas. Serve in individual-sized
  piecrusts. Serves 6.

Green Peas with Water Chestnuts

2 (10 ounce) packages frozen green peas
1 (8 ounce) can sliced water chestnuts, drained, chopped
1 (10 ounce) can cream of mushroom soup

★ Preheat oven to 350°. Prepare green peas according to package
  directions and drain. Stir in water chestnuts and soup. Heat well in
  saucepan or pour into sprayed baking dish and bake for 25 minutes.
  Serves 6.

Sugared Snap Peas with Fresh Mint

1 pound snap peas, rinsed, strings removed
2 teaspoons sesame oil
2 tablespoons butter
1 tablespoon light brown sugar
2 teaspoons soy sauce
1 tablespoon freshly chopped mint sprigs plus 1 whole sprig

★ Steam peas in pods for 3 to 5 minutes or just until tender and drain. In
  small saucepan, heat sesame oil, butter, brown sugar and soy sauce for
  1 minute over medium heat and stir until they blend.

★ Toss to coat beans with the soy-sugar blend. Add chopped mint and
  toss again. Spoon into serving bowl and garnish with mint sprig. Serve
  warm. Serves 4.

Sweet Corn Capital of the World   Hoopeville, Illinois

Minted Peas

1 teaspoon dried mint leaves
Pinch of sugar
1 (10 ounce) package frozen tiny peas, thawed
Lump of butter

★ Combine ½ cup water, mint, sugar, and a little salt and pepper in saucepan and bring to a boil. Add peas and cook for 2 to 3 minutes. Drain slightly and add butter. Serves 4 to 6.

Stuffed Poblano Rellenos

1 ¼ cups chopped walnuts
1 cup goat cheese crumbles
½ cup ricotta cheese
1 teaspoon cayenne pepper
6 large poblano chilies with stems, roasted, peeled, seeded
5 eggs, beaten
¼ cup flour
1 ¼ cups milk
Canola oil

★ Combine walnuts, goat cheese, ricotta cheese and cayenne pepper in bowl and mix well. Carefully open roasted poblano chilies and stuff cheese mixture into poblanos and close.

★ Mix eggs, flour, milk and ½ teaspoon each of salt and pepper in medium bowl. Dip chilies in egg mixture. Heat oil in deep fryer to 350°. Place chilies in hot oil and fry until golden brown. Remove from oil and drain. Serve immediately. Serves 6.

TIP: To roast chilies: Place poblano chilies over open flame or broil them in oven until outside turns dark brown and blisters on all sides. (Be careful not to burn holes in skin.) Place peppers in plastic bag, seal and allow to sweat for about 15 to 20 minutes so skin will slide off easily. Remove skins and cut through length of pepper on one side. Remove seeds, but leave veins and stem intact.

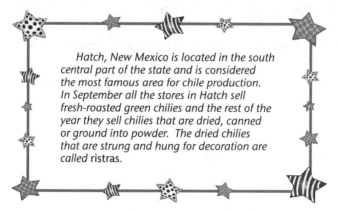

Hatch, New Mexico is located in the south central part of the state and is considered the most famous area for chile production. In September all the stores in Hatch sell fresh-roasted green chilies and the rest of the year they sell chilies that are dried, canned or ground into powder. The dried chilies that are strung and hung for decoration are called ristras.

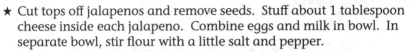

Fried Jalapenos

1 (14 ounce) can whole pickled jalapenos
1 (8 ounce) package shredded cheddar cheese
2 eggs
½ cup milk
¾ cup flour
Canola oil

★ Cut tops off jalapenos and remove seeds. Stuff about 1 tablespoon cheese inside each jalapeno. Combine eggs and milk in bowl. In separate bowl, stir flour with a little salt and pepper.

★ Roll filled jalapenos in flour mixture, then in egg mixture and again in flour. Line jalapenos on baking sheet and fry in hot oil about 350° until golden brown. Serves 5 to 6.

TIP: Wear rubber gloves when removing seeds from jalapenos.

Grilled Whole Anaheim Chilies

Serve these delicious chilies whole or sliced in strips called rajas.

8 - 10 fresh, whole Anaheim green chilies

★ Place chilies on lightly sprayed grill over low heat. Turn frequently because chilies blister and char on outside. Grill for about 2 to 3 minutes.

★ Remove from grill and slide peel away from chilies. Serve whole or cut into narrow strips. Anaheims are very mild, but remove seeds to lessen the heat. Serves 6 to 8.

Smoked Jalapenos

10 - 12 jalapenos*
¼ - ½ cup (½ - 1 stick) butter
3 - 4 cloves garlic, minced
2 tablespoons liquid smoke

★ Slice jalapenos in half and remove seeds. Spread butter on each half and sprinkle minced garlic over each half. Place jalapenos on heavy foil. Sprinkle liquid smoke over jalapenos and wrap tightly.

★ Place foil package over charcoal fire and cook for about 1 hour, if jalapenos are medium to large. Serves 8 to 10.

*TIP: Wear rubber gloves when removing seeds from jalapenos.

Crawfish Capital of the World   Breaux Bridge, Louisiana

Roasted Potatoes

18 - 20 small, red potatoes with peels
½ cup (1 stick) butter, melted
2 (4 ounce) cans diced green chilies
2 tablespoons fresh snipped parsley
½ teaspoon garlic powder
½ teaspoon paprika

★ Steam potatoes in large saucepan with small amount of water until tender. (Test with fork.) In separate saucepan, combine butter, green chilies, parsley, garlic powder, 1 teaspoon salt and ½ teaspoon pepper.

★ Heat until ingredients mix well. Place potatoes in serving dish, spoon butter mixture over potatoes and sprinkle with paprika. Serves 6 to 8.

Slap-Your-Knee Good Potatoes

6 medium potatoes
½ cup (1 stick) butter, softened
1 tablespoon flour
1 (16 ounce) package shredded cheddar cheese
¾ cup milk

★ Preheat oven to 350°. Peel and wash potatoes, slice half potatoes and place in sprayed 3-quart baking dish. Spread half of butter over potatoes and sprinkle with pepper and flour. Cover with half cheese.

★ Slice remaining potatoes, place over first layer and add remaining sliced butter. Pour milk over casserole and sprinkle more pepper. Cover with remaining cheese. Cover and bake for 1 hour. Serves 8.

TIP: This must be cooked immediately or potatoes will darken. It may be frozen after baking.

Hot Chive-Potato Souffle

3 eggs, separated
2 cups hot prepared instant mashed potatoes
½ cup sour cream
2 heaping tablespoons chopped chives

★ Preheat oven to 350°. Beat egg whites until stiff and set aside. Beat yolks until smooth and add to potatoes.

★ Fold beaten egg whites, sour cream, chives and 1 teaspoon salt into potato-egg yolk mixture and pour into sprayed 2-quart baking dish. Bake for 45 minutes. Serves 6.

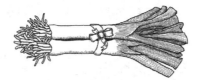

Dinner-Bell Mashed Potatoes

6 - 8 medium potatoes
1 (8 ounce) carton sour cream
1 (8 ounce) package cream cheese, softened
Butter

★ Preheat oven to 325°. Peel, cut up and boil potatoes in saucepan until tender and drain. Whip hot potatoes and add sour cream, cream cheese, 1 teaspoon salt and ½ teaspoon pepper. Continue whipping until cream cheese melts.

★ Pour in sprayed 3-quart baking dish. Dot generously with butter. Cover and bake for about 20 minutes. Bake 10 minutes longer if reheating. Serves 8 to 10.

Basic Mashed Potatoes

3 - 4 large russet potatoes
¼ cup milk
⅓ cup butter

★ Peel, cut each potato into 4 to 6 pieces and boil in medium saucepan until tender. Drain water and pour potatoes into mixing bowl. Cool and cut into smaller pieces. Beat potatoes until all blends well (may be lumpy). Add milk, butter and a little salt and pepper and whip until smooth. Serves 4 to 6.

Garlic-Mashed Potatoes

2 pounds potatoes, peeled, quartered
2 teaspoons minced garlic
1½ cups milk, warmed
½ cup sour cream
¼ cup (½ stick) butter, melted

★ Place potatoes in large saucepan and cover with salted water. Bring to a boil, lower heat to medium and slow boil 20 to 25 minutes or until potatoes are tender.

★ Place potatoes in mixing bowl and beat about 1 minute. Add garlic, warm milk, sour cream, 1 teaspoon salt and melted butter and beat until potatoes are creamy. Spoon into serving bowl. Serves 6 to 8.

Barbecue Capital of the World   Owensboro, Kentucky

Garlic Capital of the World   Gilroy, California

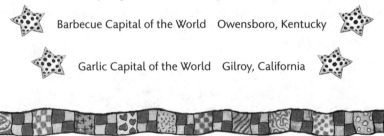

Hash-Brown Potato Bake

1 (32 ounce) bag frozen hash-brown potatoes, thawed
1 onion, chopped
½ cup (1 stick) butter, melted
1 (8 ounce) carton sour cream
1 (10 ounce) can cream of chicken soup
1 (16 ounce) package shredded cheddar cheese
1½ cups corn flakes, crushed
2 tablespoons butter, melted

★ Preheat oven to 350°. Combine hash-brown potatoes, onion, ½ cup melted butter, sour cream, cream of chicken soup and cheese in large bowl.

★ Pour in sprayed 9 x 13-inch baking dish. Combine corn flakes and 2 tablespoons melted butter in bowl and sprinkle over casserole. Bake for 50 minutes. Serves 8 to 10.

German Fried Potatoes

4 medium potatoes with peels
2 slices bacon, diced
1 medium onion, chopped

★ Boil potatoes in saucepan with enough water to cover until just tender. Drain and cut/slice both ways to make strips the size you want.

★ Fry bacon in large skillet until crisp. Add potatoes and onions and fry until potatoes are golden brown. Sprinkle with salt and pepper before serving. Serves 4 to 6.

Pan-Fried Potatoes

3 - 4 potatoes with peel
1 onion, sliced
⅓ cup Crisco®

★ Slice potatoes horizontally, not lengthwise like french-fries, about ⅛-inch thick. Heat Crisco® and carefully drop potatoes and onions into large skillet. Cover and fry potatoes for about 10 minutes.

★ Uncover, turn and separate potatoes and onions and cook uncovered for about 10 minutes. Brown potatoes and onions. Remove from skillet and drain. Season with a little salt and pepper. Serves 4.

Foods that originated or were made famous in Pennsylvania include cheese steaks, shoo-fly pie, funnel cakes and scrapple.

French Fries

4 pounds russet potatoes
Vegetable oil

★ Cut potatoes into lengths about ¼ x ¼ x 3 inches. Place in large bowl, cover with water and refrigerate for about 2 hours. Pour oil in deep saucepan to depth of 4 inches and warm over medium heat. Drain potatoes and pat dry with paper towels.

★ When oil begins to sizzle, carefully drop a few potatoes at a time in saucepan and cook about 1 to 2 minutes until crisp and golden. Drain on paper towel and sprinkle with salt. Continue cooking in small batches and serve immediately. Serves 4 to 6.

Oven Fries

5 medium baking potatoes
⅓ cup oil
Paprika

★ Preheat oven to 375°. Scrub potatoes, cut each in 6 lengthwise wedges and place in shallow baking dish. Combine oil, ¾ teaspoon salt and ¼ teaspoon pepper and brush potatoes with mixture.

★ Sprinkle potatoes lightly with paprika. Bake for about 50 minutes or until potatoes are tender and light brown. Baste twice with remaining oil mixture while baking. Serves 4 to 6.

Twice-Baked Potatoes

8 large baking potatoes
2 tablespoons butter
1 (10 ounce) can cheddar cheese soup
1 tablespoon chopped chives

★ Preheat oven to 400°. Bake potatoes bake for 1 hour and set aside to cool. Cut potatoes in half lengthwise, scoop out flesh and leave shells intact.

★ In separate bowl mash potatoes with butter, chives and a little salt and pepper. Gradually add soup and beat until light and fluffy. Stuff mashed potatoes into potato shells and place shells in 9 x 13-inch baking dish. Bake for about 15 minutes or until brown and a little crusty on top. Serves 8.

Vermont produces more maple syrup than any other state in the U.S. All the maple syrup in the world is produced in North America.

Potato Latkes

1 large egg
2 tablespoons chopped chives and grated onion
2 tablespoons flour
1 tablespoon lemon juice
2 pounds medium size potatoes, peeled
½ cup oil

★ Combine egg, chives, onion, flour, lemon juice and 1 teaspoon salt in large bowl. In food processor with shredding disk, shred potatoes and place in colander in sink; squeeze out liquid. Stir into egg mixture.

★ In large skillet, place oil and heat until very hot. Drop ¼ cup potato mixture into hot oil (about 6 at a time) and flatten each latke into rounds. Cook both sides until light brown.

★ Transfer to large baking sheet that has been lined with paper towels. Keep warm.

★ Repeat this process, stirring mixture each time before frying (you may need to add more oil after each batch).

Legacy Potato Dumplings

4 Idaho potatoes, peeled
1 cup flour
1 egg, slightly beaten
1 teaspoon dry minced onion
½ cup buttered croutons
¼ cup (½ stick) butter
2 tablespoons breadcrumbs
1 teaspoon shredded parmesan cheese

★ Boil potatoes in large saucepan in enough water to cover until just tender, drain and cool in refrigerator overnight. Peel and shred potatoes in large bowl.

★ Add flour, egg, minced onion, 2 teaspoons salt and ½ teaspoon pepper and toss gently, but thoroughly. Roll into balls about the size of medium egg. (If mixture does not stick together, add several additional tablespoons of flour and mix again.)

★ Press balls flat in hands and add several croutons to mixture. Roll into ball again, carefully drop into boiling water and cook for about 8 minutes. Remove with slotted spoon, drain and place on platter. Pour butter over top and sprinkle with parmesan cheese. Serves 4.

Old-Fashioned Butter Dumplings

¼ cup (½ stick) butter, softened
1 egg yolk
3 tablespoons flour

★ Cream butter with 1 egg yolk in bowl and beat well. Add flour a little at a time while mixing constantly. Drop small balls of dough into hot soup and cook for 10 minutes over high heat. Serve immediately.

TIP: *This is great in soups with lots of broth, but no noodles, potatoes or rice.*

Apricot-Glazed Sweet Potatoes

1½ cups apricot preserves
2 teaspoons lemon juice
½ teaspoon ground nutmeg
¼ teaspoon ground cinnamon
4 sweet potatoes, peeled

★ Preheat oven to 400°. Cook preserves and ½ cup water in heavy saucepan over medium heat until mixture begins to boil. Simmer for 5 minutes and stir constantly.

★ Remove from heat and stir in lemon juice, nutmeg and cinnamon. Slice sweet potatoes lengthwise into 8 wedges and baste thoroughly with about half apricot mixture. Bake for 20 minutes.

★ Remove from oven and baste with remaining sauce. Bake for additional 20 minutes or until tender. Serves 6 to 8.

Maple Sweet Potatoes

6 large sweet potatoes
3 tablespoons butter, softened
⅓ cup real maple syrup
3 tablespoons orange juice concentrate
1 teaspoon seasoned salt
½ teaspoon cinnamon

★ Wash potatoes, pat dry and prick with tines of fork once, so potatoes won't burst while cooking. Bake potatoes on center rack for 1 hour or until potatoes are soft to touch.

★ Remove upper one-third from each potato with sharp knife. Scoop out center of potato leaving ¼ inch rim along outside and place flesh in large bowl.

★ Add butter, syrup, orange juice, seasoned salt and cinnamon to potato and mix well. Fill potatoes with mixture and continue baking at 375° for approximately 20 minutes more. Serve warm. Serves 6.

The Best Sweet Potato Casserole

1 (29 ounce) can sweet potatoes, drained
⅓ cup evaporated milk
¾ cup sugar
2 eggs, beaten
¼ cup (½ stick) butter, melted
1 teaspoon vanilla

★ Preheat oven to 350°. Place sweet potatoes in bowl and mash slightly with fork. Add evaporated milk, sugar, eggs, butter and vanilla and mix well. Pour mixture into sprayed 7 x 11-inch baking dish.

Topping:

1 cup packed light brown sugar
⅓ cup (⅔ stick) butter, melted
½ cup flour
1 cup chopped pecans

★ Combine brown sugar, butter, flour and pecans in bowl and sprinkle over top of casserole. Bake uncovered for 35 minutes or until crusty on top. Serves 8.

Sweet Potatoes Fries

1½ pounds sweet potatoes
Canola oil

★ Wash potatoes and place in large saucepan with about 2 to 3 cups water. Cover and cook over medium heat for about 20 minutes or until tender. Remove from saucepan and cool.

★ Remove skin and cut into thin slices. Heat just enough oil to cover bottom of large skillet. Place sweet potatoes in oil when it is hot. Fry until pieces are brown on both sides. Drain on paper towels, lightly salt and serve hot. Serves 4.

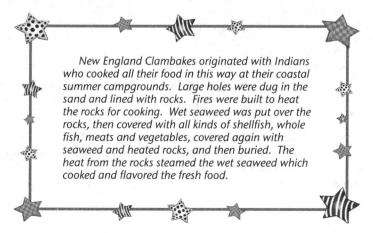

New England Clambakes originated with Indians who cooked all their food in this way at their coastal summer campgrounds. Large holes were dug in the sand and lined with rocks. Fires were built to heat the rocks for cooking. Wet seaweed was put over the rocks, then covered with all kinds of shellfish, whole fish, meats and vegetables, covered again with seaweed and heated rocks, and then buried. The heat from the rocks steamed the wet seaweed which cooked and flavored the fresh food.

Spinach with Pine Nuts

1 (16 ounce) package frozen leaf spinach, thawed
¼ cup (½ stick) butter
2 cloves garlic, finely minced
5 green onions with tops, chopped
½ teaspoon seasoning salt
¼ teaspoon celery salt
½ cup pine nuts

★ Cook spinach according to package directions. Melt butter in saucepan and add garlic, green onions, seasoning salt and celery salt. Mix well, pour over spinach and toss.

★ Place in 2-quart baking dish and sprinkle pine nuts over top. Place under broiler, brown nuts slightly and serve hot. Serves 6.

Fried Yellow Squash or Zucchini

2 large yellow squash or zucchini, sliced
1 egg, beaten
2 tablespoons milk
¾ cup cornmeal
¾ cup flour
Canola oil

★ Place squash on plate and sprinkle with a little salt and pepper. Combine egg and milk in bowl. In separate shallow bowl, combine cornmeal and flour.

★ Dip squash slices in egg-milk mixture and then in cornmeal-flour mixture. Fry in skillet in a little hot oil. Drain on paper towel. Serves 4 to 6.

Baked Squash Olé

4 - 5 cups cooked squash, drained
1 (4 ounce) can diced green chilies, drained
¾ cup shredded Monterey Jack cheese
1 (10 ounce) can cream of chicken soup
1 cup sour cream
½ cup (1 stick) butter, melted
1 package herb dressing mix

★ Preheat oven to 375°. Place squash in bowl and add 1 teaspoon salt and ½ teaspoon pepper, green chilies, cheese, soup and sour cream. Mix well.

★ In separate bowl, mix butter and herb dressing mix. Place one-half herb dressing mixture in sprayed 9 x 13-inch baking dish. Pour squash mixture on top. Sprinkle with remaining dressing mixture. Bake for 30 minutes. Serves 10.

Summer Squash Casserole

½ cup (1 stick) butter
1 (8 ounce) package herb dressing
2 pounds yellow squash, sliced, cooked, drained
2 small onions, finely chopped
1 (10 ounce) can cream of chicken soup
1 (4 ounce) can sliced water chestnuts
1 (2 ounce) jar diced pimentos

★ Preheat oven to 350°. Melt butter in saucepan and stir into dressing. Divide and place half in 8 x 12-inch baking dish.

★ Combine squash, onions, soup, water chestnuts and pimentos in bowl and pour over dressing. Cover with remaining dressing and bake for 30 to 40 minutes. Serves 8.

Stuffed Yellow Squash

5 large yellow squash
1 (16 ounce) package frozen chopped spinach, thawed
1 (8 ounce) package cream cheese, cubed
1 (1 ounce) packet onion soup mix
Shredded cheddar cheese

★ Cook whole squash in oven at 325° for 30 to 35 minutes or until tender. Cut squash lengthwise and remove seeds with spoon. Set aside shells.

★ Cook spinach according to package directions and drain very well. Add cream cheese to spinach and stir until it melts. Do not let this boil. Add soup mix and blend well.

★ Fill scooped out squash shells with spinach mixture and top with few sprinkles cheddar cheese. Place on baking sheet and bake for about 15 minutes. Serves 4 to 6.

Baked Yellow Squash

7 small yellow squash, sliced
1 small onion, diced
¼ cup (½ stick) butter, divided
½ cup half-and-half cream
¾ cup saltine cracker crumbs, divided

★ Preheat oven to 350°. Boil squash in salted water in saucepan until tender. Drain and mash. Saute onion in 2 tablespoons butter in skillet.

★ Add half-and-half cream and ¼ cup cracker crumbs to onion and mix with squash. Pour into sprayed 1½-quart baking dish, top with remaining crumbs and dot with remaining butter. Bake for 30 to 45 minutes or until top is brown. Serves 4 to 6.

Roasted Stuffed Acorn Squash

4 acorn squash
4 slices firm bread
3 tablespoons butter, divided
1 tablespoon fresh thyme or 1 teaspoon dried thyme
4 tablespoons whipping cream

★ Slice tops from acorn squash and remove seeds. Reserve tops and set aside. Add 1 inch water to baking dish and place squash, cut-side up, in dish. Cover and bake at 375° for 1 hour.

★ Tear bread into bite-size pieces and toss with 2 tablespoons melted butter in medium saucepan until brown, remove from pan and set aside for stuffing. After squash cooks 1 hour, remove from oven and allow to cool.

★ Scoop out pulp into large bowl. (If pulp is not soft, continue baking pulp in separate, ovenproof baking dish until it is soft.) Add 1 tablespoon butter, thyme, cream, sautéed bread and a little salt and pepper. Gently toss and spoon into 4 squash cavities. Place on 7 x 11-inch baking dish.

★ Return squash back to oven and continue cooking about 10 minutes or until thoroughly heated. Just before serving, place individual tops back on squash and serve warm. Serves 4.

Tuna-Stuffed Tomatoes

4 large tomatoes
2 (6 ounce) cans white meat tuna, drained
2 cups diced celery
½ cup chopped cashews
1 small zucchini with peel, chopped
½ - ⅔ cup mayonnaise

★ Cut thin slice off top of each tomato, scoop out pulp and discard. Turn tomatoes over on paper towels to drain. Combine tuna, celery, cashews and zucchini and mix well. Add ½ cup mayonnaise; add more if needed. Spoon into hollowed tomatoes and refrigerate. Serves 4.

Broccoli-Stuffed Tomatoes

4 medium tomatoes
1 (10 ounce) package frozen chopped broccoli
1 (6 ounce) roll garlic cheese, softened
½ teaspoon garlic salt

★ Preheat oven to 375°. Cut tops off tomatoes and scoop out flesh. Cook broccoli in saucepan according to package directions and drain well.

★ Combine broccoli, cheese and garlic salt in saucepan and heat just until cheese melts. Stuff broccoli mixture into tomatoes and place on baking sheet. Bake for about 10 minutes. Serves 4.

Fried Green Tomatoes

1 pound green tomatoes
1 cup flour
1 - 2 tablespoons light brown sugar
Canola oil

★ Cut ends off tomatoes, slice ⅓ inch thick and lay on paper towels to drain. Mix flour, brown sugar, and ½ teaspoon each of salt and pepper in shallow bowl.

★ Dredge tomatoes in flour thoroughly. Heat oil in skillet and carefully place each slice in skillet. When 1 side of tomato is crispy and golden in color, turn to brown other side. Drain on paper towels and serve immediately. Serves 8.

TIP: If you do most of your frying in a cast-iron skillet, add chopped onion to the
skillet to absorb some of the tomatoes' acid. It will protect your skillet.

Creamed Spinach

1 pound fresh spinach, stemmed
2 tablespoons flour
½ cup evaporated milk

★ Wash spinach and shake off excess water. Tear spinach leaves into pieces and drop into saucepan. Cover and cook over medium heat until leaves are tender. (Water on leaves will be enough liquid to steam spinach.)

★ Drain spinach and sprinkle flour over leaves. Mix in evenly and pour evaporated milk and a little salt and pepper in the mixture and cook on medium until sauce thickens. Serves 4.

Buttered Turnips

5 medium turnips, peeled, diced
2 teaspoons sugar
¼ cup (½ stick) butter, melted

★ Combine turnips with sugar, 1½ teaspoons salt and ½ teaspoon pepper in saucepan and cook until tender. Rinse well, drain thoroughly and pour into serving dish. Add butter, mash and season with a little more salt and pepper. Serves 4 to 6.

Tomatoes grown for processing are picked ripe
and red. Fresh market tomatoes are picked green.

Turnip Casserole

3 pounds turnips
¼ cup (½ stick) butter
1½ tablespoons sugar
3 eggs
1 cup seasoned breadcrumbs
1½ teaspoons lemon juice

★ Pare and cut turnips into thin slices. Boil until tender, drain and mash hot turnips with butter, sugar, 1½ teaspoons salt and a little pepper. Beat until ingredients blend well.

★ Add eggs one at a time and beat until fluffy. Stir in breadcrumbs and lemon juice. Pour into 1½-quart baking dish, cover and refrigerate. When ready to bake, preheat oven to 375°. Bake for 50 minutes. Serves 8.

Mess o' Greens

A "mess of greens" usually means a big basket full or several big handfuls of collard greens. You wash 'em, boil 'em and season 'em with a little ham hock or bacon and you've got a real nice pot of greens.

1 mess of collard greens
1 ham hock or thick-sliced bacon
½ teaspoon sugar

★ Wash greens carefully to remove all dirt and grit. Place in large pot and add about 1 inch water.

★ Add ham hock or bunch of bacon and boil. Add 1 teaspoon salt and sugar and cook on low until greens are tender. Serves 4.

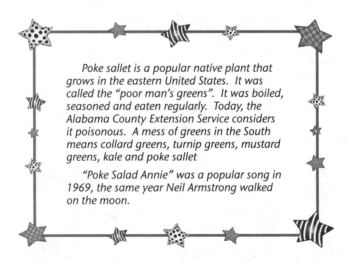

Poke sallet is a popular native plant that grows in the eastern United States. It was called the "poor man's greens". It was boiled, seasoned and eaten regularly. Today, the Alabama County Extension Service considers it poisonous. A mess of greens in the South means collard greens, turnip greens, mustard greens, kale and poke sallet

"Poke Salad Annie" was a popular song in 1969, the same year Neil Armstrong walked on the moon.

South 40 Collard Greens

2 bunches fresh collard greens
2 (10 ounce) cans chicken broth
5 - 6 strips bacon
1 onion, chopped
1 red bell pepper, seeded, chopped
1 tablespoon seasoned salt
1 teaspoon seasoned black pepper
½ teaspoon sugar
1 teaspoon hot pepper sauce, optional

★ Wash and drain collard greens, cut stems off and coarsely chop greens.
Place in large soup pot and cover with broth and 2 cups water.

★ Fry bacon in skillet, drain and crumble bacon. In same skillet with
bacon drippings, saute onion and bell pepper. Add seasoned salt,
seasoned pepper, sugar and hot pepper sauce, if you like.

★ Add onion-bell pepper mixture to soup pot and heat to a full boil.
Reduce heat, cover and simmer for 1 hour. Serves 6 to 8.

Seasoned Zucchini and Onions

8 zucchini, sliced
2 onions, chopped
¼ cup (½ stick) butter
1 (10 ounce) can fiesta nacho cheese soup
1 (6 ounce) can french-fried onions

★ Cook zucchini and onion in small amount of water in saucepan until
tender and drain. Add butter, soup and fried onions and toss. Serve hot.
Serves 6.

Ketchup was originally a sauce similar
to Worcestershire that was created in
Southeast Asia. Its popularity travelled
around the world with explorers and
sailors. Ingredients and flavors changed
as available foods changed. The Chinese-
style ketchup evolved to sauces made from
mushrooms, cucumbers, walnuts, peppers
and eventually to tomatoes. Today, tomato
ketchup is a staple in most American homes.

Chow-Chow

A delicious recipe to serve with meats and beans!

2 large heads cabbage
1½ pounds green bell peppers, chopped
4 red bell peppers, chopped
4 medium green tomatoes, chopped
4 medium onions, chopped
1½ pints vinegar
3 cups sugar

★ Chop cabbage and add 4 teaspoons salt in bowl. Working with your hands, mix and squeeze until a bit of juice comes from cabbage. Add bell peppers and tomatoes. Work a bit more and add onions.

★ Make syrup of vinegar, ½ cup water, 4½ teaspoons salt and sugar in saucepan. Let cool. Place chopped vegetable ingredients into cold syrup and bring to a rolling boil.

★ Cook for 5 minutes after boil begins. Begin to put into hot, sterilized jars from center of pot. Do NOT cook too long or syrup will cook away. Seal. Yields 4 to 6 pint jars.

Everyday Corn Relish

2 heads cabbage, chopped
12 ears corn-on-the-cob
4 red bell peppers, seeded, chopped
3 large onions, chopped
1 cup sugar
2 cups vinegar

★ Place cabbage in large saucepan. Cut corn off cob and add to cabbage. Add bell peppers and onions and mix. Add enough water to barely cover and cook on high heat until cabbage is just tender. Drain well and place in glass container.

★ In separate bowl mix sugar, vinegar and about 1 to 2 teaspoons salt and stir well. Pour over cabbage, cover and store in refrigerator. Stir occasionally. Serves 12 to 14.

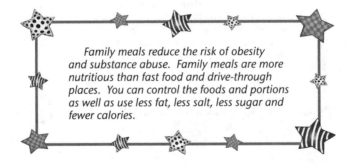

Family meals reduce the risk of obesity and substance abuse. Family meals are more nutritious than fast food and drive-through places. You can control the foods and portions as well as use less fat, less salt, less sugar and fewer calories.

County Fair Bread-and-Butter Pickles

3 medium onions, sliced
30 (6 inch) cucumbers, sliced
3¾ teaspoons alum
6½ cups vinegar
5 cups sugar
1 tablespoon celery seed
2½ teaspoons mustard seed
1½ teaspoons turmeric
2½ teaspoons ground ginger

★ Slice onions and cucumbers in bowl. Sprinkle 5 tablespoons salt and alum over both and let stand for 1 hour. Drain in colander and set aside.

★ Make syrup of vinegar, sugar, celery seed, mustard seed, turmeric and ginger in large pot and bring to a boil for 5 minutes. Pour drained cucumbers into syrup. Place in hot, sterilized jars immediately and seal. Yields 5 to 6 (8 ounce) jars.

Creamy Dilled Cucumbers

Seedless greenhouse cucumbers are wonderful in this recipe.

2 pounds cucumbers with peels, thinly sliced
1 cup reduced-fat sour cream
3 tablespoons white wine vinegar
2 tablespoons fresh dill weed
1 teaspoon sugar

★ Combine sliced cucumbers and 2 teaspoons salt in colander. Set aside to drain for 30 minutes. Transfer cucumbers to paper towels and pat dry.

★ Combine sour cream, vinegar, dill weed and sugar in large bowl. Add cucumbers and toss lightly to coat. Serve immediately. Serves 8.

Marinated Cucumbers

1 cup vinegar
½ cup sugar
1 tablespoon minced chives
6 cucumbers, peeled

★ Combine vinegar, sugar, chives and ½ teaspoon salt in large measuring cup. Slice cucumbers about ⅓ inch thick and place in large bowl. Pour marinade over cucumbers, cover and refrigerate. Serves 8.

Sides and Sauces

Spiced Pears

1 (15 ounce) can pear halves
⅓ cup packed brown sugar
¾ teaspoon ground nutmeg
¾ teaspoon ground cinnamon

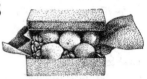

★ Drain pears, reserve syrup and set pears aside. Place syrup, brown sugar, nutmeg and cinnamon in saucepan and bring to a boil. Reduce heat and simmer uncovered for 5 to 8 minutes, stirring frequently. Add pears and simmer for 5 minutes longer or until thoroughly hot.

Baked Apples

6 apples
6 tablespoons brown sugar, divided
Whipped cream

★ Preheat oven to 350°. Wash apples and remove cores. Fill center of each apple with 1 tablespoon brown sugar. Place in sprayed baking dish.

★ Add enough boiling water to cover bottom of dish. For additional flavor, you can add a little lemon juice or cinnamon (1 teaspoon each) to water.

★ Bake uncovered, basting frequently with liquid that forms in bottom of baking dish, until apples are tender (about 20 to 30 minutes, depending on size and variety). Serve with whipped cream. Serves 6.

TIP: There are several alternatives for the brown sugar filling: sliced bananas, marmalade, jelly, preserves, honey and chopped pineapple, chopped peaches or nuts.

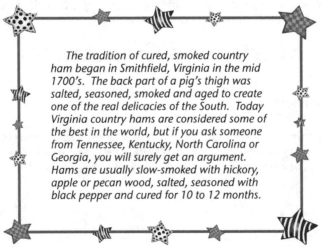

The tradition of cured, smoked country ham began in Smithfield, Virginia in the mid 1700's. The back part of a pig's thigh was salted, seasoned, smoked and aged to create one of the real delicacies of the South. Today Virginia country hams are considered some of the best in the world, but if you ask someone from Tennessee, Kentucky, North Carolina or Georgia, you will surely get an argument. Hams are usually slow-smoked with hickory, apple or pecan wood, salted, seasoned with black pepper and cured for 10 to 12 months.

Orange-Spiced Peaches

1 (28 ounce) can peach halves with juice
1 teaspoon whole cloves
6 sticks cinnamon
10 whole allspice
½ cup vinegar
⅔ cup sugar
1 orange, sliced

★ Drain peaches and set aside ½ cup syrup. Tie cloves, cinnamon and allspice in small piece of cheesecloth.

★ Combine vinegar, sugar and orange slices in large saucepan. Add drained peach halves, set aside peach syrup and spice bag. Heat to a boil, reduce heat and simmer for 5 minutes.

★ Cover and let cool to room temperature. Remove spice bag and serve peach halves with orange slices. Serve warm or cold. Serves 8.

Thanksgiving Cranberry Sauce

Cranberries are grown commercially and turn up in all sorts of dishes... but the favorite remains the cranberry sauce that's served with turkey.

2 cups fresh or frozen cranberries*
1 cup sugar
½ cup water
1 teaspoon grated orange peel, optional

★ Wash berries. Combine with sugar, water and orange peel in small saucepan and bring to a boil. Simmer 8 to 10 minutes or until the skins of the cranberries begin to pop. Stir frequently. Cool before serving. Yields 1½ cups.

TIP: If using frozen berries, increase cooking time to 20 to 25 minutes.

Home-Style Sweet Rice

1 cup rice
1 (12 ounce) can evaporated milk
¾ cup sugar
Ground cinnamon

★ Cover rice with water in saucepan, add a pinch of salt and cook until rice is almost tender. (Add water if needed.)

★ Add evaporated milk and sugar and cook until rice is tender. Pour into baking dish and serve. Sprinkle with additional sugar and a little cinnamon to taste. Serves 4.

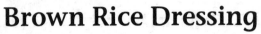

Brown Rice Dressing

1 teaspoon rosemary
3 cubes chicken bouillon 3 teaspoons granules
1½ cups brown rice
6 slices bacon
½ cup diced green onions
2 tablespoons butter, melted
1 (8 ounce) can sliced water chestnuts

★ Preheat oven to 325°. Combine 3 cups water, 1 teaspoon salt, rosemary and bouillon in saucepan and bring to a boil. Add rice, cover and simmer for 30 minutes or until all liquid absorbs into rice.

★ Fry bacon in skillet until crisp and crumble. Combine bacon, green onion, butter and water chestnuts in bowl and add to rice. Mix well and place in sprayed 7 x 11-inch baking dish. Cover and bake for 15 minutes. Serves 6.

Brown Rice and Pine Nuts

1 (5 ounce) box brown rice
1 (14 ounce) can beef broth
2 ribs celery, sliced
1 small onion, chopped
¼ cup (½ stick) butter
1 teaspoon grated lemon peel
1 tablespoon chopped fresh cilantro leaves
¼ cup toasted pine nuts

★ Cook brown rice according to package directions, using beef broth with water to total amount of liquid in package directions. Let stand for 5 minutes.

★ Saute celery and onion in butter in skillet over medium heat. Fluff rice and add celery, onion, lemon peel, cilantro and pine nuts. Serves 8.

Garlic-Seasoned Grits

1 cup grits
1 (5 ounce) roll garlic cheese
½ cup (1 stick) butter
2 eggs
Milk

★ Preheat oven to 350°. Cook grits in saucepan according to package directions. Add garlic cheese and butter and stir well.

★ Beat eggs slightly, pour into measuring cup and add enough milk to equal 1 cup. Add to grits and mix well. Pour grits mixture into sprayed baking dish and bake for 30 minutes or until light brown on top. Serves 6 to 8.

Chile-Cheese Grits

1½ cups grits
1 (16 ounce) package shredded cheddar cheese
¼ cup (½ stick) butter
3 eggs, well beaten
1 teaspoon seasoned salt
½ teaspoon hot sauce
1 (4 ounce) can diced green chilies

★ Preheat oven to 275°. Bring 6 cups water to a boil in saucepan, add grits
   slowly and cook until done. Add cheese and butter and stir until both
   melt. Fold in beaten eggs, seasoned salt, 1 teaspoon salt, hot sauce and
   green chilies.

★ Pour into sprayed 9 x 13-inch baking pan. Bake for 1 hour 20 minutes.
   (If center is not set, cook a little longer.) Serves 4 to 6.

TIP: *This may be prepared ahead of time and baked right before serving.*

New England Oyster Stuffing

*Stuffing fowl with oysters was fairly common with the rich classes
in Europe as far back as the 17th century. In colonial times,
oysters were plentiful and appeared often on all tables at mealtime.*

1 cup (2 sticks) butter
2 cups diced onion
2 cups diced celery
2 pints fresh oysters with liquor
1 teaspoon poultry seasoning
1 teaspoon lemon juice
10 slices white bread, cubed

★ Melt butter in large skillet over medium heat. Add onions and celery
   and saute until slightly tender. Add oysters with liquor, seasoning and
   lemon juice; reduce heat and cover. Simmer for about 10 minutes or
   until edges of oysters curl.

★ Pour oyster mixture into sprayed 2-quart baking dish and mix with
   bread. Pat down evenly and bake uncovered at 325° for about
   25 minutes or until heated thoroughly. Serves 6.

*Take away the heritage of a people and
they are easily persuaded.*
–Karl Marx

Holiday Apple Stuffing

1 medium onion, peeled, diced
3 ribs celery, diced
2 tablespoons canola oil, divided
1 (8 ounce) carton fresh mushrooms
3 Gala apples, peeled, seeded, diced
½ cup dried cherries or dried sweetened cranberries
½ teaspoon dried sage
¼ teaspoon dried thyme
1 (16 ounce) package bread stuffing

★ Preheat oven to 350°. In large skillet saute onion and celery in
  1 tablespoon oil until translucent. Add mushrooms and remaining
  oil and saute until translucent. Add apple to mixture and set aside.

★ Add sage and thyme to bread stuffing and mix well. Add onion, celery,
  mushrooms and a little salt and pepper to bread stuffing and mix well.
  Transfer mixture to sprayed 2-quart baking dish and bake for 30 minutes
  or until thoroughly hot. Serves 10.

Cornbread Dressing

This is a family heirloom recipe used by several generations year after year.

2 (6 ounce) packages cornbread mix
9 biscuits or 1 recipe of biscuit mix
1 small onion, chopped
2 ribs celery, chopped
2 eggs
2 teaspoons poultry seasoning
3 (14 ounce) cans chicken broth, divided

★ A day or two ahead of time prepare cornbread and biscuits according to
  package instructions.

★ Preheat oven to 350°. Crumble cornbread and biscuits into large bowl,
  using a little more cornbread than biscuits.

★ Add onion, celery, eggs, poultry seasoning and a little pepper. Stir in
  2½ cans chicken broth. (If the mixture is not "runny", add remaining
  broth. If it is still not runny, add a little milk.)

★ Bake in sprayed 9 x 13-inch glass baking dish for about 45 minutes
  or until golden brown. (This may be frozen uncooked, thawed and
  cooked when you want it.) Serve with Giblet Gravy (recipe on page
  161). Serves 10.

Giblet Gravy

2 (14 ounce) cans chicken broth, divided
2 tablespoons cornstarch
2 eggs, hard-boiled, sliced, divided
Chicken or turkey giblets, cooked, chopped

★ Mix ½ cup chicken broth with cornstarch in saucepan and stir until there are no lumps. Add remaining broth and a little pepper and heat to a boil; stir constantly until broth is thick. Add three-fourths egg slices.

★ Add cooked giblets and pour into gravy boat. Garnish with remaining egg slices in saucepan. Serves 10 to 12.

Southern Macaroni and Cheese

1 (16 ounce) package shell pasta
2 tablespoons butter
3 eggs, beaten
1 (16 ounce) carton half-and-half cream
1 (12 ounce) package shredded cheddar cheese, divided
⅛ teaspoon cayenne pepper

★ Preheat oven to 350°. Bring 4 to 5 quarts water to a boil in large pot. Add pasta and 2 teaspoons salt and cook for 6 minutes. (Pasta should be slightly undercooked.)

★ Drain pasta and stir in butter to keep it from sticking. Transfer to sprayed 2½-quart baking dish. Combine eggs, half-and-half cream, three-fourths cheese and cayenne pepper in bowl and mix well.

★ Pour mixture over pasta and sprinkle remaining cheese over top. Cover and bake for 35 minutes. Uncover and broil just enough to lightly brown top. Serves 8 to 10.

Macaroni and Cheese

There is no dispute about the origin of macaroni and cheese in America. Thomas Jefferson served it in the White House. Jefferson was an envoy to France before becoming president. When he returned to Monticello, he brought many ideas and machines to make his life better. One of the machines was a press used to make long strings of pasta. Jefferson improved the machine and introduced America to pasta.

His recipe for Macaroni and Cheese is much like our recipes today: pasta, butter, milk, seasonings, and yellow or white cheese mixed together and baked. In 1824 Mary Randolph, Jefferson's cousin, gave a recipe for Macaroni and Cheese in The Virginia Housewife, A Cookbook. *It grew in popularity for 100 years, but in 1937 Kraft started selling its Kraft Macaroni and Cheese Dinner and its popularity soared.*

Ronald Reagan was another American president who listed Macaroni and Cheese as a favorite food and served it in the White House. Today more than 1,000,000 boxes of Macaroni and Cheese Dinner are sold each day. Macaroni and Cheese is one of America's all-time favorite foods and just one more reason to thank Thomas Jefferson.

Three-Cheese Macaroni

1 (16 ounce) package macaroni
¼ cup (½ stick) butter, divided
1 (8 ounce) package longhorn cheese, cubed
1 cup cubed Swiss cheese
¼ cup grated parmesan cheese
1 tablespoon flour
1½ cups milk

★ Preheat oven to 350°. Cook macaroni according to package directions. Drain and stir in half butter to keep macaroni from sticking together. While macaroni is still warm, mix in cheeses and stir until they melt.

★ Pour mixture into sprayed 9 x 13-inch baking dish. Melt remaining butter in saucepan and add flour plus a little salt and pepper. Cook and stir for 1 minute. Slowly add milk and stir constantly.

★ Cook until thick and pour over macaroni-cheese mixture. Cover and bake for 25 minutes. Uncover and continue to bake for additional 10 minutes. Serves 8.

Easy Everyday Basic Macaroni and Cheese

See pages 163-165 for great macaroni and
cheese creations using this basic recipe.

2 cups macaroni or pasta shells
2½ cups milk
2 tablespoons flour
3 cups shredded sharp cheddar cheese
⅛ - ¼ teaspoon cayenne pepper

★ Cook macaroni shells according to package directions, drain and set aside. Pour milk into large saucepan and cook on medium-low heat. Add flour and stir until mixture thickens.

★ Preheat oven to 350°. Gradually add cheese and continue stirring until all cheese melts. Add cayenne and macaroni and stir well. Pour into baking dish and bake for 30 minutes or until bubbly. Serves 6 to 8.

Variations:

1. Use 2 cups shredded cheddar cheese and 1 cup shredded American cheese instead of 3 cups cheddar.

2. Add 2 cups cheddar cheese and 1 cup shredded parmesan cheese instead of 3 cups sharp cheddar.

Mac and 4-Cheese Blend

★ For 3 cups cheese in *Easy Everyday Basic Macaroni and Cheese* (page 162), choose any combination of cheeses: American, shredded mild cheddar, shredded extra sharp cheddar, shredded parmesan, shredded gruyere, shredded Swiss, shredded mozzarella, edam, emmental. Choose your favorite combinations. Serves 6 to 8.

Cajun Mac and Cheese

★ Use recipe for *Easy Everyday Basic Macaroni and Cheese* (page 162) and make these additions:

½ cup minced onion
½ cup minced bell pepper
½ cup minced celery
Butter
1 teaspoon cayenne pepper

★ Saute onion, bell pepper and celery in some butter in skillet until onions are translucent. Stir into melted cheese and add more cayenne. Serves 6 to 8.

Mac and Cheese Party Bites

★ Use recipe for *Easy Everyday Basic Macaroni and Cheese* (page 162) and make these additions:

1 teaspoon cayenne
10 - 12 jalapeno slices

★ Add additional seasoning with melted cheese. Pour into sprayed mini-muffin pans, place 1 jalapeno slice on top of some of the bites. Bake at 350° until edges and top of each mini-bite is toasty brown. Remove from oven and cool slightly. Serves 10 to 12.

Cowboy Mac and Cheese

★ Use recipe for *Easy Everyday Basic Macaroni and Cheese* (page 162) and make these additions:

1 pound ground beef
½ cup chopped onion
¼ - ½ cup jalapeno slices, seeded

★ Brown ground beef in large skillet, drain thoroughly. Saute onion in drippings. Add ground beef, onion and jalapenos to melted cheese. Serves 6 to 8.

Chicken-Cashew Mac and Cheese

★ Use recipe for *Easy Everyday Basic Macaroni and Cheese* (page 162) and make these additions:

> 1 cup cooked, chopped chicken
> ¾ cup cashews
> 2 teaspoons soy sauce

★ Add ingredients to melted cheese and mix thoroughly. Serves 6 to 8.

Smokey Joe's Mac and Cheese

★ Use recipe for *Easy Everyday Basic Macaroni and Cheese* (page 162) and make these additions/substitutions:

> ½ - 1 pound hickory-smoked bacon
> 2 cups shredded smoked cheddar cheese
> 1 cup shredded parmesan
> 1 pint grape tomatoes, halved

★ Fry bacon crispy in large skillet, drain thoroughly and set aside; crumble when cool. Use smoked cheddar and parmesan instead of 3 cups cheddar cheese in *Easy Everyday Basic Macaroni and Cheese*. While cheese melts, add all ingredients and mix well. Serves 8.

Twice-Baked
Mac and Cheese Potato

★ Use recipe for *Easy Everyday Basic Macaroni and Cheese* (page 162) and make these additions:

> 2 baking potatoes
> ½ cup chopped chives
> ½ - 1 cup real bacon crumbles
> 2 tablespoons butter

★ Bake potatoes, cool and cut in half lengthwise. When potatoes cool, scoop out potato leaving the potato peels as shells. Mash potatoes with fork or electric mixer and add all remaining ingredients. Season with a little salt and pepper. Stir into melting cheese.

★ Pour macaroni-potato mixture into potato shells and let overflow down both sides. (Size of potatoes determines how much mac and cheese you can put into potato shells.) Place shells on baking dish and bake at 400° just until top is brown and crispy. Yields 4 large potato shells.

Buffalo Chicken Mac and Cheese

★ Use recipe for *Easy Everyday Basic Macaroni and Cheese* (page 162) and make these additions:

> 1 -2 cups cooked, chopped chicken
> ½ - 1 teaspoon garlic powder
> ¼ - ⅓ cup Frank's® RedHot® Buffalo Wings Sauce
> 2 tablespoons butter, melted

★ Season chicken with garlic powder and marinate in mixture of Frank's® RedHot® Buffalo Wings Sauce and butter for about 30 minutes. Stir into cheese after it melts and mix well. Serves 8.

Unbelievable Lasagna

You don't have to cook the lasagna ahead of time with this recipe.

4 to 5 cups spaghetti sauce, divided
8 ounces lasagna
1 (1 pound) carton ricotta cheese
1 (8 ounce) package shredded mozzarella cheese
1 cup shredded parmesan cheese

★ Preheat oven to 350°. Pour 1 cup spaghetti sauce into 9 x 13-inch baking dish and arrange a layer of uncooked lasagna on top. Pour 1 cup spaghetti sauce, ⅓ of ricotta, ⅓ of mozzarella and ⅓ parmesan and arrange another layer of lasagna on top.

★ Repeat this step with remaining spaghetti sauce, all of ricotta, ⅓ of mozzarella and ⅓ parmesan. Arrange another layer of lasagna and top with remaining cheese. (Lasagna will expand as it cooks.) Bake for 45 to 50 minutes or until cheese is bubbly and slightly brown on top. Remove from oven and let stand for about 15 minutes before cutting into squares. Serves 6 to 8.

Easy Fettuccine Alfredo

1 (16 ounce) package fettuccine
2 tablespoons butter
¾ cup grated fresh parmesan cheese
1¼ cups whipping cream

★ Cook fettuccine according to package directions. In large saucepan over medium heat, melt butter and stir in parmesan cheese, whipping cream and a little black pepper. Cook 1 minute and stir constantly. Reduce heat, pour in fettuccine and toss gently to coat fettuccine. Serves 4 to 6.

Pasta with Basil

2½ cups small tube pasta
1 small onion, chopped
2 tablespoons canola oil
2½ tablespoons dried basil
1 cup shredded mozzarella cheese

★ Cook pasta in saucepan according to package directions and drain. Saute onion in oil in skillet. Stir in basil, 1 teaspoon salt and ¼ teaspoon pepper. Cook and stir for 1 minute.

★ Add pasta to basil mixture. Remove from heat and stir in cheese just until it begins to melt. Serve immediately. Serves 4 to 6.

Spatzle

This is a well-known Pennsylvania Dutch recipe that is
served with butter and sometimes substituted for potatoes.

1½ cups flour
2 eggs, beaten
½ cup milk
Canola oil

★ Mix flour and eggs in large bowl. Add milk, a little at a time, and beat until dough is smooth. Add 1 teaspoon salt and a dash of oil to 1 quart water in saucepan and bring to a boil.

★ Press dough through a colander or spatzle maker and drop pieces into boiling water. Cook until pieces float on surface. Remove with slotted spoon and serve immediately. Serves 4 to 6.

TIP: You can serve spatzle plain with a little butter or with a dash of nutmeg for added flavor.

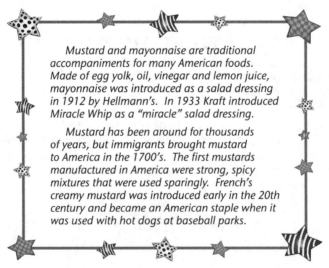

Mustard and mayonnaise are traditional accompaniments for many American foods. Made of egg yolk, oil, vinegar and lemon juice, mayonnaise was introduced as a salad dressing in 1912 by Hellmann's. In 1933 Kraft introduced Miracle Whip as a "miracle" salad dressing.

Mustard has been around for thousands of years, but immigrants brought mustard to America in the 1700's. The first mustards manufactured in America were strong, spicy mixtures that were used sparingly. French's creamy mustard was introduced early in the 20th century and became an American staple when it was used with hot dogs at baseball parks.

Spinach Enchiladas

2 (10 ounce) packages chopped spinach, thawed, pressed dry
1 (1 ounce) packet onion soup mix
1 (12 ounce) package shredded cheddar cheese
1 (12 ounce) package shredded Monterey Jack cheese
12 flour tortillas
2 cups whipping cream

★ Preheat oven to 350°. Squeeze spinach between paper towels to completely remove excess moisture.. Combine spinach and onion soup mix in medium bowl. Blend in half cheddar cheese and Jack cheese with spinach.

★ Lay out 12 tortillas and place about 3 heaping tablespoons spinach mixture down middle of tortilla and roll to close. Place each filled tortilla, seam-side down, into sprayed 9 x 13-inch baking dish.

★ Pour cream over enchiladas and sprinkle with remaining cheeses. Cover and bake for 20 minutes. Uncover and bake for additional 15 minutes. Serves 6 to 8.

Anytime Cheese Enchiladas

1 (12 ounce) carton small curd cottage cheese, drained
1½ cups sour cream, divided
1 (14 ounce) can enchilada sauce
1 (8 ounce) block cheddar cheese
12 tortillas
1 (4 ounce) can diced green chilies
1 (8 ounce) package shredded Mexican 4-cheese blend
1 (4 ounce) can chopped black olives, drained

★ Preheat oven to 350°. Combine cottage cheese, ½ cup sour cream, ½ teaspoon each of salt and pepper in small bowl and set aside.

★ In separate bowl, combine enchilada sauce and ½ cup sour cream and set aside. Cut block of cheese into 12 slices and set aside.

★ Lay several tortillas flat and spoon about 1 tablespoon cottage cheese-sour cream mixture in middle of each tortilla.

★ Add 1 slice cheese and about 1 tablespoon green chilies. Roll tortilla and place, seam-side down in sprayed 9 x 13-inch baking dish. Repeat process with all tortillas.

★ Pour enchilada sauce mixture over all tortillas in baking dish. Sprinkle cheese, olives and remaining sour cream over top. Bake for 25 to 30 minutes or until enchiladas are thoroughly hot. Serves 4 to 6.

Classic Cream Gravy

Bacon drippings
3 tablespoons flour
1½ cups milk

★ The best cream gravy is made in the same skillet used to fry chicken, steak, pork sausage or bacon. The "pan drippings" add their own special seasonings.

★ If you do not have pan "drippings", pour a little bacon grease in skillet, heat and add flour, ½ teaspoon each of salt and pepper. Stir to mix well.

★ Turn heat to high and slowly pour milk into skillet while stirring constantly until gravy thickens. When gravy reaches right consistency, pour into bowl and serve with biscuits, meat or drink it straight from bowl. Serves 4.

Basic Ranchero Sauce

Ranchero Sauce is used in Huevos Rancheros and in many Southwestern dishes with tomato-based sauce.

2 tablespoons butter
2 onions, chopped
½ cup chopped celery
2 cloves garlic, minced
2 jalapeno peppers, seeded, chopped*
1 tablespoon Worcestershire sauce
1 (28 ounce) can chopped stewed tomatoes

★ Combine all ingredients plus ½ teaspoon salt in saucepan. Heat to boil, reduce heat and simmer for 1 hour or until sauce thickens.

TIP: Wear rubber gloves when removing seeds from jalapenos.

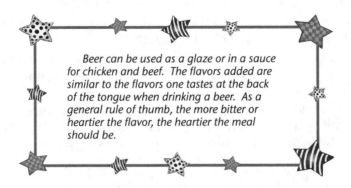

Beer can be used as a glaze or in a sauce for chicken and beef. The flavors added are similar to the flavors one tastes at the back of the tongue when drinking a beer. As a general rule of thumb, the more bitter or heartier the flavor, the heartier the meal should be.

Beer Brisket Sop

*Just sop this on a brisket when you are grilling or smoking
it to keep it moist during the cooking process. Brisket should
be cooked slowly and for a long time to be fork tender.*

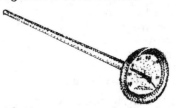

1 onion, minced
3 cloves garlic, minced
1 (12 ounce) can beer
¼ cup canola oil
¼ cup vinegar
2 tablespoons Worcestershire sauce
Chili powder

★ Place vegetables in large saucepan with ½ cup water, a little salt and
pepper and pour all remaining ingredients in saucepan.

★ Mix ingredients well and heat on low. Put sop on brisket with pastry
brush or rag wrapped around wooden spoon. Sop brisket 3 to 4 times
while cooking. Yields 1½ cups.

Barbecue Dry Rub

*Memphis is famous of its dry rubs. When you order ribs in Memphis,
they will ask "Wet or dry", meaning with dry rub or barbecue sauce.*

¼ cup paprika
2 - 3 tablespoons light brown sugar
2 tablespoons chili powder
2 tablespoons cracked black pepper
1 tablespoon cayenne pepper
1 tablespoon ground cumin
1 - 2 tablespoons garlic powder
1 tablespoon celery salt
1 - 2 teaspoons dry mustard

★ Combine all ingredients with 1 tablespoon salt in bowl and mix
thoroughly. Rub mixture into meat of your choice and wrap in plastic
wrap. Refrigerate for several hours or overnight. Yields 1 cup.

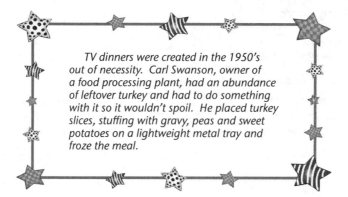

*TV dinners were created in the 1950's
out of necessity. Carl Swanson, owner of
a food processing plant, had an abundance
of leftover turkey and had to do something
with it so it wouldn't spoil. He placed turkey
slices, stuffing with gravy, peas and sweet
potatoes on a lightweight metal tray and
froze the meal.*

Barbecue Marinade

4 - 5 lemons
1 teaspoon sea salt
1 teaspoon cracked black pepper
1 tablespoon ground, dried red chile flakes
4 cloves garlic, minced
½ cup cilantro, minced
¼ cup fresh oregano
¼ cup fresh basil
¼ cup fresh chives
½ cup extra virgin olive oil

★ Juice lemons to equal ⅓ cup and pour in bowl. Add sea salt and whisk until salt dissolves. Add all remaining ingredients and whisk thoroughly. Use immediately and marinate for several hours for beef and less time for chicken. Yields 1½ cups.

Barbecue Sauce with Mustard

1 cup vinegar
⅔ cup lemon juice
2 teaspoons minced garlic
1 onion, finely grated
1 cup packed brown sugar
4 cups ketchup
1 teaspoon cayenne pepper
¼ cup mustard
2 teaspoons liquid smoke

★ Combine vinegar, lemon juice, garlic, onion and brown sugar in saucepan and bring to a boil. Add remaining ingredients, 1 tablespoon salt and 1 tablespoon pepper and boil for 5 minutes. Yields 1½ quarts.

Smoky Barbecue Sauce

1 cup vinegar
⅔ cup lemon juice
2 teaspoons minced garlic
1 onion, finely grated
1 cup packed brown sugar
4 cups ketchup
1 teaspoon cayenne pepper
¼ cup mustard
2 teaspoons liquid smoke

★ Combine vinegar, lemon juice, garlic, onion, and brown sugar in saucepan and bring to a boil. Add remaining ingredients, 1 tablespoon salt and 1 tablespoon pepper and boil for 5 minutes. Yields 1½ quarts.

Western Barbecue Sauce

1 (5 ounce) bottle Worcestershire sauce
1 cup cider vinegar
¾ cup lemon juice
¼ oil
¼ cup packed brown sugar
1 teaspoon garlic salt

★ Combine all ingredients plus 2 cups water, 2 teaspoons salt and ½ teaspoon pepper in saucepan over medium-high heat and bring to boil. Reduce heat and simmer, uncovered for about 10 minutes. Use immediately or store in air-tight container in refrigerator for 1 to 2 weeks. Yields 4 cups.

Worcestershire Butter Sauce

Serve this over fish or vegetables.

½ cup (1 stick) butter
2 tablespoons lemon juice
1 tablespoon chopped parsley
1½ teaspoons Worcestershire sauce

★ Melt butter in small saucepan and add remaining ingredients. Yields about ½ cup.

Horseradish Sauce

½ cup mayonnaise
¼ cup prepared horseradish, drained
2 tablespoons light corn syrup
2 tablespoons dry sherry or tarragon vinegar
2 teaspoons prepared mustard
¼ teaspoon hot pepper sauce

★ Combine all ingredients and a little salt and refrigerate before serving. Yields 2 cups

Cocktail Sauce for Seafood

3 tablespoons ketchup
1 tablespoon horseradish
1 tablespoon Worcestershire sauce
1 tablespoon lemon juice
¼ tablespoon hot pepper sauce

★ Combine all ingredients and refrigerate before serving. Serves 4.

Main Dishes – Beef

Grilled Flank Steak

2 pounds flank steak

Marinade:

¼ cup soy sauce
⅓ cup honey
2 tablespoons cider vinegar
1½ teaspoons garlic salt
¾ cup vegetable oil
1 small onion, finely minced

★ Score steak about ¼ inch deep on each side and remove visible fat. Combine soy sauce, honey, vinegar, garlic salt, oil and onion in shallow bowl. Marinate steak overnight in refrigerator.

★ Remove steak from marinade (discard marinade) and grill for 10 minutes on each side. Slice diagonally and thin. Serves 8

Hamburgers

Seymour, Wisconsin claims that Charlie Nagreen made the first hamburger in 1885 when his meatballs weren't selling at the Outagamie County Fair because they were too hard to handle. To boost sales he flattened the meatballs and put them between two pieces of bread.

Later in 1885 Frank and Charles Menches from Akron, Ohio sold pork sausages on a travelling circuit to county fairs. When the pork ran out at a fair in Hamburg, New York, the brothers substituted beef patties and put them between two pieces of bread and called them "hamburgers" after the city they were in at the time.

Oscar Weber Bilby made the first hamburger on a bun on July 4, 1891 in Tulsa, Oklahoma. He cooked ground beef patties on a homemade grill and made homemade yeast buns for the patties. His family still uses the original grill in their restaurant to make hamburgers today.

In 1904 the St. Louis World's Fair sold hamburgers and claimed they were the first to make them. Additional claims for the birthplace of the hamburger come from Athens, Texas and New Haven, Connecticut.

A dispute among Denver, Colorado; Louisville, Kentucky; and Pasadena, California still exists over who made the first cheeseburger.

And in 1991 Governor Frank Keating proclaimed that Tulsa, Oklahoma was the birthplace of the hamburger made with lettuce, tomato, pickles, onions, cheese and a special sauce on a hamburger bun.

Easy Swiss Steak

2 tablespoons oil
1 (2 pound/1 inch) thick round steak, trimmed, tenderized
¼ cup flour
1 envelope dry onion soup mix
1 (8 ounce) can tomato sauce

★ Preheat oven to 350°. Pour oil into 7 x 12-inch baking dish, place steak in dish and turn to get oil on both sides. Sprinkle onion soup mix over steak. Mix tomato sauce and ½ cup water. Pour over steak and cover with lid or foil. Bake for 2½ to 3 hours or until fork tender. Skim off fat and use juices as gravy. Serves 6.

Texas Beef Fajitas

If you want a short-cut, substitute Italian dressing for the marinade.

Marinade:

1 cup prepared salsa or fresh salsa
1 cup bottled Italian dressing
2 tablespoons lemon juice
2 tablespoons chopped green onions
1 teaspoon garlic powder
1 teaspoon celery salt
2 pounds skirt steak
Flour tortillas

Accompaniments for Fajitas:

Prepared salsa or fresh salsa guacamole
Grilled onions
Chopped tomatoes
Shredded cheese
Sour cream

★ Mix 1 teaspoon pepper and all marinade ingredients in large bowl and mix well. Slice skirt steak into ½ inch wide strips and marinate for several hours. Grill or pan-fry skirt steak and put on tortillas with selected accompaniments. Serves 6 to 8.

Fajitas are original to Texas and probably have their roots in the Texas cattle drives. Traditionally, fajitas are skirt steak that is marinated, grilled and cut into strips about 4 inches long and ½-inch wide. These are served with flour tortillas and a variety of vegetables. Fajitas are amazing not only for their flavor, but also because such an inexpensive cut of beef is so delicious. Fajitas are known and served all over the world.

Pepper Steak

¼ cup flour
1½ pounds round steak, cut in ½-inch strips
¼ cup canola oil
1 (15 ounce) can diced tomatoes, drained
½ cup chopped onion
1 small clove garlic, minced
1 tablespoon beef bouillon granules
1½ teaspoons Worcestershire sauce
2 large green peppers, seeded, cut in strips
Rice, cooked

★ Combine flour, ½ teaspoon salt and ¼ teaspoon pepper in bowl and coat
  steak. Heat oil in large skillet and brown meat on both sides.

★ Add tomatoes, 1 cup water, onion, garlic and bouillon. Cover and
  simmer for 1 hour 15 minutes or until meat is tender.

★ Uncover and add Worcestershire sauce and green pepper strips. Cover
  again and simmer for additional 5 minutes. Thicken gravy with
  2 tablespoons of flour and cold water. Serve over rice. Serves 4 to 6.

Salisbury Steak and Gravy

*Dr. James Henry Salisbury is given the credit for creating
this recipe for Civil War soldiers. This simple seasoned
ground-beef patty first appeared in print around 1888.*

1½ pounds extra-lean ground beef
1 egg, beaten
½ cup chili sauce
¾ cup seasoned breadcrumbs
Canola oil

★ Combine all steak ingredients in medium bowl and mix well. Shape into
  6 to 8 patties ¾-inch thick. Brown patties in a little oil in large skillet for
  about 5 minutes on each side, set aside in warm oven. Serves 4 to 6.

Brown Gravy:

2 (14 ounce) cans beef broth
¼ cup dry red wine
2 tablespoons cornstarch
1 (8 ounce) can sliced mushrooms, drained

★ Add beef broth, wine and cornstarch to skillet and stir until cornstarch
  mixture dissolves. Cook and stir over high heat until mixture thickens.
  Add mushrooms and cook until hot and gravy bubbles. Spoon gravy
  over steaks to serve.

Easy Steak and Potatoes

2 pounds round steak
⅓ cup flour
⅓ cup oil
5 potatoes, peeled, diced
¼ cup chopped onions
1 (10 ounce) cream of mushroom soup

★ Preheat oven to 350°. Dice steak, coat in flour, brown in heavy skillet and drain. Place steak in 9-inch baking dish.

★ Season potatoes with a little salt and pepper, place over steak and cover with mushroom soup diluted with ½ cup water. Bake for 1 hour 30 minutes. Serves 6 to 8.

Hungarian Goulash

1 (1½ pound) thick round steak, trimmed, cubed in ½-inch pieces
⅓ cup flour
¼ cup oil
1 teaspoon paprika
½ teaspoon garlic powder
1 onion, sliced
1 (1 pound) can whole tomatoes
⅔ cup evaporated milk

★ In large saucepan or skillet, heat oil over medium-high heat. Brown meat in oil. Mix flour, 1 teaspoon each of salt and pepper, paprika and garlic powder. Mix in with meat and add onion slices, tomatoes and 1 cup water.

★ Cover skillet and cook on medium for about 1 hour; stir occasionally. Reduce heat to simmer, mix in evaporated milk and cook for about 15 minutes; stir frequently. Serve over cooked noodles. Serves 4 to 6.

Meatloaf

There is no specific event that marks the origination of one of America's favorite comfort foods; rather, it is an evolution made of necessity. The least tender cuts of beef were ground up and stale breadcrumbs were added to soak up the fat.

Soft breadcrumbs made the beef moist while dry breadcrumbs made the meatloaf less moist. Originally an egg and seasonings were added, the meat was formed into a loaf shape and cooked in a loaf pan in the oven. As we became more health conscious, people cooked the loaf on a rack in a broiler pan to catch the drippings.

Substitutions for the liquid include wine, broth, beer and tomato sauce. The traditional meatloaf may vary in different regions, but the basics include breadcrumbs and 1 egg mixed together with tomato sauce, ketchup, bacon or mashed potatoes added on top about ten minutes before the meatloaf is done.

Chicken-Fried Steak and Cream Gravy

2 pounds round steak, tenderized
1¼ cups flour
2 eggs, slightly beaten
½ cup milk
Canola oil

★ Trim tenderized steak and cut into 6 to 8 pieces. Combine flour, 1 teaspoon salt and a little pepper in bowl. Dredge all steak pieces in flour mixture until lightly coated.

★ In separate bowl, combine eggs and milk. Dip steak into egg mixture, dredge again in flour and get plenty of flour pressed into steak. Heat about ½ inch oil in heavy skillet and fry steak pieces until golden brown.

Cream Gravy:

6 tablespoons flour
6 - 8 tablespoons pan drippings
3 cups milk

★ Move steaks to warm oven. Add flour to drippings in skillet, stir constantly and cook until flour begins to brown. Add milk slowly and stir until gravy thickens.

★ Season with ½ teaspoon salt and ¼ teaspoon pepper and serve in bowl or over steaks and mashed potatoes. Serves 4 to 6.

Chicken-Fried

Chicken-fried is a cooking method and a general all-purpose word which means anything pan-fried. Corn-fed beef just isn't "dressed" until it steps out of a cast-iron skillet wearing a golden brown coat.

Texans have been serving up chicken-fried entrees since the days beef suet and chicken fat were the only buddies to the cast-iron skillet. Choice cuts of beef don't need any decoration, but the less tender cuts of beef may require tenderizing and a little cream gravy.

Chicken-fried works for just about everything: beef, chicken, pork, seafood and even vegetables. Chicken-fried batter also enhances nearly all the farmer's market produce, like okra, yellow squash, zucchini, asparagus and tomatoes.

Smothered Fried Steak

6 cube steaks
Flour for dredging
Vegetable oil
1 large onion, sliced
1 (14 ounce) can beef broth

★ Coat steaks well in flour heavily seasoned with salt and pepper. (Use remaining flour to thicken gravy later.) Heat oil in skillet and add steaks. Fry over medium-high heat and brown steaks on both sides. Add onion and saute for 10 minutes.

★ Stir in beef broth and can of water and break up any scrapings from bottom of pan. Cover and allow steaks to simmer in liquid over low heat for 1 hour or until tender.

★ When ready to serve, combine remaining flour (about ¼ cup) with a little water and add to steaks and gravy. Stir and heat until gravy is thick. Serves 6.

Simple Beef Stroganoff

1 pound round steak, cut into thin strips
½ cup sliced onion
1 (10 ounce) can cream of mushroom soup
½ cup sour cream
Noodles, cooked

★ Brown meat and onion in skillet and drain. Add onion, soup, sour cream and ½ cup water. Simmer for 45 minutes or until tender. Serve over noodles. Serves 4 to 6.

Pot Roast

Pot roast became a well known meal in the early 1800's when New Englanders regularly cooked slowly less tender cuts of meat and added vegetables when the meat started to get tender. Coating meat with flour was used to brown the meat before cooking. The terms Yankee Pot Roast and New England Boiled Dinners weren't used extensively until the 1880's. Today pot roast may be made from rump roast, chuck roast, tri-tip roast or round steak. The most used vegetables today are potatoes, carrots and onions.

Pot roast is a simple one-pot dish symbolizing the frugal nature, sensibility and love of simplicity inherent in early settlers of America. New Englanders epitomized these qualities and one such example is their use of boiling and steaming less tender cuts of meat then adding vegetables half-way through the cooking process.

Almost every American family has had a pot roast dinner at some point in their lives. [Encyclopedia of American Food and Drink; John Mariani, Lebhar-Friedman, 1999.]

Homer's Special Beef Kebabs

Kebabs:

2 - 2½ pounds sirloin steak
Bell peppers
Fresh mushrooms
Tiny onions
Cherry tomatoes

Marinade:

1 cup red wine
2 teaspoons Worcestershire sauce
2 teaspoons garlic powder
1 cup canola oil
¼ cup ketchup

★ Cut meat into 1½ to 2-inch chunks and cut bell peppers into bite-size pieces. Combine 1 teaspoon salt and marinade ingredients in bowl, pour over steak pieces for 3 to 4 hours.

★ Alternate meat, peppers, mushrooms, onions and cherry tomatoes on skewers and cook over charcoal. Turn on all sides and baste frequently with remaining marinade. Serves 8.

Quick Broiled Sirloin

1 (1½ inch) thick sirloin or porterhouse steak
Lemon pepper
Garlic salt

★ Let steak come to room temperature. Move top oven rack to about 6 inches from broiler heat source. Preheat oven to broil. Place steak in sprayed baking dish and season both sides. Place baking dish on top rack and broil for 3 to 5 minutes.

★ Remove from oven and turn steak over. Broil another 3 to 5 minutes. Remove from oven to check for rare, medium or well done and cook accordingly.

Pan-Fried Steak

1 (1 - 1½ inch) thick sirloin
Seasoned salt
Fresh ground pepper
2 teaspoons canola oil, divided
2 - 3 cloves garlic, minced

★ Season steak with seasoned salt and ground pepper on both sides and
set aside. Pour 1 teaspoon oil in hot skillet and sauté garlic over medium
high heat until translucent.

★ Place steak in skillet and cook over high heat to sear outside to hold
juices and reduce heat to medium to cook about 3 to 5 minutes. Turn
steak and repeat steps. The more you cook steak, the tougher and drier
it will be.

Skillet Sirloin

2 teaspoons canola oil
2 teaspoons minced garlic
½ teaspoon cayenne pepper
2 tablespoons soy sauce
2 tablespoons honey
1 pound beef sirloin, thinly sliced
Rice, cooked

★ Combine oil, garlic, cayenne pepper, soy sauce and honey in bowl and
place in resealable plastic bag. Add sliced beef, seal bag and shake.
Refrigerate for 30 minutes.

★ Place beef mixture in large, sprayed skillet over medium-high heat.
Cook for 5 to 6 minutes or until desired doneness, but do not overcook.
Serve over rice. Serves 4 to 5.

Grilled Filet Mignon

4 (2 inch/8 - 10 ounce) thick filets mignon
Lemon pepper
Garlic salt

★ Let filets come to room temperature. Start charcoal grill and let coals
burn down to a slight flame with red to white hot coals. (Clean gas grill
and preheat for about 10 minutes.) Season filets on both sides.

★ Move to grill and cook about 4 to 5 minutes on one side and 3 minutes
on the other side for rare to medium rare. (Heat varies so watch steak
closely.) Do not use fork to turn steaks. Tongs keep the juices in. Serves 4.

Seasoned Beef Tenderloin

3 tablespoons dijon-style mustard
2 tablespoons prepared horseradish
1 (3 pound) center-cut beef tenderloin
½ cup seasoned breadcrumbs

★ Combine mustard and horseradish in bowl and spread over beef tenderloin. Press breadcrumbs into horseradish-mustard mixture and wrap in foil. Refrigerate for at least 12 hours.

★ When ready to bake, preheat oven to 375°. Remove wrap and place on sprayed pan. Bake for 30 minutes or to 145° for medium rare. Let tenderloin stand for 15 minutes before slicing. Serves 6.

Basic Meatloaf

1 pound lean ground beef
1 egg
1 tablespoon dried minced onion
1 teaspoon seasoned salt
1 teaspoon minced garlic
½ cup breadcrumbs
½ cup ketchup or chili sauce

★ Preheat oven to 350°. Combine ground beef, egg, minced onion, seasoned salt, ½ teaspoon pepper, garlic, breadcrumbs and ketchup in large bowl. Shape into loaf and place in shallow baking pan. Bake for 45 to 50 minutes. Serves 4 to 6.

Variations:

1. Place several slices of bacon on top of meatloaf before cooking.

2. Remove meatloaf from oven 15 minutes before it is done and pour ketchup in a line down middle for length of meatloaf. Return to oven to finish cooking.

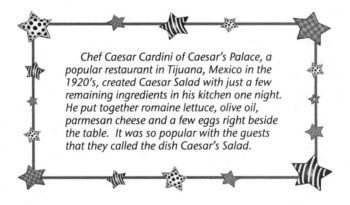

Chef Caesar Cardini of Caesar's Palace, a popular restaurant in Tijuana, Mexico in the 1920's, created Caesar Salad with just a few remaining ingredients in his kitchen one night. He put together romaine lettuce, olive oil, parmesan cheese and a few eggs right beside the table. It was so popular with the guests that they called the dish Caesar's Salad.

Miracle Meatloaf

This is even better if you make it early in the day or a day before you serve it.

1½ pounds ground beef
¼ cup seasoned breadcrumbs
1 egg
2 cups mashed potatoes
2 eggs, hard-boiled, chopped
⅓ cup mayonnaise
⅓ cup grated parmesan cheese
¼ cup finely chopped celery
2 tablespoons sliced green onion

★ Combine beef, breadcrumbs, egg and ½ teaspoon salt in bowl and mix well. Pat down beef mixture into 9 x 13-inch rectangle on foil or wax paper.

★ Combine potatoes, hard-boiled eggs, mayonnaise, cheese, celery and green onions in bowl and mix lightly. Add a little salt and pepper and spread potato mixture over beef.

★ Begin at narrow end and roll in jellyroll fashion. Refrigerate several hours or overnight. When ready to bake, preheat oven to 350°. Bake for 40 to 45 minutes. Serves 8.

Stuffed Green Peppers

4½ large bell peppers
1 large onion, diced
1 rib celery, diced
½ bunch green onions, diced
2 cloves garlic, minced
¼ cup (½ stick) butter, divided
½ - 1 pound ground beef
2 - 3 slices white breadcrumbs
1 - 2 eggs, beaten
1 carrot, grated
½ teaspoon sugar
1 cup seasoned breadcrumbs

★ Preheat oven to 350°. Parboil 4 bell peppers for 3 minutes. Cut each pepper in half horizontally and cool. Finely chop remaining ½ pepper, onion, celery and onions. Place in saucepan and saute with garlic and 2 tablespoons butter.

★ Add ground beef to mixture and brown all meat. Remove from heat and set aside. Soak breadcrumbs in ¼ cup water and 1 egg in bowl. Add breadcrumb mixture and carrot to meat mixture and mix well.

★ Add sugar and a little salt and pepper. If mixture is too stiff, add remaining egg. Fill bell pepper shells with meat mixture, cover with seasoned breadcrumbs and dot with butter. Bake for 30 to 40 minutes. Serves 6 to 8.

Tamale Pie

1¼ pounds lean ground beef
1 onion, finely chopped
Canola oil
2 (10 ounce) cans diced tomatoes and green chilies
1 (15 ounce) can pinto beans
1 (8 ounce) can whole kernel corn
1 teaspoon chili powder
1 (6 ounce) package cornbread mix

★ Preheat oven to 375°. Brown beef and onion in skillet with a little oil.
   Add tomatoes and green chilies and simmer for about 15 minutes.

★ Place 3 to 4 tablespoons beans on small plate and mash with fork to
   thicken beef-tomato mixture slightly. Add beans, corn, chili powder and
   mashed beans to beef-tomato mixture.

★ Spoon into sprayed 9 x 13-inch glass baking dish. Mix cornbread mix
   according to package directions and add extra 2 tablespoons milk for
   thinner batter. Spoon on top of beef-bean mixture. Bake for 30 minutes.
   Serves 6 to 8.

Chili Con Carne

*"Chili con carne" means chili with meat and is the same
thing as "Chili" or in Texas it is sometimes called a "Bowl
of Red". An authentic bowl of chili does not have beans.*

2 - 3 pounds cubed sirloin or tenderloin
½ cup (1 stick) butter
1 (15 ounce) can tomato sauce or 1 (15 ounce) can diced tomatoes with liquid
2 onions, chopped
4 - 6 cloves garlic, minced
¼ cup chili powder
1 tablespoon ground cumin
2 teaspoons oregano

★ Brown sirloin in butter in large skillet. Reduce heat to low and add all
   remaining ingredients plus 1 teaspoon salt. Cover and simmer for about
   2 to 3 hours. Stir occasionally and add ½ cup water, if necessary.

★ Remove cover, taste for flavor and adjust seasonings, if needed.
   Serves 8 to 10.

Chili Pie Casserole

*Nobody knows who created the Fritos® chili pie, but it has
remained one of America's most popular recipes since the 1930's.*

3 cups Fritos® Original Corn Chips, divided
1 large onion, chopped
1 cup grated American cheese, divided
1 (19 ounce) can chili

★ Place 2 cups Fritos® in bottom of 7 x 11-inch baking dish and spread
  evenly. Place onion and half of cheese over chips. Pour chili over chips
  and top with remaining chips and cheese. Bake for 15 to 20 minutes to
  heat chili throughout. Serves 4 to 6.

Beef Enchiladas

Canola oil
1½ pounds lean ground beef
1 onion, minced
1 clove garlic, minced
2 tablespoons chili powder
2 tablespoons flour
1 (15 ounce) can tomato sauce
1 teaspoon cumin
12 corn tortillas
1 (16 ounce) shredded cheddar cheese, divided

★ Preheat oven to 350°. Place a little bit of oil in skillet and brown beef,
  onion and garlic. Add ½ teaspoon salt and chili powder. Add flour and
  stir until brown. Stir in tomato sauce, cumin, ½ teaspoon each of salt
  and pepper and simmer for 5 minutes.

★ Soften tortillas by dipping in a little hot oil and drain. Place about
  2 tablespoons meat mixture in each tortilla, top with 2 tablespoons
  cheese and roll.

★ Place seam-side down in large baking dish, cover with remaining
  meat sauce and cheese. Bake for 30 minutes or until hot and bubbly.
  Serves 4 to 6.

*Mexican food is a favorite across America,
but Texas has put its stamp on Tex-Mex,
which is now considered one of the nine
American regional food cuisines. Tex-Mex is
not authentic Mexican food from the interior of
Mexico, but rather an adaptation of Mexican
food standardized to some extent by Texans.*

Cheesy Enchiladas

1½ pounds lean ground beef
1 onion, chopped
1 teaspoon ground cumin
1 teaspoon minced garlic
Canola oil
10 - 12 (8 ounce) corn tortillas
½ cup (¼ stick) butter
¼ cup flour
2 cups milk
1 cup cubed Velveeta® cheese
1 (7 ounce) can diced green chilies
1 (8 ounce) package shredded Mexican 4-cheese blend

★ Preheat oven to 350°. Brown beef and onion in skillet. Add 1 teaspoon salt, cumin and garlic and drain. In separate skillet, heat a little oil and fry tortillas only enough to soften.

★ Roll equal amount of meat mixture tightly into each softened tortilla until all meat is used. Place seam-side down in sprayed 9 x 13-inch baking dish. Melt butter in skillet, add flour and stir to remove all lumps.

★ Slowly pour in milk while stirring constantly. Add cheese and stir until cheese melts. Add green chilies and mix well. Pour sauce over enchiladas in baking dish. Top with cheese, cover and bake for about 15 to 20 minutes. Bake for 30 to 35 minutes or until hot and bubbly. Serves 4 to 6.

Beef Tacos

2 pounds ground round steak
¼ cup minced onion
2 taco seasoning packets
1 (8 ounce) can tomato sauce
24 taco shells
Shredded lettuce
Finely chopped rip tomato
Shredded cheddar cheese

★ Brown meat in skillet, add all ingredients except taco shells, lettuce, tomato and cheese. Fill taco shells as desired. Serves 8 to 10.

 Chile Capital of the World   Hatch, New Mexico

Soft Beef Tacos

2 pounds lean ground beef
2 tablespoons chili powder
1 large onion, chopped, divided
14 - 16 corn tortillas
3 large tomatoes, chopped
1 tablespoon minced cilantro
1 (12 ounce) package shredded cheddar cheese, divided

★ Preheat oven to 350°. Brown ground beef in skillet, add chili powder and
   1 tablespoon salt and cook for about 5 minutes.

★ Put several tablespoons of meat and 1 teaspoon onion in middle of each
   tortilla, roll and place side by side in sprayed 10 x 15-inch baking dish.

★ Combine tomatoes, remaining onions, and cilantro in bowl and sprinkle
   evenly over rolled tortillas. Spread cheese over top of tomatoes and bake
   for 10 to 15 minutes or until cheese melts. Serves 6 to 8.

Nothing-Fancy Beef Burritos

*Burritos are traditional Mexican sandwiches made with flour tortillas and
a filling. Burritos that are deep fried or baked are called chimichangas.*

1 pound ground beef
1 tablespoon chili powder
2 onions, chopped
1 (15 ounce) can refried beans
4 - 6 flour tortillas, warmed
1 (8 ounce) package shredded Mexican 4-cheese blend
1 tomato, chopped
Salsa

★ Brown ground beef with 1 teaspoon salt and chili powder in heavy
   skillet. Drain grease, add onions and cook until onions are translucent.

★ Heat refried beans in saucepan. Spread several tablespoons refried
   beans on warmed flour tortilla. Add ground beef, cheese and tomato,
   roll and fold up 2 ends in package. Serve with salsa. Serves 4 to 6.

*No matter how hard you try, you can't
baptize a cat.*

Family Cabbage Rolls

This is a wonderful way to get the kids to eat cabbage.

1 large head cabbage, cored
1½ pounds lean ground beef
1 egg, beaten
3 tablespoons ketchup
⅓ cup seasoned breadcrumbs
2 tablespoons dried minced onion flakes
2 (15 ounce) cans Italian stewed tomatoes
¼ cup cornstarch
3 tablespoons brown sugar
2 tablespoons Worcestershire sauce

★ Preheat oven to 325°. Place head of cabbage in large soup pot of boiling water for 10 minutes or until outer leaves are tender. Drain well. Rinse in cold water and remove 10 large outer leaves*. Set aside.

★ Slice or shred remaining cabbage. Place into sprayed 9 x 13-inch baking dish. Combine ground beef, egg, ketchup, breadcrumbs, onion flakes and 1 teaspoon salt in large bowl and mix well.

★ Pack together about ½ cup meat mixture and put on each cabbage leaf. Fold in sides and roll leaf to completely enclose filling. (You may have to remove thick vein from cabbage leaves for easier rolling.) Place each rolled leaf over shredded cabbage.

★ Place stewed tomatoes in large saucepan. Combine cornstarch, brown sugar and Worcestershire sauce in bowl and spoon mixture into tomatoes. Cook on high heat, stirring constantly until stewed tomatoes and juices thicken. Pour over cabbage rolls. Cover and bake for 1 hour. Serves 10.

TIP: To get that many large leaves, you may have to put 2 smaller leaves together to make one roll.

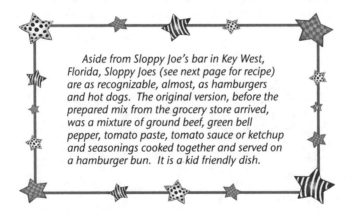

Aside from Sloppy Joe's bar in Key West, Florida, Sloppy Joes (see next page for recipe) are as recognizable, almost, as hamburgers and hot dogs. The original version, before the prepared mix from the grocery store arrived, was a mixture of ground beef, green bell pepper, tomato paste, tomato sauce or ketchup and seasonings cooked together and served on a hamburger bun. It is a kid friendly dish.

Cheeseburger Pie

1 cup plus 2 tablespoons biscuit mix, divided
1 pound ground beef
½ cup chopped onion
1 tablespoon Worcestershire sauce
2 eggs
1 cup small curd creamed cottage cheese
2 tomatoes, sliced
1 cup shredded cheddar cheese

★ Preheat oven to 375°. Mix 1 cup biscuit mix with ¼ cup cold water until soft dough forms; beat 20 strokes vigorously. Smooth dough into ball on floured wax paper or cloth and knead 5 times.

★ Roll dough 2 inches larger than inverted pie plate, about 9 x 1¼ inches. Ease into plate; flute edge if desired. Cook and stir ground beef and onion until beef is brown; drain. Stir in ½ teaspoon salt, ¼ teaspoon pepper, 2 tablespoons biscuit mix and Worcestershire sauce.

★ Spoon into piecrust. Mix eggs and cottage cheese and pour over beef mixture. Arrange tomato slices in circle on top; sprinkle with cheddar cheese. Bake about 30 minutes or until set. Serves 6 to 8.

Sloppy Joes

3 pounds ground beef
1 tablespoon minced garlic
1 large onion, finely chopped
2 ribs celery, diced
¼ cup packed brown sugar
¼ cup prepared mustard
1 tablespoon chili powder
1½ cups ketchup
3 tablespoons Worcestershire sauce
Buns

★ Brown beef, garlic and onion in very large skillet and drain. Combine celery, brown sugar, mustard, chili powder, ketchup and Worcestershire in sprayed 5-quart slow cooker. Stir in meat mixture. Cover and cook on LOW heat for 6 to 7 hours. Fills about 16 buns.

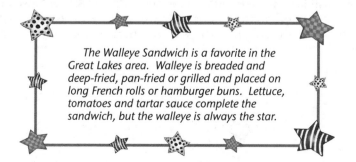

The Walleye Sandwich is a favorite in the Great Lakes area. Walleye is breaded and deep-fried, pan-fried or grilled and placed on long French rolls or hamburger buns. Lettuce, tomatoes and tartar sauce complete the sandwich, but the walleye is always the star.

Simple Cheeseburgers

2 pounds ground beef
8 slices cheese
8 hamburger buns
1 large onion, sliced
Lettuce
Tomatoes
Pickle slices
Mustard, mayonnaise or ketchup

★ Mix ground beef and a little salt and pepper and form into 8 patties. Cook on charcoal grill or in skillet until almost done. Add cheese slice on top of meat. Allow cheese to melt and put meat on warm bun. Add onions, lettuce, tomatoes and pickles. Dress with mustard, mayonnaise and/or ketchup. Serves 6 to 8.

California Cheeseburgers:

★ Replace ground beef with ground turkey. Use bean sprouts, avocado slices and tomatoes instead of bacon, onions, lettuce and pickles.

Western Cheeseburgers:

★ Replace raw onion with sautéed onion, sautéed fresh mushrooms and add chili sauce, hickory sauce or ketchup.

Southwestern Cheeseburgers:

★ Use green chili salsa and grated Mexican, four-cheese blend.

Grilled Onion Burgers

2 pounds ground beef
1 package onion soup
1 egg
½ cup breadcrumbs

★ Preheat grill. Mix ground beef, onion soup, breadcrumbs and egg in large bowl. Form mixture in 8 (¼ pound) balls. Place on wax paper and flatten to ¼ inch larger than size of hamburger bun.

★ Cook on grill for 5 to 10 minutes on each side for medium to well done burgers. Warm hamburger buns on low in oven. Garnish hamburger with lettuce, pickle, salt, pepper, mustard, mayonnaise or ketchup. Serves 8.

Hot Dogs

"The noblest of all dogs is the hot dog. It feeds the hand that bites it."
–Lawrence J. Peter

German immigrants were probably the first to sell their sausages and wrap bread around them. Late in the 1800's a German immigrant sold his spicy sausages with white gloves to make it easier to eat. After his wife suggested a roll of some kind, his baker brother-in-law created a split bun that fit the sausage perfectly and the hot dog bun was born.

Hot dogs were featured at the Chicago World's Fair in 1893, but didn't have the final name. In 1902 a newspaper cartoonist drew a long sausage with four legs. He couldn't spell dachshund so he wrote hot dog under the cartoon.

At about the same time, an ice cream vendor who wasn't selling much started selling sausages. He would yell out, "They're red hot. Get your red hot dogs!"

At a baseball game in New York, a man was selling sausages and bread and called them "meat sandwiches". A voice in the crowd yelled out "Give me a hot dog." and that seems to have solidified the name for eternity.

According to the National Hot Dog and Sausage Council, Americans eat more than 7 billion hot dogs between Memorial Day and Labor Day. When many American favorites have one day dedicated to them, the hot dog celebrates the whole month of July as National Hot Dog Month.

Today, hot dogs are part of the American culture. Wherever there are food stands, there are hot dogs. And just as surely there will be regional differences.

Great American Hot Dog

8 all-beef franks
8 hot dog buns
Mustard
Shredded cheese
Chopped onion

★ Boil or steam franks in water about 4 to 5 minutes, grill franks for about 8 to 10 minutes over medium hot coals or microwave franks in paper towels for 30 to 35 seconds. Spread mustard on both sides of bun, place frank on bun and top with chili and onions. Serves 6 to 8.

Coney Island Hot Dogs

All-beef franks
Hot dog buns
All-beef chili
Shredded cheese
Chopped onions

★ Steam or cook franks on griddle. Place in bun and stack remaining ingredients on frank.

Michigan Coney Island Hot Dog

*Coney Island hot dog refers to ingredients used, not New
York City, and is known in much of the North and Midwest.
Coney Island does refer to the home of the hot dog.*

All-beef franks
Hot dog buns
Mustard
All-beef chili, no beans
Chopped onions

★ Grill franks (never steam or boil) and place on steamed bun. Add all-beef chili with no beans, mustard and lots of chopped onions.

Cincinnati Cheese Coney

All-beef franks
Buns
Cincinnati chili
Mustard
Shredded cheese

★ Steam or grill franks and place on buns. Pile Cincinnati chili, mustard and a lot of cheese on top.

Chicago-Style Hot Dogs

All-beef franks
Poppy seed buns, steamed
Mustard
Green sweet pickle relish
Crunchy dill pickle spear
Chopped onion
Tomato wedges
Sport peppers
Ketchup

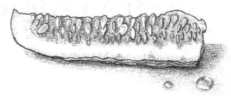

★ Steam or cook franks on griddle. Place in bun and stack remaining ingredients on frank.

Washington, D.C. Hot Dogs

Half-smoke, spicy sausage franks
Hot dog buns
All-beef chili
Chopped onions
Mustard

★ Steam or grill franks, place in bun and stack all remaining ingredients in bun.

Arizona Hot Dogs

All-beef franks
Bacon slices
Polilo rolls
Pinto beans
Tomatoes, sliced
Chopped onions
Jalapenos
Mustard
Mayonnaise

★ Wrap bacon slices around franks and steam or grill until bacon is crispy.
  Place franks in rolls and stack remaining ingredients on top.

New York State "Hots"

*Hot dogs are called white or red hots depending on the ingredients
of the franks. Hots are found in the Rochester, New York area and
are the official hot dogs of many of the local national sports teams.*

White hots: mixed uncured, unsmoked pork, veal, beef franks
Red hots: all beef or all pork or mixture of both franks
Buns
Mustard
Chopped onion
Hot sauce

★ Steam or boil franks, place in buns and stack remaining ingredients
  on top.

Slaw Dogs

Slaw dogs are found only in the South.

All-beef franks
Hot dog buns
Coleslaw

★ Steam or grill franks and place on buns. Pile coleslaw on top.

Red Snapper Hot Dogs

*These are found only in Maine and have this name
because of the bright red casings on the franks.*

Maine franks
Hot dog buns
Butter

★ Butter both sides of buns. Steam franks and place in buns.

Traditional Shepherd's Pie

Traditionally an Irish dish and found in many Irish pubs.

1½ pounds ground beef
1 large onion, chopped
1 cup chopped carrots
1 cup sliced mushrooms or 1 (6 ounce) can sliced mushrooms
2 tablespoons butter
½ cup frozen green peas
2 teaspoons Worcestershire sauce
½ cup beef broth
2 tablespoons flour
4 cups mashed potatoes

★ Preheat oven to 400°. Brown beef skillet; drain fat and set aside beef. In same skillet, saute onion, carrots and mushrooms in butter until onions are translucent. Add peas, beef, Worcestershire sauce, broth, and salt and pepper. Simmer for 10 minutes.

★ Mix flour with ¼ cup water and add to mixture; cook and stir until thickened. Place in 9 x 13-inch baking dish. Spread mashed potatoes on top and swirl into peaks. Bake for 25 to 30 minutes or until potatoes are golden. Serves 6.

Super Beef Casserole

1½ pounds lean ground beef
1 onion, chopped
1 (15 ounce) can tomato sauce
½ teaspoon dried basil
1 (8 ounce) package medium noodles
1 (16 ounce) carton small curd cottage cheese
1 (8 ounce) carton sour cream
1 cup shredded cheddar cheese

★ Preheat oven to 350°. Brown beef and onion in large skillet and drain. Stir in tomato sauce, basil and ample amount of salt and pepper. Stir well and simmer for 25 minutes.

★ Cook noodles according to package directions, drain and rinse in cold water. Spoon noodles into sprayed 3-quart baking dish.

★ Combine cottage cheese and sour cream in bowl and spoon over noodles. Pour beef mixture over cottage cheese mixture and top with cheddar cheese. Bake for 25 to 30 minutes. Serves 8.

Why do hamburgers beat hot dogs at every sport?

Because hot dogs are the wurst.

Spaghetti and Meatballs

Meatballs:

2 pounds lean ground round
½ pound ground pork
4 eggs
2 cups grated parmesan cheese
1½ cups dry breadcrumbs
1 onion, chopped
2 cloves garlic, pressed
½ bunch fresh parsley, minced
½ cup milk
1½ tablespoons ketchup

★ Toss all ingredients lightly and shape into balls. Brown in olive oil and set aside.

Sauce:

1 onion, minced
1 clove garlic, pressed
1 tablespoon olive oil
2 (6 ounce) cans tomato paste
1½ to 2 quarts
1 tablespoon minced sweet basil
1 tablespoon ground oregano

★ In heavy saucepan saute onion and garlic in olive oil until soft and clear. Add tomato paste, 1½ to 2 quarts water, a little salt and pepper, basil and oregano and mix well. Add browned meatballs and simmer for 1 one hour or until sauce thickens. Serve over cooked spaghetti. Serves 6 to 8.

Easy Spaghetti Meat Sauce

This recipe appeared in the 1960's and it remains popular today.

1 pound ground beef
1 clove garlic, minced
1 envelope onion soup mix
¼ teaspoon oregano
1 (28 ounce) can tomato puree

★ Brown ground beef in large skillet or saucepan and drain. Add remaining ingredients and 1 cup water. Simmer, covered, and stir occasionally. Cook about 30 minutes and pour over spaghetti. Serves 4 to 6.

Philly Cheese Steak

A visit to Philadelphia is not complete without
eating a Philly Cheese Steak sandwich.

Oil
1 onion, sliced thin, separated
*Chipped beef: rib eye, sirloin roast beef or eye of round steak
4 premium Italian rolls, split
4 slices American cheese, provolone or Cheez Whiz®

★ With hot oil in large skillet, saute onion until it is translucent. (*Chipped beef is frozen, sliced paper thin and cooked on grill or skillet.) Add about 16 thin slices of beef or enough for 4 sandwiches to onion and mushrooms. Cook until pink is gone.

★ Place beef, onion and mushrooms into split Italian roll and top with cheese. Serves 4.

Variation:

★ Sauteed mushrooms and bell peppers, pizza sauce, ketchup, and Italian pickled peppers are sometimes added. To be totally authentic you have to use a Philly roll, but they are only available in Philadelphia. Send us a post card.

Yankee Pot Roast

1 (4 - 5 pound) boneless chuck roast
Garlic powder
6 medium potatoes, peeled, quartered
8 carrots, peeled, quartered
3 onions, peeled, quartered

★ Preheat oven to 375°. Set roast in roasting pan with lid and sprinkle liberally with seasoned salt, seasoned pepper and garlic powder. Add 2 cups water and bake for 30 minutes.

★ Reduce heat to 325° and bake for 3 hours. Add potatoes, carrots and onions and bake for additional 30 minutes. Place roast on serving platter and place potatoes, carrots and onion around roast.

Gravy:

3 tablespoons cornstarch

★ Combine cornstarch and ¾ cup water and add to juices remaining in roaster. Add ½ teaspoon each of salt and pepper. On stovetop, cook on high and stir constantly until gravy is thick. Serve in gravy boat with roast and vegetables. Serves 8.

So-Cal Marinated Tri-Tip Roast

2 cloves garlic, minced
⅔ cup soy sauce
¼ cup canola or virgin olive oil
¼ cup packed light brown sugar
2 tablespoons red wine vinegar
1 (2 - 3 pound) tri-tip roast

★ Mix garlic, soy sauce, oil, brown sugar and vinegar in bowl. Pour into resealable plastic bag with tri-tip. Marinate in refrigerator overnight. Turn plastic bag several times to rotate meat. Cook slowly over charcoal fire until meat is rare to medium rare. Cut thin slices across grain. Serves 6.

Grilled Tri-Tip and Potatoes

1 (2 pound) beef tri-tip roast
1 tablespoon coarsely ground black pepper
3 cloves garlic, minced
4 - 5 large baking potatoes, sliced lengthwise about ½ inch thick
Olive oil
½ cup sour cream
¼ cup basil pesto sauce

★ Season tri-tip with black pepper and garlic and rub into meat. Cook over medium-low grill for about 30 minutes or until meat thermometer reads 140° in the center. Cook slowly, but it is most tender when it is rare or medium-rare.

★ At same time rub potatoes with olive oil and cook on grill or in the oven until brown on the outside and tender on the inside.

★ Wrap tri-tip loosely in foil for several minutes. Mix sour cream and pesto sauce in bowl and dabble over potatoes. Serves 4 to 6.

Brown Beer Beef Marinade

½ cup dark beer
½ cup teriyaki sauce
¼ cup packed brown sugar
1 teaspoon seasoned salt
1 teaspoon garlic powder

★ Mix all ingredients and pour into large freezer bag. Place tri-tip beef in bag, seal and marinate in refrigerator for about 4 hours. Move bag frequently.

Prime Rib of Beef

⅓ cup chopped onion
⅓ cup chopped celery
½ teaspoon garlic powder
1 (6 - 8 pound) beef rib roast
1 (14 ounce) can beef broth

★ Preheat oven to 350°. Combine onion and celery in bowl and place in sprayed roasting pan. Combine 1 teaspoon salt, garlic powder and a little black pepper and rub over roast. Place roast over vegetables with fat-side up.

★ Bake for 2 hours 30 minutes to 3 hours or until meat reaches desired doneness. (Medium-rare is 145°; medium is 160°; well done is 170°.)

★ Let stand for about 15 minutes before carving. Skim fat from pan drippings and add beef broth. Stir to remove browned bits and heat. Strain and discard vegetables. Serve au jus with roast. Serves 10 to 12.

Real Simple Brisket

1 (4 - 6 pound) trimmed beef brisket
Seasoned pepper
1 (1 ounce) packet onion soup mix
¼ cup Worcestershire sauce

★ Preheat oven to 375°. Place brisket in roasting pan. Generously sprinkle brisket with seasoned pepper. Spread onion soup mix over top of brisket.

★ Pour Worcestershire sauce in and add about 1 cup water. Bake for 1 hour. Reduce heat to 300° and cook for 3 to 4 hours or until brisket is tender. Cool for 15 minutes and cut thin slices across the grain. Serves 8 to 10.

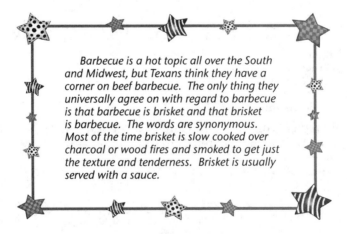

Barbecue is a hot topic all over the South and Midwest, but Texans think they have a corner on beef barbecue. The only thing they universally agree on with regard to barbecue is that barbecue is brisket and that brisket is barbecue. The words are synonymous. Most of the time brisket is slow cooked over charcoal or wood fires and smoked to get just the texture and tenderness. Brisket is usually served with a sauce.

Smoked Brisket

You'll get as many different opinions about smoking briskets as you will about barbecue. This is one version that's simple, but very good. Brisket is usually served with pickles, sliced onions, potato salad and baked beans.

1 (4 - 5 pound) beef brisket
Seasoned salt
Cracked black pepper

★ Season brisket at room temperature for about 1 hour before cooking. Soak mesquite or hickory chips in water or beer for at least 1 hour.

★ Start 5 to 10 pounds of charcoal in fire box at 1 end of smoker. When coals burn down to red hot, add wet mesquite or hickory to fire.

★ Put brisket on rack away from fire, close lid and begin smoking process. Add wood chips several times to make sure enough smoke is circulating. Smoke for about 3 to 4 hours.

★ Remove brisket from smoker and cook in covered, roasting pan with about 1 cup water at 300° for about 1 to 2 hours or until fork tender. Check water to make sure pan and brisket do not dry out. Remove from oven and cool for about 1 hour before slicing. Slice across the grain in thin pieces. Serves 6 to 8.

New England Boiled Dinner

Boiled dinners started with the colonists and has become a New England tradition. It is associated with the Irish and St. Patrick's Day in many New England towns.

1 (3½ - 4 pound) corned beef brisket with seasoning packet
4 - 6 red potatoes, peeled, quartered
4 carrots, peeled, quartered
2 large turnips, peeled, quartered
1 medium head cabbage, quartered

★ Preheat oven to 325°. Place corned beef in large roasting pan and cover with water. Cover and cook until fork tender, about 3 hours. (If a seasoning packet does not come with the brisket, add following seasonings: 1 bay leaf, 6 whole cloves, 10 to 12 peppercorns.)

★ When brisket is fork tender, place it on serving platter and cover to keep warm. Add vegetables to roasting pan and bring to a boil. Reduce heat to medium and cook until vegetables are tender.

★ Slice meat into thin pieces. Drain vegetables and place around brisket. Serves 6 to 8.

TIP: Before you add vegetables, taste broth for seasonings. If it's too salty, add water extra potatoes.

Slow-Cooker Corned Beef Brisket

Corned beef is a beef brisket cured in a salt water or brine solution.

4 ribs celery, chopped
3 onions, quartered
1 (2 - 3 pound) corned beef brisket, trimmed
2 tablespoons whole black peppercorns
2 bay leaves
1 large head green cabbage
8 - 10 small red or new potatoes, quartered
10 - 12 small carrots
2 tablespoons butter, melted

★ Place celery and onions in 5-quart slow cooker and place brisket on top. Sprinkle peppercorns and bay leaves on top of brisket and add 3 to 4 cups water. Cook on LOW for 8 to 9 hours or until brisket is fork-tender.

★ Place brisket on platter and discard liquid. Let stand for about 10 to 20 minutes before slicing. Place cabbage, potatoes, carrots and ¼ cup water in large microwave-safe bowl. Microwave on HIGH for about 7 minutes. Stir and rotate in microwave.

★ Microwave again on HIGH for about 5 minutes or until vegetables are tender. Pour butter over vegetables, season with a little salt and pepper and arrange around corned beef on platter. Serve immediately. Serves 6 to 8.

The Reuben Sandwich

2 slices rye bread
1 slice Swiss cheese
Generous thin slices corned beef
2 tablespoons or more sauerkraut
Thousand Island dressing

★ Butter 1 slice bread on 1 side. Place butter-side down in skillet over low heat. Layer cheese, corned beef and sauerkraut on bread.

★ Spread dressing on 1 side of second slice and butter on the other side. Place butter-side up on sauerkraut. Cook until bottom browns, turn carefully and brown other side. Serves 1.

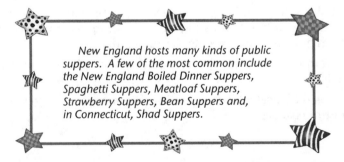

New England hosts many kinds of public suppers. A few of the most common include the New England Boiled Dinner Suppers, Spaghetti Suppers, Meatloaf Suppers, Strawberry Suppers, Bean Suppers and, in Connecticut, Shad Suppers.

Pan-Fried Liver and Onions

4 - 6 slices (¼ inch thick) organic calves' liver
Flour
Canola oil
2 large onions, sliced thin

★ Season calf liver slices and dredge with flour in shallow bowl. Brown both sides in small amount of oil in heavy skillet.

★ Slice onions and separate into rings. Place rings on top of liver, cover and simmer for 20 minutes. Serve immediately.

Variation:

★ Fry a few strips of bacon crisp and set aside. Fry calf liver and onions in the bacon drippings instead of oil. Crumble bacon on top.

Liver and Onions with Gravy

Bacon drippings or vegetable oil
1 pound calves' liver
Flour
1 (10 ounce) can French onion soup
½ soup can water

★ Heat bacon drippings or oil in large skillet over medium-high heat. Season liver with a little salt and pepper and dredge in flour. Brown both sides in skillet.

★ Pour soup and ½ soup can of water over liver and stir to loosen crumbs. Cover and reduce heat. Cook for about 15 to 20 minutes more or until gravy thickens. Serves 4.

Traditional Weiner Schnitzel

1½ pounds (½ inch) thick veal cutlets
½ cup flour
2 eggs, beaten
1 cup dry fine breadcrumbs
¾ cup (1½ sticks) butter
1 lemon, thinly sliced

★ Pound cutlets to very thin. Add a little salt and pepper to flour in bowl and stir. Dredge cutlets on both sides in flour.

★ Dip in eggs and pour breadcrumbs on both sides. Melt butter in large skillet and saute cutlets over low heat for about 5 to 7 minutes on each side.

★ Remove from skillet and keep warm on oven-proof platter in oven at 250° until ready to serve. Serve with slices of lemon. Serves 4.

State Fair Corny Dogs

Corny dogs originated at the State Fair of Texas in Dallas in 1946.

1 cup flour
1 cup yellow cornmeal
¼ cup sugar
4 teaspoons baking powder
2 eggs
½ cup milk
¼ cup canola oil
1 (10 count) beef wieners
10 ice cream sticks
Canola oil

★ Preheat oven to 375°. Mix flour, cornmeal, sugar, baking powder, eggs, milk, oil and ¾ teaspoon salt in deep bowl and blend well.

★ Put each wiener on ice cream stick. Dip into batter; then drop into deep fryer and cook until golden brown. Remove from fryer and drain. Serves 4 to 5.

Main Dishes – Chicken

Bacon-Wrapped Chicken

6 boneless, skinless chicken breast halves
1 (8 ounce) carton whipped cream cheese with onion and chives, softened
Butter
6 bacon strips

★ Preheat oven to 375°. Flatten chicken to ½-inch thickness. Spread 3 tablespoons cream cheese over each piece. Dot with butter and a little salt and roll. Wrap each with 1 bacon strip and place seam-side down in sprayed 9 x 13-inch baking dish.

★ Bake for 40 to 45 minutes or until juices run clear. To brown, broil 6 inches from heat for about 3 minutes or until bacon is crisp. Serves 6.

 Chicken Capital of the World   Gainesville, Georgia

Orange Chicken

4 large boneless, skinless chicken breast halves
2 eggs, beaten
Canola oil
1 cup cornstarch
½ cup flour
1 teaspoon cayenne pepper

★ Cut chicken into bite-size pieces and season with salt and pepper. Mix eggs, 1 tablespoon oil, cornstarch and flour into batter consistency. Stir in cayenne.

★ Dredge chicken pieces through flour mixture and fry in wok or skillet with a little hot oil. Brown on all sides and drain on paper towels.

Orange Sauce:

1 orange
5 cloves garlic, minced
1 teaspoon ground ginger
3 tablespoons soy sauce
½ cup sugar
½ vinegar
1 tablespoon cornstarch
Rice, cooked

★ Wash orange and shave off outside peel (zest) without inside white pith while chicken cools. Add garlic and ginger to clean wok or skillet and cook until translucent.

★ Add zest, soy sauce, sugar and vinegar. Add 1 tablespoon cornstarch to ½ cup water and stir until it dissolves. Add to wok or skillet to cook down and thicken; stir well. Stir in chicken to coat well and serve over rice. Serves 4.

Barbecued-Grilled Chicken

6 boneless, skinless chicken breast halves
3 cups ketchup
½ cup packed brown sugar
¼ cup Worcestershire sauce
2 tablespoons vinegar
1 teaspoon hot sauce

★ Wash chicken breasts and dry with paper towels. Combine remaining ingredients in saucepan, add a little salt and pepper and mix well. Bring to a boil, reduce heat to low and cook for 15 minutes.

★ Fire up grill and smoke chicken over mesquite wood, if possible. Baste chicken frequently with sauce. Turn chicken periodically and cook chicken for 8 to 10 minutes per side. Any leftover barbecue sauce keeps well in refrigerator. Serves 6.

One-Dish Chicken Bake

1 (6 ounce) package chicken stuffing mix
4 boneless, skinless chicken breast halves
1 (10 ounce) can cream of mushroom soup
⅓ cup sour cream

★ Preheat oven to 375°. Toss contents of seasoning packet, stuffing mix and 1⅔ cups water in bowl and set aside. Place chicken in sprayed 9 x 13-inch baking dish.

★ Over low heat mix soup and sour cream in saucepan and heat just enough to pour over chicken. Spoon stuffing evenly over top. Bake for 40 minutes. Serves 4.

Easy Chicken Pot Pie

1 (15 ounce) package refrigerated piecrust
1 (19 ounce) can cream of chicken soup
2 cups cooked, diced chicken breasts
1 (10 ounce) package frozen mixed vegetables, thawed

★ Preheat oven to 325°. Place 1 piecrust in 9-inch deep-dish pie pan. Fill with chicken soup, chicken and mixed vegetables. Gently stir to mix.

★ Cover with second layer of piecrust, fold edges under and crimp. With knife, cut 4 slits in center of piecrust. Bake for 1 hour 15 minutes or until crust is golden brown. Serves 8.

TIP: When you're too busy to cook a chicken, grab a rotisserie chicken from the grocery store.

Chicken Divan

2 (10 ounce) packages frozen broccoli florets
4 boneless, skinless chicken breast halves, cooked, sliced
2 (10 ounce) cans cream of chicken soup
1 cup mayonnaise
1 teaspoon lemon juice
½ teaspoon Worcestershire sauce
1½ cups shredded sharp cheddar cheese, divided
½ cup seasoned breadcrumbs
1 teaspoon butter, melted

★ Preheat oven to 350°. Cook broccoli until tender and drain. Arrange broccoli in sprayed 9 x 13-inch baking dish. Place chicken slices on top.

★ Combine soup, mayonnaise, lemon juice, curry powder or Worcestershire sauce and ¾ cup cheese in bowl and pour over chicken.

★ In separate bowl, combine breadcrumbs and butter and layer over chicken. Sprinkle remaining cheese over top and bake for 25 to 30 minutes. Serves 4.

Almond-Crusted Chicken

1 egg
¼ cup seasoned breadcrumbs
1 cup sliced almonds
4 boneless, skinless chicken breast halves
1 (5 ounce) package grated parmesan cheese

★ Preheat oven to 325°. Place egg and 1 teaspoon water in shallow bowl and beat. In separate shallow bowl, combine breadcrumbs and almonds. Dip each chicken breast in egg, then in almond mixture and place in sprayed 9 x 13-inch baking pan.

★ Bake for 20 minutes. Remove chicken from oven and sprinkle parmesan cheese over each breast. Bake for additional 15 minutes or until almonds and cheese are golden brown.

Sauce:

1 teaspoon minced garlic
⅓ cup finely chopped onion
2 tablespoons olive oil
1 cup white wine
¼ cup teriyaki sauce

★ Saute garlic and onion in oil in saucepan. Add wine and teriyaki sauce and bring to a boil. Reduce heat and simmer for about 10 minutes or until mixture reduces by half. When serving, divide sauce between 4 plates and place chicken breasts on top. Serves 4 to 6.

Easy Roasted Chicken

This is one of the easiest recipes and always delicious.

1 (1½ - 2½) pound whole chicken
Favorite seasonings

★ Preheat oven to 350°. Rub favorite seasonings (see variations below) over and inside chicken. Place in roasting pan with water covering about half the chicken. Bake for 1 hour, add water if needed. Remove lid and continue to cook until top is brown and juices run clear.

Seasonings:

1. Salt and pepper, garlic powder

2. Lemon pepper, garlic salt, onion salt or flakes

3. Chili powder, cumin and sage

4. Coriander, cumin, cardamom and turmeric

Sesame-Pecan Chicken

⅓ cup (⅔ stick) butter
1 cup flour
1 cup finely ground pecans
¼ cup sesame seeds
1 tablespoon paprika
1 egg, beaten
1 cup buttermilk*
6 - 8 boneless, skinless chicken breast halves
⅓ cup coarsely chopped pecans
Fresh parsley or sage

★ Preheat oven to 350°. Melt butter in 9 x 13-inch baking dish and set
   aside. Combine flour, finely ground pecans, sesame seeds, paprika,
   1 teaspoon salt and ¼ teaspoon (1 ml) pepper in shallow dish.

★ In separate bowl, combine egg and buttermilk. Dip chicken in egg
   mixture, dredge in flour mixture and coat well. Place chicken in baking
   dish and turn over to coat with butter. Sprinkle with coarsely chopped
   pecans and bake for 40 minutes or until golden brown. Garnish with
   fresh parsley or sage. Serves 6 to 8.

*TIP: Chicken may be cut into strips, prepared the same way and used as an appetizer.
   A honey-mustard dressing would be nice for dipping. This recipe could also be
   used for fish, like orange roughy, if cooking time is reduced to half.*

**TIP: To make buttermilk, mix 1 cup milk with 1 tablespoon lemon juice or
   vinegar and let milk stand for about 10 minutes.*

Chicken-Ham Tetrazzini

1 (7 ounce) package spaghetti, broken
½ cup slivered almonds, toasted
1 (10 ounce) can cream of mushroom soup
1 (10 ounce) can cream of chicken soup
¾ cup milk
2 tablespoons dry white wine
2½ cups cooked, diced chicken
2 cups cooked, diced ham
½ cup chopped green bell pepper
½ cup halved pitted ripe olives
1 (8 ounce) package shredded cheddar cheese

★ Preheat oven to 350°. Cook spaghetti according to directions; rinse
   cooked spaghetti with cold water. Combine almonds, soups, milk and
   wine in large bowl. Stir in spaghetti, chicken, ham, bell pepper and
   pitted olives.

★ Pour mixture into sprayed 9 x 13-inch baking dish. Sprinkle cheddar
   cheese on top and bake for 35 minutes or until hot and bubbly. Serves 10.

Chicken Tetrazzini

6 - 8 boneless, skinless chicken breast halves
4 tablespoons (¼ stick) butter
1 (4 ounce) can sliced mushrooms
1 tablespoon parsley flakes
2 (10 ounce) cans cream of chicken soup
½ pint sour cream
1 (12 ounce) package spaghetti
Parmesan cheese

★ Preheat oven to 400°. Place chicken in large saucepan and cover with water. Boil until chicken is tender. Cool and cut in bite-size pieces. Melt butter in large skillet, add drained mushrooms and saute about 10 minutes.

★ Stir in parsley flakes and chicken. Cover and let stand for 10 minutes. Add cream of chicken soup and sour cream and stir. Break spaghetti in bite-size pieces and cook according to package directions.

★ Drain and cool. Combine with chicken mixture and place in buttered, casserole dish. Sprinkle with parmesan cheese and bake uncovered until hot. Serves 6 to 8.

Old-Fashioned Chicken Spaghetti

8 - 10 ounces spaghetti
1 bell pepper, seeded, chopped
1 onion, chopped
1 cup chopped celery
½ cup (1 stick) butter
1 (10 ounce) can tomato soup
1 (10 ounce) can diced tomatoes and green chilies
1 (4 ounce) can chopped mushrooms, drained
½ teaspoon garlic powder
1 tablespoon chicken bouillon granules
4 - 5 cups chopped chicken
1 (8 ounce) package cubed Velveeta® cheese
1 (8 ounce) package shredded cheddar cheese

★ Preheat oven to 325°. Cook spaghetti according to package directions and drain. Saute bell pepper, onion and celery with butter in medium saucepan.

★ Add soup, tomatoes and green chilies, mushrooms, ½ teaspoon each of salt and pepper, garlic powder, bouillon granules, and ½ cup water and mix. Combine spaghetti, vegetable-soup mixture, chicken and cheeses in large bowl.

★ Place in 2 sprayed 2-quart baking dishes. Freeze one; cover and bake the other for 40 to 50 minutes. To cook frozen casserole, thaw first. Serves 10.

Easy Chicken and Dumplings

3 cups cooked, chopped chicken
2 (10 ounce) cans cream of chicken soup
3 teaspoons chicken bouillon granules
1 (8 ounce) can refrigerated buttermilk biscuits

★ Combine chopped chicken, both cans of soup, chicken bouillon granules and 4½ cups water in large, heavy pot. Boil mixture and stir to mix well.

★ Separate biscuits and cut in half, cut again making 4 pieces out of each biscuit. Drop biscuit pieces, 1 at a time, into boiling chicken mixture and stir gently.

★ When all biscuits are dropped, reduce heat to low and simmer, stirring occasionally, for about 15 minutes. Serves 4 to 6.

TIP: Deli turkey will work just fine in this recipe. It's a great time-saver!

King Ranch Chicken

The King Ranch, established in 1853 from a Spanish land grant, is the largest ranch in the U.S. Today the ranch covers more than 800,000 acres in South Texas with additional holdings in Brazil and 3 states in the U.S. This recipe was developed at the ranch.

8 (8 inch) corn tortillas, divided
Chicken broth
1 onion, chopped
1 green bell pepper, seeded, chopped
2 tablespoons butter
1 (14 ounce) can cream of chicken soup
1 (10 ounce) can cream of mushroom soup
1 tablespoon chili powder
3 - 4 pound fryer, cooked, boned, diced
1 (12 ounce) package shredded cheese
1 (10 ounce) can diced tomatoes and green chilies

★ Preheat oven to 350°. Layer half tortillas dipped in hot chicken broth just long enough to soften in sprayed 10 x 15-inch baking pan. Saute onion and bell pepper with butter in skillet. Stir in soups, chili powder and diced chicken.

★ Pour layer of half soup-chicken mixture over tortillas and half cheese. Repeat layers and pour tomatoes and green chilies over casserole. Bake for 40 to 45 minutes or until hot and bubbly. Serves 6 to 8.

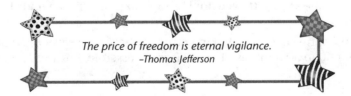

The price of freedom is eternal vigilance.
–Thomas Jefferson

Easy Cola Chicken

4 - 6 boneless, skinless chicken breast halves
1 cup ketchup
1 cup cola
2 tablespoons Worcestershire sauce

★ Preheat oven to 350°. Place chicken in 9 x 13-inch baking dish. Mix ketchup, cola and Worcestershire sauce in bowl and pour over chicken. Cover and bake for 50 minutes. Serves 6.

Grilled Chicken Fajitas

6 boneless, skinless chicken breast halves
Cayenne pepper
1 red or green bell pepper
1 onion
12 flour tortillas, warmed
Avocado, sliced
Salsa
Sour cream

★ Pound chicken breasts between pieces of wax paper. Sprinkle both sides of chicken breasts with salt and pepper. Slice bell pepper into strips and slice onion twice to make 3 thick slices.

★ Grill chicken breasts, bell pepper and onion over charcoal fire. Cook for 5 to 10 minutes on each side, or until the chicken juices run clear. Remove from grill and let cool for about 5 minutes. Cut chicken breasts into thin strips.

★ To assemble, place several strips chicken, bell pepper and onion in center of tortilla. Top with some avocado, salsa or sour cream. Fold over and serve. Serves 4 to 6.

TIP: Traditional fajitas do not include sour cream, guacamole or chopped avocado, but you don't have to be traditional.

TIP: You can also marinade the chicken in Italian dressing for 1 hour before seasoning. It's a great way to tenderize chicken and is super quick and easy.

Easy Chicken Quesadillas

3 boneless, skinless chicken breast halves
1 teaspoon chili powder
4 (10 inch) flour tortillas
2 cups shredded 4-cheese blend
2 tomatoes, thinly sliced

★ Season chicken with chili powder and a little salt and pepper. Spray skillet or heat 1 tablespoon oil in skillet over medium heat. Cook chicken about 4 minutes per side or until juices are clear. Set aside to cool; cut into thin slices.

★ Spray skillet and place 1 flour tortilla on bottom. Spread about ½ cup shredded cheese over one-half of tortilla. Place one-fourth of chicken slices and tomato slices on top of cheese. Fold tortilla half over cheese-chicken mixture and heat until cheese melts. Serves 4.

Sour Cream Chicken Enchiladas

4 - 5 boneless, skinless chicken breast halves
1 onion, chopped
¼ cup plus 1 tablespoon butter, divided
1 (4 ounce) can diced green chilies
1 (12 ounce) package shredded cheddar cheese
2 teaspoons chili powder, divided
1 (16 ounce) carton sour cream, divided
10 - 12 flour tortillas
¼ cup flour
1 (12 ounce) package shredded Monterey Jack cheese, divided

★ Preheat oven to 350°. Cook chicken in enough water to cover chicken in saucepan, drain and set aside 1½ cups broth. Allow chicken to cool and chop into small pieces.

★ Saute onion in 3 tablespoons butter in skillet, add chicken, green chilies, cheddar cheese, 1 teaspoon chili powder and 1 cup sour cream and mix well.

★ Wrap tortillas in slightly damp paper towel and microwave on HIGH for about 1 minute or until softened. Spoon chicken-cheese mixture onto tortillas and roll to enclose filling. Place seam-side down in sprayed 10 x 15-inch baking pan.

★ Combine flour and 2 tablespoons butter, melted in saucepan, mix well and add set aside broth; cook, stirring constantly, until thick and bubbly.

★ Fold in one-half Monterey Jack cheese, remaining 1 cup sour cream and remaining chili powder; spoon over enchiladas.

★ Bake for 30 minutes. Remove from oven and sprinkle with remaining Monterey Jack cheese. Serves 8 to 10.

Spiced Drumsticks

⅔ cup fine breadcrumbs
⅔ cup finely crushed corn chips
1 (1 ounce) packet taco seasoning mix
1 (16 ounce) jar taco sauce, divided
2 pounds chicken drumsticks, skinned

★ Preheat oven to 375°. Combine breadcrumbs, crushed corn chips and dry taco seasoning mix in bowl. Place ½ cup taco sauce in flat bowl.

★ Dip drumsticks in taco sauce, one at a time, then dredge in crumb mixture. Discard taco sauce used for dipping. Place on lightly sprayed baking sheet and bake for 30 to 35 minutes. Serve with remaining taco sauce. Serves 6 to 8.

Easy Rosemary Baked Chicken

1 (2½ - 3 pound) whole chicken
1 lemon, sliced
1 McCormick® Recipe Inspirations (Rosemary Baked Chicken) seasoning packet

★ Preheat oven to 350°. Place chicken in sprayed roasting pan and place several lemon slices on chicken. Use other slices to squeeze lemon juice over chicken. Sprinkle seasonings over chicken.

★ Place squeezed lemon slices in chicken cavity. Bake, covered, for 45 minutes. Remove lid from roasting pan and cook another 20 to 30 minutes until top is golden brown and juices are clear. Serves 4 to 6.

TIP: McCormick® Recipe Inspirations have pre-measured seasonings with a recipe on the back of the packets. The packet for this recipe has rosemary, paprika, garlic and pepper already measured for the recipe. This is really handy when you don't have all the seasonings or you don't want to buy a seasoning you may   never use again.

Ritzy Chicken Bake

8 boneless, skinless chicken thighs
2 cups Ritz cracker crumbs
¾ cup shredded parmesan cheese
1 (16 ounce) bottle ranch dressing
1 teaspoon lemon juice

★ Season chicken with a little salt and pepper. Process or roll out crackers and make crumbs. Mix cracker crumbs and parmesan cheese in pie pan. In separate dish mix about ½ cup ranch dressing and lemon juice. Preheat oven to 350°.

★ Rub dressing mixture on chicken to cover. Dredge in cracker mixture and cover surface of chicken. Place in sprayed baking pan and bake for about 20 minutes or until juices are clear. Serves 4 to 6.

Prairie Spring Chicken

2 pounds chicken thighs
Canola oil
¾ cup chili sauce
¾ cup packed brown sugar
1 (1 ounce) packet onion soup mix
Rice, cooked

★ Preheat oven to 325°. Brown chicken pieces in skillet with a little oil and place in sprayed 9 x 13-inch baking dish.

★ Combine chili sauce, brown sugar, soup mix and ½ cup water in bowl and pour over chicken. Cover and bake for 20 minutes. Remove cover and bake for additional 15 minute to brown. Serve over rice. Serves 8.

Beer-in-the-Rear Chicken

Straight from The Authorized Texas Ranger Cookbook *by Cheryl and Johnny Harris, this recipe captures the spirit and imagination of retired Texas Ranger Bill Gunn.*

1 whole frying chicken
Olive oil
Rosemary
Thyme
Onion flakes
Garlic flakes
Onion, apple or celery slices
1 (12 ounce) can light beer

★ Buy a whole frying-size chicken. This will work equally well on the grill or in the kitchen oven. You can prepare the chicken to suit individual tastes. You are limited only by your imagination.

★ Some suggestions are to rub the chicken with olive oil and sprinkle with rosemary and thyme, or sprinkle with onion flakes and garlic flakes (inside and out). Place slice of onion, apple or celery in cavity of chicken.

★ After preparing chicken open a can of light beer (removing tab and opening one or two additional holes) and insert can of beer upright into cavity of the chicken and place upright in shallow pan in oven at 325° for 2 hours or until done.

★ If barbecuing, place chicken upright on grill (after placing beer can in cavity). Baste with sauce about 30 minutes before done. Serves 4.

 Beef Capital of the World   Hereford, Texas

Barbecued Chicken

1 (2 pound) whole chicken, quartered
½ cup ketchup
¼ cup butter (½ stick), melted
2 tablespoons sugar
1 tablespoon mustard
½ teaspoon minced garlic
¼ cup lemon juice
¼ cup white vinegar
¼ cup Worcestershire sauce
Several dashes hot pepper sauce, optional

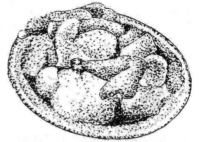

★ Preheat oven to 325°. Sprinkle chicken quarters with a little salt and pepper and brown in skillet. Place in large sprayed baking pan.

★ Combine ketchup, butter, sugar, mustard, garlic, lemon juice, vinegar Worcestershire and hot pepper sauce in bowl. Pour over chicken. Cover and bake for 50 minutes. Serves 4.

Southern Fried Chicken

1 whole chicken, cut up or 2 - 3 pounds chicken pieces
2 eggs, beaten
¼ cup half-and-half cream
Flour
Vegetable oil or shortening

★ Wash chicken pieces and dry with paper towels. Sprinkle all sides with salt and pepper. Combine eggs and cream in bowl. Dip chicken into egg mixture, dredge in flour and coat well.

★ Carefully place chicken in heavy skillet with ¼ inch hot oil or shortening over medium high heat. Add more oil as needed. Brown chicken pieces over medium high heat on both sides. Lower heat, cover and cook slowly for 20 to 25 minutes or until tender and juices run clear.

Gravy:

3 tablespoons flour
1½ cups milk

★ Remove chicken from skillet and add flour and ½ teaspoon each of salt and pepper and stir constantly. Increase heat to high. Add milk, cook and stir until gravy is thick. Serve hot. Serves 4 to 6.

Variations:

1. Double dip chicken pieces in egg and flour and return to egg and flour again. You'll need more eggs and cream. If you don't have cream, water will work.

2. Add hot sauce to egg mixture or add cayenne pepper to flour.

Oven-Fried Chicken

1 medium fryer chicken, cut into serving pieces
1 (1 ounce) packet ranch buttermilk salad dressing mix
1 cup buttermilk*
½ cup mayonnaise
2 - 3 cups crushed corn flakes

★ Preheat oven to 350°. Pat chicken pieces dry and place on paper towels. Combine ranch dressing mix, buttermilk and mayonnaise in shallow bowl and mix well.

★ Dip chicken pieces in dressing and cover well. Roll each piece in corn flakes and coat all sides well. Arrange pieces so they do not touch in sprayed 9 x 13-inch baking dish.

★ Bake for 1 hour. If chicken pieces are not brown, cook for additional 15 minutes. Serves 6 to 8.

*TIP: To make buttermilk, add 2 tablespoons lemon juice or vinegar to an 8-ounce glass of milk and set aside for 10 minutes.

Chicken-Fried Chicken and Cream Gravy

1 medium fryer chicken, cut up
2 tablespoons milk
2 eggs, beaten
Flour
Canola oil or shortening

★ Sprinkle a little salt and pepper over each piece of chicken. Add milk to beaten eggs in bowl and dip chicken into egg mixture. Roll in flour and coat chicken well.

★ Heat about ¼ inch oil or shortening in heavy skillet and brown chicken on both sides. Lower heat and cook until tender, about 25 minutes.

Gravy:

3 tablespoons flour
1 - 1½ cups milk

★ Remove chicken from skillet and add flour and ½ teaspoon each of salt and pepper. Turn burner to high heat and add milk, stirring constantly, until gravy thickens. Serves 4 to 5.

Chicken Poppy Kash

8 - 10 skinless, boneless chicken thighs
1 onion, chopped
¼ cup chicken broth
3 cups egg noodles
3 tablespoons cornstarch
1 (8 ounce) container sour cream

★ Brown chicken in skillet with a little oil. Place in sprayed slow cooker.
Add onion and broth. Cover and cook for 7 to 8 hours.

★ About 30 minutes before serving, cook noodles and drain. Remove
chicken from slow cooker and keep warm. Mix cornstarch with
3 tablespoons cold water until cornstarch dissolves. Pour into slow
cooker and mix with juices.

★ Cover and cook for about 15 minutes or until juices thicken a little. Add
sour cream and stir well. Place chicken in slow cooker to mix well with
creamy gravy. Serve over cooked noodles. Serves 4 to 6.

Chicken Stew

6 - 8 boneless, skinless chicken thighs
Oil
1 (8 ounce) carton fresh mushrooms, stemmed, sliced
1 (12 ounce) package baby carrots
4 - 5 ribs celery, chopped
1 (10 ounce) can mushroom with roasted garlic soup

★ Cut chicken into bite-size pieces and sear outside of pieces in large skillet
with a little oil. Drain and set aside. Add mushrooms, carrots and celery
to sprayed slow cooker. Place browned chicken pieces on top.

★ In separate saucepan, heat soup and ½ soup can water and stir until
soup is creamy. Pour soup over chicken. Cover and cook on LOW for 6 to
8 hours or until chicken is tender. Serves 6 to 8.

Fried Chicken

*There's no real creation date for fried chicken. Frying dates back
to ancient times, but there is an evolution for fried chicken in America.
The first well noted mention of fried chicken appears in 1709 when
Governor William Byrd II of Virginia served fried chicken on his plantation.*

*Maryland-style fried chicken is described early in the 1700's as well.
This old-fashioned recipe starts with melting butter in a heavy skillet and
cooking salt pork until golden brown. The salt pork was removed and disjointed
pieces of chicken were dipped in milk and flour before cooking in the hot fat.*

*History seems to reflect that fried chicken was a staple in the South
more than in the North. Slaves raised chickens in the South and maybe
that accounts for some of the popularity, but not until the popularity
of fast foods in the 1960's did fried chicken catch on in the North.*

Chicken Cutlets with Dijon Sauce

4 - 6 boneless, skinless chicken breast halves
3 tablespoons butter, divided
2 tablespoons olive oil
1 bunch green onions with tops, chopped
2 ribs celery, chopped
1 red bell pepper, seeded, minced
1 tablespoon dijon-style mustard

★ Season chicken with a little salt and pepper. Cut each piece in half and place between 2 sheets of wax paper. Pound each piece to about ¼-inch thick.

★ Place in skillet over medium-high heat with 1 tablespoon butter and 1 tablespoon oil. Fry each piece about 2 to 3 minutes on one side, turn and cook for about 1 minute on the other side; drain well. Keep chicken warm.

★ Add remaining butter and oil to skillet. Add onions, bell pepper, celery and mustard and cook just until onions are translucent. (Add extra butter if needed.) Pour over chicken to serve. Serves 4 to 6.

Parmesan Chicken Cutlets

6 - 8 boneless, skinless chicken breast halves
Olive oil
2 cups Italian-style breadcrumbs
1 cup shredded parmesan cheese
1 cup flour
2 eggs, beaten

★ Season chicken breasts with a little salt and pepper. Cut chicken breasts in half and place between 2 sheets of wax paper. Pound each piece to about ⅛ inch to ¼ inch thickness.

★ Mix breadcrumbs and parmesan in pie plate. Pour flour on plate and dredge chicken in flour. Pour eggs into separate pie plate. Dip floured chicken in eggs and then in breadcrumb mixture.

★ Heat a little oil in large skillet over medium-high heat. Fry each piece several minutes and turn to fry other side about 1 minute. Remove from skillet and drain. Serves 6 to 8.

Southern Fried Chicken

The term "Southern Fried Chicken" was first printed in 1925 and cream sauces had turned into milk gravy. Batters were used, but the most chicken pieces were dipped in milk and flour or dipped in egg and flour or both. A dash of hot sauce was sometimes added to the liquid, but seasonings always depended on local customs.

Today, fried chicken as we know it is the American version, but there are as many versions of fried chicken as there are local cuisines all around the world.

[www.foodtimeline.org] [www.experienceproject.com]

Chicken Skillet with Broccoli

6 boneless, skinless chicken breast halves
2 teaspoons lemon pepper, divided
1 tablespoon canola oil
1 cup chicken broth
1 (16 ounce) package frozen broccoli florets
2 cups instant white rice

★ Season chicken with 1 teaspoon lemon pepper and a little salt and pepper. Place in skillet with oil over medium heat, cover and cook for about 3 minutes on both sides. Place chicken on ovenproof plate and keep warm.

★ In same skillet, pour in broth, ¾ cup water and broccoli. Bring mixture to boil. Add rice and bring to boil again. Place chicken on top, cover and cook for about 10 minutes or until juices of chicken are clear. Serves 4 to 6.

Variation:

★ After chicken is done, remove to plate again and keep warm. Pour 1 (4 ounce) jar Cheez Whiz® over rice and broccoli and heat until cheese melts. Return chicken to skillet and serve. Serves 4 to 6.

Easy Marinated Chicken Breasts

6 - 8 boneless, skinless chicken breast halves
1 (16 ounce) bottle creamy Italian dressing
1 lemon

★ Season chicken breasts with a little salt and pepper. Cut breast halves in half and place in sprayed 9 x 13-inch baking dish.

★ Pour Italian dressing over chicken and marinate in refrigerator for 30 minutes to 1 hour.

★ Preheat oven to 350°. Before baking, cut lemon in half and squeeze juice over chicken. Bake for 30 to 45 minutes or until juices are clear. Serves 6 to 8.

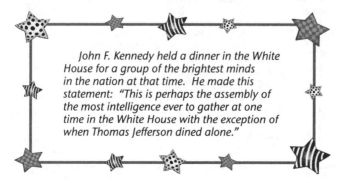

John F. Kennedy held a dinner in the White House for a group of the brightest minds in the nation at that time. He made this statement: "This is perhaps the assembly of the most intelligence ever to gather at one time in the White House with the exception of when Thomas Jefferson dined alone."

Best Smoked Chicken

3 whole chickens, halved
Seasoned pepper
½ cup (1 stick) butter
2 teaspoons Worcestershire sauce
2 dashes hot sauce
2 tablespoons lemon juice
½ teaspoon garlic salt
1 cup (8 ounces) 7UP®

★ Sprinkle chickens with seasoned pepper and leave at room temperature for 1 hour. Melt butter in small saucepan and add Worcestershire sauce, hot sauce, lemon juice, garlic salt and 7UP®.

★ Cook chickens on grill using mesquite charcoal. Turn often and baste with sauce mixture several times. Grill for about 1 hour and baste to keep chicken moist. Chickens are done when juices run clear. Serves 6 to 10.

Fried Chicken Livers

1 pound chicken livers, washed, dried
2 tablespoons buttermilk*
2 eggs, beaten
Flour
Canola oil

★ Season chicken livers with a little pepper. Add buttermilk to beaten eggs in bowl and dip livers into egg mixture. Roll in flour and coat livers well.

★ Heat about ¼ inch oil in heavy skillet and brown livers on both sides. Lower heat and cook until tender, about 15 to 20 minutes.

★ Remove from skillet, drain on paper towels, add a little salt and pepper again and serve immediately. Serves 4.

*TIP: To make buttermilk, mix 1 cup milk with 1 tablespoon lemon juice or vinegar and let stand for about 10 minutes.

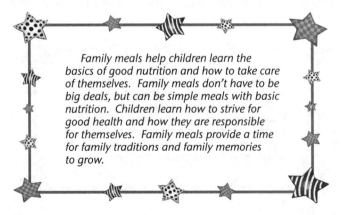

Family meals help children learn the basics of good nutrition and how to take care of themselves. Family meals don't have to be big deals, but can be simple meals with basic nutrition. Children learn how to strive for good health and how they are responsible for themselves. Family meals provide a time for family traditions and family memories to grow.

Southern Stuffed Peppers

6 large green bell peppers
½ pound chicken livers, chopped
6 slices bacon, diced
1 cup chopped onion
1 cup sliced celery
1 clove garlic, crushed
1 (4 ounce) can sliced mushrooms
2 cups cooked rice
Dash of cayenne pepper

★ Wash peppers, cut slice from stem end and remove seeds. Cook peppers for about 5 minutes in small amount of boiling salted water in large saucepan. Remove from water and drain.

★ Cook chicken livers, bacon, onion, celery and garlic in skillet until vegetables are tender. Add mushrooms, rice, 1 teaspoon salt, ¼ teaspoon pepper and a dash of cayenne pepper. Stuff peppers with mixture.

★ Arrange in baking pan, seal and freeze. Thaw before baking. When ready to bake, preheat oven to 375°. Add ½ inch water to pan, cover and bake for 20 to 25 minutes. Serves 6.

Main Dishes – Turkey

Thanksgiving Turkey

1 (15 to 18 pound) turkey
1 cup butter, softened

★ Put turkey in refrigerator to thaw 3 to 4 days before cooking. When ready to cook, remove metal clamp from legs. Run cold water into breast and neck cavities to wash and to remove giblets and neck. (Interior should be cold to slightly icy.) Refrigerate until ready to cook.

★ To cook turkey, preheat oven to 425°. Rub entire turkey with butter and lightly salt and pepper. Place turkey in roaster, breast side up. Cover bottom of pan with ½ to 1 cup water. Place 1 or 2 ribs celery and ½ peeled white onion inside cavity. Cover with lid or foil. Follow cooking time chart below and baste occasionally with drippings while turkey is cooking.

Cooking Times for Turkey:

Weight of turkey	Cooking time at 325°	
6 to 8 pounds	3 to 3½ hours	Serves 6 to 8
8 to 12 pounds	3½ to 4½ hours	Serves 8 to12
12 to 16 pounds	4½ to 5½ hours	Serves 16 to 20
16 to 20 pounds	5½ to 6½ hours	Serves 20 to 26
20 to 24 pounds	6½ to 7 hours	Serves 26 to 32

Smoked Turkey

This may sound incredible, but it works! The trick
is teaching your husband to smoke the turkey! Thanksgiving
is much more enjoyable with a "little help in the kitchen"!

1 butter-basted turkey
1 onion, peeled, halved
2 - 3 small ribs celery
Poultry seasoning
2 - 3 strips bacon

★ Buy turkey that will fit on covered grill. Soak hickory chips in water while charcoal gets "good and hot". Place washed and dried turkey in disposable aluminum foil roasting pan.

★ Rub poultry seasoning, salt and pepper on turkey inside and out and insert onion and celery in cavity of turkey. Lay strips of bacon across top of turkey.

★ Pour a little water in pan to prevent sticking and place on grill. Close grill cover and cook for 11 minutes per pound. Baste occasionally during cooking time. (This cooking method produces a beautiful brown turkey. The meat will look slightly pink, but if the juices run clear, the turkey is done.)

★ Pan drippings in roaster are ready to make gravy. By using this procedure, Thanksgiving cooking is much easier because your oven is free for other dishes. Just throw away the messy pan when you are finished! (You can discard the onion and celery.)

Deep-Fried Turkey

Be sure to read the instructions with your turkey fryer before
using this recipe. Always cook outside on dirt or concrete.

1 (8 - 12) pound turkey
Seasonings
Peanut oil

★ Wash or soak turkey in brine for several hours and dry thoroughly. Season turkey. (Place turkey in cooker and fill with water about 2 inches over turkey. Remove turkey and mark fill line.) Dry cooker and add oil to fill line. (Over filling could cause fire.) Turn burner on high.

★ When oil starts to pop and bubble, carefully place turkey in basket and lower into hot oil with tools provided with cooker. (Wear fire-proof gloves and lots of protection.). Cook turkey about 3 minutes per pound. Remove turkey and place in large baking dish. Internal breast temperature should be 170° and thigh temperature should be 180°. Serves 8 to 12.

Glazed Turkey Tenders

Canola oil
1 pound turkey tenders
Rice, cooked

★ Place a little oil in heavy skillet and cook turkey tenders for about 5 minutes on each side or until they brown.

Glaze:

⅔ cup honey
2 teaspoons peeled grated fresh ginger
1 tablespoon marinade for chicken
1 tablespoon soy sauce
1 tablespoon lemon juice

★ Combine all glaze ingredients, mix well and pour into skillet. Bring mixture to a boil, reduce heat and simmer for 15 minutes. Serve over rice. Serves 6.

TIP: As a time-saver, you might want to try the package of rice that can be microwaved for 90 seconds and it's ready to serve.

California Turkey Burgers

2 pounds ground turkey
1 (16 ounce) jar hot chipotle salsa, divided
8 slices Monterey Jack cheese
Sesame seed hamburger buns

★ Preheat broiler. Combine ground turkey with 1 cup salsa in large bowl. Mix well and shape into 8 patties. Place patties in skillet or broiler pan and broil for 12 to 15 minutes. Turn once during cooking.

★ Top each patty with cheese slice and heat just long enough to melt cheese. Place burgers on buns, spoon heaping tablespoon salsa over cheese and top with remaining half of bun. Serves 6 to 8.

Variation:

★ Avocado slices and bean sprouts are great with this burger as well.

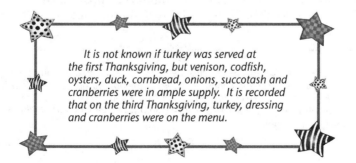

It is not known if turkey was served at the first Thanksgiving, but venison, codfish, oysters, duck, cornbread, onions, succotash and cranberries were in ample supply. It is recorded that on the third Thanksgiving, turkey, dressing and cranberries were on the menu.

Turkey Croquettes

These are very easy to make. Make several
batches and freeze them for another meal.

1½ cups cooked, chopped turkey
1 (10 ounce) can cream of chicken soup
1 cup turkey stuffing mix
2 eggs
1 tablespoon minced onion
Flour
Vegetable oil

★ Mix turkey, soup, stuffing mix, eggs and onion in bowl and refrigerate
  for several hours. Shape into patties or rolls. Dredge in flour and fry in
  deep oil until brown. Serves 6 to 8.

Turkey Jerky

Turkey breasts, cooked
Salt or seasoned salt
Freshly ground black pepper

★ Preheat oven to 175°. Slice turkey breasts across the grain in very thin
  slices about ¼ inch thick.

★ Place on baking sheet and sprinkle both sides lightly with salt and a lot
  of freshly ground black pepper.

★ Cook in oven until turkey gets to the right consistency. It should be very
  dense, dark brown, but not burned. (The time is different with the size
  of pieces. Beef jerky takes 4 to 6 hours or more, but turkey jerky usually
  takes much less time. Check it after 2 hours.)

Roasted Turkey Supreme

If you have leftover turkey, you will like this.

4 cups chopped cooked turkey
½ cup (1 stick) butter, melted
1 (6 ounce) box cornbread stuffing mix, crushed

★ Preheat oven to 350°. Dip medium to large-size pieces of turkey in
  melted butter and roll in cornbread stuffing crumbs. Place in sprayed
  9 x 13-inch baking dish. Bake for 15 to 20 minutes just to heat through.
  Serves 4 to 6.

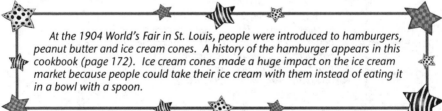

At the 1904 World's Fair in St. Louis, people were introduced to hamburgers,
peanut butter and ice cream cones. A history of the hamburger appears in this
cookbook (page 172). Ice cream cones made a huge impact on the ice cream
market because people could take their ice cream with them instead of eating it
in a bowl with a spoon.

Main Dishes – Pork

Pork Loin with Apricot Glaze

1 (3½ - 4 pound) center-cut pork loin
1 tablespoon olive oil
1 teaspoon dried rosemary
1 cup dry white wine or cooking wine
1½ cups apricot preserves

★ Preheat oven to 350°. Rub pork loin with olive oil and sprinkle a little pepper and rosemary over roast. Place loin in shallow roasting pan. Pour wine and 1 cup water into pan, cover and roast for 1 hour.

★ Remove pan from oven and spoon about 1 cup pan drippings into small bowl. Add apricot preserves to bowl and mix well. Pour mixture over pork, reduce oven to 325°. Cover and return to oven. Continue to roast for additional 1 hour and baste 2 to 3 times with pan drippings.

★ Set aside pork for 15 minutes before slicing. Remove roast from drippings, place in glass baking dish and slice.

★ Serve immediately or pour drippings into separate container and refrigerate both. When ready to serve, heat drippings and pour over roast. Warm roast at 350° for 20 minutes. Serves 8.

Aloha Pork Tenderloin

This is great served over rice.

2 (1 pound) lean pork tenderloins
1 tablespoon canola oil
1 (15 ounce) can pineapple chunks with juice
1 (12 ounce) bottle chili sauce
1 teaspoon ground ginger
Rice, cooked

★ Cut pork in 1-inch cubes. Season pork tenderloins with salt and pepper and brown on medium-high heat in skillet with oil. Add pineapple with juice, chili sauce and ginger.

★ Cover and simmer for 30 minutes. Serve over rice. Serves 4 to 6.

Award-Winning Pork Tenderloin

⅔ cup soy sauce
⅔ cup canola oil
2 tablespoons crystallized ginger, finely chopped
2 tablespoons real lime juice
1 teaspoon garlic powder
2 tablespoons minced onion
2 pork tenderloins

★ Combine all marinade ingredients in bowl and pour over pork tenderloins. Marinate for about 36 hours. When ready to serve, cook over charcoal fire for about 45 minutes. Serves 8 to 10.

Grilled Pork Loin

½ teaspoon garlic powder
¼ teaspoon celery salt
½ teaspoon onion salt
2 tablespoons lemon juice
1 (5 pound) pork loin

★ Combine garlic powder, celery salt, onion salt and lemon juice in bowl. Rub mixture into loin and place in covered glass dish. Refrigerate for at least 8 hours or overnight.

★ Grill loin over hot coals for 30 minutes or until thickest portion of meat reaches 140°. (Center part of tenderloin will be slightly pink.) Set aside for at least 10 minutes before cutting. Serves 8 to 10.

Parmesan-Covered Pork Chops

½ cup grated parmesan cheese
⅔ cup Italian seasoned dried breadcrumbs
1 egg
4 - 5 thin-cut pork chops
Canola oil

★ Combine cheese and dried breadcrumbs in shallow bowl. Beat egg with 1 teaspoon water on shallow plate. Dip each pork chop in beaten egg then in breadcrumb mixture.

★ Cook with a little oil in skillet over medium-high heat for about 5 minutes on each side or until golden brown. Serves 4 to 5.

Grilled Pork Chops

4 (1 inch) thick center-cut pork chops
2 to 3 tablespoons olive oil
1 lemon

★ Start charcoal fire or heat gas grill. Allow pork chops to reach room temperature. When fire is ready, dry pork chops with paper towel and season with olive oil, a little lemon juice and a lot of salt and pepper.

★ Place pork chops on grill and sear both sides for a minute or two to seal the juices inside. Move to cooler part of grill and cook 5 to 10 minutes or until chops are firm to the touch and juices are slightly pink on the inside.

★ (Cooking time will vary with type of fire, thickness of chops and covered and uncovered grill. The main thing is not to overcook which dries out pork chops.) Remove chops from grill, drizzle with a little more lemon juice and serve immediately. Serves 4.

Barbecued Pork Chops

6 pork chops
1 tablespoon chili powder
1 teaspoon paprika
¼ cup packed brown sugar
½ cup vinegar
1 (10 ounce) can tomato soup

★ Preheat oven to 350°. Place pork chops in baking dish. Combine remaining ingredients with 1 teaspoon salt in bowl and pour over chops. Bake for 1 hour 30 minutes. Serves 6.

Apple Valley Pork Chops

These pork chops just melt in your mouth!

6 thick-cut pork chops
Flour
Canola oil
3 baking apples

★ Preheat oven to 325°. Dip pork chops in flour and coat well. Brown pork chops in oil in skillet and place in sprayed 9 x 13-inch baking dish. Add ⅓ cup water to casserole. Cover and bake for 45 minutes.

★ Peel, halve and seed apples and place half apple over each pork chop. Return to oven for 5 to 10 minutes. (DO NOT overcook apples). Serves 6.

Tangy Pork Chops

4 - 6 pork chops
¼ cup Worcestershire sauce
¼ cup ketchup
½ cup honey

★ Preheat oven to 325°. Brown pork chops in skillet. Place in shallow baking dish. Combine Worcestershire, ketchup and honey in bowl. Pour over pork chops.

★ Cover and bake for 20 minutes; uncover and bake for additional 15 minutes. Serves 4 to 6.

Skillet Pork Chops

⅔ cup biscuit mix
½ cup crushed saltine crackers
1 egg
6 boneless (½ inch) thick pork chops

★ In shallow bowl, combine baking mix, crushed crackers and a generous amount of salt and pepper. In another shallow bowl, beat egg with 2 tablespoons water.

★ Heat skillet with small amount of oil. Dip each pork chop in egg mixture and then in cracker mixture. Place in heated skillet and cook for 8 to 10 minutes on each side. Serves 6.

Pineapple-Pork Chops

6 - 8 thick, boneless pork chops
Canola oil
1 (6 ounce) can frozen pineapple juice concentrate, thawed
3 tablespoons brown sugar
⅓ cup wine or tarragon vinegar
⅓ cup honey
Rice, cooked

★ Preheat oven to 325°. Place pork chops in a little oil in skillet and brown. Remove to shallow baking dish.

★ Combine pineapple juice, brown sugar, vinegar and honey in bowl. Pour over pork chops. Cover and cook for about 50 minutes. Serve over hot rice. Serves 6 to 8.

 Pork Barbecue Capital of the World   Memphis, Tennessee

Pork Chop Casserole

¾ cup rice
6 pork chops, floured
2 tablespoons vegetable oil
1 large onion, chopped
1 medium bell pepper, cut in rings
1 (15 ounce) can diced tomatoes
1 (10 ounce) can beef broth

★ Preheat oven to 350°. Place rice in 2-quart shallow baking dish. Brown floured chops in oil in skillet and place on top of rice. Brown onion and bell pepper in remaining oil and pour over pork chops.

★ Combine tomatoes and 1 teaspoon salt in bowl and pour over pork chops. Pour beef broth over entire casserole. Cover and bake for 1 hour. Serves 6.

Pork Chops and Red Cabbage

6 (1 inch) thick pork chops
Vegetable oil
⅓ cup flour
⅓ cup sugar
½ cup cider vinegar
1 small red cabbage, shredded
2 Rome apples with peel, sliced

★ Brown pork chops on both sides with a little oil in skillet. Lower heat, cover and simmer for 15 minutes.

★ Combine flour, sugar, and liberal amount of salt in bowl. In separate bowl, combine vinegar and ¼ cup water.

★ In larger bowl, combine cabbage and apples and toss with flour-sugar mixture and then vinegar mixture. Spoon over pork chops, cover and simmer for 30 minutes. Serves 6.

The World Championship Barbecue Cooking Contest is held annually in Memphis, Tennessee in May. It is billed as the largest pork barbecue cooking contest on the planet.

Fried Pork Chops

4 - 6 (1 inch) thick pork chops
¼ cup milk
2 eggs, beaten
Flour
Canola oil or shortening

★ Sprinkle a little salt and pepper over pork chop. Add milk to beaten eggs in bowl and dip chop into egg mixture. Roll in flour and coat well.

★ Heat about ¼ inch oil or shortening in heavy skillet and brown pork chops on both sides. Lower heat and cook until tender, about 25 minutes.

Gravy:

3 tablespoons flour
1 - 1½ cups milk

★ Remove chops from skillet and add flour and ½ teaspoon each of salt and pepper. Turn burner to high heat and add milk, stirring constantly, until gravy thickens. Serves 4 to 6.

Barbecued Pork Roast Sandwiches

3 onions, divided
5 pound pork roast, boned, trimmed
6 whole cloves
1 (16 ounce) bottle barbecue sauce
Buns

★ Slice 2 onions and place half onion slices in slow cooker. Add meat, cloves and 2 cups water; top with remaining sliced onions. Cover and cook overnight or for 8 to 12 hours on LOW.

★ Discard drippings. Remove and shred meat. Chop remaining onion. Return meat to slow cooker along with chopped onions and barbecue sauce. Cook on HIGH for 2 hours and stir occasionally. Serve roast on buns. Serves 10 to 12.

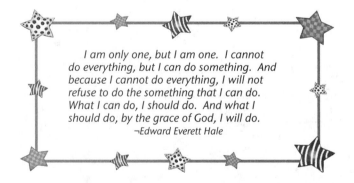

I am only one, but I am one. I cannot do everything, but I can do something. And because I cannot do everything, I will not refuse to do the something that I can do. What I can do, I should do. And what I should do, by the grace of God, I will do.
¬Edward Everett Hale

Carolina Pulled Pork

*Lots of people in the South eat their coleslaw
right on the bun with the pork. It's great!*

4 onions, divided
1 (3 - 4 pound) pork roast or shoulder
Carolina-style barbecue sauce with mustard
Buns
Coleslaw
Dill pickles

★ Slice 1 onion into rings, place in bottom of slow cooker and place roast
  on top. Slice another onion into rings and place over top of roast; fill
  slow cooker about half way or a little more with water. Cook on
  LOW overnight.

★ Remove roast and pour out all but 1 to 2 inches liquid from slow cooker.
  When roast is cool, pull meat apart with fingers or shred it with fork.
  Return roast to slow cooker and pour barbecue sauce over meat.

★ Chop 1 onion, season with salt and pepper and add to meat. Cook on
  HIGH for several hours until onion is tender. Serve on large buns with
  coleslaw, dill pickles and slices of remaining onion. Serves 8 to 12.

TIP: *If your barbecue sauce is thick, you may need a little more liquid from slow
  cooker so meat will not be dry.*

Apple-Glazed Pork Roast

1 (12 ounce) jar apple jelly
4 teaspoons dijon-style mustard
3 teaspoons lemon juice, divided
¼ teaspoon garlic powder
1 (3 - 4 pound) pork loin roast
Lemon

★ Preheat oven to 350°. Melt jelly in small saucepan over low heat. Stir
  in mustard and 1 teaspoon lemon juice and set aside. Rub roast with a
  little pepper and garlic powder.

★ Place on rack in foil-lined shallow roasting pan and bake for about
  45 minutes. Remove from oven, brush with jelly mixture and bake
  for 20 minutes.

★ Brush once more with jelly mixture, reduce heat to 325° and bake for
  additional 1 hour. Remove roast to warm platter.

★ Scrape any browned drippings into remaining jelly mixture. Add
  2 teaspoons lemon juice to mixture, bring to a boil and turn heat off. To
  serve, sauce plate and place thin slices of roast on top or serve roast on
  platter with sauce. Serves 6 to 8.

Supreme Ham Casserole

2 cups cooked, cubed ham
1 onion, chopped
1 red bell pepper, seeded, chopped
2 ribs celery, chopped
1 (6 ounce) box white and wild rice mix
1 (4 ounce) jar diced pimentos, drained
1 (8 ounce) package shredded colby cheese
2 (10 ounce) cans cream of chicken soup

★ Preheat oven to 350°. Combine all ingredients plus amount of water called for on box of rice in bowl. Mix well. Spoon mixture into sprayed 9 x 13-inch baking dish. Cover and bake for 1 hour. Serves 8.

Apricot-Baked Ham

1 (12 - 15 pound) whole ham, bone-in, fully cooked
Whole cloves
2 tablespoons dry mustard
1¼ cups apricot jam
1¼ cups packed light brown sugar

★ Preheat oven to 450°. Trim skin and excess fat from ham. Place ham on rack in large roasting pan. Insert whole cloves in ham every inch or so. Be sure to push cloves into ham surface as far as they will go.

★ Combine dry mustard and apricot jam in bowl and spread over surface of ham. Pat brown sugar over jam. Turn oven to 325° and bake for 15 minutes per pound.

★ A sugary crust forms on ham and keeps juices inside. When ham is tender, remove from oven, allow ham to stand for 20 minutes and remove from pan to carve. Serves 10 to 12.

Honey Ham Slice

⅓ cup orange juice
⅓ cup honey
1 teaspoon prepared mustard
1 (1-inch thick) slice cooked ham

★ Combine orange juice, honey and mustard in saucepan and cook slowly for 10 minutes; stir occasionally. Place ham in broiling pan about 3 inches from heat. Brush with orange glaze. Broil 8 minutes on first side. Turn ham slice over. Brush with glaze again and broil for another 6 to 8 minutes. Serves 4.

Smithfield Virginia Country Ham

*Smithfield Country Hams are the most famous in
the U.S. and can only be cured in Smithfield, Virginia.*

1 Smithfield Virginia Country Ham

★ When you first unwrap a country ham, you may think something is
wrong with it because the outside is covered in mold. When hams are
aged, mold is part of the process, but is in no way harmful to the ham
or to you. Wash and scrape this outside coating of mold off with warm
water. Soak ham for about 12 to 24 hours to pull out some of the salt
in the ham. (Change water several times to pull out more salt.) Cook
the country ham in one of the following ways. Serves depends on size of
ham. Plan on ½ to ¾ pounds per person with bone-in ham.

Boiling:

★ Place ham skin-side down in large roasting pan and cover with water.
Cook in simmering hot water (not boiling) for 25 minutes per pound or
until internal temperature reaches 160°.

★ Add water if necessary to keep ham covered. Remove ham from roasting
pan and remove outside skin and fat.

★ Serve as is or sprinkle brown sugar, honey or molasses and breadcrumbs
on the outside and bake in oven at 400° until outside is brown. Carve
into thin slices and serve immediately.

Roasting:

★ Preheat oven to 300°. Wrap ham in foil with opening at top and place in
large baking pan. Pour 4 cups water into foil and seal.

★ Bake for 20 minutes per pound or until meat thermometer reaches
160°. Remove from oven and scrape off outside skin and fat. Carve
into thin slices and serve.

Pan Frying:

★ Carve ham into very thin slices, trim outside rind and fry in large skillet
with a little oil over medium low heat for about 10 to 15 minutes or until
ham slice is cooked throughout. Serve immediately.

Slicing:

★ "Start slicing several inches away from hock or small end. Make first
slice straight through to the bone. Slant the knife for each succeeding
cut. Decrease slant as slices become larger." www.smithfield.com

Ham and Red-Eye Gravy

Ham steak, ⅓-inch thick
1 tablespoon canola oil
½ onion, finely minced
½ teaspoon minced garlic
1 tablespoon cornstarch
1 (10 ounce) can beef broth
⅓ cup strong coffee

★ Cut ham steak in serving-size pieces. Brown and cook ham in oil in heavy skillet on both sides. Transfer from skillet to serving plate.

★ In same skillet, combine onion, garlic, cornstarch, beef broth and coffee and cook on low heat until mixture thickens slightly.

★ To serve, pour gravy over ham, biscuits, mashed potatoes or grits. Serves 3 to 4.

Easy Baked Ham

1 (3-4 pound) cooked ham
½ cup packed brown sugar
1 teaspoon Worcestershire sauce
1 (20 ounce) can pineapple slices, drained
Whole cloves

★ Preheat oven to 350°.

★ Place ham in large roasting pan with 2 cups water. Cover and bake for 3 to 4 hours or until it is tender. Check ham every hour and add water if needed. Remove from oven and let cool for about 15 minutes.

★ Combine brown sugar and Worcestershire sauce in bowl. Cut pineapple slices into halves, forming crescents.

★ Spread brown sugar mixture over ham and place pineapple halves in rows over brown sugar. Pierce each pineapple half slice with cloves.

★ Bake for additional 20 minutes or until sugar glaze is brown. Serves 6 to 10.

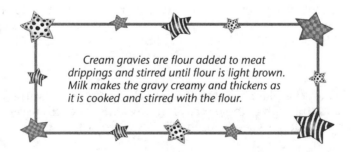

Cream gravies are flour added to meat drippings and stirred until flour is light brown. Milk makes the gravy creamy and thickens as it is cooked and stirred with the flour.

Praline Ham

2 (½ inch) thick ham slices, cooked
½ cup maple syrup
3 tablespoons brown sugar
1 tablespoon butter
⅓ cup chopped pecans

★ Preheat oven to 325°. Bake ham slices in shallow pan for 10 minutes.
   Bring syrup, brown sugar and butter in small saucepan to a boil and
   stir often. Stir in pecans and spoon over ham. Bake for additional
   20 minutes. Serves 4 to 6.

Easiest Baked Ham

★ Buy ½ picnic, shank or butt portion ham, unwrap and place it in
   roasting pan. Cover and bake at 350° for 3 to 4 hours. Check it after
   each hour to check on juices. If it is drying out, add 1 to 2 inches of
   water. The meat will fall off the bone when it is done.

Schnitz un Knepp

(Ham, apples and dumplings)
This hearty dish is a traditional Pennsylvania Dutch favorite.

4 cups dried apples
1 (3 pound) smoked ham
2 tablespoons brown sugar

Dumplings:

2 cups flour
4 teaspoons baking powder
1 egg, well beaten
3 tablespoons butter, melted
½ cup milk

★ Place apples in a pot and cover with water; soak at least 3 hours or
   overnight.

★ In stock pot, cover ham with water and simmer for 2 hours. Add apples
   and the water in which they were soaked; bring to boil and simmer for
   1 hour. Stir in brown sugar.

★ Mix together flour, baking powder, 1 teaspoon salt and ¼ teaspoon pepper.

★ In separate bowl, combine egg, butter and milk. Stir egg mixture into
   flour mixture all at once; mix just until it blends. Drop tablespoonfuls
   into simmering liquid with ham and apples; cover pot tightly and
   simmer for 20 minutes until dumplings are done. Serves 8 to 10.

Raisin Sauce for Ham

1 cup raisins
¼ cup vinegar
¼ cup packed brown sugar
1 teaspoon mustard
1 teaspoon Worcestershire sauce
1 tablespoon flour
1 tablespoon butter

★ Cook raisins in 1 cup water for 10 minutes over medium heat. Remove from heat and set aside.

★ Combine ½ teaspoon salt and remaining ingredients in bowl and add to raisins. Cook mixture until thick and add butter, if desired. Yields 2½ cups.

Ginger Baby Back Ribs

1 tablespoon butter
1 onion, chopped
1 cup apricot preserves
¼ cup soy sauce
¼ cup honey
3 tablespoons red wine
1 tablespoon fresh grated ginger
1 tablespoon dried orange peel
4 - 5 pounds baby back pork ribs

★ Preheat oven to 375°. Melt butter in saucepan and cook onion until tender, but not brown. Add apricot preserves, soy sauce, honey, wine, ginger and orange peel. Cook and stir constantly until mixture heats thoroughly.

★ Place ribs in large baking pan and pour preserve mixture over ribs. Cover and bake for 30 minutes. Reduce heat to 275° and bake 3 hours to 3 hours 30 minutes or until rib meat is tender. (If ribs have not browned, remove cover and bake for additional 15 minutes.) Serves 6 to 8.

Country Spareribs

4 - 5 pounds pork spareribs
¾ cup ketchup
¼ cup lemon juice
⅓ cup packed brown sugar
1 tablespoon Worcestershire sauce
1½ teaspoons garlic powder
1 teaspoon minced green onion

★ Place ribs in sprayed 9 x 13-inch baking dish. Mix remaining ingredients and 1 teaspoon each of salt and pepper in bowl and pour over ribs. Cover and refrigerate for 24 hours.

★ When ready to cook, preheat oven at 350°. Cook for about 1 hour. Lower heat to 200° and cook for about 3 hours. Turn ribs once while baking and baste with sauce. Serves 6 to 8.

Smoked Baby Back or Country-Style Ribs

The simplicity of this is unbelievable and the flavor is outstanding!

6 - 8 racks baby back or country-style ribs
Sugar

★ Lay out racks of ribs on baking sheets and season with salt and pepper thoroughly. Sprinkle with salt, pepper and sugar. Rub in seasonings and set aside for about 30 minutes.

★ Use charcoal with water-soaked, mesquite or hickory wood chips or mesquite, hickory or oak wood fire and burn to red hot coals without strong flame.

★ Place ribs on grill away from direct fire and cook with heat and smoke of wood. Add wood chips every hour or so. Cook for about 4 to 5 hours. Outside of ribs should be caramelized and crusty, but ribs should be moist. Serves 10 to 12.

TIP: Use barbecue sauce if you particularly like sauce, but this simple combination of salt, pepper and sugar surpasses the slightly sweet, spicy, gooey taste of barbecue sauce. Add barbecue sauce about 30 to 45 minutes before ribs are done so it won't burn.

Education's purpose is to replace an empty mind with an open one.
–Malcolm Forbes

No-Hassle Baby Back Ribs

1 rack baby back ribs
1 bottle favorite barbecue sauce

★ Cut ribs into smaller pieces that fit into roasting pan. Cover ribs with water in roasting pan and boil for about 45 to 50 minutes. Drain and place in sprayed 9 x 13-inch baking dish, coat with favorite barbecue sauce and cover with foil. (Cut into smaller portions if needed.)

★ Refrigerate for several hours or overnight. Bake, covered, at 250° for 3 hours. Remove foil last 10 minutes or so of cooking to brown.

Saucy Ham Loaf

Make this Mustard Sauce the day before you make the Ham Loaf.

Sweet-and-Hot Mustard Sauce:

4 ounces dry mustard
1 cup vinegar
3 eggs, beaten
1 cup sugar

★ Combine mustard and vinegar in bowl and mix until smooth. Set aside overnight. Add eggs and sugar and cook in double boiler and stir constantly for 8 to 10 minutes or until mixture coats spoon. Cool and refrigerate in covered jars.

Ham Loaf:

1 pound ground ham
½ pound ground beef
½ pound ground pork
2 eggs
1 cup bread or cracker crumbs
2 teaspoons Worcestershire sauce
1 (5 ounce) can evaporated milk
3 tablespoons chili sauce
Bacon strips for top of loaf, optional

★ Ask butcher to grind 3 meats together for ham loaf. Preheat oven to 350°. Combine all loaf ingredients except bacon in bowl. Form into loaf in 9 x 13-inch baking pan. Strip bacon on top and bake for 1 hour. Serves 8 to 10.

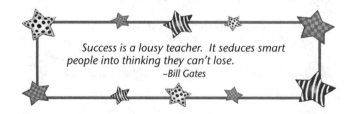

Success is a lousy teacher. It seduces smart people into thinking they can't lose.
–Bill Gates

Classic Hot Tamales

Warm these in a slow cooker and use them as an appetizer.
You'll find the men gathered around the slow cooker.

2 pounds corn husks
16 New Mexico dried red chilies
1 onion, chopped
3 cloves garlic, minced
2 cups meat stock, divided*
3 pounds boneless pork, beef or chicken with stock, cooked, shredded
1 pound lard (no substitute)
3 pounds masa harina
3 tablespoons baking powder

★ (*Use meat stock from cooked pork, beef or chicken.) Wipe silks from corn husks, wash in warm water and dry. Wash dried chilies, remove seeds and stems. Place in saucepan and bring to a boil in water and simmer for about 10 minutes.

★ Pour water and chilies into blender and process. Strain into large bowl to remove pieces of skin. Saute onions and garlic in 1 tablespoon lard or shortening in skillet. Add 2 cups chile sauce mixture, 1 cup broth, 2 tablespoons salt and shredded meats and simmer for about 15 to 20 minutes. If mixture becomes too thick, add more broth.

★ Whip melted lard fluffy. Add masa, 2 tablespoons salt and baking powder. Whip until mixture is light and fluffy. (Masa should float when dropped into glass of cold water.) Add remaining chile sauce and broth and mix well. Masa should be a stirring consistency. Add broth if needed.

★ Place heaping spoonful masa in middle of husk and spread close to top, out to edges and about 1½ inches from bottom. Place 2 spoonfuls filling on top of masa and spread top to bottom.

★ Roll husk and fold up bottom 1½ inches. Place in baking dish with fold facing down. Repeat process until all filling is used. Stack tamales upright in slow cooker with folded end down. Pour a little water in bottom, cover and steam on HIGH for 3 to 4 hours or until tamales unroll from husks. Yields about 36 tamales.

Why do I have to follow CNN on Twitter? If I
want to follow CNN, I can follow them on CNN.
–Jon Stewart

Easy Chorizo Sausage

This traditional spicy, pork sausage is used in casseroles, stews, soups and enchilada and huevos (egg) dishes. This homemade version is much better than prepared chorizos sold in stores.

4 - 6 New Mexico dried red chilies
2 - 3 cloves garlic, minced
1 teaspoon ground cumin
1 pound ground pork
1 pound ground beef
¼ cup tequila

★ Mix all ingredients plus ¾ teaspoon salt in large bowl. Use hands to blend 2 meats and seasonings. When mixture is same color throughout, roll into 2 big balls, cover and refrigerate for several hours or overnight. Freeze any unused chorizo.

Sausage Souffle

8 slices white bread, cubed
2 cups shredded sharp cheddar cheese
1½ pounds link sausage cut in thirds
4 eggs
2¼ cups milk
¾ teaspoon dry mustard
1 (10 ounce) can cream of mushroom soup
½ cup milk

★ Place bread cubes in sprayed 9 x 13-inch baking dish and top with cheese. Brown sausage in skillet and drain. Place sausage on top of cheese.

★ Beat eggs with milk and mustard in bowl and pour over sausage. Cover and refrigerate overnight. When ready to bake, preheat oven to 300°.

★ Dilute soup with milk and pour over bread and sausage. Bake for 1 hour or until set. Serves 8 to 10.

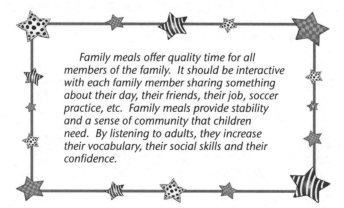

Family meals offer quality time for all members of the family. It should be interactive with each family member sharing something about their day, their friends, their job, soccer practice, etc. Family meals provide stability and a sense of community that children need. By listening to adults, they increase their vocabulary, their social skills and their confidence.

Party Pizza

1 pound ground sausage
1 (14 ounce) jar pizza sauce
1½ teaspoon oregano
¼ teaspoon garlic powder
1 cup chopped onion
½ cup shredded parmesan cheese
½ cup grated mozzarella cheese
1 (10 inch) pizza crust

★ In medium skillet cook and drain sausage and set aside. To pizza sauce, add oregano and garlic powder. Spread pizza sauce evenly over pizza crust. Sprinkle sausage, onion, parmesan cheese and mozzarella cheese on top of pizza sauce. Bake at 350° until cheese melts and pizza is bubbly on top. Serves 2.

Variation:

★ Add pepperoni slices, ground beef, Canadian bacon slices, green olives, black olives, bell pepper, mushrooms, jalapenos, pineapple, ham and/or anchovies.

Bratwurst Heroes

1 (6 - 8 count) package bratwurst sausages
Hot dog buns
1 cup prepared marinara sauce
1 (8 ounce) jar roasted bell peppers
6 - 8 slices pepper Jack cheese

★ Heat bratwurst on grill until hot and turn frequently. When brats are just about done, toast buns cut side down on grill.

★ Heat marinara sauce in saucepan and place brats on toasted buns. Layer bell peppers, marinara sauce and cheese over bratwurst. Serves 6 to 8.

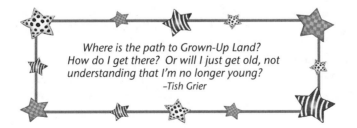

Where is the path to Grown-Up Land?
How do I get there? Or will I just get old, not
understanding that I'm no longer young?
–Tish Grier

Summertime Brats

6 pork or beef bratwursts or Italian sausages
Olive oil
2 Vidalia® or 1015 Texas SuperSweet onions, sliced
½ (12 ounce) can or bottle dark beer
Buns

★ Cook sausages in large skillet with a little olive oil until brown on outside. Drain on paper towels.

★ Saute onions in a little olive oil in same skillet until translucent. Place sausages back in skillet. Pour in beer, cover and cook on medium for about 20 minutes or until liquid thickens to syrup consistency. Serve immediately on buns. Serves 4 to 6.

Undercover Dogs

1 large onion, thinly sliced
1 tablespoon olive oil
2 (12 ounce) bottles or cans beer
4 cooked pork or beef bratwurst
1 tablespoon dijon-style mustard
4 (8 inch) flour tortillas, warmed
4 slices cheddar cheese

★ Saute onion in oil in large skillet on medium-low heat for 3 to 5 minutes or until onions are translucent. Pour beer into saucepan and bring almost to boil. Add bratwurst, cover and cook for 5 minutes, but do not boil. (Beer will turn bitter if boiled.)

★ Drain bratwurst and grill over medium heat until brown; turn occasionally. Spread mustard on tortillas and place cheese, onions and bratwurst on tortilla and roll up. Serve immediately. Serves 4.

Sauerkraut and Kielbasa

2 (16 ounce) cans sauerkraut
2 (12 ounce) cans beer
1 tablespoon light brown sugar
1 (1 pound) package kielbasa sausage, sliced

★ Wash sauerkraut thoroughly and drain in colander. Place in large saucepan and pour beer over top. (Make sure beer more than covers sauerkraut.) Add brown sugar and stir.

★ Cook over high heat until it boils. Reduce heat and simmer for 1 hour 15 minutes. Place sausage in sauerkraut and cook for additional 15 to 20 minutes. Drain sauerkraut and serve hot. Serves 4.

Low Country Boil

3 pounds kielbasa or link sausage
4 potatoes with peels
3 onions
3 cups cut green beans, drained

★ Cut sausage into bite-size pieces. Wash potatoes and peel onions. Place sausage, potatoes, whole onions and green beans into large stockpot, cover with water and boil until potatoes are tender. Season according to your own taste. Serves 8 to 10.

Main Dishes – Seafood

Easy Breezy Salmon or Trout on a Plank

If you haven't tried cooking on a western red cedar or alder plank, you're missing a treat.

¾ cup (1½ sticks) butter, softened
⅓ cup snipped fresh basil
4 - 5 cloves garlic, minced or crushed
1 (2 pound) skinless salmon fillet

★ Soak cedar plank for about 30 minutes, turn plank over and soak for additional 30 minutes. Prepare charcoal grill while cedar plank is soaking. Mix butter, basil and garlic in small bowl and spread it on both sides of salmon.

★ When coals are hot, but not flaming, place salmon on plank and plank on grill. Close lid and cook about 5 minutes. Check plank to make sure it's not burning and fire to make sure it's not too hot. (Use spray bottle with water to douse plank if it catches on fire.)

★ Add a little salt and pepper on both sides and turn salmon to cook other side. Check again after 5 minutes or so and cook until salmon flakes, but is still moist inside. Cooking time varies with fire. Serves 3 to 4.

Favorite Salmon Croquettes

What shape are your croquettes? Are they round logs, flat patties or triangular-shaped logs? No matter how you shape them, these are great!

1 (15 ounce) can salmon
¼ cup shrimp cocktail sauce or chili sauce
1 (10 ounce) can cream of chicken soup, divided
1 egg
½ onion, finely chopped
Several dashes hot sauce
1⅓ cups cracker crumbs
Flour
Vegetable oil

★ Drain salmon well in colander and remove skin and bones. Combine salmon, ½ teaspoon each of salt and pepper, cocktail sauce, half soup, egg, onion, hot sauce and cracker crumbs in bowl and mix well.

★ Pat mixture into logs with 3 sides about 3 inches long and roll in flour. Make about 10 to 12 logs.

★ Pour just enough oil in large skillet to cover bottom. Turn to medium heat, place croquettes in skillet and fry. Turn twice so you have 3 sides that brown. (Add extra oil halfway through cooking if needed.)

★ It will take about 15 minutes to fry on 3 sides. (Of course you could deep-fry croquettes if you want.) Serves 6 to 8.

TIP: Use remaining cream of chicken soup by diluting with equal amount of milk and have a cup of soup as an appetizer.

Pacific Northwest Salmon Burgers

1 pound fresh cooked salmon
1 egg, slightly beaten
¼ cup lemon juice
⅔ cup seasoned breadcrumbs
Hamburger buns
Mayonnaise
Lettuce
Sliced tomatoes

★ In bowl, combine salmon, 2 tablespoons salmon liquid, egg, lemon juice, breadcrumbs and a little salt and pepper. Form into patties and cook in a little oil on both sides until golden. Serve hot on buns with mayonnaise, lettuce and sliced tomatoes.

TIP: If you can't get fresh salmon, use 1 (15 ounce) can salmon with liquid.

 Salmon Capital of the World   Ketchican, Alaska

Deep-Fried Steelhead

Steelhead trout are also known as freshwater salmon.

Steelhead fillets
Milk
Garlic salt
Eggs, beaten
Flour
Instant potato flakes
Canola oil

★ Soak fillets in milk overnight. Season with a little garlic salt and pepper.
Dip fillets into eggs and dredge through flour.

★ Roll fillets in potato flakes and carefully drop into hot oil in deep fryer.
Fry until golden brown. Drain and serve hot.

Grilled Fish

1 whole, cleaned fish (about 1 pound)
Onion, minced
Celery, diced
Parsley, snipped
Fresh garlic cloves, minced
Butter
Bacon

★ Use these basic ingredients with any size fish. Fill cavity of fish with
onion, celery, parsley, garlic and butter and season with a little salt
and pepper.

★ Wrap entire fish with bacon slices. Wrap several times in heavy-duty foil
to prevent any leakage. Cook over hot charcoal fire for about 20 minutes
on each side. The larger the fish, the longer it will need to cook. Serves 2.

Easy Grilled Salmon

1 (2 - 4 pound) whole salmon fillet
Garlic powder
1 cup packed brown sugar
½ cup apple cider vinegar
½ cup honey
Liquid smoke

★ Lightly season fillet with garlic powder. Combine ingredients for basting
sauce. Baste one side generously and place on grill, basted side down.
Baste side up and cook for about 5 minutes. Baste generously again.

★ Turn with tongs and spatula or in fish cooker rack. Don't puncture fish.

★ Baste top sides and cook about 3 to 5 minutes or until fish is barely
translucent in center. (Over cooking will dry out fish.) Serves 8 to 12.

Brook Trout Wrapped in Foil

1 onion, sliced
1 rib celery, chopped
1 carrot, chopped
¼ teaspoon thyme
1 bay leaf
3 sprigs parsley, snipped
2 (12 ounce) brook trout, dressed
½ cup wine
2 teaspoons butter
⅓ cup half-and-half cream
2 teaspoons flour

★ Preheat oven to 400°.

★ Make pouch out of heavy-duty foil large enough for vegetables and fish. Place onion, celery, carrot, thyme, bay leaf and parsley on first. Place trout on top and pour wine over fish.

★ Seal foil pouch so no liquids escape. Place in sprayed baking dish and cook for about 20 to 30 minutes until fish flakes, but is not dry.

★ A few minutes before fish is ready, melt butter in saucepan over low heat. Add half-and-half cream and flour slowly and whisk to dissolve lumps. Remove from heat and pour liquid from pouch into saucepan.

★ Whisk into sauce, add vegetables and pour over fish. Serve immediately. Serves 3 to 4.

Baked Rainbow Trout

1 pound trout fillets
3 tablespoons plus ¼ cup butter, divided
1 teaspoon tarragon
2 teaspoons capers
2 tablespoons lemon juice

★ Preheat oven to 375°.

★ Place fish fillets with 3 tablespoons butter in sprayed shallow pan and sprinkle with salt and pepper.

★ Bake for about 6 to 8 minutes, turn and bake until fish flakes. (Do not overcook.)

★ For sauce, melt ¼ cup butter with tarragon, capers and lemon juice in saucepan and serve over warm fish. Serves 4 to 6.

Rainbow Trout Skillet

2 (1 pound) rainbow trout fillets
½ cup (1 stick) plus 3 tablespoons butter, divided
10 - 12 large cloves garlic, minced
3 small green onions with tops, minced
3 tablespoons white wine
1 egg, lightly beaten
1 - 3 tablespoons canola oil
1 lemon, sliced

★ Wash and pat dry trout fillets and set aside. Melt ½ cup butter in skillet and saute garlic and green onions over medium heat until they are translucent. Add white wine and simmer while fish cooks.

★ Beat egg slightly with 1 tablespoon water in bowl and dip each fillet into egg mixture.

★ In separate skillet, heat a little oil and 1 tablespoon butter and place fillets to cook over medium heat.

★ Turn once, add 1 to 2 tablespoons butter, if needed, and remove when fish flakes in thickest part. Arrange on platter, keep fish warm and pour warm garlic sauce over fish just before serving. Garnish with lemon slices. Serves 2.

Grilled Tuna with Salsa

1 red bell pepper
1 yellow bell pepper
1 large sweet onion, minced
4 - 5 cloves garlic, minced
1 teaspoon extra-virgin olive oil
¼ cup snipped cilantro
1 lemon or lime
4 - 6 tuna steaks

★ Remove seeds and veins from bell peppers. Chop peppers, mix with all remaining ingredients except fish and squeeze some lemon juice over all. Add a little salt and pepper. Wrap in foil and cook with tuna.

★ Cook tuna steaks on each side for about 3 minutes over hot coals or until grill marks show. Check center of steaks and remove from grill just when pink in center is almost gone. Do not overcook and dry out fish. Serve hot with salsa on top. Serves 4 to 6.

Tuna Toast

1 (10 ounce) can cream of chicken soup
1 (6 ounce) can tuna in water, drained
2 slices thick Texas toast
1 tomato, cubed

★ Combine soup, ½ soup can water and tuna in saucepan and stir to break
up chunks of tuna. Brown Texas toast on both sides. Pour soup mixture
over toast. Sprinkle tomatoes over soup mixture. Serve immediately.
Serves 4.

Tuna Fish Sandwich

1 (6½ ounce) can flaked white tuna, drained
2 eggs, hard-boiled, chopped
2 tablespoons sweet relish
¼ cup chopped onion
3 tablespoons mayonnaise
4 slices sandwich bread

★ Combine tuna, eggs, relish, onion, relish and mayonnaise; mix well.
Toast four slices sandwich bread. Spread tuna mixture on two pieces of
toast and cover with another slice of toast. Serves 2.

Tuna-Noodle Casserole

1 (7 ounce) package elbow macaroni
1 (8 ounce) package shredded Velveeta® cheese
2 (6 ounce) cans tuna, drained
1 (10 ounce) can cream of celery soup
1 cup milk

★ Preheat oven to 350°. Cook macaroni according to package directions.
Drain well, add cheese and stir until cheese melts.

★ Add tuna, celery soup and milk and continue stirring. Spoon into
sprayed 7 x 11-inch baking dish. Cover and bake 35 minutes or until
bubbly. Serves 4.

Beware the young doctor and the old barber.
–Benjamin Franklin

Easy Tuna Casserole

1 (10 ounce) can condensed cream of celery or mushroom soup
¼ cup milk
2 eggs, hard-boiled, sliced
1 cup cooked green peas
1 (8 ounce) can tuna packed in water, drained, flaked
½ cup crushed potato chips

★ Preheat oven to 350°. Blend soup and milk in 1-quart baking dish. Stir
   in eggs, peas and tuna. Bake for 25 minutes or until hot throughout.
   Stir and top with potato chips; bake additional 5 minutes. Serves 4.

Lemon-Dill Halibut or Cod

½ cup mayonnaise
2 tablespoons lemon juice
½ teaspoon grated lemon peel
1 teaspoon dill weed
1 pound halibut fillets

★ Combine mayonnaise, lemon juice, lemon peel and dill weed in bowl
   and mix until they blend well. Place fish on sprayed grill or broiler rack.
   Brush with half sauce.

★ Grill or broil for 5 to 8 minutes, turn and brush with remaining sauce.
   Continue grilling or broiling for 5 to 8 minutes or until fish flakes easily
   with fork. Serves 4.

Baked Cod Fillets

*Cape Cod got its name from the abundance of cod in the
area. You can use any kind of white fish in this recipe.*

1 pound fish fillets
3 tablespoons butter
1 teaspoon tarragon
2 teaspoons capers
2 tablespoons lemon juice

★ Preheat oven to 375°. Place fish fillets in sprayed shallow pan and
   sprinkle with salt and pepper. Bake for about 8 to 10 minutes, turn and
   bake for additional 6 minutes or until fish flakes.

★ For sauce, melt butter with tarragon, capers and lemon juice in
   saucepan and serve over warm fish. Serves 3 to 4.

 Flounder Capital of the World   Wachapreague, Virginia

Bay Red Snapper

1 (8 ounce) can tomato sauce
1 (4 ounce) can diced green chilies
1 clove garlic, minced
1 pound red snapper fillets

★ Mix tomato sauce, green chilies and garlic in small bowl. Put snapper fillets on microwave-safe dish and brush tomato sauce mixture evenly over red snapper. Cover with plastic wrap.

★ Microwave on HIGH for about 3 minutes, rotate dish and microwave for 2 minutes. Check snapper to see if it flakes easily. If not, microwave for additional 2 minutes and check to see if meat is flaky. Serves 4.

Seaside Red Snapper

1 (3 - 5 pound) whole butterflied red snapper
½ cup (1 stick) butter, melted
Flour
Sea salt
Cracked black pepper
Fresh dill weed
3 - 4 tablespoons white wine
1 cucumber, sliced

★ Preheat oven to 350°.

★ Rinse and pat dry inside and outside of red snapper. Brush melted butter on inside and outside of snapper, but set aside some for later.

★ Sprinkle flour, sea salt and black pepper on inside and outside of snapper thoroughly. Place fresh dill weed inside fish and close.

★ Pour white wine in sprayed baking dish. Carefully lay snapper in dish and bake for 20 minutes. Remove dish from oven, baste with set aside butter and add a little more white wine, if needed.

★ Return to oven and bake for additional 20 to 25 minutes or until fish flakes. Remove dill weed. Carefully place whole snapper on serving plate and garnish with cucumber slices and dashes of paprika. Serves 8.

I never did give them hell. I just told the truth and they thought it was hell.
–Harry S Truman

Rockfish Flounder

1 (2 - 3 pound) whole flounder
3 or more strips bacon
4 medium potatoes
2 - 4 onions
1 (8 ounce) can tomato sauce
1 lemon, cut in wedges

★ Preheat oven to 325°. Salt fish on both sides and cut slits on top. Place
in sprayed glass baking dish. With knife blade, press strips of bacon into
slits. Bake until fish browns. Remove from oven.

★ Steam potatoes and onion until tender and arrange ring of potatoes and
onion over baked fish. Pour tomato sauce and enough water over fish to
keep it moist. (Use water from onions and potatoes. Make sure water is
still warm.) Add pepper, as desired.

★ Return dish to oven and bake for 20 minutes or until done. Baste once.
Garnish dish with lemon wedges and parsley before serving. Serves 6 to 8.

Baked Flounder

This works with most fish fillets.

½ cup fine dry breadcrumbs
¼ cup grated parmesan cheese
¼ teaspoon seasoned salt
1 pound flounder
⅓ cup mayonnaise

★ Preheat oven to 375°. In shallow dish combine crumbs, cheese and
seasoned salt. Brush both sides of fish with mayonnaise. Coat with
crumb mixture.

★ Arrange in single layer in shallow baking pan and bake for 20 to
25 minutes or until fish flakes easily. Serves 2 to 3.

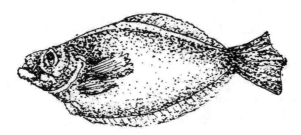

Easy Grilled Stripers

¾ cup minced onion
¾ cup finely chopped mushrooms
½ cup minced celery
1 teaspoon oil
1½ - 2 pounds striped bass fillets
1 lemon
1 tomato, sliced
Butter

★ Preheat grill. Wrap onion, mushrooms and celery in foil with oil until onions are translucent. Add a little salt and pepper and mix. At the same time place sheet of foil over grill and place striper fillets.

★ Coat with butter and garlic powder and cook about 3 to 5 minutes per side. (Don't overcook.) Squeeze a little lemon juice over fillets. Place tomato slices on top after fillets are turned and salt and pepper lightly. Cook until fillets are opaque and flake easily. Serves 4 to 6.

Unbeatable Fried Catfish

8 - 10 catfish fillets
2 cups crushed cracker crumbs or cornmeal
⅓ cup flour
1 cup buttermilk*
Canola oil

★ Dry fish with paper towels and sprinkle with a little salt and pepper. Mix cracker crumbs or cornmeal and flour in bowl.

★ Dip fillets in buttermilk and in crumb mixture and make sure both sides have lots of batter. Heat about ½-inch of oil in skillet and fry fish until light brown and crisp. Serves 4 to 6.

*TIP: To make buttermilk, mix 1 cup milk with 1 tablespoon lemon juice or vinegar and let stand for about 10 minutes.

Lake House Fried Fish

1½ pounds fish fillets
Beer
¾ cup cornmeal
½ cup flour
Shortening or canola oil

★ Dip fillets in beer, then in mixture of cornmeal, flour, ½ teaspoon each of salt and pepper and coat well.

★ Deep fry in oil for 3 to 4 minutes or pan fry at high heat until golden brown. Turn pan-fried fish once. Serves 4.

Crisp Oven-Fried Fish

¼ cup milk
1 egg, beaten
1 cup corn flake crumbs
¼ cup parmesan cheese
2 pounds fish fillets
⅓ cup (⅔ stick) butter, melted
Lemon slices or wedges

★ Preheat oven to 425°. Combine milk and egg in shallow dish. In separate shallow dish, combine corn flake crumbs and cheese.

★ Dip fillets in milk-egg mixture, roll in crumb-cheese mixture and place side-by-side in sprayed baking dish. Set aside leftover crumb-cheese mixture. Drizzle with melted butter over fish.

★ Pour remaining crumb-cheese mixture over top and bake for 12 to 15 minutes. Serve with lemon slices. Serves 6 to 8.

Marinated Swordfish

½ cup extra virgin olive oil
2 cloves fresh garlic chopped
¼ cup chopped fresh basil
½ cup chopped onion
4 (½ pound) swordfish fillets
Lime

★ Combine oil, garlic, basil and onion in bowl. Mix well. Add swordfish to marinade and coat steaks well. Cover bowl and marinate in refrigerator for 2 to 4 hours.

★ Grill steaks on medium high for 4 to 5 minutes (if steaks are thick) on each side or until firm to the touch. Don't overcook swordfish; it will dry out. Squeeze lime juice over top before plating. Serves 4.

Red Fish Barbecue

2 pounds red fish fillets
1 (8 ounce) bottle Italian dressing
1 (12 ounce) can beer
Several dashes hot sauce

★ Place fish in glass baking dish. Pour Italian dressing, beer and hot sauce over fish. Cover and marinate in refrigerator for at least 2 hours. When ready to cook, drain fish, discard marinade and place in microwave-safe dish. Microwave fish for about 4 to 5 minutes per pound and rotate plate. Serves 8.

Swordfish-Bacon Kebabs

1 (1 pound) ½- inch thick swordfish steak
2 teaspoons minced garlic
1 tablespoon lemon juice
1 tablespoon olive oil
8 slices bacon
12 cherry tomatoes

★ Cut fish into 2-inch pieces and combine in shallow bowl with garlic, lemon juice and oil. Cover and place in refrigerator; marinate for about 20 minutes.

★ Cook bacon on medium heat until soft, but not crisp. Drain and reserve pan drippings. Cut bacon into 2-inch pieces. Thread swordfish, bacon and tomatoes on to 4 (10 inch) skewers. Brush kebabs with reserved bacon drippings.

★ Grill on rack about 6 inches above hot coals for about 4 minutes. Turn kebabs and grill another 4 minutes or until swordfish cooks through. Serve immediately. Serves 2 to 3.

Easy Fish Tacos

¾ pound boned white fish
2 tablespoons lime juice
Garlic powder
Canola oil
6 - 8 corn tortillas
Shredded lettuce
Finely chopped tomatoes
Salsa

★ Season fish with lime juice and garlic powder. Cook fish with a little oil in skillet for about 2 to 3 minutes on each side until fish flakes easily. Shred each piece of fish and set aside.

★ Wrap about 5 tortillas in slightly damp paper towel and heat tortillas in microwave for 45 seconds. Repeat for remaining tortillas for about 30 seconds.

★ When ready to serve, place about 2 tablespoons shredded fish, lettuce and tomatoes in tortilla and fold over. Serve with salsa. Yields about 6 to 8 fish tacos.

Use only fish from the best schools.

Lemon-Baked Fish

1 pound sole or halibut fillets
¼ cup (½ stick) butter, melted, divided
1 teaspoon dried tarragon
2 tablespoons lemon juice

★ Preheat oven to 375°. Place fish fillets in sprayed, shallow pan. Sprinkle with a little salt, pepper and butter. Bake for 8 to 10 minutes. Turn and bake for additional 6 minutes or until fish flakes. Combine remaining butter with tarragon and lemon juice. Serve over warm fish fillets. Serves 4.

Seafood Batters

Batters create a crunchy crust on the outside and moist inside when pan-fried or deep-fried. Batters also vary by region or family tradition.

Simple Basic Batter

★ Sprinkle a little salt and pepper in flour and dredge seafood in it to coat. Shake off excess flour and fry. You can substitute breadcrumbs, cracker crumbs or cornmeal for the flour. Carefully place in hot oil, cook and drain on paper towels.

Beer Batter

1 cup flour
8 ounces beer

★ Sprinkle a little salt and pepper in flour in bowl and mix with beer. Add a little more flour or beer to get the consistency you like. Dip seafood in batter and pan-fry or deep-fry in hot oil. Drain on paper towels.

3-Step Seafood Batter

Flour
1 egg, beaten
Breadcrumbs or seasoned breadcrumbs

★ Sprinkle a little salt and pepper in flour in bowl. Dip seafood in beaten egg and then in flour. Roll seafood in breadcrumbs and fry in hot oil. Drain on paper towels.

 Catfish Capital of the World   Belzoni, Mississippi

Spicy Seafood Batter

1 cup flour
1 cup cornmeal
1 tablespoon garlic salt
2 cups milk
1 tablespoon cayenne pepper
1 tablespoon hot sauce

★ Mix flour and cornmeal with a little garlic salt and pepper in bowl. In separate bowl, mix milk, cayenne pepper and hot sauce.

★ Dip seafood into flour and shake once to remove excess flour. Transfer seafood to milk mixture and cover all sides. Dredge seafood through flour again, dust off excess and fry in hot oil.

Tempura Batter

⅔ cup flour
⅓ cup cornmeal
1 tablespoon baking powder
1 egg, beaten

★ Mix flour, cornmeal, baking powder and a little salt and pepper in bowl. In separate bowl, add 1 cup ice water to egg and whip to mix. Dredge seafood in ice water-egg mixture and coat with flour-cornmeal mixture. Fry in hot oil.

Boiled Lobsters

4 - 5 (1½ pounds) live lobsters
1 tablespoon sea salt
½ - 1 cup (1- 2 sticks) butter
2 lemons, sliced

★ Cook lobsters in large pot with enough water to cover lobster. Add several tablespoons sea salt to water and bring to rolling boil.

★ Place lobsters in boiling water and cover. Boil until lobsters turn bright red. Remove from water, drain and cool before handling. Twist and pull off claws and legs and set aside.

★ Twist and pull tail from body. Lay lobster upside down in palm of hand to expose underbelly. Cut soft shell up the middle and remove meat. Bend claws and legs in half and remove meat with lobster or nut pick or any tool that will fit into the shell. Serves 4.

Steamed Lobsters

1 onion, quartered
3 ribs celery, quartered
2 tablespoons pickling spice
1½ cups (3 sticks) butter, melted
2 (1 pound) live lobster

★ Cover vegetables, pickling spice and 1 teaspoon salt with at least 2 to 3 inches water in large soup pot. Bring to a rolling boil. Place lobster in steamer basket, add to pot and cover tightly.

★ Steam for about 10 to 15 minutes. Add water, if needed. Check for doneness with small claw. Serve with melted butter. Serves 4.

TIP: If you want to kill lobsters before putting them into a steamer, make a large cut from 1½ inches behind eyes to between eyes and through head.

Classic Maine Lobster Rolls

1 pound fully cooked lobster meat
⅔ cup mayonnaise
2 - 3 small green onions, thinly sliced
1 rib celery, chopped
1 tablespoon finely chopped dill pickle
4 New England-style buns
4 tablespoons unsalted butter, softened
4 Boston lettuce leaves, washed, dried

★ Combine lobster meat, mayonnaise, scallions, celery, pickle, dash of salt and pepper in large bowl and mix well. Heat buns spread with butter in heavy skillet to warm. Spread buns with lobster salad and add lettuce leaf. Serve immediately. Serves 4.

TIP: This recipe is wonderful stuffed in a hollowed out tomato as a light entree.

Hush puppies made of cornmeal are a welcome accompaniment to a fish meal. Hush puppies are said to have originated when hunters threw pan scraps to their dogs to keep them quiet.

Crab Angel Pasta

½ cup (1 stick) butter
½ onion, finely chopped
1 bell pepper, seeded, chopped
1 teaspoon dried parsley flakes
1 teaspoon dried basil
1 teaspoon celery salt
1 teaspoon lemon pepper
2 (16 ounce) cans diced tomatoes
1 (16 ounce) can Italian stewed tomatoes
½ cup dry white wine
1 pound cooked crabmeat or lobster
1 pound angel hair pasta, cooked
Freshly grated parmesan cheese

★ Melt butter in large saucepan and sauté onion and bell pepper. Stir in parsley, basil, celery salt, lemon pepper and tomatoes and bring to a boil. Add wine and simmer for 5 minutes.

★ Add crabmeat and simmer for 2 minutes. Place warm pasta in serving dish and top with crab mixture. Serve with parmesan cheese. Serves 6 to 8.

Seaside Stuffed Crab

¼ bell pepper, seeded, finely diced
1 small onion, finely diced
2 ribs celery, finely diced
¼ cup (½ stick) butter
8 ounces lump crabmeat
1 tablespoon marinade for chicken
1 tablespoon ketchup
1 (8 ounce) carton whipping cream
1 cup seasoned breadcrumbs
Crab shells

★ Preheat oven to 350°. Saute bell pepper, onion and celery in butter in saucepan and set aside. Combine remaining ingredients (except shells) in bowl and add onion-celery mixture. Spoon into crab shells and bake for 30 to 35 minutes. Serves 2 to 4.

Let us resolve to be masters, not victims, of our history, controlling our own destiny without giving way to blind suspicions and emotions.
–John F. Kennedy

East Coast Crab Cakes

1 pound crabmeat
1 large egg, lightly beaten
2 tablespoons minced onion
2 tablespoons mayonnaise
1 tablespoon Worcestershire sauce
1 tablespoon mustard
½ - ¾ teaspoons hot sauce
½ teaspoon freshly ground pepper
¾ cup buttery cracker crumbs
Vegetable oil

★ Combine 1 teaspoon salt and remaining ingredients except cracker crumbs and oil in bowl and mix well. Place cracker crumbs in shallow bowl.

★ Shape crab mixture into 6 patties and roll in cracker crumbs. Fry in skillet for about 3 minutes on each side. Drain. Serves 6.

Elegant Crab Quiche

Easy and delicious.

1 cup shredded Swiss cheese
1 (9 inch) refrigerated piecrust
5 eggs
1½ cups milk or half-and-half cream
½ cup sliced mushrooms
1 (6 ounce) can crabmeat

★ Preheat oven to 375°. Sprinkle cheese into piecrust. Beat eggs in bowl and mix with milk, ½ teaspoon and ⅛ teaspoon pepper.

★ Pour over cheese in piecrust and sprinkle with mushrooms and crabmeat. Bake for 35 to 55 minutes until firm. Serves 6.

Deviled Crab

¼ cup minced, seeded green bell pepper
¼ cup minced onion
1 cup diced celery
1 teaspoon Worcestershire
2 (6 ounce) cans crab meat, drained, flaked
2 cups herb-seasoned stuffing, crushed
1 cup mayonnaise

★ Preheat oven to 350°. Mix all ingredients and spoon into 8 oven-proof shells. Bake for 30 minutes or until tops brown slightly. Serves 6.

Crab Cake Capital of the World   Baltimore, Maryland

Crab Louis

This terrific crab dish is easy and a people-pleaser.

1 (10 ounce) can cream of celery soup
½ cup chili sauce
¼ cup mayonnaise
2 tablespoons minced onion
¼ cup whipping cream, whipped
4 cups cooked flaked crab meat
4 eggs, hard-boiled
2 tomatoes

★ Mix soup, chili sauce, mayonnaise, onion and a little pepper and fold in
  whipped cream. Add crab meat and refrigerate. Place crab on bed of
  lettuce. Garnish with egg and tomato wedges. Serves about 4.

Seacoast Crab Devils

2 tablespoons butter
3 tablespoons flour
1 cup chicken broth
⅓ cup whipping cream
⅛ teaspoon cayenne pepper
2 egg yolks
1 (4 ounce) can sliced mushrooms
1 tablespoon dried parsley
2 (6 ounce) cans crabmeat, well-drained, flaked
6 crab shells or ramekins
⅓ cup seasoned breadcrumbs

★ Preheat oven to 350°. Melt butter in skillet over medium heat. Slowly
  mix in flour, broth and cream and stir well. Add ½ teaspoon salt,
  cayenne pepper and egg yolks and continue to stir and cook until thick.

★ Add mushrooms, parsley and crabmeat to mixture and blend well. Pour
  into lightly buttered shells or ramekins. Cover with breadcrumbs and
  bake for 10 minutes or until light brown. Serves 6.

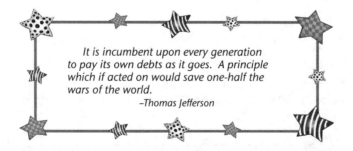

*It is incumbent upon every generation
to pay its own debts as it goes. A principle
which if acted on would save one-half the
wars of the world.*
–Thomas Jefferson

Crabmeat Delight

2 tablespoons chopped green bell pepper
2 tablespoons butter
2 tablespoons flour
Dash cayenne pepper
½ teaspoon mustard
½ teaspoon Worcestershire sauce
1 cup chopped tomatoes, drained
1 cup shredded cheddar cheese
1 egg, slightly beaten
1⅔ cups scalded milk
1 cup flaked crabmeat
6 patty shells or toasted rounds

★ Brown bell pepper in butter in saucepan and add flour and mix until smooth. Combine cayenne pepper, mustard, Worcestershire, ¼ teaspoon salt, tomatoes, cheese and egg in bowl and add to bell pepper mixture.

★ Cook mixture in double boiler for 10 minutes. Stir constantly and add milk slowly. Add crabmeat and heat thoroughly. Serve on patty shells or toast rounds. Serves 6.

Aunt Edna's Crabmeat Casserole

Don't let the number of ingredients discourage you.
This is just as easy as it can be.

½ cup chopped celery
½ cup chopped green bell pepper
¼ cup chopped onion
Butter
1 pound crabmeat
3 - 4 eggs, hard-boiled, chopped
1½ cups seasoned breadcrumbs
1 cup mayonnaise
1 tablespoon dry mustard
1 tablespoon vinegar
1 tablespoon lemon juice
1 tablespoon dry horseradish
½ cup white wine
½ cup buttered breadcrumbs
Paprika

★ Preheat oven to 350°. Saute celery, green pepper and onion with butter in skillet until tender but not brown.

★ Combine all ingredients except buttered breadcrumbs and paprika in sprayed 1½-quart baking dish.

★ Top with buttered breadcrumbs and sprinkle with paprika. Bake for 20 minutes or until it is thoroughly hot. Serves 6 to 8.

Crab Casserole

1 pound fresh mushrooms
Butter
2 pounds crabmeat, flaked
2 cups mayonnaise
1 (1 pint) carton whipping cream
2 tablespoons chopped onion
2 tablespoons parsley
4 eggs, hard-boiled, diced
1 (6 ounce) package herb stuffing mix

★ Preheat oven to 350°. Slice and saute mushrooms in butter in saucepan. Mix all ingredients in bowl, but save a little stuffing to be used for topping.

★ Pour in sprayed 9 x 13-inch pan and top with remaining stuffing mix. Bake for 40 minutes. Serves 8 to 10.

King Crab Casserole

1 (10 ounce) package frozen broccoli spears or asparagus
½ cup shredded sharp cheddar cheese
6 tablespoons (¾ stick) butter, divided
2 tablespoons minced onion
2 tablespoons flour
¼ teaspoon curry powder
1 cup milk
1 tablespoon lemon juice
1 (6 ounce) package frozen king crab, thawed, drained
2 slices bread

★ Preheat oven to 350°. Cook broccoli or asparagus according to package directions and drain. Arrange in sprayed 8 x 8-inch baking dish and sprinkle cheese over top.

★ Melt ¼ cup butter in saucepan, add onions and saute until soft. Add flour, curry powder, ½ teaspoon salt and milk and stir constantly until thick. Stir in lemon juice and crab. Pour heated mixture over broccoli or asparagus.

★ Spread 2 tablespoons butter over bread and cut into cubes. Sprinkle over crab mixture and bake for 30 minutes. Serves 8.

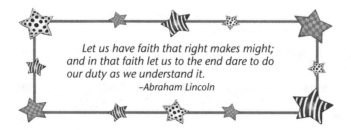

Let us have faith that right makes might; and in that faith let us to the end dare to do our duty as we understand it.
–Abraham Lincoln

California Sushi Rolls

4 nori sheets
1 tablespoon wasabi powder
2 seedless cucumbers
2 avocados
2 Alaska king crab legs, thawed
Lemon juice
3 cups cooked sushi rice
¼ cup sesame seeds, toasted
Soy sauce
Wasabi
Ginger

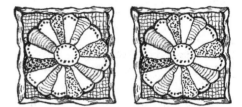

★ Hold nori sheets over high heat with tongs and dry roast until pieces turn green. Place 1 sheet on sudare or bamboo mat. Mix wasabi powder with 1 tablespoon water in bowl to make paste.

★ Peel cucumbers, avocados and crab and slice into thin strips. Sprinkle a little lemon juice over avocados. Spread ¾ cup sushi rice over nori sheet and leave 1 inch bare at far side making small ledge of rice. Spread about 1 teaspoon wasabi paste down center of rice.

★ Sprinkle one-fourth of sesame seeds evenly over rice. Lay one-fourth of crab meat on side closest to you. Lay one-fourth of cucumber and one-fourth avocado firmly next to it. Roll mat over once away from you, but leave 1 inch nori sheet sticking out.

★ Press ingredients together to make roll firm and tight. Press mat to tighten roll. Remove mat, again press roll to make it tight and form circle or square. Cut into bite-size pieces and serve with soy sauce, wasabi and ginger. Yields 4 rolls and about 32 pieces.

Deep-Fried Shrimp

1 cup milk
2 eggs, beaten
1½ cups flour
2 teaspoons seasoned salt
1 - 1½ pounds medium shrimp, peeled, veined
About 40 saltine crackers, heavily crushed
Canola oil
Cocktail sauce

★ Combine milk and eggs in shallow bowl. In separate shallow bowl, combine flour and seasoned salt. Place crushed crackers in third bowl.

★ Dip shrimp in flour mixture, then in milk-egg mixture and finally in cracker crumbs and cover well. Deep-fry shrimp in oil until golden brown and serve with cocktail sauce or tartar sauce. Serves 4.

Barbecued Shrimp

2 (8 ounce) cans tomato sauce
1 cup corn oil
⅓ cup red wine vinegar
2 tablespoons ketchup
2 cloves garlic, minced
¼ cup minced cilantro
1 teaspoon freshly ground black pepper
18 - 22 shrimp

★ Combine tomato sauce, corn oil, red wine vinegar and ketchup in bowl and mix well. Stir in garlic, cilantro, 2 teaspoons salt and black pepper and mix well. Add shrimp, cover with barbecue sauce and refrigerate for at least 2 to 3 hours.

★ Stir shrimp to coat with sauce several times while marinating. Put shrimp in 9 x 13-inch baking dish, place under broiler or on grill and cook for 3 to 5 minutes per side or until light brown. Serve immediately. Serves 4.

Shrimp Cocktail with Red Sauce

1 cup ketchup
¾ cup chili sauce
2 - 3 tablespoons horseradish sauce
4 - 5 teaspoons lemon juice
1 teaspoon Worcestershire sauce
½ teaspoon hot sauce
1 pound cooked, shelled, veined shrimp

★ Mix all ingredients except shrimp in medium bowl. Refrigerate for several hours for flavors to blend. Pour into shrimp cocktail serving bowl with sauce in center and shrimp arranged around it. If you have a large bowl, fill it with ice before arranging cocktail sauce bowl and shrimp. Serves 2 to 3.

Carolina Shrimp Boil

2 pounds kielbasa or link sausage, cut in bite-size pieces
8 large ears corn-on-the cob, halved
14 - 16 new (red) potatoes with peels
2 onions
Shrimp boil or Old Bay® crab boil
4 - 5 pounds shrimp in shells

★ Place sausage, corn-on-the-cob, potatoes, onions, 1 to 2 tablespoons salt, shrimp boil and enough water to cover in large stockpot. Bring to a boil and cook for 15 to 20 minutes or until potatoes are almost tender.

★ Add shrimp and cook for additional 5 minutes or until shrimp turn pink. Drain and serve. Serves 10 to 12.

Fisherman's Beer Shrimp

2 (12 ounce) cans beer
4 tablespoons pickling spice
1 lemon, sliced
2 pounds fresh shrimp

★ Pour beer in large stew pot and turn on medium high heat, but do not boil. (Beer will be bitter.) Add pickling spice, lemon slices and ½ teaspoon salt. When mixture steams, add shrimp and stir well. Make sure there is enough liquid to cover or almost cover shrimp.

★ Add beer, if necessary. Cook just until shrimp turn pink, remove from pot and drain. Serves 4 to 6. (For larger amounts, use 2 to 3 tablespoons pickling spice per pound and enough beer to cover shrimp.)

Fried Butterfly Shrimp

2 pounds jumbo shelled, veined shrimp
1 cup flour
½ teaspoon sugar
Oil or shortening
1 egg

★ Slit shrimp down back without cutting all the way through. Wash and dry with paper towels.

★ Combine flour, sugar and a little salt. Add 1 cup ice water, 2 tablespoons oil and egg and beat until smooth. Dip shrimp, one at a time, into mixture.

★ Place carefully in deep fryer or skillet with hot oil and cook for 3 to 5 minutes or until golden brown. Drain on paper towels. Serve hot with your favorite sauce. Serves 4 to 6.

Skillet Shrimp

2 pounds uncooked shrimp, peeled, veined
⅔ cup herb-garlic marinade with lemon juice
2 teaspoons olive oil
¼ cup minced green onion with tops

★ Heat marinade and olive oil in large skillet. Place shrimp in hot skillet and cook until shrimp turn pink. Stir in green onions and serve over rice or pasta. Serves 3 to 4.

 Seafood Capital of the World   Crisfield, Maryland

Top-Shelf Tequila Shrimp

1½ pounds medium shrimp, shelled, veined
¼ cup (½ stick) butter
2 tablespoons canola oil
2 cloves garlic, minced
3 tablespoons tequila
1½ tablespoons lime juice
½ teaspoon chili powder
¼ cup coarsely chopped fresh cilantro
Rice, cooked
Lime wedges

★ Rinse and pat shrimp dry with paper towels. Heat butter and oil in large skillet over medium heat. Add garlic and shrimp and cook for about 2 minutes, stirring occasionally.

★ Stir in tequila, lime juice, ½ teaspoon salt and chili powder. Cook for additional 2 minutes or until most liquid evaporates and shrimp are pink and glazed. Add cilantro, serve over rice and garnish with lime wedges. Serves 4 to 6.

Pan-Seared Shrimp Ancho

3 - 4 ancho chilies
½ cup extra-virgin olive oil
6 - 8 cloves garlic, minced
2 pounds fresh shrimp, shelled, veined
Cracked black pepper
Rice, cooked

★ Clean ancho chilies well with dry cloth, heat for several minutes in lightly oiled skillet and soak in hot water for about 30 minutes.

★ Dry chilies, remove stems and seeds and slice in long, thin strips. Place in large cast-iron or heavy skillet with garlic and about ¼ to ½ cup hot oil. Cook for about 1 to 2 minutes.

★ Add shrimp and cook until they turn pink. Season with a little salt and cracked black pepper and serve over rice or with bread and salad. Serves 8.

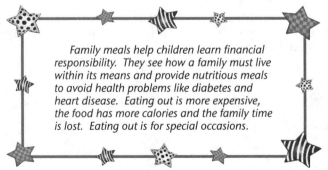

Family meals help children learn financial responsibility. They see how a family must live within its means and provide nutritious meals to avoid health problems like diabetes and heart disease. Eating out is more expensive, the food has more calories and the family time is lost. Eating out is for special occasions.

Shrimp Scampi

½ cup (1 stick) butter
3 cloves garlic, pressed
¼ cup lemon juice
2 pounds shrimp, peeled, veined

★ Melt butter in skillet, saute garlic and add lemon juice. Arrange shrimp in single layer in shallow baking dish. Pour garlic-butter over shrimp and salt lightly.

★ Broil for 2 minutes, turn shrimp and broil for additional 2 minutes. Reserve garlic butter and serve separately. Serves 8.

Northwest Steamers

These soft-shell clams are called steamers in the Pacific Northwest and the East Coast. Soft-shell clams are the best for steaming.

4 pounds live soft-shelled clams
1¼ cups (2½ sticks) unsalted butter, divided
1 small onion, chopped
4 - 5 cloves garlic, minced
¼ cup snipped parsley
1 teaspoon red pepper flakes
1 bottle white wine
Italian bread

★ Scrub shells of clams well to remove sand and grit. Rinse and soak them in water and a little kosher or sea salt to remove last bits of grit. (Do not use iodized salt.)

★ Add ¼ cup butter to large steamer pot, melt over medium heat and bring to slow boil. Cook onions until translucent. Add garlic, parsley and red pepper flakes and pour wine over all. Immediately pour clams into steaming pot, close lid and steam for about 5 to 8 minutes or until clams open.

★ Remove clams with large slotted spoon or tongs and divide among 4 individual bowls. Discard any clams that do not open. Melt remaining butter and pour into 4 small bowls. Serve clams with melted butter and Italian bread. Serves about 8 to 10.

What is the best way to communicate with a fish?

Drop it a line.

Steamed Soft-Shell Clams

Littlenecks are small hard-shell clams less than 2 inches in diameter.
Larger clams are called cherrystones and quahogs on the East Coast and
Pacific Littlenecks or common "littlenecks" on the West Coast.

2 pounds fresh littleneck clams
4 tablespoons olive oil, divided
4 - 5 cloves garlic, minced
4 green onions with tops, diced
1 cup dry champagne
¼ cup chopped parsley
2 tablespoons lemon juice
½ cup (1 stick) butter

★ Wash clams and scrub shells to remove all sand. Pour a little oil into large soup pot and heat over medium-high heat. Saute garlic and onions in hot oil until onions are translucent.

★ Pour remaining oil in pot and heat. Add clams, cook for about 2 minutes and toss frequently. Add champagne and cook for additional 3 minutes. Reduce heat, cover and steam for about 5 minutes.

★ Remove clams with open shells using slotted spoon and continue to cook remaining clams, covered, for additional 5 minutes. Remove open shells and discard unopened clams.

★ Boil stock in pot until it reduces to about 1 cup. (This may take 5 to 10 minutes.) Simmer and add parsley and lemon juice.

★ Drop butter into liquid a little at a time. Continue stirring until butter melts. Taste and season with a little salt and pepper. Pour over clams or in serving bowls for dipping. Serve in open shells. Serves 6.

Steamed Mussels

2 - 3 pounds fresh mussels in shells
1 - 1½ cups (1 stick) butter, divided
4 - 6 cloves garlic, minced
½ - ¾ cup white wine

★ Wash and scrub mussels. (See handling of clams in above recipe.)

★ Saute ¼ - ½ cup butter and garlic in large saucepan until garlic is translucent. Pour wine into saucepan and bring to small boil. Add mussels, close lid and steam until mussels open. Discard any that do not open.

★ Do not drain; serve with French bread and remaining butter, melted. Serves 4.

Marshland Muddle

"Muddle" is a term used by early settlers meaning "a mess of fish".
"A mess of" is a unit of measure that all Southerners understand.

2 large bell peppers, seeded, chopped
4 ribs celery, chopped
2 onions, chopped
2 cloves garlic, minced
Vegetable oil
6 cups clam juice
10 - 12 clams, cleaned
10 - 12 mussels, cleaned
10 - 12 shrimp
1 - 1½ pounds flounder

★ Cook bell peppers, celery, onions and garlic in a little oil in large stockpot until onions are translucent. Pour in clam juice and clams. Cook until clams open. Add mussels, shrimp and flounder. Cook until shrimp turns pink. Serves 8 to 10.

TIP: Throw away any clams or mussels that do not open.

Fried Oysters

Measurements just don't work with this recipe,
so just make sure you have enough of everything.

Fresh oysters, shucked
Cracker crumbs or cornmeal
Canola oil

★ Wash and pat dry oysters. Pour cracker crumbs or cornmeal in shallow bowl and add a little salt and pepper. Roll oysters in crumbs and coat well.

★ Heat oil in deep fryer. When oil is very hot, carefully add oysters one at a time and place them so they do not touch. When oysters are crispy and golden brown, remove from oil and drain. Serve hot.

Baked Oysters

1 cup oysters, drained, rinsed
2 cups cracker crumbs
¼ cup (½ stick) butter, melted
½ cup milk

★ Make alternate layers of oysters, cracker crumbs and butter in 7 x 11-inch baking dish. Pour warmed milk over layers and add lots of salt and pepper. Bake at 350° for about 35 minutes. Serves 2.

Scalloped Oysters

½ cup (1 stick) butter
1 cup cracker crumbs
½ cup seasoned breadcrumbs
1 pint oysters, drained, set aside liquid
2 tablespoons light cream, divided

★ Preheat oven to 400°. Melt butter in saucepan and pour into small bowl with cracker crumbs and breadcrumbs. Toss mixture to coat well.

★ Place one-third crumb mixture in sprayed shallow baking dish and cover with half oysters. Sprinkle with salt and pepper.

★ Add 1 tablespoon of oyster liquor to mixture and 1 tablespoon light cream. Repeat process for second layer, top with remaining crumb mixture and bake for 30 minutes. Serves 6.

Scallop Rolls

1 tablespoon minced garlic
1 tablespoon chopped chives
2 tablespoons chopped fresh parsley leaves
1 - 2 tablespoons olive oil
2 tablespoons butter
1 pound fresh bay scallops
1 lemon
¼ cup white wine
4 large buns

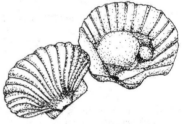

★ Saute garlic, chives and parsley in oil and butter just until garlic is translucent, about 1 minute. Add scallops and cook for 1 minute.

★ Add juice of 1 lemon and wine and cook for another 2 to 3 minutes or until scallops are just cooked through, but not overcooked. Remove from heat and serve on soft rolls. Serves 4.

Quick Cocktail Sauce

1½ cups cocktail sauce
4 tablespoons lemon juice
3 tablespoons horseradish
2 teaspoons Worcestershire
½ teaspoon grated onion
4 drops hot sauce

★ Combine all ingredients and a little salt and pepper and refrigerate for several hours. Yields 2 cups.

Tartar Sauce

⅓ cup sweet pickle relish, drained
2 tablespoons minced onion
1½ cups mayonnaise

★ Combine all ingredients in bowl and mix well. Yields 2 cups.

Quick Remoulade Sauce

½ cup mayonnaise
2 tablespoons chunky salsa
1 teaspoon chopped fresh parsley
1 teaspoon dijon-style mustard

★ Mix all ingredients and refrigerate. Yields ¾ cup.

Quick Horseradish Mayo

½ cup mayonnaise
1 tablespoon chopped fresh chives
1 tablespoon prepared horseradish
⅛ teaspoon seasoned salt

★ Mix all ingredients and refrigerate. Yields ¾ cup.

Sweets – Cakes

Vanilla Cupcakes Surprise

1 (18 ounce) box white cake mix
⅓ cup canola oil
1 teaspoon vanilla
3 large egg whites
1 cup white chocolate chips

★ Preheat oven to 350°. Place blue paper baking cups in 24 muffin cups. Beat cake mix, 1¼ cups water, oil, almond extract and egg whites in bowl on low speed for 30 seconds.

★ Increase speed to medium and beat for 2 minutes. Stir in white chocolate chips. Divide batter among muffin cups.

★ Bake for 19 to 22 minutes or until toothpick inserted in center comes out clean. Cool for 10 minutes before removing from pan. Cool for 30 minutes before frosting. Yields 24 cupcakes.

Strawberry Cupcake Frosting

2 cups (4 sticks) butter, softened
7 cups powdered sugar
1 teaspoon vanilla
½ cup fresh strawberry puree

★ Blend butter with electric mixer until creamy and fluffy. Add powdered sugar slowly and mix well. Add vanilla and strawberry puree and mix. Frost cupcakes. Yields enough for 24 cupcakes.

Triple Chocolate Cupcakes

1 (18 ounce) box triple chocolate fudge cake mix
⅓ cup canola oil
3 eggs
1 12 ounce) package swirled chocolate and white chocolate chips
1 (16 ounce) can chocolate fudge frosting
24 candles
1 (6 ounce) container chocolate fudge frosting

★ Preheat oven to 350°. Place paper baking cups in 24 muffin cups. Combine cake mix, 1¼ cups water, oil and eggs in bowl. Beat on low speed for 30 seconds. Increase speed to medium and beat for 2 minutes. Stir in chocolate chips and spoon into muffin cups.

★ Bake for 19 to 23 minutes or until toothpick inserted in center comes out clean. Cool in pan for about 10 minutes. Cool completely before frosting. Spread frosting in round swirling motions on each cupcake. Yields 24 cupcakes.

Red Velvet Cupcakes

1 (1 ounce) bottle red food coloring
1 (18 ounce) box devil's food cake mix
½ cup canola oil
3 eggs
1 (16 ounce) container classic white frosting

★ Preheat oven to 350°. Place paper baking cups in 16 muffin cups. Pour food coloring into measuring cup and add enough water to make 1¼ cups liquid.

★ Beat cake, water-food coloring mixture, oil and eggs in bowl. Beat on low speed for 30 seconds; increase speed to medium and beat for 2 minutes. Divide batter among muffin cups.

★ Bake for 15 to 20 minutes or until toothpick inserted in center comes out clean. Cool for 10 minutes before removing from pan. Cool completely before frosting. Frost in round swirling motions. Yields 16 cupcakes.

Carrot Cake Cupcakes

1 (18 ounce) box carrot cake mix
3 eggs
½ cup canola oil
1 (8 ounce) can crushed pineapple with liquid
¾ cup chopped pecans
1 (16 ounce) ready-to-serve cream cheese frosting
24 edible sugar or fondant carrots, optional

★ Preheat oven to 350°. Place paper baking cups in 24 muffin cups. Mix
  cake mix, eggs, oil, pineapple and ½ cup water in bowl and beat on low
  speed for 1 minute. Increase speed to medium and beat for 2 minutes.

★ Fold in pecans and raisins and spoon into muffin cups. Bake for 19 to
  23 minutes or until toothpick inserted in center comes out clean. Cool
  in pan for 5 minutes. Remove cupcakes from pan and cool completely
  before frosting. Use round swirling motions to froze. Yields 24 cupcakes.

TIP: *The easiest topping for these cupcakes is to sprinkle powdered sugar and*
pecan pieces over the top. You can make a carrot topper by adding orange
food coloring to a little frosting, squeeze frosting out of plastic bag with a
bottom corner cut off and make the shape of carrot. Use green food coloring
to make the stem.

Peanut Butter Cupcakes
with Chocolate

1 (21 ounce) package double fudge brownie mix
2 eggs
3 (9 ounce) packages miniature peanut butter cups
1 (16 ounce) ready-to-serve buttercream frosting
½ cup peanut butter
1 (2 ounce) jar chocolate sprinkles

★ Preheat oven to 350°. Prepare brownie mix according to package
  directions using 2 eggs. Spoon into miniature foil cupcake liners and fill
  three-fourths full. Place peanut butter cup in center of each and push
  into batter.

★ Bake for 20 to 25 minutes or until toothpick inserted in center comes out
  clean. Cool completely before frosting. Mix buttercream frosting and
  peanut butter and spread on cupcakes. Yields 16.

The most interesting information comes
from children, for they tell all they know and
then stop.
–Mark Twain

Strawberry Shortcakes

2½ cups biscuit mix
¼ cup sugar
3 tablespoons butter, softened
½ cup milk

★ Preheat oven to 350°. In mixing bowl, combine biscuit mix and sugar and cut in butter until mixture is crumbly. Add milk and stir just until soft dough forms.

★ Drop heaping tablespoons of batter onto sprayed baking sheet. Bake about 15 minutes or until light brown. Yields about 4 to 6.

Strawberry Glaze:

1 tablespoon cornstarch
1 teaspoon almond extract
¾ cup sugar
1 (16 ounce) container frozen strawberries, thawed
1 (8 ounce) carton frozen whipped topping, thawed

★ To make glaze, place cornstarch, almond extract, sugar and 2 tablespoons water in saucepan. Add strawberries, bring mixture to a boil and stir constantly. Reduce heat, cook and stir until mixture thickens. Remove from heat and refrigerate.

★ When ready to serve, split shortcakes in half and spoon about ½ cup Strawberry Glaze over bottom half of each shortcake. Top with an ample amount of whipped topping and place top half of shortcake on top. Spoon any remaining glaze over top.

Easy Chocolate Frosting

⅓ cup plus 1 tablespoon butter, softened
⅓ cup evaporated milk
2¾ cups powdered sugar
⅓ cup unsweetened cocoa powder
1 teaspoon vanilla

★ Cream butter until light and fluffy. Add evaporated milk a little at a time and alternately add powdered sugar. Mix in cocoa powder and vanilla. Adjust consistency with milk or sugar. Yields frosting for 1 cake or 12 cupcakes.

In the 1800's the first bakery was started on the yeast coast.

Gingerbread Shortcake

2 cups flour
1 teaspoons baking powder
1 teaspoon baking soda
1 teaspoon ground ginger
2 teaspoons ground cinnamon
1 cup molasses
⅓ cup butter, softened
½ cup buttermilk*
1 egg
1 (8 ounce) carton whipping cream

★ Preheat oven to 375°. Sift dry ingredients in mixing bowl. In separate pan, heat molasses and butter almost to boiling. Add milk and egg to dry ingredients and stir quickly into hot molasses mixture.

★ Bake in 2 sprayed 8-inch cake pans for 20 to 25 minutes. Cool and cover each with whipped cream to serve. Serves 12.

TIP: To make buttermilk, add 1 tablespoon lemon juice or vinegar to 8 ounces milk and set aside for about 10 minutes.

Applesauce Cake

½ cup shortening
1½ cups packed brown sugar
1 egg
1 teaspoon baking soda
1 cup thick applesauce
1 teaspoon ground cinnamon
½ teaspoon ground cloves
1½ - 2 cups flour

★ Preheat oven to 350°. Cream shortening, brown sugar and egg in bowl. In separate bowl, dissolve baking soda in applesauce and add to shortening mixture.

★ Sift 1 teaspoon salt, cinnamon and cloves with part of flour and add to first shortening mixture. Add enough additional flour to make a fairly stiff batter. Pour batter into sprayed, floured loaf pan and bake for 50 to 60 minutes. Serves 6 to 8.

TIP: For a quick frosting, use prepared vanilla frosting and add ½ teaspoon ground cinnamon.

 Apple Capital of the World   Wenatchee, Washington

Best Fresh Apple Cake

1½ cups canola oil
2 cups sugar
3 eggs
2½ cups flour, sifted
½ teaspoon baking soda
2 teaspoons baking powder
½ teaspoon ground cinnamon
1 teaspoon vanilla
3 cups peeled, grated apples
1 cup chopped pecans

★ Preheat oven to 350°. Mix oil, sugar and eggs in bowl and beat
  well. In separate bowl, combine flour, ½ teaspoon salt, baking soda,
  baking powder and cinnamon. Gradually add flour mixture to
  creamed mixture.

★ Add vanilla, fold in apples and pecans and pour into sprayed, floured
  tube pan. Bake for 1 hour. While cake is still warm, invert onto
  serving plate.

Glaze:

2 tablespoons butter, melted
2 tablespoons milk
1 cup powdered sugar
1 teaspoon vanilla
¼ teaspoon lemon extract

★ Mix all ingredients in bowl and drizzle over cake while cake is still warm.
  Serves 18 to 20.

Easy Applesauce-Spice Cake

1 (18 ounce) box spice cake mix
3 eggs
1¼ cups applesauce
⅓ cup oil
1 cup chopped pecans

★ Preheat oven to 350°. Combine cake mix, eggs, applesauce and oil.
  Beat at medium speed for 2 minutes. Stir in pecans. Pour into sprayed,
  floured 9 x 13-inch baking pan. Bake for 40 minutes. Serves 18 to 20.

*TIP: If you want an easy frosting, mix ½ to 1 teaspoon cinnamon to prepared
  vanilla frosting.*

 Bratwurst Capital of the World   Sheboygan, Wisconsin

Apricot Nectar Cake

Make recipe the day before you eat so icing has time to seep into cake. It's wonderful and will store just fine.

1 (18 ounce) box lemon cake mix
1 cup apricot nectar
4 eggs
¾ cup vegetable oil
½ cup sugar

★ Preheat oven to 350°. Combine all ingredients in bowl and mix well. Bake in sprayed, floured tube pan for 1 hour. Cool for 5 minutes, remove from pan and glaze while hot.

Glaze:

Juice from 1 lemon
1½ cups powdered sugar

★ Combine ingredients in bowl and pour slowly over hot cake so glaze seeps into cake. Spread remaining glaze on sides of cake. Serves 18 to 20.

Maine Blueberry Coffee Cake

¾ cup sugar
¼ cup shortening
1 egg
2 cups fresh or frozen blueberries

★ Preheat oven to 375°. Cream sugar and shortening with electric mixer on high. Add egg and continue to beat. Combine flour, baking powder and salt in separate bowl.

★ Reduce mixer speed to low and add flour mixture alternately with egg to creamed mixture. Beat on low until mixed well. Gently fold in blueberries and spread batter evenly in sprayed 9 x 9-inch cake pan.

Topping:

⅓ cup flour
½ cup sugar
1 teaspoon cinnamon

★ Mix in separate bowl and sprinkle over top of batter. Bake for 40 to 45 minutes or until toothpick inserted in center comes out clean. Serves 12 to 14.

 Steak Capital of the World   Lincoln, Nebraska

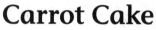

Carrot Cake

2 cups sifted flour
2 cups sugar
1 teaspoon baking powder
1 teaspoon baking soda
1 teaspoon ground cinnamon
4 eggs
1½ cups vegetable oil
2 cups grated carrots

★ Preheat oven to 350°. Sift ¼ teaspoon salt and dry ingredients in bowl. In separate bowl, combine eggs and oil.

★ Add dry ingredients and mix thoroughly. Stir in carrots. Pour into 3 sprayed, floured 9-inch layer cake pans and bake for 30 to 40 minutes.

Frosting:

1 (8 ounce) package cream cheese, softened
½ cup (1 stick) butter
1 teaspoon vanilla
1 (16 ounce) package powdered sugar
1 cup chopped pecans

★ Beat cream cheese and butter in bowl. Add vanilla and powdered sugar. Frost cake and sprinkle with pecans. Serves 18 to 20.

Easy Chocolate-Cherry Cake

1 (18 ounce) box milk chocolate cake mix
1 (20 ounce) can cherry pie filling
3 eggs

★ Preheat oven to 350°. Combine cake mix, pie filling and eggs in bowl and mix with spoon. Pour into sprayed, floured 9 x 13-inch baking dish.

★ Bake for 35 to 40 minutes. Cake is done when toothpick inserted in center comes out clean.

Icing:

5 tablespoons butter
1¼ cups sugar
½ cup milk
1 (6 ounce) package chocolate chips

★ When cake is done, combine butter, sugar and milk in medium saucepan. Boil for 1 minute, stirring constantly. Add chocolate chips and stir until chips melt. Pour over hot cake. Serves 18 to 20.

Nutty Cherry Cake

2 cups sugar
½ cup (1 stick) butter, softened
2 eggs
2½ cups flour
2 teaspoons baking soda
1 (16 ounce) can bing cherries, drained
1 cup chopped pecans

★ Preheat oven to 350°. Combine sugar, butter and eggs in bowl and beat for several minutes. Add flour and baking soda and mix well. Fold in cherries and pecans.

★ Pour into sprayed, floured 9 x 13-inch baking pan and bake for 35 minutes. Cake is done when toothpick inserted in center comes out clean.

Cherry Sauce:

1 (16 ounce) can cherry pie filling
⅓ cup sugar

★ Combine cherry pie filling, sugar and ⅓ cup water in saucepan. Heat to dissolve sugar, but not to boiling stage. When ready to serve, pour ⅓ cup hot sauce over each piece of cake. Serves 18 to 20.

Date Cake

4 eggs, separated
1½ cups packed brown sugar
⅔ cup shortening
3¼ cups flour
5 teaspoons baking powder
1 teaspoon ground cinnamon
½ teaspoon ground nutmeg
¾ cup milk
1½ cups chopped dates
Prepared vanilla icing, optional

★ Preheat oven to 350°. Cream egg yolks, brown sugar and shortening in mixing bowl. Mix and sift flour, baking powder, 1 teaspoon salt, cinnamon and nutmeg.

★ Add dry ingredients to first mixture alternately with milk. Beat egg whites and stir into batter. Stir in dates. Turn batter into sprayed loaf pan. Bake for 50 to 60 minutes. Cool and frost as desired. Serves 8 to 10.

Hummingbird Cake

3 cups flour
2 cups sugar
1 teaspoon ground cinnamon
1 teaspoon baking soda
3 eggs
1½ cups vegetable oil
3 cups mashed bananas
3 cups chopped pecans
1 (8 ounce) can crushed pineapple with juice

★ Preheat oven to 325°. Sift flour, sugar, 1 teaspoon salt, cinnamon and baking soda in bowl. Add eggs and oil and mix well.

★ Fold in bananas, pecans and pineapple. Bake in sprayed large tube pan for 1 hour 15 minutes. Cool and frost.

TIP: An alternate method is to bake in 3 (8 or 9 inch) cake pans at 350° for 25 to 30 minutes.

Frosting:

½ cup (1 stick) butter, softened
1 (8 ounce) package cream cheese, softened
1 (1 pound) box powdered sugar
1 teaspoon vanilla
1 cup chopped pecans

★ Combine butter and cream cheese in bowl and beat until smooth. Add powdered sugar, vanilla and nuts. Spread over layers, top and sides of cooled cake. Serves 12 to 14.

Easy Deluxe Coconut Cake

1 (18 ounce) box yellow cake mix
1 (14 ounce) can sweetened condensed milk
1 (15 ounce) can coconut cream
½ cup shredded coconut
1 - 2 (8 ounce) cartons frozen whipped topping, thawed

★ Preheat oven to 350°. Prepare cake according to box directions with ingredients called for on box. Pour into sprayed, floured 9 x 13-inch baking pan.

★ Bake for 30 to 35 minutes or until toothpick inserted into cake comes out clean. While cake is hot, punch holes in cake about 2 inches apart. Pour sweetened condensed milk over cake and spread around until all milk has soaked into cake.

★ Pour can of coconut cream over cake and sprinkle shredded coconut on top. Cool and frost with whipped topping. Refrigerate. Serves 18 to 20.

Lemon Cake

Cake:

1 (18 ounce) box yellow cake mix
4 eggs
1 (3 ounce) package lemon gelatin
¾ cup vegetable oil

★ Preheat oven to 350°. Combine all ingredients with ¾ cup water in bowl and beat until fluffy. Pour into sprayed, floured 9 x 13-inch baking pan.

★ Bake for 30 to 35 minutes. Remove cake from oven and jab with fork to bottom at 1-inch intervals.

Glaze:

2 cups powdered sugar
1 teaspoon grated lemon peel
Juice of 2 lemons
1 (7 ounce) package flaked coconut

★ Combine powdered sugar, lemon peel and juice in bowl. Spoon glaze mixture over warm cake, sprinkle with coconut and serve warm. Serves 16 to 18.

Lemon-Pecan Holiday Cake

1 (1.5 ounce) bottle lemon extract
4 cups pecan halves
2 cups (4 sticks) butter
3 cups sugar
3½ cups flour, divided
1½ teaspoons baking powder
6 eggs
½ pound candied green pineapple, chopped
½ pound candied red cherries, halved

★ Preheat oven to 275°. Pour lemon extract over pecans in medium bowl, toss and set aside. Cream butter and sugar in large bowl until fluffy.

★ In separate bowl, sift 3 cups flour and baking powder. Add eggs to butter-sugar mixture, one at a time, alternating with flour mixture.

★ Place pineapple and cherries in separate bowl, add ½ cup flour and mix until flour covers fruit well. Fold fruit and pecans into batter and pour in sprayed, floured tube cake pan.

★ Bake for 2 hours 30 minutes to 2 hours 45 minutes. Cake is done when toothpick inserted in center comes out clean. Cool and remove carefully from pan. Serves 20.

Lemon-Blueberry Bundt Cake with Honey-Lemon Glaze

1 (18 ounce) box lemon cake mix
1 (3.4 ounce) vanilla flavor instant pudding mix
1 (8 ounce) container vanilla yogurt
3 eggs
½ cup oil
2 cups blueberries, fresh or frozen
2 tablespoons flour

★ Preheat oven to 350°. In large bowl, combine cake mix, pudding mix, yogurt, eggs and oil. Beat on low speed to blend, then beat on medium speed for 2 minutes.

★ In small bowl, toss blueberries gently with flour to coat. Stir carefully into batter. Pour batter into sprayed, floured 12-cup capacity bundt cake pan.

★ Bake for 50 to 55 minutes or until toothpick inserted in center comes out clean. Cool cake in pan for 10 minutes, then turn out onto serving platter. Let cool and spoon Honey-Lemon Glaze over cake.

Honey-Lemon Glaze:

2 tablespoon sugar
¼ cup honey
1 tablespoon lemon juice
1 tablespoon butter

★ In small saucepan, bring sugar, honey, lemon juice and butter to a boil, stirring constantly. Boil gently for 1 minute; remove from heat. Let cool for several minutes, then spoon over cake. Serves 18 to 20.

TIP: *After spooning glaze over the cake, scoop up some of the glaze pooled around the bottom of the cake and spoon it over the cake again.*

Easy Chess Cake

1 (18 ounce) box yellow cake mix
4 eggs, divided
½ cup (1 stick) butter, softened
1 (8 ounce) package cream cheese, softened
1 (1 pound) box powdered sugar

★ Preheat oven to 350°. Beat cake mix, 2 eggs and butter until creamy. Press into greased 9 x 13-inch baking pan. In separate bowl, beat 2 eggs, cream cheese and powdered sugar. Pour over cake. Bake for 35 minutes. Serves 18 to 20.

Festive Christmas Cake

This is easy to make and great if you make the day before.

1 (18 ounce) box lemon supreme pound cake mix
1 (12 ounce) package mixed candied fruit, dredged in flour

★ Prepare cake batter according to package directions. Fold candied fruit into batter and pour into cake pan. Bake according to package directions. (Some fruit may be set aside for garnish.)

Frosting:

3 tablespoons butter, softened
1 cup powdered sugar
1½ tablespoons sherry
Candied fruit for garnish

★ Cream butter and powdered sugar in bowl. Add sherry gradually until frosting is of spreading consistency. Spread over top of cake and garnish with candied fruit. Serves 18 to 20.

Simple Chocolate-Orange Cake

1 (16 ounce) loaf frozen pound cake, thawed
1 (12 ounce) jar orange marmalade
1 (16 ounce) can chocolate fudge frosting

★ Cut cake horizontally into 3 layers. Place 1 layer on cake platter and spread with half of marmalade. Place second layer over first and spread on remaining marmalade.

★ Top with third cake layer and spread frosting liberally on top and sides of cake. Refrigerate. Serves 8 to 10.

Easy Golden Rum Cake

1 (18 ounce) box yellow cake mix with pudding
3 eggs
⅓ cup oil
½ cup rum
1 cup chopped pecans

★ Preheat oven to 325°. Beat cake mix, eggs, 1⅓ cups water, oil and rum; blend well. Stir in pecans. Pour into sprayed, floured 10-inch tube or bundt pan. Bake for 1 hour. Sprinkle powdered sugar over cooled cake if you want topping. Serves 18 to 20.

 Cherry Capital of the World   Traverse City, Michigan

Pina Colada Cake

1 (18 ounce) box pineapple cake mix
3 eggs
⅓ cup canola oil
1 (14 ounce) can sweetened condensed milk
1 (15 ounce) can cream of coconut
1 cup flaked coconut
1 (8 ounce) can crushed pineapple, drained
1 (8 ounce) carton frozen whipped topping, thawed

★ Preheat oven to 350°. Combine cake mix, eggs, 1¼ cups water and oil in bowl. Beat for 3 to 4 minutes and pour into sprayed, floured 10 x 15-inch baking pan. Bake for 35 minutes.

★ When cake is done, punch holes in top with fork so frosting will soak into cake. Mix sweetened condensed milk, cream of coconut, coconut and pineapple in bowl.

★ While cake is still warm, pour mixture over top of cake. Refrigerate for about 1 hour, spread whipped topping over cake and return to refrigerator. Serves 12 to 14.

Out-of-This-World Cake

2 cups sugar
1 cup (2 sticks) butter, softened
5 eggs
1 cup milk
1 (13.5 ounce) box graham cracker crumbs
1 tablespoon baking powder
1 (15 ounce) can crushed pineapple, drained
1 (6 ounce) package frozen flaked coconut, thawed
1½ cups chopped nuts
1 tablespoon vanilla

★ Preheat oven to 350°. Combine all ingredients in bowl and mix well using electric mixer. Pour into sprayed, floured tube pan and bake for about 1 hour 20 minutes or when toothpick inserted in center comes out clean. Cool before removing from pan. Serves 18.

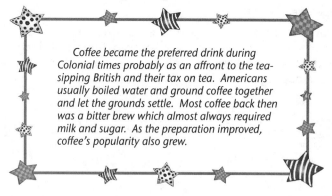

Coffee became the preferred drink during Colonial times probably as an affront to the tea-sipping British and their tax on tea. Americans usually boiled water and ground coffee together and let the grounds settle. Most coffee back then was a bitter brew which almost always required milk and sugar. As the preparation improved, coffee's popularity also grew.

Poppy Seed Cake

3 cups sugar
1¼ cups shortening
6 eggs
3 cups flour
¼ teaspoon baking soda
1 cup buttermilk*
3 tablespoons poppy seeds
2 teaspoons almond extract
2 teaspoons vanilla
2 teaspoons butter flavoring

★ Preheat oven to 325°. Cream sugar and shortening in bowl until mixture is light and fluffy. Add eggs, one at a time, and blend mixture well. In separate bowl, sift flour, baking soda and ½ teaspoon salt.

★ Alternately add dry ingredients and buttermilk to sugar mixture. Add poppy seeds and flavorings and blend well. Pour into sprayed, floured bundt pan. Bake for about 1 hour 15 minutes. Cake is done when toothpick inserted in center comes out clean.

Glaze:

1½ cups powdered sugar
⅓ cup lemon juice
1 teaspoon vanilla
1 teaspoon almond extract

★ Combine all ingredients in bowl and mix well. Pour over top of cooled cake and let some glaze run down sides of cake. Serves 20.

*TIP: To make buttermilk, mix 1 cup milk with 1 tablespoon lemon juice or vinegar and let milk stand for about 10 minutes.

Easy Poppy Seed Bundt Cake

1 (18 ounce) box yellow cake mix
1 (3.4 ounce) package instant coconut cream pudding mix
½ cup oil
3 eggs
2 tablespoons poppy seeds

★ Preheat oven at 350°. Beat cake mix, pudding mix, 1 cup water, oil and eggs in mixing bowl. Beat on low speed until moist. Beat on medium speed for 2 minutes. Stir in poppy seeds.

★ Pour into sprayed, floured bundt an. Bake for 50 minutes or until a toothpick inserted near center comes out clean. Cool for 10 minutes; remove from pan. Dust with powdered sugar when cool. Serves 18 to 20.

Pumpkin Chess Cake

1 (18 ounce) box yellow cake mix
¾ cup (1½ sticks) butter, softened, divided
4 eggs, divided
1 (15 ounce) can pumpkin
2 teaspoons ground cinnamon
½ cup packed brown sugar
⅔ cup milk
½ cup sugar
⅔ cup chopped pecans

★ Preheat oven to 350°. Set aside 1 cup cake mix. Mix rest of cake mix, ½ cup butter and 1 egg and press into sprayed 9 x 13-inch baking pan.

★ Mix pumpkin, 3 eggs, cinnamon, brown sugar and milk in bowl and pour over batter in pan. Use remaining cake mix, sugar, remaining butter and pecans to make topping and crumble over cake. Bake for 1 hour. Serves 10 to 12.

Mom's Pound Cake

This is an old-fashioned pound cake that is great.

1 cup (2 sticks) butter
2 cups sugar
5 eggs
1 teaspoon vanilla
2 cups flour
1 cup chopped pecans

★ Preheat oven to 350°. Cream butter, sugar, eggs and vanilla in large bowl. In separate bowl, mix flour and ½ teaspoon salt. Slowly mix flour mixture with sugar mixture.

★ Pour evenly into sprayed, floured bundt pan. Sprinkle pecans on top. Bake for about 40 minutes. Cake is done when toothpick inserted in centers comes out clean. Serves 18.

Pound Cake

Pound cakes have been made in the South long before the first recorded recipes of the 18th century. They were named pound cakes because of the equal weights of the ingredients: 1 pound flour, 1 pound butter, 1 pound sugar and 1 pound eggs. In The Virginia Housewife *published in 1824, Mary Randolph uses these ingredients and measurements and suggests adding grated lemon peel, nutmeg and brandy. She also suggests baking as a cake or as a pudding in a large mold and boiling it and serving with butter and sugar.*

Double Chocolate Pound Cake

1 cup (2 sticks) butter, softened
½ cup shortening
1 (3 ounce) package cream cheese, softened
3 cups sugar
2 teaspoons vanilla
5 large eggs
½ cup cocoa
3 cups flour
1 teaspoon baking powder
1 cup buttermilk*
1 (6 ounce) package chocolate chips
Powdered sugar

★ Preheat oven to 325°. Beat butter, shortening, cream cheese and sugar in bowl on high speed for 5 minutes. Add vanilla and eggs and beat well.

★ In separate bowl, mix cocoa, flour, baking powder and ½ teaspoon salt. Add half dry ingredients to batter, then buttermilk and end with remaining dry ingredients. Beat well after each addition. Fold in chocolate chips.

★ Pour into sprayed, floured 10-inch tube pan and bake for 1 hour 30 minutes. Cake is done when toothpick inserted in center comes out clean. Cool cake in pan for 15 minutes; then turn onto cake plate and cool completely. Dust with sifted powdered sugar. Serves 18 to 20.

*TIP: To make buttermilk, mix 1 cup milk with 1 tablespoon lemon juice or vinegar and let milk stand for about 10 minutes.

Nutty Pound Cake

1 cup (2 sticks) butter, softened
2 cups sugar
5 large eggs
1 teaspoon vanilla
1 teaspoon butter flavoring
1 teaspoon almond extract
2 cups flour, divided
2 cups chopped pecans
Powdered sugar

★ Preheat oven to 325°. Cream butter and sugar in bowl and beat in eggs, one at a time. Stir in vanilla, butter and almond flavorings. Add 1¾ cups flour and beat well.

★ Combine remaining flour with pecans and fold into batter. Bake in sprayed, floured bundt pan for 70 to 75 minutes. Cool, remove cake from pan and dust with powdered sugar. Serves 18.

Pumpkin-Pie Pound Cake

1 cup shortening
1¼ cups sugar
¾ cup packed brown sugar
5 eggs, room temperature
1 cup canned pumpkin
2½ cups flour
2 teaspoons ground cinnamon
1 teaspoon ground nutmeg
1 teaspoon baking soda
½ cup orange juice, room temperature
2 teaspoons vanilla
1½ cups chopped pecans

★ Preheat oven to 325°. Cream shortening, sugar and brown sugar in bowl for about 4 minutes. Add eggs, one at a time and mix well after each addition. Blend in pumpkin.

★ In separate bowl, mix flour, spices, ¼ teaspoon salt and baking soda and mix well. Gradually beat dry ingredients into batter until ingredients mix well. Fold in orange juice, vanilla and pecans. Pour into sprayed, floured bundt pan.

★ Bake for 70 to 75 minutes or until toothpick inserted in center comes out clean. Allow cake to stand in pan for about 15 minutes. Turn cake out onto rack to cool completely before frosting.

Frosting:

1 (1 pound) box powdered sugar
6 tablespoons (¾ stick) butter, melted
¼ teaspoon orange extract
2 - 3 tablespoons orange juice

★ Thoroughly mix all ingredients in bowl using only 2 tablespoons orange juice. Add more orange juice if frosting seems too stiff. Serves 18.

Strawberry-Angel Delight Cake

1 cup sweetened condensed milk
¼ cup lemon juice
1 pint fresh strawberries, halved
1 prepared angel food cake
1 pint whipping cream, whipped

★ Combine sweetened condensed milk and lemon juice in bowl. Fold in strawberries. Slice cake in half horizontally.

★ Spread strawberry filling on bottom layer and place top layer over filling. Cover with whipped cream and top with extra strawberries. Serves 16.

Easy Strawberry Pound Cake

1 (18 ounce) box strawberry cake mix
1 (3.4 ounce) package instant pineapple pudding mix
⅓ cup canola oil
4 eggs
1 (3 ounce) package strawberry gelatin

★ Preheat oven to 325°. Mix all ingredients plus 1 cup water in bowl and
  beat for 2 minutes on medium speed. Pour into sprayed, floured bundt
  pan.

★ Bake for 55 to 60 minutes. Cake is done when toothpick inserted in
  center comes out clean. Cool for 20 minutes before removing cake
  from pan. If you would like an icing, use prepared vanilla icing.
  Serves 18 to 20.

*TIP: If you like coconut better than pineapple, use coconut cream pudding mix
instead of pineapple.*

Strawberry Cake

1 (18 ounce) box white cake mix
1 tablespoon flour
1 (3 ounce) box strawberry gelatin
1 (10 ounce) package frozen strawberries, thawed, divided
1 cup corn oil
4 eggs

★ Preheat oven to 350°. Spray and flour 2 (8 or 9 inch) layer pans or
  spray and flour sides of pans and cut out circle of wax paper to fit
  bottom of pans.

★ Combine cake mix, flour and gelatin in bowl and mix well. In separate
  bowl, mix ¾ cup strawberries, ½ cup water and corn oil. Add to cake
  mixture and blend well.

★ Add eggs one at a time and beat for 1 minute after each egg. Pour into
  pans and bake for 35 minutes.

Frosting:

½ cup (1 stick) butter
2½ - 3 cups powdered sugar
2 tablespoons milk

★ Cream butter and sugar with milk in bowl. Add small amount of
  remaining strawberries for color. If frosting is too thin, add more
  powdered sugar. Frost cake and refrigerate for several hours before
  serving. Serves 18 to 20.

Red Velvet Cake
with Cream Cheese Icing

1½ cups sugar
1 cup shortening
2 eggs
1 teaspoon vanilla extract
2 tablespoons red food coloring
1 tablespoon cocoa powder
2½ cups flour
1 teaspoon baking soda
1 teaspoon vinegar

★ Preheat oven to 350°. Mix sugar, shortening, eggs and vanilla in large bowl until creamy. In separate bowl, mix cocoa and food coloring and combine with sugar mixture. In separate bowl, mix flour and 1 teaspoon salt.

★ Add ⅓ of the flour mixture to the sugar mixture and mix. Add one-half buttermilk to flour-sugar mixture and mix. Repeat steps with flour mixture and buttermilk 2 more times and mix.

★ Mix baking soda and vinegar in small cup and fold it in cake batter as soon as it stops fizzing. Pour cake batter into 2 sprayed (9-inch) cake pans and level tops of cake with spatula. Bake for 25 to 30 minutes or until toothpick inserted into center comes out clean.

★ Place cake pans on rack to cool. Refrigerate or freeze for about 1 hour before spreading frosting for best results.

Cream Cheese Icing:

1 (8 ounce) package cream cheese, softened
1 (8 ounce) package mascarpone cheese, softened
1 teaspoon vanilla extract
1 cup powdered sugar
1½ cups whipping cream

★ Beat cream cheese and mascarpone until smooth and creamy. Add remaining ingredients and mix well. Spread over cooled cake. Serves 10 to 12.

 Date Capital of the World   Indio, California

Fudge Cake

½ cup shortening
1¼ cups packed brown sugar
1 teaspoon vanilla
2 eggs
3 ounces unsweetened chocolate, melted
2 cups sifted flour
1½ teaspoons baking powder
½ teaspoon baking soda
1 cup milk

★ Cream shortening and brown sugar in mixing bowl. Add vanilla. Add eggs, one at a time, and beat thoroughly after each addition. Gradually beat in chocolate.

★ Sift flour, baking powder and baking soda and add alternately with milk to first mixture. Beat until smooth. Turn into sprayed loaf pan or layer cake pans. In loaf pan, bake at 325° for 1 hour. In layer cake pans, bake at 350° for 25 minutes.

Mississippi Mud Cake

The history of the Mississippi Mud Cake or Mississippi Mud Pie is uncertain. The story is told it originated in the Vicksburg-Natchez area. The original cake resembled the muddy banks of the Mississippi River. It had layers of chocolate cake and pudding, topped with chocolate icing that looked crusted and cracked similar to the riverbanks in the hot summertime.

2 cups sugar
⅓ cup cocoa
1½ cups (3 sticks) butter
4 eggs
1 teaspoon vanilla
1½ cups flour
1⅓ cups flaked coconut
1½ cups chopped pecans
1 (7 ounce) jar marshmallow cream

★ Preheat oven to 350°. Cream sugar, cocoa, and butter in bowl and add eggs and vanilla. Mix well. Stir in flour, coconut, and pecans.

★ Pour in 9 x 13-inch baking pan and bake for 40 minutes. When done, spread marshmallow cream over hot cake. Cool before frosting.

Frosting:

1 (1 pound) box powdered sugar
⅓ cup cocoa
½ cup (1 stick) butter, softened
½ cup evaporated milk
1 teaspoon vanilla

★ Sift powdered sugar and cocoa in bowl. Cream butter with dry ingredients, then stir in evaporated milk and vanilla. Spread over cake. Serves 16 to 18.

Devil's Food Cake

2 cups cake flour
1 teaspoon baking soda
1 cup sugar
½ cup packed brown sugar
½ cup vegetable shortening
⅔ cup buttermilk or thick sour milk
1 teaspoon vanilla
2 eggs
3 (1 ounce) squares unsweetened chocolate

★ Preheat oven to 350°. Sift flour, soda ¾ teaspoon salt and sugar into mixing bowl. Add brown sugar, shortening, ½ cup buttermilk, vanilla and eggs.

★ Beat for 2 minutes at medium speed on electric mixer or by hand. Combine chocolate and ½ cup boiling water; stir until smooth. Add remaining milk and chocolate mixture. Beat 1 more minute.

★ Turn batter into 2 sprayed, floured 9-inch layer pans. Bake for about 25 minutes. Let stand for 5 minutes. Turn out and cool before icing. Frost with Creamy Chocolate Frosting. Serves 10.

Creamy Chocolate Frosting:

1 cup semi-sweet chocolate chips
1 (8 ounce) carton sour cream

★ In small saucepan, combine chocolate chips and sour cream. Cook over medium-low heat, stirring constantly, until chocolate melts and mixture is smooth. Remove from heat and let cool until just warm to the touch.

Easy Pineapple Cake

2 cups sugar
2 cups flour
1 (20 ounce) can crushed pineapple with liquid
1 teaspoon baking soda
1 teaspoon vanilla

★ Preheat oven to 350°. Combine all cake ingredients in bowl and mix with spoon. Pour into sprayed, floured 9 x 13-inch baking pan. Bake for 30 to 35 minutes.

Easy Pineapple Cake Icing:

1 (8 ounce) package cream cheese, softened
½ cup (1 stick) butter, melted
1 cup powdered sugar
1 cup chopped pecans

★ Beat cream cheese, butter and powdered sugar in bowl. Add chopped pecans and pour over hot cake. Serves 12.

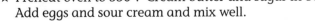

Rich Turtle Cake

1 (18 ounce) box German chocolate cake mix
½ cup (1 stick) butter, softened
½ cup canola oil
1 (14 ounce) can sweetened condensed milk, divided
1 cup chopped pecans
1 (16 ounce) bag caramels

★ Preheat oven to 350°. Combine cake mix, butter, 1½ cups water, oil and half can sweetened condensed milk in bowl and beat well.

★ Fold in pecans and pour half batter into sprayed, floured 9 x 13-inch baking dish. Bake for 25 minutes.

★ Combine caramels and remaining sweetened condensed milk in saucepan, spread evenly over baked cake and cover with remaining batter. Bake for additional 20 to 25 minutes.

Frosting:

½ cup (1 stick) butter
¼ cup cocoa
4 - 5 tablespoons milk
1 (1 pound) box powdered sugar
1 teaspoon vanilla

★ Melt butter in saucepan, add cocoa and milk and mix well. Add powdered sugar and vanilla and stir well. (If frosting seems too stiff, add 1 tablespoon milk.) Spread over warm, but not hot, cake. Serves 12 to 14.

Sour Cream-Chocolate Chip Cake

This is so easy!

1 cup (2 sticks) butter
1¼ cups sugar
3 eggs, lightly beaten
1 (8 ounce) carton sour cream
2 cups cake flour
½ teaspoon baking soda
1 teaspoon baking powder
1 teaspoon vanilla
1 (12 ounce) package miniature chocolate chips
1 cup chopped pecans

★ Preheat oven to 350°. Cream butter and sugar in bowl until smooth. Add eggs and sour cream and mix well.

★ Sift flour, baking soda and baking powder into mixture. Add vanilla, chocolate chips and pecans. Pour into sprayed tube pan and bake for 1 hour. Serves 18.

Old-Fashioned Buttermilk Cake

1 cup buttermilk*
3 tablespoons vanilla
½ teaspoon baking soda
1 cup shortening
2 cups sugar
4 eggs
3 cups flour
¾ cup chopped walnuts

★ Preheat oven to 325°. Pour buttermilk, vanilla and baking soda in glass and set aside. Place shortening in large bowl and cream until smooth. Add sugar slowly and continue to cream until mixture is fluffy.

★ Add eggs one at a time and beat after each addition. When mixture is fluffy, gradually add flour and 1 teaspoon salt a little at a time and stir well after each addition. Fold in nuts.

★ Pour into sprayed, floured 10-inch tube pan. Bake for about 1 hour or until toothpick inserted in center comes out clean. Serves 18 to 20.

*TIP: To make buttermilk, mix 1 cup milk with 1 tablespoon lemon juice or vinegar and let milk stand for about 10 minutes.

Family Chess Cake

Crust:

1 (18 ounce) box yellow or chocolate cake mix
½ cup (1 stick) butter, softened
1 egg

★ Preheat oven to 350°. Crumble cake mix in bowl and stir in butter and egg. Pat into sprayed 9 x 13-inch baking pan.

Filling:

1 (8 ounce) package cream cheese, softened
1 (1 pound) box powdered sugar
2 eggs
3 - 4 tablespoons lemon juice for yellow cake or brewed coffee for chocolate cake

★ Beat cream cheese, powdered sugar, eggs, and lemon juice or coffee in bowl. Blend thoroughly and pour mixture over crust. Bake for 35 to 40 minutes or until brown. Serves 16 to 18.

 Snack Food Capital of the World   York, Pennsylvania

Easiest Favorite Cake

*Keep these ingredients on hand all the time so you can
bake at the last minute. It is so good and so easy.*

1 (18 ounce) box yellow cake mix
3 eggs
⅓ cup canola oil
1 box dry coconut-pecan frosting mix

★ Preheat oven to 350°. Combine cake mix, eggs, 1¼ cups water and oil in
  bowl and beat well. Stir in frosting mix and mix well.

★ Pour into sprayed, floured bundt pan and bake for 45 minutes. Cake is
  done when toothpick inserted in center comes out clean. Serves 18.

Down-Home Molasses Cake

½ cup shortening
½ cup sugar
3 eggs, separated
¾ teaspoon baking soda
⅔ cup molasses
2¼ plus cups flour
1 teaspoon ground cinnamon
¼ teaspoon ground cloves
¼ teaspoon ground mace
½ cup milk
½ cup raisins

★ Preheat oven to 350°. Cream shortening, sugar and egg yolks in bowl.
  In separate bowl, combine baking soda with molasses and add to
  shortening mixture.

★ Sift flour with cinnamon, cloves, mace and 1 teaspoon salt. Add
  alternately with milk to shortening mixture. Beat egg whites and stir
  into batter.

★ Dredge raisins lightly with flour and stir lightly into batter. Pour batter
  into sprayed, floured loaf pan and bake for 50 to 60 minutes. Serves 6 to 8.

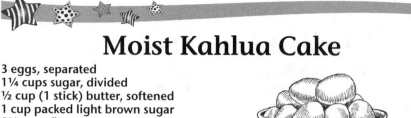

Moist Kahlua Cake

3 eggs, separated
1¼ cups sugar, divided
½ cup (1 stick) butter, softened
1 cup packed light brown sugar
2¼ cups flour
½ cup cocoa
1½ teaspoons baking soda
⅔ cup strong cold brewed coffee
⅔ cup Kahlua® liqueur

★ Preheat oven to 350°. Beat egg whites in bowl until frothy, pour in ¾ cup sugar and beat until stiff peaks form. Set aside. In separate bowl, cream butter, brown sugar and ½ cup sugar until fluffy. Beat in egg yolks one at a time.

★ Sift flour, cocoa and baking soda in bowl. Add to creamed mixture alternately with coffee and Kahlua® liqueur and blend well. Fold egg whites into batter.

★ Pour into sprayed, floured bundt pan and bake for 55 to 60 minutes. Cake is done when toothpick inserted in center comes out clean. Cool for about 10 to 15 minutes before removing cake from pan. Cool completely before frosting.

Icing:

1 cup powdered sugar
2 tablespoons cocoa
2 - 3 tablespoons Kahlua® liqueur

★ Blend powdered sugar, cocoa and Kahlua® liqueur in bowl, drizzle over top and let some drip down sides of cake. Serves 18 to 20.

Angel Food Cake

1 cup sifted flour
1¼ cups sugar, divided
8 egg whites
¾ teaspoon cream of tartar
1 teaspoon vanilla

★ Preheat oven to 325°. Sift flour and ¾ cup sugar several times. Beat egg whites with ½ teaspoon salt in bowl until frothy. Add cream of tartar and beat until peaks form. Fold in remaining sugar to form meringue. Then gently and gradually fold in flour mixture.

★ When it is partly blended, add vanilla. Use gentle folding motion to mix; stirring tends to release air that is needed for leavening.

★ Bake in sprayed, floured tube pan for 1 hour. After baking, invert cake and remove from pan when almost cold. Serves 18 to 20.

Rummy Yum Cake

1 cup chopped pecans or walnuts
1 (18 ounce) box yellow cake mix
1 (3 ounce) package vanilla instant pudding mix
½ cup dark rum
4 eggs
½ cup vegetable oil

★ Preheat oven to 325°. Sprinkle nuts in sprayed, floured 10-inch tube or 12-cup bundt pan.

★ Combine ½ cup cold water and remaining ingredients in bowl and pour over nuts and bake for 1 hour. Cool. Invert cake on serving plate.

Glaze:

½ cup (1 stick) butter
1 cup sugar
½ cup dark rum

★ Melt butter in saucepan and stir in ¼ cup water and sugar. Boil for 5 minutes and stir constantly. Remove from heat and add rum.

★ Prick top of cake and drizzle glaze evenly over top and sides. Allow cake to absorb glaze and repeat until glaze is completely used. Serves 18 to 20.

Plain Sponge Cake

1 cup sifted flour
4 large eggs, separated
1 cup sugar, divided
2 tablespoons lemon juice
1 teaspoon lemon peel, grated
Powdered sugar, optional

★ Preheat oven to 350°. Sift flour. Beat egg yolks until thick and lemon-colored. Gradually add half sugar, beat thoroughly and add lemon juice and peel. Beat until thick.

★ Beat egg whites and ¼ teaspoon salt until they start to peak but will still flow. Fold in rest of sugar, then yolk mixture. Fold in flour gently.

★ Pour batter into baking pan as soon as it is mixed. A large or medium-size loaf or tube pan is best. The center opening allows mixture to heat evenly.

★ Sift powdered sugar over top to make desirable crust. The oven should be ready for the cake as soon as it is mixed and in pan.

★ Bake for 50 to 60 minutes. After baking, invert cake to cool, but remove from pan before it is entirely cool. Serves 18.

Boston Cream Pie

This "pudding cake" is a cake, but was originally made in pie tins because they were plentiful in the mid 1800's and the tradition carries on today.

1½ cups sugar
¾ cup (1½ sticks) butter, softened
1 teaspoon vanilla
2 large eggs
2 cups flour*
2½ teaspoons baking powder
¾ cup milk

★ Preheat oven to 350°F. Combine sugar, butter and vanilla in mixing bowl and beat until mixture is light and fluffy. Beat eggs, one at a time, into mixture thoroughly.

★ Sift flour, baking powder, ½ teaspoon salt and beat into sugar-butter mixture, alternately with milk.

★ Pour into sprayed, floured 10-inch spring-form baking pan. Bake 50 to 60 minutes or until a toothpick comes out clean. Remove from oven and cool on wire rack. After cool, remove from pan.

Custard for Pie:

⅓ cup sugar
3 tablespoons cornstarch
1 cup milk
3 large eggs
½ cup whipping cream
1 teaspoon vanilla
3 tablespoons butter

★ Combine sugar, cornstarch, milk, eggs, cream, vanilla and ½ teaspoon salt in saucepan and whisk until smooth. Over medium heat, stir constantly and let custard boil for 2 minutes. Remove from heat and whisk in butter. Set custard aside to cool, but whisk occasionally.

Glaze for Pie:

6 ounces bittersweet chocolate
2 tablespoons butter
1½ tablespoons light corn syrup

★ Place chocolate, butter, corn syrup and ¼ teaspoon salt in double broiler and stir until mixture melts and is smooth. Remove from heat.

★ To put cake together, cut cake in half horizontally with long serrated knife. Place half cake on cake platter with cut side facing up. Spread custard on top. Place other half of cake with cut side down on top of custard. Coat top with glaze and allow a little to drip down the sides. Serves 18 to 20.

TIP: Cake flour is lighter and works better, if you have it.

Emergency Cheesecake

1 (8 ounce) package cream cheese, softened
1 (14 ounce) sweetened condensed milk
½ cup lemon juice
1 teaspoon vanilla
1 (6 ounce) graham cracker piecrust
1 (21 ounce) can favorite pie filling

★ Blend all ingredients with mixer except piecrust. Pour into graham
   cracker crust and refrigerate. Top with favorite pie filling. Serves 8 to 10.

Cheesecake

2 (8 ounce) packages cream cheese, softened
3 eggs
½ cup sugar
½ teaspoon almond extract
½ pint sour cream
2 tablespoons sugar
1 teaspoon vanilla

★ Preheat oven to 350°. Blend cream cheese, eggs, sugar and almond
   extract. Pour into pie shell and bake 30 minutes. Remove from oven and
   reduce heat to 300°. Mix well sour cream, sugar and vanilla. Pour into
   sunken shell. Bake at 300° for 10 minutes. Serves 8 to 10.

Toppings:

★ Cheesecake may be served by itself or with toppings such as cherry
   pie filling, blueberry pie filling, fresh strawberries, fresh blueberries or
   sauces such as lemon, caramel, chocolate, etc.

Red Cherry Cheesecake

This is so simple and so beautiful. People will really be impressed.

2 (8 ounce) packages cream cheese, softened
½ cup sugar
½ teaspoon vanilla
2 eggs
1 (9 inch) graham cracker piecrust
1 (20 ounce) can cherry pie filling

★ Preheat oven to 350°. Beat cream cheese, sugar, vanilla and eggs with
   mixer until creamy. Pour into piecrust. Bake for 35 to 40 minutes and
   cool. Refrigerate for about 30 minutes or more. Top with cherry pie
   filling. Serves 6 to 8.

Pumpkin Cheesecake

This combination of pumpkin pie and cheesecake brings together two of America's favorite desserts.

Crust:

1 cup ground gingersnaps crumbs
1 cup ground graham cracker crumbs
⅓ cup plus 1 tablespoon butter, softened
2 tablespoons sugar

★ Mix all ingredients until mixture sticks together. Pour into springform pan and press down evenly on bottom of pan. Refrigerate.

Pumpkin Filling:

4 (8 ounce) packages cream cheese, softened
1 cup packed light brown sugar
1 (15 ounce) can pumpkin
1 tablespoon pumpkin pie spice*
1 teaspoon vanilla extract
4 eggs

★ Preheat oven to 350°. Beat cream cheese with mixer until creamy. Add brown sugar, pumpkin, pumpkin pie spice and vanilla until they blend well. Add eggs, one at a time, and beat on low speed after each addition. Place springform pan on baking sheet and pour pumpkin filling into pan.

★ Bake for 1 hour 20 minutes or until edges of cheesecake are puffy and center is almost firm. Do not test with toothpick or knife to avoid cracking. (Do not overcook.) Loosen cheesecake sides with knife, but keep the rim in place. Refrigerate 3 or 4 hours before serving. Serves 8 to 10.

TIP: If you don't want to buy pumpkin pie spice, use ½ teaspoon ground cinnamon, ¼ teaspoon ground ginger, ⅛ teaspoon ground nutmeg and ⅛ teaspoon ground cloves.

Caramel Sauce for Cheesecakes

2 cups sugar
1½ tablespoons light corn syrup
2 tablespoons butter
⅔ cup whipping cream

★ Combine sugar, corn syrup, ½ cup water and butter in saucepan over medium heat; stir almost constantly until mixture turns light brown. Pour in whipping cream a little at a time and continue stirring until mixture gets to right consistency to pour over cheesecake.

Very Blueberry Cheesecake

34 vanilla wafers, crushed
6 tablespoons (¾ stick) butter, melted
1 (.3 ounce) packet unflavored gelatin
2 (8 ounce) packages cream cheese, softened
1 tablespoon lemon juice
1 (7 ounce) jar marshmallow creme
¼ cup powdered sugar
1 (16 ounce) can blueberries, drained
1 (8 ounce) carton frozen whipped topping, thawed

★ Place crumbs in sprayed 9-inch springform pan. Pour melted butter in pan, mix well and pat down. Soften gelatin in ¼ cup cold water in saucepan. Place over low heat just until it dissolves.

★ Combine cream cheese, lemon juice, marshmallow creme, powdered sugar and gelatin in bowl and beat until smooth.

★ Puree blueberries in blender. Fold whipped topping and pureed blueberries into cream cheese mixture and pour into springform pan. Refrigerate for several hours before serving. Serves 12 to 14.

Praline Cheesecake

1¼ cups graham cracker crumbs
¼ cup sugar
¼ cup (½ stick) butter, melted
3 (8 ounce) packages cream cheese, softened
1¼ cups packed dark brown sugar
2 tablespoons flour
3 large eggs
2 teaspoons vanilla
½ cup finely chopped pecans
Pecan halves
Maple syrup

★ Preheat oven to 350°. Combine crumbs, sugar and butter in bowl and press in 9-inch springform pan. Bake for 10 minutes.

★ Combine cream cheese, brown sugar and flour in bowl and blend on medium speed. Add eggs, one at a time, and mix well after each addition. Blend in vanilla, stir in pecans and pour mixture over crust. Bake for 50 to 55 minutes.

★ Remove from oven and loosen cake from rim of pan. Let cake cool before removing from pan. Refrigerate. Place pecan halves around edge of cake (about 1 inch from edge and 1 inch apart) and pour syrup over top.

★ When you slice cheesecake, pour 1 tablespoon of syrup over each slice so some will run down sides. Serves 16 to 18.

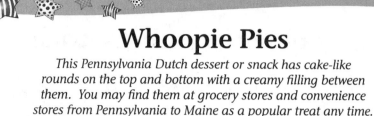

Whoopie Pies

This Pennsylvania Dutch dessert or snack has cake-like rounds on the top and bottom with a creamy filling between them. You may find them at grocery stores and convenience stores from Pennsylvania to Maine as a popular treat any time.

1 cup shortening, divided
1¼ cups sugar
2 eggs, separated
1 cup milk
2 teaspoons vanilla, divided
2 cups flour
¼ cup cocoa
1 teaspoon baking powder
1 teaspoon baking soda
2 cups powdered sugar, divided

★ Preheat oven to 375°. Cream ½ cup shortening and sugar in large bowl. Beat egg yolks until lightly colored and pour into sugar mixture; add milk and 1 teaspoon vanilla. Mix well and beat again.

★ In separate bowl, mix flour, cocoa, baking powder, baking soda and ½ teaspoon salt. Gradually pour a little flour mixture at a time into shortening-sugar mixture and beat after each addition.

★ Drop spoonfuls of mixture onto unsprayed cookie sheets and bake for about 8 minutes or until done. Cream remaining ½ cup shortening, two-thirds of powdered sugar, 1 teaspoon vanilla and ½ teaspoon salt in large bowl.

★ Beat egg whites until stiff. Pour remaining one-third of powdered sugar into egg whites and beat. Add shortening mixture to egg whites and beat for about 2 minutes. Make "sandwiches" of the cakes and filling. Wrap each individually and eat right away. Yields 8 to 12 pies.

Easy Chocolate Dessert Sauce

This chocolate sauce works on just about anything you want to pour it on.

1 cup semi-sweet chocolate chips
¾ cup whipping cream
1 teaspoon vanilla

★ Melt chocolate chips over low heat with whipping cream; stir constantly. When chocolate is creamy, add vanilla and move from heat. Cool slightly and pour over ice cream, cakes, pies or cookies. Yields about 1 cup.

Sweets – Pies

Grandma's Buttermilk Pie

4 eggs
1 cup sugar
3 tablespoons flour
2 tablespoons butter, melted
3 tablespoons lemon juice
1¼ cups buttermilk*
½ teaspoon lemon extract
1 (9 inch) baked piecrust, chilled

★ Preheat oven to 350°. Beat eggs in large bowl until light and fluffy. Gradually add sugar and blend in flour, butter and lemon juice. Add buttermilk slowly and mix until it blends well. Stir in lemon extract.

★ Pour into piecrust; bake for 45 minutes or until knife inserted in center come out clean. Serve room temperature or chilled, but refrigerate any leftovers. Serves 8.

TIP: To make buttermilk, mix 1 cup milk with 1 tablespoon lemon juice or vinegar and let stand for about 10 minutes.

Southern Whiskey Pie

5 eggs
1¾ cups sugar
1 tablespoon vinegar
¼ cup bourbon
⅓ cup (⅔ stick) butter, melted
1 (9 inch) refrigerated piecrust

★ Preheat oven to 325°. Beat eggs in bowl until light and gradually add sugar. Stir in vinegar, bourbon and butter and mix well.

★ Pour into piecrust and bake for 35 minutes until light brown on top. Serve warm or at room temperature. Serves 6.

TIP: Protect piecrust from excess browning by placing 1-inch strip of foil around edges.

In the late 1780's, Reverend Elijah Craig, a Baptist minister, developed corn liquor or bourbon whiskey in Scott County, Kentucky.

Cream Puff Pie

*This recipe gives you the same accolades of
individual cream puffs without the time.*

Crust:

¼ cup shortening
½ cup flour
2 eggs

★ Preheat oven to 400°. Mix ½ cup boiling water, shortening and ⅛ teaspoon salt in saucepan over heat. Stir in flour all at once. Stir until mixture pulls away from sides and forms into a ball.

★ Remove from heat and cool slightly. Beat in eggs, one at a time, until smooth. Spread in bottom of sprayed 9-inch pie pan but not onto sides.

★ Bake for 50 to 60 minutes. Sides will rise up and curl in slightly. Cool slowly away from drafts.

Filling:

1 (4 ounce) package instant vanilla pudding
1 cup whipped cream
Strawberries
1 cup frozen whipped topping, thawed

★ Mix vanilla pudding according to package directions. Fold in whipped cream. Pour cream filling into crust and top with strawberries. Top with additional whipped topping. Serves 8.

Pink Lemonade Pie

1 (6 ounce) can pink lemonade frozen concentrate
1 (14 ounce) can sweetened condensed milk
1 (12 ounce) package frozen whipped topping, thawed
1 (6 ounce) graham cracker piecrust

★ Combine lemonade concentrate and sweetened condensed milk in large bowl and blend well. Fold in whipped topping and pour into piecrust. Refrigerate overnight. Serves 8 to 10.

*No matter how old a mother is, she watches
her middle-aged children for signs of improvement.*
–Florida Scott-Maxwell

Real Strawberry-Margarita Pie

¼ cup frozen pink lemonade concentrate, thawed
2 tablespoons tequila
2 tablespoons triple sec liqueur
1 teaspoon grated lime peel
1 pint fresh strawberries, sliced
1 quart strawberry ice cream, softened
1 (6 ounce) ready graham cracker piecrust, chilled
Strawberries

★ Combine and mix lemonade, tequila, triple sec, lime peel and strawberries in large bowl. Fold in softened ice cream. Work quickly so ice cream will not melt completely.

★ Spoon mixture into chilled crust and freeze. Take out of freezer about 10 minutes before serving to slice. Garnish with strawberries. Serves 6.

Key Lime Pie

4 egg yolks, beaten
2 (14 ounces) cans sweetened condensed milk
1 cup key lime juice
1 (9-inch) prepared piecrust
Whipped cream

★ Preheat oven to 375°. Combine egg yolks, milk and key lime juice and mix. Pour into unbaked shortbread crust and bake for 15 minutes; refrigerate. Top with dollops of whipped cream and lime slices.

TIP: Authentic Key lime pie is yellow, not green. The egg yolks create the color, but you can add a few drops of green food coloring if you prefer.

Cherry-Pecan Pie

1 (14 ounce) can sweetened condensed milk
¼ cup lemon juice
1 (8 ounce) carton frozen whipped topping, thawed
1 cup chopped pecans
1 (20 ounce) can cherry pie filling
2 (6 ounce) graham cracker piecrusts

★ Combine condensed milk and lemon juice and stir well. Fold in whipped topping. Fold pecans and pie filling into mixture. Spoon into piecrusts. Refrigerate overnight. Serves 6 to 8.

 Raisins Capital of the World   Fresno and Selma, California

Macaroon Crunch Pie

½ cup plus 2 tablespoons shredded coconut, divided
1 (9 inch) baked piecrust
3 cups orange sherbet, softened
1½ cups whipping cream
⅓ cup powdered sugar
1 cup crushed crisp macaroon cookies
½ cup chopped pecans

★ Preheat oven to 325°.

★ Toast ½ cup coconut in shallow pan for 5 to 10 minutes or until light brown. Stir often to keep from burning. Remove from oven and sprinkle toasted coconut into piecrust. Cover with sherbet and place in freezer.

★ Beat cream and powdered sugar in bowl until thick. Set aside 1 cup for topping.

★ Fold crushed cookies and pecans into remaining cream-sugar mixture. Spoon over sherbet and top with set aside whipping cream and 2 tablespoons coconut. Freeze for 6 hours. Serves 8.

TIP: *This pie will store and freeze well. Also, substitute your choice of sherbet flavor.*

Pennsylvania Dutch Shoo-Fly Pie

1 cup flour
½ cup packed brown sugar
1 teaspoon baking soda
Shortening
½ cup molasses
1 (9 inch) frozen piecrust, unbaked

★ Preheat oven to 350°. Mix flour, brown sugar, baking soda and a pinch of salt in bowl. Add just enough shortening to make mixture crumbly.

★ Mix molasses and ½ cup boiling water in saucepan. While hot, pour molasses into piecrust. Spread flour crumbles over top of molasses. Bake until firm in middle and toothpick inserted in center comes out clean. Serves 8.

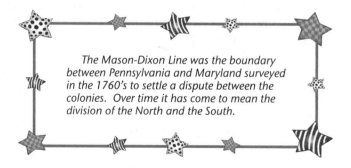

The Mason-Dixon Line was the boundary between Pennsylvania and Maryland surveyed in the 1760's to settle a dispute between the colonies. Over time it has come to mean the division of the North and the South.

German Chocolate Pie

1 (4 ounce) package German sweet chocolate
½ cup (1 stick) butter
1 (12 ounce) can evaporated milk
1½ cups sugar
3 tablespoons cornstarch
2 eggs
1 teaspoon vanilla
1 (9 inch) refrigerated piecrust
1 (3.5 ounce) can flaked coconut
¾ cup chopped pecans

★ Preheat oven to 350°. Melt chocolate with butter in saucepan over low heat and gradually blend in milk.

★ Combine sugar, cornstarch and ⅛ teaspoon salt in bowl and mix thoroughly. Beat in eggs and vanilla, gradually blend into chocolate mixture and pour into piecrust.

★ Combine coconut and pecans in bowl and sprinkle over filling. Bake for 45 to 50 minutes. Filling will be soft but will set while cooking. Cool for at least 4 hours before slicing. Serves 8.

Chocolate Pie

¾ cup sugar
3 tablespoons flour
¼ cup (½ stick) butter
3 egg yolks, beaten
1 (12 ounce) can evaporated milk
5.5 ounces chocolate syrup
1 tablespoon vanilla
1 (9 inch) baked piecrust
Whipped cream or frozen whipped topping, thawed

★ Mix sugar and flour in saucepan. Add butter, ¼ teaspoon salt, egg yolks, evaporated milk, chocolate syrup and vanilla. Stir until all ingredients are moist.

★ Bring to a boil and cook for 8 to 10 minutes. Stir constantly. Cool and stir several times. Pour into piecrust. Top with whipped cream or whipped topping. Garnish with shaved chocolate, if desired. Serves 8.

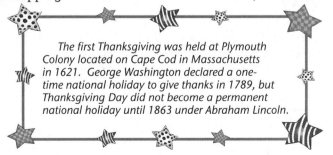

The first Thanksgiving was held at Plymouth Colony located on Cape Cod in Massachusetts in 1621. George Washington declared a one-time national holiday to give thanks in 1789, but Thanksgiving Day did not become a permanent national holiday until 1863 under Abraham Lincoln.

Chocolate Meringue Pie

2 egg yolks
2 cups milk, divided
½ cup sugar
⅓ cup self-rising flour*
2 tablespoons butter
¾ teaspoon vanilla
1 (8 inch) baked piecrust
½ cup semi-sweet chocolate chips
½ cup pecan pieces

★ Combine egg yolks with ¼ cup milk in double boiler. Add sugar, flour and ½ teaspoon salt and mix thoroughly. Add remaining milk.

★ Cook over boiling water for about 6 to 7 minutes and stir constantly until thick. Cover and cook for additional 5 minutes.

★ Remove from boiling water and stir in butter and vanilla. Pour into piecrust and sprinkle chocolate chips and pecans over filling.

Meringue:

2 egg whites
¼ cup sugar

★ Preheat oven to 425°. Beat egg whites in bowl until foamy. Add sugar and beat until meringue forms stiff peaks. Spread over pie and bake for 10 minutes or until light brown. Serves 6 to 8.

TIP: If you don't have self-rising flour, add ½ teaspoon baking powder and ⅛ teaspoon salt to ⅓ cup all-purpose flour and mix well.

Brownie Pie

Really a special treat!

1 cup sugar
½ cup flour
2 eggs, beaten slightly
½ cup (1 stick) butter, melted
1 cup chopped pecans
1 cup chocolate chips
1 teaspoon vanilla
1 (9 inch) refrigerated piecrust
Frozen whipped topping, thawed

★ Preheat oven to 350°. Combine sugar and flour in bowl and add eggs. Add slightly cooled melted butter and mix well. Add pecans, chocolate chips and vanilla and pour into piecrust. Bake for 45 minutes and top with whipped topping. Serves 6.

Chocolate Angel Pie

2 egg whites
⅛ teaspoon cream of tartar
½ cup sugar
½ cup finely chopped walnuts or pecans
1½ teaspoons vanilla, divided
4 (1 ounce) squares German sweet chocolate
1 (8 ounce) carton whipping cream, whipped

★ Preheat oven to 325°. Beat egg whites with ⅛ teaspoon salt and cream of tartar in bowl until foamy. Add sugar gradually, beating until very stiff peak holds. Fold in nuts and ½ teaspoon vanilla.

★ Spread in sprayed 8 or 9-inch pie pan or into 8 individual pie pans. Build up sides to ½ inch above pan to form a meringue shell. Bake for 50 to 55 minutes. Cool.

★ Melt chocolate in 3 tablespoons water in double boiler over low heat and stir constantly. Cool until thick. Add 1 teaspoon vanilla and fold into whipped cream. Pile into meringue shell. Refrigerate for at least 2 hours before serving. Serves 8.

TIP: You can prepare this recipe 1 to 2 days ahead.

Chocolate Chess Pie

1 (8 - 9 inch) refrigerated piecrust
½ cup (1 stick) butter
1 (1 ounce) square unsweetened chocolate
1 cup sugar
2 eggs
1 teaspoon vanilla
Whipped cream
½ cup nuts

★ Preheat oven to 450°. If desired, bake crust for about 5 minutes. Remove crust from oven and reduce heat to 350°. Melt butter and chocolate in double boiler.

★ Blend in sugar, eggs, vanilla and a dash of salt and thoroughly combine with butter and chocolate. Pour into piecrust and bake for 25 to 30 minutes. Top with whipped cream and nuts. Serves 8.

I am not young enough to know everything.
–Oscar Wilde

Mississippi Mud Pie

*The Mississippi Mud Pie and Mississippi Mud Cake
both allude to the muddy banks of the Mississippi River.
No one knows for sure which came first: the pie or cake.*

4 ounces chocolate wafers
½ cup (1 stick) butter
1 quart coffee ice cream, softened
1½ cups chocolate fudge ice cream topping
Frozen whipped topping, thawed
Sliced almonds

★ Process wafers to crumbs. Melt butter in saucepan, add wafer crumbs
and stir well. Press buttered wafer crumbs in bottom and sides of 9-inch
pie pan and cool.

★ Spread ice cream on top of wafer crust. Freeze for several hours or until
firm. Spread fudge topping over top and freeze overnight. Serve with
whipped topping and garnish with sliced almonds. Serves 6.

Sinful Sundae Pie

You must do this ahead of time so it will freeze.

1 cup evaporated milk
1 (6 ounce) package semi-sweet chocolate pieces
1 cup miniature marshmallows
1 quart vanilla ice cream, softened
1 (9 inch) vanilla wafer crumb crust (recipe follows)
Chopped walnuts or slivered almonds, toasted

★ Combine evaporated milk, chocolate and ¼ teaspoon salt in saucepan.
Stir over low heat until mixture melts and is thick. Remove from heat
and add marshmallows. Stir until they melt and are smooth. Cool to
room temperature.

★ Spoon half ice cream into crust. Cover with half chocolate mixture.
Repeat layers. Garnish with nuts and freeze until firm, at least 5 hours.

Vanilla Wafer Crumb Crust:

1½ cups vanilla wafer crumbs
¼ cup (½ stick butter, softened

★ Preheat oven to 350°. Combine ingredients until they blend well and
press into 9-inch pie pan. Bake for 10 minutes. Cool. Serves 8.

Strawberry Capital of the World   Oxnard, California

White Chocolate Pie

4 ounces white chocolate
20 large marshmallows
½ cup milk
1 (8 ounce) carton frozen whipped topping, thawed
½ cup chopped pecans
½ cup maraschino cherries, chopped, well drained
1 (9 inch) baked piecrust

★ Melt white chocolate, marshmallows and milk in double boiler and cool. Add whipped topping, pecans and cherries, pour in piecrust and freeze. Remove from freezer 5 to 10 minutes before serving. Serves 6 to 8.

Mom's Pecan Pie

1 cup pecan halves
1 (9 inch) refrigerated piecrust
1 cup corn syrup
¾ cup sugar
3 tablespoons butter, melted
1 teaspoon vanilla
3 eggs, slightly beaten

★ Preheat oven to 375°. Place pecans in piecrust and make sure pecans are evenly distributed in crust. Combine corn syrup, sugar, butter, vanilla and eggs in bowl and mix well. Pour into piecrust and rearrange pecans, if necessary.

★ Place 1-inch strips of foil around edges of piecrust to prevent excessive browning. Bake for 10 minutes, reduce heat to 325° and bake for 45 minutes or until center sets. Serves 8.

Fluffy Pecan Pie

3 large egg whites
1 teaspoon cream of tartar
1 cup sugar
12 soda crackers, crushed
1½ teaspoons vanilla
1½ cups chopped pecans

★ Preheat oven to 350°. Beat egg whites with cream of tartar in bowl until frothy. Gradually add sugar and continue beating until stiff peaks form.

★ Fold in crackers, vanilla and pecans mix well. Pour into 9-inch glass pie pan. Bake for about 30 minutes or until pie is firm. Serves 8.

Peanut Pie

You will need to make this in advance and freeze.

1 (3 ounce) package cream cheese
½ cup peanut butter
1 cup powdered sugar
½ cup milk
1 (8 ounce) carton frozen whipped topping, thawed
1 (6 ounce) ready graham cracker piecrust
¼ cup finely chopped peanuts

★ Beat cream cheese, peanut butter, powdered sugar and milk in bowl until smooth. Fold in whipped topping.

★ Pour into piecrust and top with peanuts. Freeze. Do not thaw before cutting and serving pie. Serves 6.

Apple Crumb Pie

6 cooking apples
2 teaspoons lemon juice
½ cup sugar
1 cup all-purpose flour
1 cup packed brown sugar
½ teaspoon ground cinnamon
½ teaspoon ground ginger
½ teaspoon ground mace
½ cup butter
1 (9 inch) prepared pie crust

★ Preheat oven to 400°. Pare apples, cut in eights and remove core. In large mixing bowl place apples and sprinkle with lemon juice. Sprinkle with sugar and toss to mix.

★ Arrange apples in unbaked pie shell. Mix flour, brown sugar, spices and butter, mix until crumbly. Spoon evenly over apples. Bake 45 minutes. Serves 6 to 8.

Middle age is when you've met so many people that every new person you meet reminds you of someone else.
–Ogden Nash

All-American Apple Pie

1 (15 ounce) package refrigerated double piecrust
¾ cup sugar
2 tablespoons flour
1 teaspoon ground cinnamon
6 tart apples, (gala, granny smith)
1 tablespoon butter, softened
1 large egg white, lightly beaten

★ Preheat oven to 400°. Line 9-inch pie pan with 1 piecrust; trim extra crust even with edge. Mix sugar, flour and cinnamon in large bowl. Peel, core and slice apples. Gently toss with sugar mixture.

★ Pour into pie crust and dot with butter. Place remaining piecrust over filling. Trim, seal and flute edges. Cut slits in top.

★ Bake for 20 to 25 minutes or until crust is golden brown and filling is bubbly. Cool on wire rack. Refrigerate leftovers. Serves 8.

Old-Fashioned Cherry Pie

4 cups pitted cherries
1¼ cups sugar
¼ cup flour
¼ teaspoon cinnamon
2 (9 inch) frozen piecrusts
2 tablespoons butter

★ Preheat oven to 425°. Gently mix cherries and sugar in large bowl. Stir in flour and cinnamon. Spoon mixture over bottom crust in pie pan. Dot with butter and place top crust over pie filling.

★ Fold edges of top crust under edges of bottom crust to seal. Flute edges with fingers and cut several slits in top crust. Bake for 15 minutes and remove pie from oven.

★ Cover edges of piecrust with foil to prevent excessive browning. Return to oven and bake for 20 to 25 minutes or until pie bubbles and crust is golden brown. Serves 8.

It's surprising how much of memory is built around things unnoticed at the time.

Creamy Blueberry Pie

4 cups fresh blueberries
1 (9 inch) refrigerated piecrust
1 cup sugar
⅓ cup flour
2 eggs, beaten
½ cup sour cream

★ Preheat oven to 350°. Place blueberries in piecrust. Combine sugar and flour in bowl. In separate bowl, blend eggs and sour cream and add sugar mixture to eggs. Spoon over blueberries.

Topping:

½ cup sugar
½ cup flour
¼ cup (½ stick) butter, softened

★ Combine sugar, flour and butter in bowl. Mix well. Crumble evenly over sour cream mixture. Bake for 1 hour or until light brown. Serves 8.

Banana Split Pie

3 small bananas
1 (6 ounce) graham cracker piecrust
1 quart vanilla ice cream, softened
Fudge sauce
Frozen whipped topping, thawed
½ cup chopped pecans
6 maraschino cherries with stems

★ Slice bananas and place on 6-ounce graham cracker piecrust. Spoon softened ice cream over bananas. Freeze for 2 to 3 hours.

★ Spread some fudge sauce over ice cream and top with layer of whipped topping and pecans. When ready to serve, place cherry on top of each piece of pie. Serves 6.

Banana Split

Dr. David Strickler worked at Tassel Pharmacy in Latrobe, Pennsylvania filling prescriptions and jerking sodas and scooping ice cream behind the pharmacy's soda fountain. To attract college students from St. Vincent College, Strickler made several ice cream sundae concoctions. None were as popular as the one he served with a banana split longwise and placed parallel on a dish with ice cream in the center. To give it a little razzle-dazzle, he poured crushed pineapple over the vanilla ice cream, chocolate syrup over the chocolate ice cream and strawberry sauce over the strawberry ice cream. To finish it off he put a dollop of whipped cream on top of each scoop of ice cream and a stemmed maraschino cherry on top. The original price was 10 cents.

Cranberry Pie

2 cups fresh or frozen cranberries
1½ cups sugar, divided
½ cup chopped walnuts or pecans
2 eggs
1 cup flour
¼ cup shortening, melted
½ cup (1 stick) butter, melted

★ Preheat oven to 325°. Spread cranberries in sprayed 10-inch deep-dish pie pan. Sprinkle with ½ cup sugar and nuts.

★ Beat eggs well in bowl, add remaining sugar gradually and beat thoroughly. Add flour, shortening and butter to sugar mixture and mix well. Pour over top of cranberries and bake for 1 hour or until crust is golden brown. Serves 8.

Lemon Meringue Pie

1½ cups sugar
¼ cup butter, softened
⅓ cup cornstarch
4 eggs, separated
¼ cup lemon juice
2 tablespoons lemon zest
1 (9-inch) baked pie shell

★ Combine sugar, ½ teaspoon salt, 1 cup water and butter. Heat until sugar dissolves. Blend cornstarch with ½ cup cold water and slowly add to hot mixture. Cook on low heat until clear.

★ Beat egg yolks and slowly add to mixture and cook another 3 minutes, stirring constantly. Remove from heat and add lemon juice and zest. Pour in baked pie shell. Set aside. Preheat oven to 375°.

Meringue:

4 egg whites
1 teaspoon vanilla
¼ teaspoon cream of tartar
⅔ cup sugar

★ Blend egg whites, vanilla and cream of tartar. With mixer on high speed, mix until peaks form. Gradually add sugar while beating constantly. Beat until sugar dissolves. Spread on lemon filling and seal sides. Brown in oven for 10 to 15 minutes. Serves 8.

Cranberry Capital of the World   Middleboro, Massachusetts

Old-Fashioned Lemon-Chess Pie

1¼ cups sugar
3 large eggs
½ cup corn syrup
1 tablespoon cornmeal
¾ cup sour cream
½ teaspoon vanilla
¼ cup lemon juice
1 (9 inch) refrigerated piecrust

★ Preheat oven to 350°. Beat sugar and eggs in bowl and mix well. Fold in corn syrup, cornmeal, sour cream, vanilla and lemon juice and mix well. Pour into piecrust.

★ Cut 1½-inch strips of foil and cover edges of crust to keep crust from excessive browning. Bake for 45 to 50 minutes or until knife inserted in center comes out clean. Serves 8.

Easy Creamy Lemon Pie

1 (8 ounce) package cream cheese, softened
1 (14 ounce) can sweetened condensed milk
¼ cup lemon juice
1 (20 ounce) can lemon pie filling
1 (6 ounce) ready graham cracker piecrust

★ Beat cream cheese in bowl until smooth and creamy. Add sweetened condensed milk and lemon juice and beat until mixture is creamy.

★ Fold in lemon pie filling and stir well. Pour into piecrust and refrigerate for several hours before slicing and serving. Serves 6 to 8.

Easy Peanut Butter Pie

⅔ cup crunchy peanut butter
1 (8 ounce) package cream cheese, softened
½ cup milk
1 cup powdered sugar
1 (8 ounce) carton frozen whipped topping, thawed
1 graham cracker piecrust

★ Blend peanut butter, cream cheese, milk and powdered sugar together and fold in whipped topping. Pour into piecrust. Refrigerate several hours before serving. Serves 8.

Peanut Capital of the World   Dothan, Alabama
Terrell County, Georgia   Sylvester, Georgia
Suffolk, Virginia

Peach Parfait Pie

1 (9 inch) unbaked piecrust
3½ cups peeled, sliced fresh peaches
¾ cup sugar
1 (3 ounce) package lemon gelatin
1 (1 pint) carton vanilla ice cream, softened
1 (8 ounce) carton frozen whipped topping, thawed

★ Bake piecrust according to package directions and cool or use a ready graham cracker crust. Sweeten fresh peaches with sugar and let stand for 15 minutes.

★ In saucepan, combine 1 cup water and gelatin, heat to a boil and stir until it dissolves. Spoon ice cream into mixture and stir until ice cream melts.

★ Refrigerate until mixture mounds slightly when dropped from spoon. Fold in peaches. Spoon mixture into piecrust and refrigerate until firm. Top with whipped topping. Serves 8.

Apricot Fried Pies

These fall in the "fried pies" category, but they're baked.
It's an old family recipe and the name just stuck.

1 (8 ounce) package dried apricots
1½ cups sugar

★ Place apricots, sugar and about 2 to 3 cups water in saucepan, bring to a boil, lower heat and simmer about 1 hour or until apricots are tender and liquid is gone. Stir frequently. (Add water if necessary so apricots cook long enough to get tender.) Mash peaches and cool completely.

Piecrust:

If you don't want to make the piecrust, buy 2 (9 inch) unbaked piecrusts.

2 cups flour
½ cup oil
¼ cup milk

★ Preheat oven to 350°. Mix ingredients well. Place large sheet of wax paper on counter and place dough in center. Place second sheet on top. Hold bottom sheet of wax paper against counter with stomach to keep it from sliding.

★ Turn several times to roll out to about ⅛ inch thick. Cut into 6-inch diameter circles, spoon several dollops of apricots in center and fold over.

★ Press fork into cut edges to seal and sprinkle a little extra sugar over pies. Bake for 10 to 15 minutes or until pies are slightly brown. Cool on rack. Yields 8 to 10 individual pies.

Easy Pineapple-Coconut Pie

1 (9 inch) refrigerated deep-dish piecrust
½ cup (1 stick) butter, melted
2 cups sugar
4 eggs, slightly beaten
1 (10 ounce) can flaked coconut
1 (8 ounce) can pineapple chunks, slightly drained

★ Preheat oven to 350°. Mix all ingredients in bowl and pour into piecrust. Bake for 45 minutes to 1 hour or until golden brown. Serves 8.

Old-Time Pineapple-Chess Pie

1½ cups sugar
1 tablespoon cornmeal
2 tablespoons flour
6 tablespoons (¾ stick) butter, melted
2 eggs, beaten
1 (8 ounce) can crushed pineapple with juice
1 (9 inch) refrigerated piecrust

★ Preheat oven to 350°. Combine sugar, cornmeal, flour and pinch of salt in bowl and mix. Stir in butter, eggs and pineapple and beat. Pour into piecrust and bake for 45 minutes. Serves 8.

Thanksgiving Pumpkin Pie

This is a traditional pumpkin pie. It's very easy.

¾ cup sugar
2 teaspoons ground cinnamon
½ teaspoon ground ginger
½ teaspoon ground cloves
2 large eggs
1 (15 ounce) can pumpkin
1 (12 ounce) can evaporated milk
1 (9-inch) unbaked deep-dish piecrust
Whipped cream or frozen whipped topping, thawed

★ Preheat oven to 425°. Mix sugar, cinnamon, ginger, cloves and ½ teaspoon salt in small bowl. In larger bowl, beat eggs; stir in sugar mixture and pumpkin. Stir in evaporated milk a little at a time. Pour into piecrust.

★ Bake at 425° for 15 minutes and reduce temperature to 350°. Bake for additional 40 to 50 minutes or until toothpick inserted in center comes out clean. Cool for several hours before serving or refrigerate. Top with whipped cream. Serves 8.

Creamy Pumpkin Pie

1 (8 ounce) package cream cheese, softened
2½ cups powdered sugar, divided
1 (8 ounce) carton frozen whipped topping, thawed
2 (6 ounce) ready butter-flavored piecrusts
¼ cup milk
1 (5 ounce) package instant vanilla pudding
1 (15 ounce) can pumpkin
2 teaspoons ground cinnamon

★ Combine cream cheese and 2 cups powdered sugar in bowl and beat
  until smooth and creamy. Fold in whipped topping and pour half cream
  cheese mixture in each piecrust.

★ In same bowl, combine milk, instant pudding mix and remaining ½ cup
  powdered sugar and beat until smooth.

★ Fold in pumpkin and cinnamon. Spread half pumpkin mixture over
  each pie. Refrigerate for 3 or 4 hours before serving. Eat one pie and
  freeze the other. Serves 12.

Mother's Pumpkin Chiffon Pie

This is a light, fluffy pumpkin pie and great any time.

1 (1 ounce) packet unflavored gelatin
2 eggs
1¼ cups sugar
1¼ cups canned pumpkin
⅔ cup milk
½ teaspoon ground ginger
½ teaspoon ground nutmeg
⅓ teaspoon ground cinnamon
1 (8 ounce) carton whipping cream
1 (9 inch) baked piecrust

★ Soften gelatin in ¼ cup cold water in bowl and set aside. In separate
  bowl, beat eggs for 3 minutes. Add sugar, pumpkin, milk, ginger,
  nutmeg, cinnamon and ½ teaspoon salt and mix well.

★ Pour mixture in double boiler and stir constantly until mixture reaches
  custard consistency. Mix in softened gelatin, dissolve in hot pumpkin
  mixture and cool.

★ When mixture is cool, whip cream in bowl until very stiff and fold into
  pumpkin mixture. (Do not use whipped topping.) Pour into piecrust
  and refrigerate for several hours before slicing. Serves 8.

*TIP: Original "chiffon" pies had egg whites whipped and folded into pie. Because
  raw eggs are not good in uncooked recipes, this recipe cooks the whole eggs
  and adds whipped cream. It is delicious!*

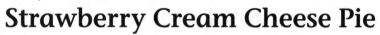

Strawberry Cream Cheese Pie

1 (10 ounce) package frozen sweetened strawberries, thawed
2 (8 ounce) packages cream cheese, softened
⅔ cup powdered sugar
1 (8 ounce) carton frozen whipped topping, thawed
1 (6 ounce) ready chocolate piecrust

★ Drain strawberries and set aside ¼ cup juice and several strawberries.
  Combine cream cheese, juice and powdered sugar in bowl and beat well.

★ Fold in strawberries and whipped topping and spoon into crust.
  Refrigerate overnight. Garnish with fresh strawberries to serve.
  Serves 6 to 8.

Strawberry Pie

1 cup sugar
¼ cup cornstarch
¼ cup strawberry gelatin
1 tablespoon lemon juice
2 cups sliced strawberries
2 (8 - 9 inch) baked piecrusts or 1 deep-dish crust
Frozen whipped topping, thawed

★ Combine sugar, cornstarch, gelatin, lemon juice and 1½ cups water in
  saucepan, cook until thick and stir occasionally. Cool.

★ Place berries in piecrusts and pour thickened mixture on top.
  Refrigerate for at least 3 hours. Serve with whipped topping and garnish
  with halved or whole strawberries, if desired. Serves 8.

Simple Sweet Potato Pie

1 (15 ounce) can sweet potatoes, drained, mashed
3 eggs
1 cup sugar
1 tablespoon butter, melted
1 (9 inch) piecrust

★ Preheat oven to 350°. In large bowl combine sweet potatoes, eggs, sugar
  and butter. Beat until all ingredients blend well. Pour into piecrust and
  bake until brown, about 1 hour.

★ If desire, remove pie from oven about 5 minutes early and top
  with ½ cup pecans and 1 cup marshmallows. Return to oven until
  marshmallows are light brown. Serves 6 to 8.

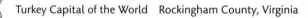

 Turkey Capital of the World   Rockingham County, Virginia

Sweets – Cobblers and Crisps

Easy Cinnamon-Apple Cobbler

2 (20 ounce) cans apple pie filling
½ cup packed brown sugar
1½ teaspoons ground cinnamon
1 (18 ounce) box yellow cake mix
½ cup (1 stick) butter, melted

★ Preheat oven to 350°. Spread apple pie filling in sprayed, floured
   9 x 13-inch baking dish. Sprinkle with brown sugar and cinnamon
   and top with dry cake mix. Drizzle melted butter over top of cake mix.
   Bake for 50 minutes or until light brown and bubbly. Serves 16.

Double-Berry Cobbler

1 (12 ounce) package frozen raspberries
1 (12 ounce) package frozen blackberries
⅓ cup sugar
⅓ cup flour
¼ cup (½ stick) butter, melted
½ (15 ounce) package refrigerated piecrust

★ Preheat oven to 375°. Combine raspberries, blackberries, sugar, flour
   and butter in large bowl and mix well. Spoon berry mixture into sprayed
   9 x 13-inch baking dish.

★ Roll 1 piecrust to fit on top of berry mixture and sprinkle with extra
   sugar. Bake for 1 hour or until golden brown and bubbly. Serves 16.

Easy Cherry Cobbler

2 (20 ounce) cans cherry pie filling
1 (18 ounce) box white cake mix
¾ cup (1½ sticks) butter, melted
1 (4 ounce) package slivered almonds
Frozen whipped topping, thawed

★ Preheat oven to 350°. Spread pie filling in sprayed 9 x 13-inch baking
   pan. Sprinkle cake mix over pie filling.

★ Drizzle butter over top and sprinkle with almonds. Bake for 45 minutes.
   Top with whipped topping to serve. Serves 16.

There are about 250 cherries in a cherry pie.

Easy Peach Cobbler

½ cup (1 stick) butter, melted
1 cup flour
2¼ cups sugar, divided
2 teaspoons baking powder
1 cup milk
3 - 4 cups fresh, ripe sliced peaches
1 teaspoon ground cinnamon

★ Preheat oven to 350°. Combine butter, flour, 1 cup sugar, baking powder and ¼ teaspoon salt in bowl; mix in milk and blend well.

★ Spoon into sprayed 9 x 13-inch glass baking dish. Combine sliced peaches, 1¼ cups sugar and cinnamon and pour over dough. Bake for 1 hour. Crust will come to top. Serves 10 to 12.

Quick-Easy Peach-Pineapple Cobbler

1 (20 ounce) can peach pie filling
1 (20 ounce) can crushed pineapple with juice
1 cup chopped pecans
1 (18 ounce) box yellow cake mix
1 cup (2 sticks) butter, melted
Frozen whipped topping, thawed, or ice cream

★ Preheat oven to 375°. Pour pie filling into sprayed 9 x 13-inch baking dish and spread evenly. Spoon pineapple and juice over pie filling.

★ Sprinkle pecans over pineapple and then sprinkle cake mix over pecans. Drizzle melted butter over cake mix. Do NOT stir. Bake for 40 minutes or until light brown and crunchy. Serve hot or at room temperature with whipped topping or ice cream. Serves 10 to 12.

TIP: For variety, substitute apple, apricot or cherry pie filling for peach.

Easy Peach Crisp

4¾ cups peeled, sliced peaches
3 tablespoons lemon juice
1 cup flour
1¾ cups sugar
1 egg, beaten

★ Preheat oven to 350°. Place peaches in 9-inch baking dish and sprinkle lemon juice over top.

★ Mix flour, sugar, egg and dash of salt. Spread mixture over top of peaches with a little butter. Bake until golden brown, about 20 to 30 minutes. Serves 10 to 12..

Simple Apple Crisp

Peeling apples is the most difficult part of this recipe.

5 cups peeled, cored, sliced apples
½ cup (1 stick) butter, melted
1 cup quick-cooking oats
½ cup packed brown sugar
⅓ cup flour

★ Preheat over to 375°. Place apple slices in sprayed, floured 8-inch or 9-inch square baking pan. Combine butter, oats, brown sugar and flour in bowl and sprinkle mixture over apples.

★ Bake for 40 to 45 minutes or until apples are tender and topping is golden brown. Serves 9.

TIP: For a change, add 1 teaspoon cinnamon and ½ cup raisins or dried cranberries to apples before sprinkling with topping.

Just Peachy Peach Crisp

You will love this easy peachy dish.

1½ quarts peaches, peeled, sliced
1½ cups sugar, divided
Lemon juice
Ground nutmeg
Ground cinnamon
½ cup (1 stick) butter, melted
¾ cup self-rising flour
Whipped cream or ice cream

★ Preheat oven to 350°. Arrange peaches and ½ cup sugar in 3-quart baking dish. Sprinkle lemon juice, nutmeg and cinnamon as desired.

★ Mix butter, flour and remaining sugar in bowl and spread topping over peaches. Bake for 30 to 35 minutes or until brown. Serve plain or with whipped cream or ice cream. Serves 8 to 10.

TIP: If you don't have self-rising flour, add 1½ teaspoons baking powder and ½ teaspoon salt to 1 cup all-purpose flour and mix well.

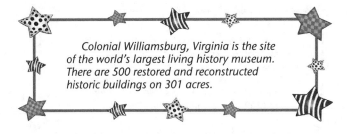

Colonial Williamsburg, Virginia is the site of the world's largest living history museum. There are 500 restored and reconstructed historic buildings on 301 acres.

Blueberry Crumble

Great crumbles. Great flavors.

1 (13 ounce) box wild blueberry muffin mix
⅓ cup plus ¼ cup sugar, divided
1½ teaspoon ground cinnamon, divided
¼ cup (½ stick) butter, melted
⅔ cup chopped pecans
1 (16 ounce) can blueberry pie filling
Vanilla ice cream

★ Preheat oven to 350°. Combine muffin mix, ⅓ cup sugar, ½ teaspoon cinnamon and butter in bowl and mix until crumbly. Add pecans and set aside. Pour blueberry pie filling into sprayed, floured 7 x 11-inch glass baking dish.

★ Pour can drained blueberries from muffin mix over top of pie filling. Sprinkle ¼ cup sugar and 1 teaspoon cinnamon over top; then, with your hands, crumble muffin mixture over top of pie filling. Bake for 35 minutes. To serve, hot or at room temperature, top with a dip of vanilla ice cream. Serves 8.

Apple Tarts

1 (10 ounce) package frozen puff pastry shells
½ cup Craisins®
¼ cup apple brandy
¼ cup sugar
1 (20 ounce) can apple pie filling
½ teaspoon cinnamon

★ Preheat oven to 400°. Place pastry shells on baking sheet and bake for 20 minutes. Remove centers and cool.

★ Combine Craisins®, apple brandy and sugar in saucepan and let soak for 10 minutes. Add pie filling and cinnamon to saucepan and mix well. Fill each pastry shell with pie mixture. Serves 8.

TIP: If you like, serve the tarts with a dollop of whipped topping or a scoop of vanilla ice cream.

The fluffernutter is a favorite sandwich of New England, especially in Massachusetts where it has been proposed as the official state sandwich. It is made with equal amounts of peanut butter and marshmallow creme between two slices of white bread.

Date-Pecan Tarts

1 (8 ounce) package chopped dates
2½ cups milk
½ cups flour
1½ cups sugar
3 eggs
1 teaspoon vanilla
1 cup chopped pecans
8 tart shells, baked, cooled
3 tablespoons powdered sugar
1 (8 ounce) carton frozen whipped topping, thawed

★ In saucepan, cook dates, milk, flour and sugar until thick and stir constantly. Add beaten eggs and ½ teaspoon salt. Cook mixture for 5 minutes on medium heat and stir constantly.

★ Stir in vanilla and pecans and pour into tart shells. Let cool. Add powdered sugar and top each tart with heaping tablespoonful whipped topping. Serves 8.

Sweets – Cookies and Bars

Old-Fashioned Ice Box Cookies

These are the cookies you roll up in a log and refrigerate before you bake them.

1 cup shortening
¼ cup packed brown sugar
1 cup sugar
1 egg
1½ teaspoons vanilla
2 cups flour
2 teaspoons baking powder
1 cup chopped pecans

★ Preheat oven to 350°. Combine shortening, brown sugar, sugar, egg, ¼ teaspoon salt and vanilla in bowl and mix well. Add flour and baking powder and mix until it blends well. Add pecans and mix.

★ Divide dough in half and roll in log shape on wax paper. Roll remaining half into another log. Refrigerate for several hours.

★ Slice into ¼-inch slices. Place on cookie sheet and bake for 15 minutes or until slightly brown. Yields 2 to 3 dozen.

Just Good Butter Cookies

1 cup (2 sticks) butter, softened
1 (1 pound) box powdered sugar
1 egg
1 teaspoon almond extract
1 teaspoon vanilla
2½ cups plus 1 tablespoon flour
¾ teaspoon cream of tartar
1 teaspoon baking soda
Sugar

★ Cream butter, powdered sugar, egg, almond extract and vanilla in bowl and mix well. In separate bowl, sift flour, cream of tartar and baking soda and add to creamed mixture. Cover and refrigerate for several hours.

★ When ready to bake, preheat oven to 350°. Roll cookie dough into ¼-inch thickness and use cookie cutters to make desired shapes. Place on sprayed cookie sheet.

★ Bake for 7 to 8 minutes, but do not brown. Sprinkle a little sugar over each cookie while still hot. Yields 2 dozen cookies.

Sugar Cookies

½ cup (1 stick) butter, softened
1 cup sugar
1 egg
1 tablespoon cream
½ teaspoon vanilla
2 cups flour
1 teaspoon baking powder

★ Preheat oven to 375°. Cream butter in bowl and slowly add sugar. Beat until light and fluffy. In separate bowl, combine egg, cream and vanilla; add to butter mixture and beat to mix.

★ In separate bowl, combine flour, baking powder and ¼ teaspoon salt. Add flour mixture to butter mixture a little at a time and mix after each addition.

★ Drop teaspoonfuls of mixture onto sprayed cookie sheet and bake for about 8 to 10 minutes. Yields about 5 dozen cookies.

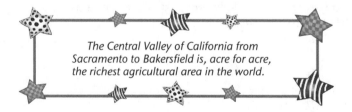

The Central Valley of California from Sacramento to Bakersfield is, acre for acre, the richest agricultural area in the world.

Holiday Spritz Cookies

½ cup plus 2 tablespoons (1¼ sticks) butter, softened
1¼ cups sugar
1 egg, well beaten
1 teaspoon almond flavoring
Food coloring
3 cups flour
1 teaspoon baking powder

★ Preheat oven to 350°. Cream butter and sugar in bowl. Add egg and almond flavoring and beat well. Add food coloring of your choice to add a holiday touch.

★ Stir flour and baking powder into creamed mixture. Using cookie press, press dough in desired shapes on unsprayed cookie sheet. Bake for about 8 minutes or until cookies are light brown. Yields 3 dozen cookies.

TIP: Use some of the decorative icings or sprinkles found in grocery store to decorate cookies.

Classic Shortbread Cookies

*Basic shortbread cookies just have 4 ingredients:
butter, flour, sugar and vanilla.*

2 cups (4 sticks) butter, softened
1+ cup powdered sugar
4 cups flour
2 teaspoons vanilla extract

★ Use electric mixer to beat butter in bowl until creamy. Gradually add powdered sugar and beat vigorously after each addition until sugar completely dissolves.

★ Add flour, a little at a time, and beat well after each addition. Shape into a round disc and refrigerate dough for at least 1 hour. When ready to bake, preheat oven to 350°.

★ Sprinkle counter surface with equal parts of flour and powdered sugar and turn one-third of dough at a time onto surface.

★ Pat into ½-inch thickness and cut cookies with 1½-inch biscuit cutter or small glass. Place on unsprayed cookie sheet and prick tops of cookies with fork to make a design.

★ Bake for 15 to 20 minutes or until light golden color. Remove from oven and cool slightly before lightly dusting with powdered sugar. Yields 3 dozen cookies.

Almond-Fudge Shortbread

1 cup (2 sticks) butter, softened
1 cup powdered sugar
1¼ cups flour
1 (12 ounce) package chocolate chips
1 (14 ounce) can sweetened condensed milk
½ teaspoon almond extract
1 (2.5 ounce) package chopped almonds, toasted

★ Preheat oven to 350°. Beat butter, powdered sugar and ¼ teaspoon salt in bowl and stir in flour. Pat into sprayed 9 x 13-inch baking pan and bake for 15 minutes.

★ Melt chocolate chips with sweetened condensed milk in medium saucepan over low heat and stir until chips melt. Stir in almond extract.

★ Spread evenly over shortbread and sprinkle with almonds. Refrigerate for several hours or until firm and cut into bars. They may be stored at room temperature. Yields 2 dozen cookies.

Pecan Tassies

1 (8 ounce) package cream cheese, softened
5 tablespoons butter, softened
1¾ cups flour
3 eggs, beaten
2 cups packed brown sugar
¼ cup (½ stick) butter, melted
2 teaspoons vanilla
1¾ cups coarsely chopped pecans

★ Preheat oven to 325°.

★ Beat cream cheese and 5 tablespoons butter in bowl until light and fluffy. Add flour a little at a time and mix well.

★ Form about 36 balls. Press into miniature muffin cups so sides and bottoms to form tart shape.

★ Beat eggs, brown sugar, butter and vanilla in bowl. Divide pecans equally into 36 tarts.

★ Fill tarts with egg-sugar mixture and bake for 25 minutes. Cool and remove tarts from pans very carefully. Yields 36 miniature tarts.

Shortbread Crunchies

1 cup (2 sticks) butter, softened
1 cup vegetable oil
1 cup sugar
1 cup packed brown sugar
1 egg
1 teaspoon vanilla
1 cup quick-cooking oats
3½ cups flour
1 teaspoon baking soda
1 cup crushed corn flakes
1 (3.5 ounce) can flaked coconut
1 cup chopped pecans

★ Preheat oven to 350°. Cream butter, oil, sugar and brown sugar in bowl; then add egg and vanilla and mix well. Add oats, flour, baking soda and 1 teaspoon salt and mix. Add cornflakes, coconut and pecans and mix.

★ Drop teaspoonfuls of mixture onto cookie sheet. Flatten with fork dipped in water and bake for 15 minutes or until only slightly brown. Yields 4 dozen.

Melting Moments

1 cup flour
½ cup corn starch
½ cup powdered sugar plus extra
¾ cup (1½ sticks) butter, softened

★ In large bowl stir flour, corn starch and powdered sugar. In separate bowl beat butter with mixer on medium speed until creamy. Add flour mixture slowly and beat until all is incorporated. Refrigerate 1 hour.

★ Preheat oven to 300°. Shape dough into 1-inch ball and place about 2 inches apart on unsprayed baking sheet. Lightly flour back of spatula and flatten each ball a little. (Flour will keep dough from sticking.) Bake for 20 minutes or until edges are light brown. (Sprinkle powdered sugar on top. Yields about 3 dozen.

Hershey, Pennsylvania is the Chocolate Capital of the United States. Not only does it feature the world's largest chocolate factory, Hershey includes Hershey's Chocolate World and Hershey Park.

Mexican Wedding Cookies

*Similar to Melting Moments, these cookies melt
in your mouth. They are also called Sand Tarts, Russian
Tea Cakes, Pecan Butterballs, Snowballs and Snowdrops.*

1 cup ground pecans or walnuts
2 cups flour
⅓ cup powdered sugar plus extra
¼ teaspoon salt
1 cup (2 sticks) butter, softened
1 teaspoon vanilla

★ Preheat oven to 275°. Spread ground nuts out loosely on baking sheet
and toast in oven for about 10 minutes. (This brings out the flavor of
nuts.) Mix flour, powdered sugar and salt in bowl. Place butter, vanilla
and nuts in mixer bowl and beat until creamy. Mix flour mixture in
with butter gradually until mixture mixes well. Refrigerate dough for
about 1 hour.

★ Preheat oven to 350°. Roll dough into 1-inch balls or shape into crescent
moon shape and place on baking sheet. Bake for about 15 minutes or
until edges of cookies start to turn brown. Cool on wire rack.

★ When cookies are almost cool, pour powdered sugar on second baking
sheet. Place all cookies on powdered sugar and sprinkle powdered over
tops of cookies. Yields about 3 dozen.

Young Whippersnappers

¾ cup packed brown sugar
¾ cup sugar
1½ cups shortening
2 large eggs
1½ cups flour
½ teaspoon baking soda
2¾ cups oats
½ cup chopped pecans
½ cup peanut butter
1½ teaspoons vanilla
1 (6 ounce) package chocolate chips

★ Preheat oven to 350°. Cream brown sugar, sugar and shortening in
bowl. Add eggs and beat. In separate bowl, sift flour, baking soda and
½ teaspoon salt and add to sugar mixture.

★ Stir in oats, pecans, peanut butter, vanilla and chocolate chips.
Drop teaspoonfuls of dough onto sprayed cookie sheet and bake
for 12 to 14 minutes or until edges of cookies begin to brown. Yields
4 dozen cookies.

Chocolate Chip Cookies

½ cup sugar
¼ cup packed brown sugar
½ cup shortening
1 egg, well beaten
1 cup flour
½ teaspoon baking soda
1 (8 ounce) package semi-sweet chocolate chips
1 teaspoon vanilla

★ Preheat oven to 375°. Add sugar and brown sugar gradually to shortening while creaming until light and fluffy. Add egg and mix well.

★ Sift flour with ½ teaspoon salt and baking soda. Combine mixtures thoroughly. Add chocolate chips and vanilla. Drop teaspoonfuls of dough onto sprayed cookie sheet.

★ Bake for 10 to 12 minutes. Yields about 40 cookies.

Chocolate Cookies

½ cup vegetable oil
4 (1 ounce) squares unsweetened chocolate, melted
2 cups sugar
4 eggs
2 teaspoons vanilla
2 cups flour
2 teaspoons baking powder
1 cup chopped nuts
1 cup powdered sugar

★ Preheat oven to 350°. Mix oil, chocolate and sugar. Blend in 1 egg at a time. Add vanilla, flour, baking powder, ½ teaspoon salt and nuts and mix well. Refrigerate overnight.

★ Make balls using about 1 teaspoon dough. Roll in confectioner sugar. Place on unsprayed cookie sheet 2 inches apart. Bake for 10 to 12 minutes. Yields 7 dozen.

Toll House Chocolate Chip Cookies

In 1930 Ruth and Kenneth Wakefield bought the Toll House Inn near Whitman, Massachusetts. While making chocolate cookies, Ruth realized she did not have her standard baker's chocolate, so she grabbed a Nestle Crunch milk chocolate candy bar just introduced by Nestle in 1938. She broke the chocolate bar into small pieces, stirred them into the cookie dough and baked them. She published her recipe for Chocolate Crunch Cookies in a few local papers when Andrew Nestle struck a deal with her to print her recipe on every bag of Nestle's chocolate and in return she was provided with chocolate for life. After providing a chopper with Nestle's chocolate, Nestle began packaging Chocolate Morsels in 1939 similar to what we have today. Originally built in 1709, the Toll House burned to the ground in 1984. Ruth Graves Wakefield died in 1977, but her Toll House Chocolate Chip Cookies live on.

5-Minute No-Bake Chocolate Cookies

2 cups sugar
½ cup milk
5 heaping tablespoons cocoa
½ cup (1 stick) butter
½ cup chunky peanut butter
1 teaspoon vanilla
3 cups quick-cooking oats

★ Combine sugar, milk, cocoa and butter in saucepan. Cook until mixture boils. Remove from heat and add peanut butter, vanilla and oats. Drop teaspoonfuls of dough onto wax paper and cool. Do not bake! Yields 2 dozen cookies.

Bourbon Balls

Rum Balls and Bourbon Balls are the same except for the alcohol. These were especially popular during the 1960's.

½ pound vanilla wafers
1¼ cups powdered sugar, divided
2 tablespoons cocoa
1 cup finely chopped pecans
½ cup light corn syrup
¼ cup bourbon

★ Roll vanilla wafers into fine crumbs with rolling pin. Mix all ingredients, except ¼ cup powdered sugar in bowl, and set aside for 1 hour.

★ Coat hands with remaining powdered sugar and shape mixture into 1-inch balls. Before serving, roll in powdered sugar. Yields 2 to 3 dozen.

Rum Balls

This is so easy!

½ pound vanilla wafers
1¼ cups powdered sugar, divided
2 tablespoons cocoa
1 cup finely chopped pecans
½ cup light corn syrup
¼ cup rum

★ Roll vanilla wafers into fine crumbs with rolling pin. Mix all ingredients, except ¼ cup powdered sugar in bowl, and set aside for 1 hour.

★ Coat hands with remaining powdered sugar and shape mixture into 1-inch balls. Before serving, roll in powdered sugar. Yields 2 to 3 dozen.

Advent Spice Cookies

This recipe is easily doubled. It's so good!

¾ cup shortening
1 cup packed brown sugar
1 egg
¼ cup molasses
2¼ cups flour
2 teaspoons baking soda
½ teaspoon ground cloves
1 teaspoon ground cinnamon
1 teaspoon ground ginger
Sugar

★ Preheat oven to 375°. Thoroughly mix shortening, brown sugar, egg and molasses in bowl. In separate bowl, sift flour, baking soda, cloves, cinnamon, ginger and ¼ teaspoon salt and stir into first mixture.

★ Refrigerate dough and shape into large marble-size balls. Roll in sugar and place balls about 2 inches apart on sprayed cookie sheet. Bake for 10 to 12 minutes. Cool for 2 minutes on cookie sheet. Yields 2 to 3 dozen cookies.

Classic Gingersnaps

¾ cup packed brown sugar
¾ cup butter or shortening
¾ cup light molasses
1 egg
¾ cup flour
2 teaspoons baking soda
1 teaspoon ground cinnamon
1 teaspoon ground ginger
½ teaspoon ground cloves
¼ cup sugar

★ Mix brown sugar and butter or shortening in bowl until smooth and creamy. Pour molasses and egg into mixture and beat well. In separate bowl, combine flour, baking soda, cinnamon, ginger, cloves and ¼ teaspoon salt.

★ Gradually add to butter mixture and stir after each addition. Mix well. Refrigerate overnight or for several hours. When ready to bake, preheat oven to 350°.

★ Form dough in 1 to 2-inch balls and roll in sugar. Place 2 inches apart on sprayed cookie sheet. Bake for 10 to 12 minutes. Yields 3 dozen cookies.

Gram's Best Molasses Cookies

1 cup sugar
1 cup packed brown sugar
1 cup (2 sticks) butter, softened
1 egg, beaten
3 cups flour
1 teaspoon ground ginger
2 teaspoons ground cinnamon
½ teaspoon baking soda
½ cup dark molasses

★ Preheat oven to 350°. Mix sugar, brown sugar and butter in bowl. Add egg and mix well. In separate bowl, combine flour, ginger, cinnamon and baking soda.

★ Add flour mixture to sugar-butter bowl in small batches and stir well after each addition.

★ Roll in balls and drop on cookie sheet to bake. If you prefer, roll dough to about ¼-inch thickness on wax paper and cut out different shapes with cookie cutters.

★ Bake until slightly firm. Time will vary depending on size of cookies. Watch carefully. You don't want any burned stars in the batch! Yields 4 dozen cookies.

Molasses Crisps

¼ cup (½ stick) butter
½ cup sugar
¾ cup molasses
1 cup flour

★ Preheat oven to 350°. Melt butter in saucepan. Add sugar and molasses and bring to a boil. Cool slightly. Add flour and ¼ teaspoon salt. Drop teaspoonfuls of dough onto sprayed cookie sheet. Bake for 12 to 15 minutes. Yields 36 cookies.

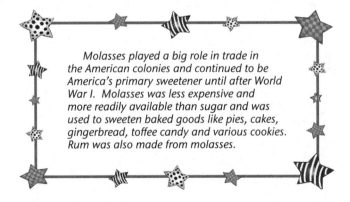

Molasses played a big role in trade in the American colonies and continued to be America's primary sweetener until after World War I. Molasses was less expensive and more readily available than sugar and was used to sweeten baked goods like pies, cakes, gingerbread, toffee candy and various cookies. Rum was also made from molasses.

Classic Snickerdoodles

Dutch colonial settlers are credited with bringing snickerdoodles to America. The origin of the unusual name is unknown, but snickerdoodles have survived and changed little throughout America's history.

½ cup (1 stick) butter, softened
½ cup shortening
1¾ cups sugar, divided
2 eggs
2¼ cups flour
2 teaspoons cream of tartar
1 teaspoon baking soda
2 teaspoons cinnamon

★ Preheat oven to 350°. Mix butter, shortening, 1½ cups sugar and eggs in medium mixing bowl and beat until creamy. Stir in flour, cream of tartar, baking soda and ¼ teaspoon salt.

★ Shape dough by rounded teaspoonfuls into balls. In small bowl, mix ¼ cup sugar and cinnamon and roll balls in mixture to cover.

★ Place balls 2 inches apart onto unsprayed cookie sheet and use bottom of jar or glass to mash cookies flat. Bake 8 to 10 minutes or until edges just begin to brown. Yields 24 to 30 cookies.

TIP: The surface of this cookie often cracks as it rises.

Old-Fashioned Hermits

1 cup (2 sticks) butter, softened
1½ cups sugar
3 eggs
3 cups flour
½ teaspoon baking soda
1 teaspoon ground allspice
1 teaspoon ground cinnamon
1 teaspoon ground cloves
1 teaspoon ground nutmeg
1½ cups raisins
½ cup chopped walnuts

★ Preheat oven to 350°. Cream butter, sugar and eggs in bowl and beat until light and fluffy. In separate bowl, sift flour, 1½ teaspoons salt, baking soda, allspice, cinnamon, cloves and nutmeg and add to creamed mixture.

★ Add raisins and walnuts and mix well. Drop dough by teaspoonfuls onto sprayed cookie sheet. Bake for 15 to 20 minutes. Yields 70 cookies.

Classic Oatmeal Cookies

1 cup packed brown sugar
1 cup sugar
1 cup shortening
2 eggs
2 teaspoons vanilla
1 teaspoon baking soda
1½ cups flour
3 cups quick-cooking oats
1 cup chopped pecans

★ Preheat oven to 350°. Combine brown sugar, sugar, shortening, eggs,
   2 tablespoons water and vanilla in bowl and beat well. Add 1 teaspoon
   salt, baking soda and flour and mix well. Add oats and pecans and mix.

★ Drop teaspoonfuls of dough onto sprayed cookie sheet and bake for 14 to
   15 minutes or until cookies brown. Yields 4 dozen cookies.

Oatmeal-Chocolate Chip Cookies

½ cup (1 stick) butter, softened
¾ cup sugar
¾ cup packed brown sugar
1 egg
½ teaspoon vanilla
1 cup flour
½ teaspoon baking soda
1½ cups quick-cooking oats
1 (6 ounce) package chocolate chips
½ cup chopped pecans

★ Preheat oven to 350°. Combine butter, sugar, brown sugar, egg,
   1 tablespoon water and vanilla in bowl and beat well. Add flour and
   baking soda and mix well. Add oats, chocolate chips and pecans and
   mix well.

★ Drop teaspoonfuls of mixture onto cookie sheet and bake for 12 to
   15 minutes or until light brown. Yields 2 dozen.

Peanut Clusters

1 (24 ounce) package almond bark
1 (12 ounce) package milk chocolate chips
5 cups salted peanuts

★ In double boiler, melt almond bark and chocolate chips. Stir in peanuts
   and drop by teaspoons onto waxed paper until cool. Store in airtight
   container.

Oatmeal-Raisin Cookies

1½ cups flour
½ teaspoon baking powder
¼ teaspoon ground nutmeg
1 cup (2 sticks) butter, softened
1 cup sugar
1 cup packed brown sugar
2 large eggs
3 cups quick-cooking oats
1½ cups dark raisins

★ Preheat oven to 325°. Combine flour, baking powder and ½ teaspoon salt in bowl and set aside. In separate bowl, beat butter, sugar and brown sugar until creamy.

★ Beat in eggs, one at a time. Reduce speed to low and slowly mix in flour mixture. Mix in oats and raisins. Using ¼ cup measure of dough, roll dough into balls and place on cookie sheet 2½ inches apart.

★ Flatten cookies slightly using your palm and bake for 22 to 25 minutes. Let cookies cool on cookie sheets for 10 minutes and transfer to wire rack. Cool completely before storing. Yields 2 dozen large cookies.

Crunchy Cashew Cookies

1 cup (2 sticks) butter, softened
1 cup sugar
¾ cup packed brown sugar
1 egg
2¼ cups flour
½ teaspoon baking soda
½ teaspoon cream of tartar
2 teaspoons vanilla
1 teaspoon almond extract
1½ cups chopped cashews

★ Preheat oven to 350°. Combine butter, sugar, brown sugar and egg in bowl and beat well. Blend in flour, baking soda and cream of tartar. Add vanilla, almond extract and cashews and mix thoroughly.

★ Drop teaspoonfuls of dough onto sprayed cookie sheet and bake for 10 to 12 minutes or until golden brown. Yields 3 dozen cookies.

Regular milk is sometimes called sweet milk to show it is different from buttermilk or any other form of milk.

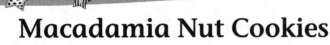

Macadamia Nut Cookies

½ cup shortening
½ cup (1 stick) butter, softened
2½ cups flour, divided
1 cup packed brown sugar
½ cup sugar
2 eggs
1 teaspoon vanilla
½ teaspoon butter flavoring
½ teaspoon baking soda
2 cups white chocolate chips
1 (3 ounce) jar macadamia nuts, chopped

★ Preheat oven to 350°. Beat shortening and butter in bowl. Add half flour and mix well. Add brown sugar, sugar, eggs, vanilla, butter flavoring and baking soda.

★ Beat until mixture combines well. Add remaining flour, mix well and stir in white chocolate chips and nuts. Drop teaspoonfuls of dough onto cookie sheet and bake for 8 minutes. Yields 3 dozen cookies.

Peanut Butter Cookies

½ cup (1 stick) butter, softened
¼ cup shortening
⅔ cup sugar
1 cup packed brown sugar
1 egg
1 cup crunchy peanut butter
1¾ cups flour
½ teaspoon baking powder
¾ teaspoon baking soda

★ Preheat oven to 350°. Cream butter, shortening, sugar, brown sugar and egg in bowl and beat well. Add peanut butter and mix. Add flour, baking powder, baking soda and ¼ teaspoon salt and mix well.

★ Using small cookie scoop, place cookies onto cookie sheet. Use fork to flatten cookies and criss-cross fork marks twice. Bake for 12 minutes. Store covered. Yields 2 to 3 dozen.

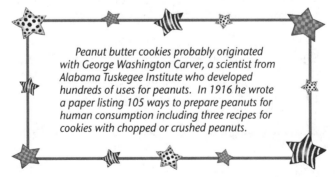

Peanut butter cookies probably originated with George Washington Carver, a scientist from Alabama Tuskegee Institute who developed hundreds of uses for peanuts. In 1916 he wrote a paper listing 105 ways to prepare peanuts for human consumption including three recipes for cookies with chopped or crushed peanuts.

Pecan Drops

This is another of the easy cookie recipes you can whip up in a jiffy.

½ cup (1 stick) butter, softened
½ cup plus 2 tablespoons shortening
1 cup powdered sugar
2½ cups cake flour
2 teaspoons vanilla
1 cup chopped pecans

★ Preheat oven to 325°. Cream butter and shortening in bowl until smooth. Beat in powdered sugar gradually. Stir in flour thoroughly and add vanilla and pecans.

★ Drop teaspoonfuls of mixture onto cookie sheet. Bake for 15 to 20 minutes or until delicate light brown. Yields 3 to 4 dozen.

Applesauce Yummies

4 cups flour
2 teaspoons baking soda
1 teaspoon ground cinnamon
1 teaspoon ground nutmeg
½ teaspoon ground allspice
1 cup (2 sticks) butter, softened
1½ cups sugar
1½ cups packed brown sugar
3 eggs, beaten
2 cups applesauce
1 cup golden raisins
1½ cups chopped walnuts

★ Preheat oven to 400°. Combine flour, baking soda, 1 teaspoon salt, cinnamon, nutmeg and allspice in bowl. In separate bowl, combine butter, sugar and brown sugar, beat until fluffy. Stir in eggs and applesauce.

★ Add dry ingredients and mix well. Stir in raisins and walnuts. Drop teaspoonfuls of dough onto sprayed cookie sheet and bake for 8 to 10 minutes or just until cookies brown lightly. Yields 5 dozen cookies.

Americans eat about 19 pounds of fresh apples per person every year. Europeans eat an average of 46 pounds annually.

Washington State produces more apples than any other state.

Christmas Cookies

1 cup (2 sticks) butter, softened
1½ cups sugar
¼ teaspoon ground nutmeg
1 teaspoon vanilla
3 eggs
1 teaspoon baking soda
2½ cups flour
1½ cups chopped pecans
1½ cups raisins
2 cups chopped dates
1 cup candied pineapple
1 cup candied cherries

★ Preheat oven to 350°. Cream butter and sugar in bowl. Add nutmeg, vanilla, eggs, baking soda and flour and mix well.

★ Combine pecans, raisins, dates, pineapple and cherries in bowl with large spoon and add to batter. Drop teaspoonfuls on sprayed cookie sheet and bake for 12 minutes or until done. Yields 3 to 4 dozen.

Classic Date Log Cookies

1 cup dates
¼ cup sugar
1 (3 ounce) package cream cheese, softened
½ cup butter
1 cup flour
Powdered sugar

★ Preheat oven to 275°. Cook dates and sugar in ¼ cup water in saucepan over medium heat until a smooth paste forms.

★ Beat cream cheese and butter in bowl until smooth. Add flour and a little salt and mix well. On lightly floured wax paper, roll out dough and cut in 3-inch squares.

★ Place 1 teaspoon date mixture on each square and roll into logs. Seal ends with fork. Bake for 20 minutes. Roll in powdered sugar and serve. Yields 2 dozen cookies.

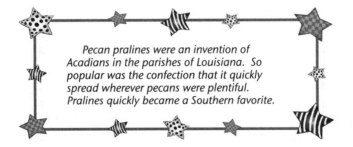

Pecan pralines were an invention of Acadians in the parishes of Louisiana. So popular was the confection that it quickly spread wherever pecans were plentiful. Pralines quickly became a Southern favorite.

Fig Newtons

½ cup (1 stick) butter, softened
1½ cups sugar
1 egg, beaten
½ cup milk
1 teaspoon vanilla
3 cups flour
3 teaspoons baking powder
1 cup dried figs, chopped

★ Preheat oven to 400°. Cream butter and 1 cup sugar in bowl. Add egg and beat until light. Combine milk and vanilla. Sift ½ teaspoon salt, flour and baking powder and add alternately with milk to creamed mixture. Blend well.

★ Roll dough out to ⅛-inch thickness on lightly floured board in shape of rectangle. Put figs in saucepan with remaining sugar and 1 cup boiling water. Boil for 5 minutes. Cool.

★ Spread cooked mixture over half of dough. Cover with remaining half of dough. Cut into rectangles. Bake for 12 to 15 minutes. Yields 20 cookies.

Thumbprint Fruit Cookies

⅔ cup butter, softened
1¼ cups sugar plus more for sprinkling
2 eggs
3 cups flour
2 teaspoons baking powder
Grated zest of 1 lemon
1 tablespoon freshly squeezed lemon juice
1¼ cups strawberry jam

★ Cream butter, sugar and eggs in bowl until light and fluffy. In separate bowl, sift flour, 1½ teaspoons salt and baking powder and add to first mixture. Add zest and lemon juice. Mix until smooth.

★ Roll into ball and wrap in wax paper or plastic wrap. Refrigerate for at least 1 hour. When ready to bake, preheat oven to 350°. Roll to ⅛-inch thickness on lightly floured board.

★ Cut into circles. Make small indention in center of cookie with thumb and put 1 teaspoon jam in center of circle. Top with another circle and press edges firmly together. Bake for 12 to 15 minutes. Yields 60 cookies.

Easy Orange Balls

*There's nothing hard about these delicious
cookies and they will keep for several weeks.*

1 (12 ounce) box vanilla wafers, crushed
½ cup orange juice concentrate, thawed
1 cup powdered sugar, divided
¾ cup shredded coconut
½ cup chopped pecans
Additional powdered sugar

★ Combine vanilla wafers, orange juice, powdered sugar, coconut and
pecans in bowl. Blend mixture well, shape into balls and store in
covered container. Before serving, roll in additional powdered sugar.
Yields 2 to 3 dozen.

Easy Angel Macaroons

1 (16 ounce) package 1-step angel food cake mix
1½ teaspoons almond extract
2 cups flaked coconut

★ Preheat oven to 350°. Beat cake mix, ½ cup water and almond extract
in bowl for 30 seconds. Scrape bowl and beat on medium speed for
1 minute. Fold in coconut.

★ Drop rounded teaspoonfuls of dough onto parchment paper-lined
cookie sheet and bake for 10 to 12 minutes or until cookies set. Remove
parchment paper with cookies to wire rack to cool. Yields 3 dozen
cookies.

Potato Chip Cookies

Freeze these if you want to eat them in several weeks.

1 cup (2 sticks) butter, softened
½ cup sugar
1¾ cups flour
1 teaspoon vanilla
½ cup finely chopped pecans
½ cup crushed potato chips
¼ cup powdered sugar

★ Preheat oven to 350°. Cream butter, sugar, flour and vanilla in bowl and
mix well. Add pecans, stir and add potato chips.

★ Drop heaping tablespoons on cookie sheet. Press flat with fork. Bake
for 13 minutes and sprinkle with powdered sugar. Yields 2 to 3 dozen.

Cheerleader Brownies

Great, chewy, chocolaty brownies! They won't last long!

⅔ cup canola oil
2 cups sugar
4 eggs, beaten
⅓ cup corn syrup
½ cup cocoa
1½ cups flour
1 teaspoon baking powder
2 teaspoons vanilla
1 cup chopped pecans

★ Preheat oven to 350°. Mix oil, sugar, eggs and corn syrup in large bowl.
   In separate bowl, mix cocoa, flour, 1 teaspoon salt and baking powder.

★ Slowly pour cocoa mixture into sugar mixture and mix thoroughly. Stir
   in vanilla and pecans.

★ Pour into sprayed 9 x 13-inch baking pan and bake about 50 minutes
   or until toothpick inserted in center comes out clean. Yields 12 to
   14 brownies.

Blonde Brownies

These are unbelievably delicious and so easy.
They store well and you can even freeze them.

1 cup (2 sticks) butter
1 (1 pound) box light brown sugar
2 eggs
2 cups flour
2 teaspoons baking powder
1 teaspoon vanilla
1 cup chopped pecans

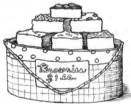

★ Preheat oven to 350°. Melt butter in heavy saucepan. Add brown
   sugar and stir in eggs, flour and baking powder. Add vanilla, a pinch
   of salt and pecans. Pour in sprayed 9 x 13-inch baking pan. Bake
   for 25 minutes. Yields 16.

Toasted Pecans

24 pecan halves
1 cup (2 sticks) butter
Salt

★ Preheat oven to 250°. Place pecans in baking pan and toast for
   30 minutes to dry out. Melt butter in saucepan and coat pecans
   thoroughly. Remove from butter and place on baking pan. Toast
   for 1 hour or until pecans are crispy. Serves 8 to 10.

Snickers Brownies

1 (18 ounce) box German chocolate cake mix
¾ cup (1½ sticks) butter, melted
½ cup evaporated milk
4 (2.7 ounce) Snickers® candy bars

★ Preheat oven to 350°. In large bowl combine cake mix, butter and evaporated milk. Beat on low speed until ingredients blend well. Pour half the batter into greased, floured 9 x 13-inch baking pan. Bake for 10 minutes.

★ Cut Snickers® bars in ¼-inch slices. Remove from oven and place candy bar slices evenly over brownies. Drop remaining half of batter by spoonfuls over candy bars and spread as evenly as possible. Return to oven and bake for minutes longer. Cool and cut into squares. Yields about 20 brownies.

Glazed-Butterscotch Brownies

3 cups packed brown sugar
1 cup (2 sticks) butter, softened
3 eggs
3 cups flour
2 tablespoons baking powder
1½ cups chopped pecans
1 (7 ounce) can flaked coconut

★ Preheat oven to 350°. Combine and beat sugar and butter in bowl until fluffy. Add eggs and blend. Combine flour, baking powder and ½ teaspoon salt and add to sugar-egg mixture, 1 cup at a time.

★ Add pecans and coconut. Spread batter in sprayed 10 x 15-inch baking pan and bake for 20 to 25 minutes. Batter will be hard to spread.

Glaze:

½ cup packed brown sugar
⅓ cup evaporated milk
½ cup (1 stick) butter
1 cup powdered sugar
½ teaspoon vanilla

★ Combine brown sugar, evaporated milk, butter and ⅛ teaspoon salt in saucepan and bring to a boil.

★ Cool slightly and add powdered sugar and vanilla and beat until smooth. Spread glaze over cooled brownies. Yields 14 brownies.

 Lettuce Capital of the World   Salinas, California

Almond-Coconut Squares

2 cups graham cracker crumbs
3 tablespoons brown sugar
½ cup (1 stick) butter, melted
1 (14 ounce) can sweetened condensed milk
1 (7 ounce) package shredded coconut
1 teaspoon vanilla

★ Preheat oven to 325°. Combine graham cracker crumbs, brown sugar
   and butter in bowl and mix well. Pat mixture evenly into sprayed
   9 x 13-inch baking pan and bake for 10 minutes. Cool.

★ Combine sweetened condensed milk, coconut and vanilla in bowl and
   pour over baked crust. Bake for additional 25 minutes. Cool.

Topping:

1 (6 ounce) package chocolate chips
1 (6 ounce) package butterscotch chips
4 tablespoons (½ stick) butter
6 tablespoons crunchy peanut butter
½ cup slivered almonds

★ Melt all topping ingredients in double boiler and spread mixture over
   baked ingredients. Cool and cut into squares. Yields 20 squares.

Toffee Squares

1 cup (2 sticks) plus 2 tablespoons butter, softened, divided
1 cup packed brown sugar
1 egg yolk, beaten
1 teaspoon vanilla
2 cups flour
1 (8 ounce) chocolate bar
1 cup chopped nuts

★ Preheat oven to 350°. Cream 1 cup butter and brown sugar in bowl until
   light. Add egg yolk, vanilla and flour.

★ Spread dough thin on cookie sheet and bake for 15 to 20 minutes. Cool
   slightly. Melt chocolate with 2 tablespoons butter in double boiler and
   spread on cookie surface. Sprinkle with nuts and cut into squares.
   Yields 10 to 12.

*What did Snow White say when her
photographs were ready?*

"I knew one day my prints would come."

Butter-Pecan Turtle Bars

2 cups flour
1½ cups packed light brown sugar, divided
¾ cup (1½ sticks) plus ⅔ cup (1⅓ sticks) butter, divided
1½ cups coarsely chopped pecans
4 (1 ounce) squares semi-sweet chocolate

★ Preheat oven to 350°. Combine flour, ¾ cup brown sugar and ½ cup butter in bowl and blend until crumbly. Pat down crust mixture evenly in sprayed, floured 9 x 13-inch baking pan. Sprinkle pecans over crust and set aside.

★ Combine remaining brown sugar and ⅔ cup butter in small saucepan. Cook over medium heat and stir constantly. Bring mixture to a boil for 1 minute and stir constantly.

★ Drizzle caramel sauce over pecans and crust and bake for 18 to 20 minutes or until caramel layer is bubbly. Remove from oven and cool. Melt chocolate squares and ¼ cup butter in saucepan and stir until smooth. Pour over bars and spread around. Cool and cut into bars. Yields 12 bars.

Macadamia Bars

Crust:

1 cup (2 sticks) butter, softened
⅔ cup sugar
2 cups flour

★ Preheat oven to 350°. Cream butter, sugar and flour in bowl. Press into sprayed 9 x 13-inch baking dish and bake for 20 minutes.

Filling:

4 eggs
1 cup flaked coconut
3 cups packed light brown sugar
2 (3.2 ounce) jars macadamia nuts, chopped
¼ cup flour
3 teaspoons vanilla extract
1 teaspoon baking powder

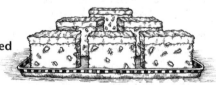

★ Lightly beat eggs in medium bowl and add remaining filling ingredients. Pour over hot, baked crust and bake for additional 25 to 30 minutes.

★ Cool completely and cut into small squares or you can cut in larger squares and serve with dip of ice cream. Yields 20 bars.

TIP: You could substitute 1½ cups walnuts for macadamia nuts. Either way, these bars are moist, chewy and absolutely sinful.

Pecan Bars

Crust:

3 cups flour
¾ cup (1½ sticks) butter, softened
⅓ cup sugar

★ Preheat oven to 350°. Blend flour, butter, sugar and ¾ teaspoon salt in bowl and press firmly in sprayed 12 x 18-inch jellyroll pan. Bake for 25 minutes or until golden brown.

Filling:

4 eggs, beaten
1½ cups packed brown sugar
1½ cups light corn syrup
3 tablespoons butter, melted
1½ teaspoons vanilla
2½ cups chopped pecans

★ Mix all ingredients except pecans in bowl. Spread pecans over crust, pour in egg mixture and spread evenly.

★ Bake for additional 25 minutes or until filling sets. Cool and cut into squares. Yields 12 to 14 bars.

Lemon Bars

1 cup (2 sticks) butter
2 cups flour
½ cup powdered sugar
2 cups sugar
6 tablespoons flour
4 eggs, lightly beaten
6 tablespoons lemon juice
½ teaspoon grated lemon peel
Powdered sugar

★ Preheat oven to 350°. Melt butter in 9 x 13-inch baking pan in oven. Add 2 cups flour and powdered sugar, stir into melted butter in pan and mix well. Press down evenly and firmly and bake for 15 minutes.

★ For filling, combine sugar, 6 tablespoons flour, eggs, lemon juice and lemon peel in bowl. Mix and pour over crust. Bake for 20 minutes more. Cool and dust with powdered sugar. To serve, cut into squares. Yields 24 to 28 bars.

The world's largest pecan tree is the national champion pecan tree located just north of Weatherford, Texas.

Buttery Walnut Squares

1 cup (2 sticks) butter, softened
1¾ cups packed brown sugar
1¾ cups flour

★ Preheat oven to 350°. Combine butter and brown sugar in bowl and beat until smooth and creamy. Add flour and mix well. Pat mixture down evenly in sprayed, floured 9 x 13-inch glass pan and bake for 15 minutes.

Topping:

1 cup packed brown sugar
4 eggs, lightly beaten
2 tablespoons flour
2 cups chopped walnuts
1 cup flaked coconut

★ Combine sugar and eggs in medium bowl. Add flour and mix well. Fold in walnuts and coconut and pour over crust. Bake for 20 to 25 minutes or until set in center. Cool in pan and cut into squares. Yields 20 squares.

TIP: Serve these delicious squares with a scoop of ice cream for a great dessert.

Gingerbread

2 cups sifted cake flour
2 teaspoons baking powder
¼ teaspoon baking soda
2 teaspoons ground ginger
1 teaspoon ground cinnamon
⅓ cup shortening
½ cup sugar
1 egg, beaten
⅔ cup molasses
¾ cup buttermilk

★ Preheat oven to 350°. Sift flour, baking powder, baking soda, spices and ½ teaspoon salt in mixing bowl. Cream shortening thoroughly, add sugar gradually and whip until light and fluffy.

★ Add egg and molasses, add flour mixture alternately with milk. Beat after each addition until smooth. Pour batter into 9 x 13-inch baking pan. Bake for 1 hour 15 minutes. Serve with whipped cream. Serves 6.

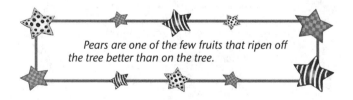

Pears are one of the few fruits that ripen off the tree better than on the tree.

Magic Cookie Bars

You can use the same baking pan to mix and bake these cookies.

1½ cups crushed corn flakes
3 tablespoons sugar
½ cup (1 stick) butter, melted
1 cup coarsely chopped walnuts or pecans
1 (6 ounce) package semi-sweet chocolate chips
1⅓ cups flaked coconut
1 (14 ounce) can sweetened condensed milk

★ Preheat oven to 350°. Combine corn flakes, sugar, and butter in bowl
and mix thoroughly. Pour mixture into 9 x 13-inch baking pan. With
back of tablespoon, press mixture evenly and firmly in bottom of pan
to form crust.

★ Sprinkle nuts, chocolate chips and coconut evenly over crumb crust.
Pour sweetened condensed milk evenly over nuts and bake for
25 minutes or until light brown around edges. Cool and cut into
bars. Yields 16 to 18 bars.

Million-Dollar Bars

½ cup (1 stick) butter
2 cups graham cracker crumbs
1 (6 ounce) package chocolate chips
1 (6 ounce) package butterscotch chips
1 cup chopped pecans
1 (7 ounce) can flaked coconut
1 (14 ounce) can sweetened condensed milk

★ Preheat oven to 325°. Melt butter in sprayed 9 x 13-inch baking dish.
Sprinkle crumbs over butter and stir.

★ Add layers of chocolate chips, butterscotch chips, pecans and coconut.
Pour sweetened condensed milk over top and bake for about 30 minutes.
Cool in pan and cut bars. Yields 12 to 14 bars.

Cinnamon Pecans

1 pound pecan halves
1 egg white, slightly beaten
2 tablespoons cinnamon
¾ cup sugar

★ Preheat oven to 325°. Combine pecan halves with egg white and mix
well. Sprinkle with mixture of cinnamon and sugar and stir until egg
whites coat pecans. Spread on baking sheet and bake for about
20 minutes. Cool. Store in covered container.

Chocolate-Caramel Bars

Truly unusual and delicious!

1 (14 ounce) bag light caramels (about 50 pieces)
1 (5 ounce) can evaporated milk, divided
1 (18 ounce) box German chocolate cake mix
¾ cup (1½ sticks) butter, melted
1 cup chopped nuts
1 cup chocolate chips

★ Preheat oven to 350°. Melt caramels with ⅓ cup evaporated milk in double boiler. Combine cake mix, butter and remaining evaporated milk and mix well.

★ Spread half cake mixture into sprayed 9 x 13-inch baking dish. Bake for 6 minutes and remove from oven. Sprinkle with nuts and chocolate chips and spread caramel mixture on top. Spread remainder of cake mixture and bake for 15 to 18 minutes. Remove from oven and cool before cutting into bars. Yields 18 bars.

TIP: If you use cake mix with pudding, bake for 18 to 20 minutes.

Cheesecake-Pecan Bars

1 cup flour
5 tablespoons butter, softened
½ cup packed brown sugar
1 (8 ounce) package cream cheese, softened
1 egg
1 tablespoon milk
½ teaspoon vanilla
½ cup chopped pecans

★ Preheat oven to 350°. Combine flour, butter and brown sugar in bowl. Press into 8 x 8-inch baking pan. Bake for 10 minutes.

★ Beat cream cheese, egg, milk and vanilla in bowl until smooth and scrape sides of bowl often. Spread over baked flour layer and sprinkle with pecans.

★ Bake for 25 minutes. Cool and refrigerate for at least 2 hours before cutting into bars. Store in refrigerator. Yields 8 to 9 bars.

Goodness is the only investment that never fails.
–Henry David Thoreau

Yummy Chess Squares

1 (18 ounce) box butter cake mix
4 eggs, divided
½ cup (1 stick) butter, melted
2 teaspoons vanilla, divided
1 (8 ounce) package cream cheese, softened
1 (1 pound) box powdered sugar

★ Preheat oven to 300°. Combine cake mix, 1 egg, butter and 1 teaspoon vanilla in bowl and mix well. Batter will be very thick. Spread in sprayed, floured 9 x 13-inch baking dish.

★ Combine remaining 3 eggs, 1 teaspoon vanilla, cream cheese and powdered sugar in bowl and beat well. Spread over cake mixture. Bake for 1 hour. Refrigerate and serve. Yields 12 to 14 squares.

Raspberry-Crunch Bars

1¼ cups plus 2 tablespoons flour, divided
⅔ cup sugar
½ cup (1 stick) butter
¾ cup raspberry jam
3 eggs
⅔ cup packed light brown sugar
1 teaspoon vanilla
¼ teaspoon baking powder
1¼ cups chopped pecans

★ Preheat oven to 350°. Combine 1¼ cups flour and sugar in bowl. Cut in butter until mixture is crumbly. Press into sprayed 9-inch baking pan and bake for 20 minutes or until edges are light brown. Spread raspberry jam over hot crust.

★ Beat eggs, brown sugar, vanilla, remaining 2 tablespoons flour and baking powder. Stir until well blended.

★ Stir in pecans. Spoon over jam and spread evenly. Bake for additional 18 minutes or until golden brown. Cool and cut into bars.

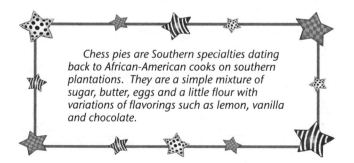

Chess pies are Southern specialties dating back to African-American cooks on southern plantations. They are a simple mixture of sugar, butter, eggs and a little flour with variations of flavorings such as lemon, vanilla and chocolate.

Sweets – Desserts

Traditional Vanilla Custard

1 tablespoon flour
1 cup sugar
5 whole eggs
1 gallon milk
1 teaspoon vanilla

★ Combine flour and sugar in bowl and stir. In separate bowl, beat eggs well and add milk. Combine with flour-sugar mixture and stir until sugar dissolves.

★ Pour mixture into double boiler, stir constantly and cook until thick. Remove from heat, stir in vanilla and pour into custard cups. Serves 8.

Flan

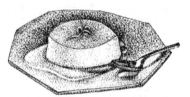

2 tablespoons butter
1 cup sugar, divided
1 (14 ounce) can sweetened condensed milk
1 (13 ounce) can evaporated milk
4 eggs, very well beaten
1 teaspoon vanilla

★ Preheat oven to 350°. Rub butter in heavy saucepan on bottom and sides. Melt ½ cup sugar in saucepan over medium heat until it caramelizes. Add remaining sugar and stir until there is clear brown syrup. Pour equal parts into 6 individual, custard bowls.

★ Combine sweetened condensed milk, evaporated milk, eggs and vanilla in bowl and mix well. Pour mixture over cooled, melted sugar mixture in custard bowls.

★ Place bowls in another container half-filled with water. Bake for 1 hour. Flan is done when toothpick inserted in center comes out clean.

★ Serve by carefully turning bowls upside-down onto plate and removing flan from bowls. The caramelized sugar will be on top. Serves 6.

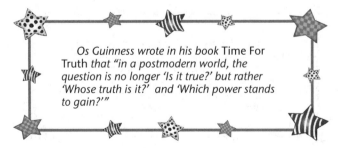

Os Guinness wrote in his book Time For Truth *that "in a postmodern world, the question is no longer 'Is it true?' but rather 'Whose truth is it?' and 'Which power stands to gain?'"*

Creamy Banana Pudding

1 (14 ounce) can sweetened condensed milk
1 (3.5 ounce) package instant vanilla pudding mix
1 (8 ounce) carton frozen whipped topping, thawed
36 vanilla wafers
3 bananas, sliced

★ Combine sweetened condensed milk and 1½ cups cold water in bowl. Add pudding mix and beat well. Refrigerate for 5 minutes and fold in whipped topping. Spoon 1 cup pudding mixture into 3-quart glass serving bowl.

★ Top with one-third vanilla wafers, one-third bananas and one-third remaining pudding. Repeat layers twice, ending with pudding. Cover and keep refrigerated. Serves 8 to 10.

Bread Pudding with Whiskey Sauce

3 tablespoons butter
1 loaf French bread
1 quart milk
3 eggs
2 cups sugar
2 tablespoons vanilla
1 cup raisins

★ Preheat oven to 350°. Melt butter in 3-quart baking dish and cool. Soak bread in milk in bowl and crush with hands. Mix thoroughly. Add eggs, sugar, vanilla and raisins and stir well.

★ Pour mixture over melted butter and bake 55 to 60 minutes or until very firm. Cool, cube pudding and pour into individual dessert dishes. When ready to serve, add Whiskey Sauce.

Whiskey Sauce:

1 cup sugar
½ cup (1 stick) butter
1 egg, well beaten
Whiskey

★ Heat sugar and butter in double boiler until sugar completely dissolves. Add egg, beating quickly so egg doesn't curdle. Cool and add whiskey to taste. Serves 8.

Oma's Bread Pudding

1½ cups breadcrumbs
3 cups hot milk
2 eggs, beaten
⅔ cup sugar
1 tablespoon butter
½ teaspoon vanilla
½ cup chopped nuts
Whipped cream

★ Preheat oven to 350°. Combine breadcrumbs, milk, eggs, sugar, butter and ¼ teaspoon salt in bowl. Mix well.

★ Add vanilla and nuts. Turn mixture into sprayed baking dish. Bake for 35 to 40 minutes or until firm. Serve with whipped cream. Serves 6.

Easy Rice Pudding

2¼ cups milk
½ cup rice
⅓ cup packed brown sugar
1 egg
1 teaspoon vanilla
¼ teaspoon cinnamon
¼ cup golden raisins

★ Mix milk and rice in saucepan and bring to boil almost; reduce heat and simmer for 20 to 25 minutes or until rice is tender. Stir often; do not scorch milk or let rice stick to pan.

★ In mixing bowl combine brown sugar and egg; add a little rice-milk mixture at a time to equal about ¼ to ½ cup and mix well. Pour sugar and milk mixture into saucepan and cook on low for about 10 minutes or until pudding thickens. Do not boil and stir frequently.

★ Remove from heat and stir in vanilla, raisins and cinnamon. Serve warm or cold. Serves 2.

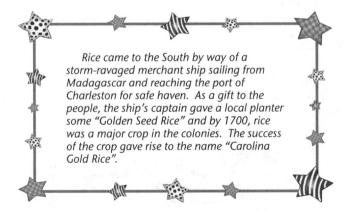

Rice came to the South by way of a storm-ravaged merchant ship sailing from Madagascar and reaching the port of Charleston for safe haven. As a gift to the people, the ship's captain gave a local planter some "Golden Seed Rice" and by 1700, rice was a major crop in the colonies. The success of the crop gave rise to the name "Carolina Gold Rice".

Old-Fashioned Rice Pudding

1 cup rice
1 quart milk
½ cup (1 stick) butter
5 eggs
¾ cup sugar
½ cup raisins
1 teaspoon vanilla
2 teaspoons ground cinnamon

★ Preheat oven to 350°. Combine rice, milk and butter in saucepan. Bring to a boil; cover and cook over low heat until rice is tender and absorbs most of milk.

★ Add eggs, sugar, raisins and vanilla to mixture and pour into sprayed 2-quart baking dish. Sprinkle cinnamon on top and bake for 25 minutes. Serves 8.

Great Grape-Nuts Pudding

Grape-Nuts® cereal was introduced in 1897 at the height
of a health craze inspired by dietary reformer Sylvester Graham.
In this recipe, based on an old recipe first published in Yankee
magazine, the cereal settles in the pan to create a tasty bottom layer.

1 cup Grape-Nuts® cereal
1 quart milk, scalded
4 eggs
½ cup sugar
1 tablespoon vanilla
1 teaspoon nutmeg
2 tablespoons butter, softened

★ Preheat oven to 350°. Place Grape-Nuts® in 2-quart bowl and pour scalded milk over cereal. Stir and let stand 5 minutes.

★ With electric mixer, beat eggs, sugar, vanilla, nutmeg and 1 teaspoon salt. Slowly stir into cereal-milk mixture and pour into buttered 2-quart baking dish.

★ Place baking dish into larger pan of hot water that reaches halfway up dish. Bake 55 to 60 minutes or just until mixture is set or until knife inserted one inch from center comes out clean. Serve warm. Serves 6.

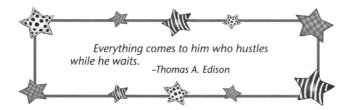

Everything comes to him who hustles
while he waits.
–Thomas A. Edison

Great-Grandmother's Sweet Potato Pudding

This recipe is so old it came with the wagon trains.

2 cups grated sweet potato
¾ cup packed brown sugar
2 small eggs, beaten
1 teaspoon ground cloves
1 teaspoon ground allspice
1 teaspoon ground cinnamon
½ cup milk
⅓ cup orange juice
⅓ cup (⅔ stick) butter, melted

★ Preheat oven to 350°. Combine all ingredients in bowl and mix well. Pour into sprayed baking dish and bake for 1 hour. Serves 8.

Tapioca Custard Pudding

⅓ cup minute tapioca
2 cups scalded milk, slightly cooled
2 eggs, slightly beaten
½ cup sugar
1 tablespoon butter

★ Preheat oven to 325°. Add tapioca to milk and cook in double boiler over low heat for 30 minutes. Combine eggs with sugar and ½ teaspoon salt. Stir gradually into hot tapioca mixture.

★ Turn pudding into 9-inch sprayed baking dish. Add butter. Put in pan of hot water. Bake for 30 minutes. Serves 6.

TIP: For additional flavor, you can add one cup of almost any chopped, canned or stewed fruits or berries, drained.

White Velvet

1 (8 ounce) carton whipping cream
1½ teaspoons unflavored gelatin
⅓ cup sugar
1 (8 ounce) carton sour cream
¾ teaspoon rum flavoring
Fresh fruit

★ Heat cream over medium heat. Soak gelatin in ¼ cup cold water. When cream is hot, stir in sugar and gelatin until it dissolves. Remove from heat. Fold in sour cream and flavoring. Pour into individual molds, cover with plastic wrap and refrigerate. Unmold to serve and top with fresh fruit.

Caramel-Apple Mousse

¾ cup (1½ sticks) butter
⅔ cup sugar
2½ teaspoons lemon juice
½ teaspoon ground cinnamon
2 tablespoons rum
5 - 6 medium apples, peeled, thinly sliced
¼ cup sugar
1 teaspoon vanilla
1 (8 ounce) carton frozen whipped topping, thawed
Peanut brittle, slightly crushed

★ Melt butter in large skillet and add sugar, lemon juice and ¼ cup water. Cook for 10 minutes or until sugar dissolves and syrup is slightly thick and golden; stir often. Remove from heat and add cinnamon, rum and apples.

★ Cook apples in syrup for 3 to 4 minutes or until they thoroughly coat and are soft. Remove apples from syrup and cool.

★ In separate bowl, add sugar and vanilla to whipped topping and fold apples into whipped topping. Spoon mixture into parfait glasses or crystal sherbet glassess and refrigerate for several hours. Sprinkle generously with crushed peanut brittle before serving. Serves 8.

Lemon-Raspberry Parfaits

What a quick, easy 5-minute recipe!

1 cup whipping cream, chilled
⅓ cup lemon-flavored yogurt
⅓ cup sugar
2 bananas
1 pint fresh raspberries

★ In mixing bowl, beat whipping cream with yogurt and sugar until soft peaks form. Divide half of mixture into 4 parfait glasses.

★ Slice bananas and arrange layer on top of whipped cream mixture in each glass. Top with remaining cream mixture divided equally among glasses. Sprinkle raspberries over top of each. Refrigerate until ready to serve. Serves 4..

 Sweet Potato Capital of the World   Vardamon, Mississippi

Orange Bavarian Cream

1½ cups vanilla wafer crumbs (about 34 wafers), divided
2 (6 ounce) cartons orange yogurt
1 (3.5 ounce) package vanilla instant pudding mix
¼ cup powdered sugar
1 (8 ounce) carton frozen whipped topping, thawed
½ teaspoon orange flavoring
3 (11 ounce) cans mandarin oranges, drained, divided

★ Crush vanilla wafers in food processor or crush in resealable plastic bag. Beat yogurt and pudding mix in bowl for 30 seconds. Fold in powdered sugar, whipped topping and orange flavoring.

★ Layer mixture in 8 parfait glasses with oranges and crushed vanilla wafers. Save enough orange slices and crumbs to top each serving. Serves 8.

Coffee Surprise

*This is a super dessert – no slicing, no "dishing up" –
just bring it right from the fridge to the table.*

1 (10 ounce) package large marshmallows
1 cup strong brewed coffee
1 (8 ounce) package chopped dates
1¼ cups chopped pecans
1 (8 ounce) carton whipping cream, whipped

★ Melt marshmallows in hot coffee. Add dates and pecans and refrigerate. When mixture thickens, fold in whipped cream. Pour into 6 sherbet glasses. Place plastic wrap over top and refrigerate. Serves 6.

Twinkies Dessert

1 (10 count) box Twinkies®
4 bananas, sliced
1 (5 ounce) package vanilla instant pudding, prepared
1 (20 ounce) can crushed pineapple, drained
1 (8 ounce) carton frozen whipped topping, thawed

★ Slice Twinkies® in half lengthwise and place in sprayed 9 x 13-inch pan cream-side up. Layer sliced bananas.

★ Pour vanilla pudding over bananas and add pineapple. Top with whipped topping and refrigerate. Cut into squares to serve. Serves 8 to 10.

*Johnny Appleseed (1774-1845) was born
John Chapman in Leominster, Massachusetts.
For 49 years, he planted apple trees from New
England to the Ohio Valley. He is the Official
State Folk Hero of Massachusetts.*

Toffee-Cream Surprise

1 cup buttermilk*
1 (3 ounce) package French vanilla instant pudding
1 (12 ounce) carton frozen whipped topping, thawed
1 (12 ounce) package toffee toppers, fudge covered, shortbread cookies
1 (10 ounce) jar maraschino cherries, drained, halved
1 cup chopped pecans
1 cup miniature marshmallows

★ Combine buttermilk and vanilla pudding in bowl. Beat with whisk until it mixes thoroughly. Fold in whipped topping.

★ Lightly crumble cookies with knife blade of food processor. Don't pulverize cookies. You may have to break a few cookies up by hand. Leave some cookies in chunks.

★ Fold cookies, cherries, pecans and marshmallows into pudding mixture. Refrigerate in covered bowl and serve in individual sherbet dishes. Best served same day. Serves 12.

TIP: To make buttermilk, mix 1 cup with 1 tablespoon lemon juice or vinegar and let milk stand for about 10 minutes.

Charlotte Russe

1 tablespoon unflavored gelatin
½ cup milk, warm
1 (8 ounce) carton whipping cream
¼ cup sugar
½ jigger (1½ tablespoons) brandy
Ladyfingers or pound cake

★ Dissolve gelatin in warm milk in bowl and cool slightly. In separate bowl, whip cream and add sugar and brandy.

★ Fold whipped cream mixture into gelatin mixture and pour into dish lined with ladyfingers or thinly sliced pound cake. Refrigerate for 3 to 4 hours or until well set. Serves 6 to 8.

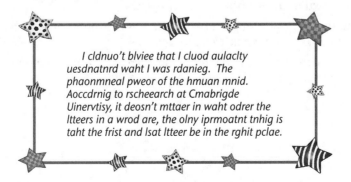

I cldnuo't blviee that I cluod aulaclty uesdnatnrd waht I was rdanieg. The phaonmneal pweor of the hmuan mnid. Aoccdrnig to rscheearch at Cmabrigde Uinervtisy, it deosn't mttaer in waht odrer the ltteers in a wrod are, the olny iprmoatnt tnhig is taht the frist and lsat ltteer be in the rghit pclae.

Old-Fashioned Apple Pandowdy

This old-fashioned apple dessert may have received its name because it is so simple and not all that pretty, but its taste keeps people coming back for more.

3 cups peeled, sliced apples
½ cup molasses
¾ teaspoon cinnamon
½ teaspoon nutmeg
½ cup (1 stick) butter, melted
½ cup milk
1 egg
½ cup sugar
1½ cups flour
2 teaspoons baking powder

★ Preheat oven to 350°. Mix apples, molasses, cinnamon and nutmeg in sprayed 2-quart baking dish. Bake for 20 minutes.

★ Whisk butter, milk, egg and sugar in bowl and set aside. Mix flour, baking powder and ½ teaspoon salt. Pour into milk mixture and mix well. Pour over apple mixture and bake for about 30 minutes or until bubbly. Serves 6 to 8.

Apple Dumplings

1½ cups packed brown sugar, divided
¼ cup chopped pecans
2 tablespoons butter, softened
6 baking apples, cored
1 (15 ounce) package refrigerated piecrusts

★ Preheat oven to 425°. Mix ½ cup packed brown sugar, pecans and butter in bowl and spoon mixture into each apple. Roll piecrusts to ⅛-inch thickness.

★ Cut into 6 squares approximately 7 inches each. Wrap 1 square around each apple, pinch edges to seal and place in baking dish. Place remaining 1 cup packed brown sugar and ½ cup water in saucepan over medium heat and stir until sugar dissolves.

★ Pour syrup over dumplings. Bake for 35 to 40 minutes or until tender and baste occasionally with syrup. Serves 6.

TIP: For even more flavorful dumplings, add 1 teaspoon ground cinnamon or apple pie spice along with sugar, pecans and butter.

Apple Bake

1 (8 ounce) can refrigerated crescent dinner rolls
3 tablespoons plus ½ cup sugar, divided
2 teaspoons ground cinnamon, divided
1 apple, peeled, cored
½ cup whipping cream
1 tablespoon almond extract
1 egg, beaten
½ cup sliced almonds

★ Preheat oven to 375°.

★ Separate crescent dinner rolls and place on sprayed baking sheet. Flatten each roll into 8 triangles, but do not let them touch.

★ Mix 3 tablespoons sugar and 1 teaspoon cinnamon in small bowl. Sprinkle mixture over each triangle and pat into dough.

★ Cut apple into 8 slices and place each slice on wide end of triangle. Wrap sides on left and right over apple and roll starting with wide end. Press and seal seams.

★ Place each triangle seam-side down around 9-inch round baking dish with 1 in middle. Bake for 15 to 20 minutes.

★ Mix ½ cup sugar, whipping cream, almond extract and egg in bowl with whisk until ingredients blend well.

★ Drizzle mixture evenly over apples. Sprinkle almonds and remaining 1 teaspoon cinnamon over top.

★ Bake for additional 14 to 15 minutes or until golden brown. If necessary, cover pan with foil during last 5 minutes of baking time to prevent excessive browning. Serve warm. Serves 8.

Blueberry Souffle

2 tablespoons butter, melted
3 tablespoons flour
1 cup milk
¼ cup sugar
⅔ cup blueberries
3 egg yolks
3 egg whites, stiffly beaten

★ Preheat oven to 350°. Blend butter and flour. Add milk slowly and bring to a boil, stirring constantly. Add sugar and ½ teaspoon salt. Mix blueberries with 3 tablespoons hot water and add to mixture. Cool.

★ Add egg yolks and beat until light. Fold in egg whites. Turn into 8-inch sprayed baking pan. Set in a larger sized pan of hot water. Bake for 40 to 45 minutes. Serves 6.

Old-Fashioned Ice Cream

4 large eggs, separated
2 tablespoons flour
2¾ cups sugar
1 tablespoon vanilla
3 quarts milk, divided
1 gallon freezer container
1 (1 pint) carton whipping cream
Rock salt

★ Beat egg yolks in bowl until light and fluffy. In separate bowl, combine flour, sugar and vanilla, add to egg yolks and 1 quart milk and beat well.

★ In separate bowl, beat egg whites until stiff and fold into yolk-milk mixture. Pour into double boiler and heat, stirring constantly, until mixture thickens. Pour into ice cream freezer.

★ Add whipping cream and enough milk to reach 3 inches from top of freezer. Cover tightly and pack freezer with ice and rock salt and freeze. Serves 10 to 14.

TIP: To make peach, banana or peppermint ice cream, add 2 cups diced fruit before adding remaining milk.

Buttermilk Ice Cream

1 quart buttermilk*
1 pint whipping cream
1 teaspoon vanilla
1 cup sugar

★ Combine buttermilk, whipping cream, vanilla, ¼ teaspoon salt and sugar in bowl and stir until sugar dissolves. Pour into ice trays and freeze. When cream is partially frozen, remove from freezer and beat. Return to trays and freeze. Serves 6.

*TIP: To make 1 quart buttermilk, mix 1 quart milk with ¼ cup lemon juice or vinegar and let milk stand for about 10 minutes.

Homemade Ice Cream Additions

★ Just add any of these extras to homemade ice cream for a surprise treat.

Marmalade	Rhubarb
Fresh mint	Crushed toffee bits
Crushed peppermint	Avocado
Pistachios	Coffee syrup

Homemade Peach Ice Cream

1½ quarts mashed, ripe peaches
2 tablespoons vanilla
2 (14 ounce) cans sweetened condensed milk
1 (12 ounce) can evaporated milk
½ cup sugar
½ gallon milk

★ Combine peaches, vanilla, ½ teaspoon salt, sweetened condensed milk, evaporated milk and sugar in ice cream freezer container and mix well. Add milk to mixture line in container. Freeze according to manufacturer's directions. Serves 10 to 12.

Mango Cream

2 ripe, soft mangoes
½ gallon vanilla ice cream, softened
1 (6 ounce) can frozen lemonade concentrate, thawed
1 (8 ounce) carton frozen whipped topping, thawed

★ Peel mangoes, cut slices around seed and chop slices. Mix ice cream, lemonade and whipped topping in large bowl and fold in mango chunks.

★ Quickly spoon mixture into parfait glasses, cover with plastic wrap and freeze. Serves 8 to 10.

Banana Split Sundae

1 firm banana
1 scoop each: vanilla, chocolate, strawberry ice cream
2 tablespoons each: chocolate syrup, strawberry syrup, butterscotch sauce
Whipped cream
Maraschino cherries with stems
2 tablespoons chopped nuts

★ Peel banana and slice in 2 pieces lengthwise. Put 1 scoop each of vanilla, chocolate and strawberry ice cream between slices of banana. Pour chocolate syrup, strawberry syrup and butterscotch sauce over scoops of ice cream. Top with whipped cream, maraschino cherries and nuts.

The first soft-serve ice cream machine was used in a Dairy Queen in Olympia, Washington.

Hot Fudge Sundae

1 cup semi-sweet chocolate chips
1 tablespoon butter
¼ cup sugar
½ cup evaporated milk
Vanilla ice cream
Chopped nuts
Frozen whipped topping, thawed
Maraschino cherries

★ In heavy saucepan over low heat, melt chocolate, butter and sugar, stirring constantly. Remove from heat, pour in milk and stir until smooth.

★ In separate bowl, place 1 or 2 scoops vanilla ice cream, pour hot fudge over top, sprinkle nuts, whipped topping and maraschino cherry on top. Serve immediately.

Ice Cream with Hot Raspberry Sauce

2 pints fresh raspberries
¾ cup sugar
2 tablespoons cornstarch
Ice cream

★ Soak raspberries with sugar in ½ cup water in saucepan for about 20 minutes. Pour small amount of water from raspberries into small cup. Add cornstarch and stir well to dissolve cornstarch and any lumps.

★ Pour raspberries and cornstarch mixture into blender and process to desired consistency. Strain over saucepan while pouring processed raspberries into saucepan.

★ Bring to a boil, reduce heat to low and cook for 2 to 4 minutes or until sauce thickens; stir constantly. Serve over ice cream. Serves 4.

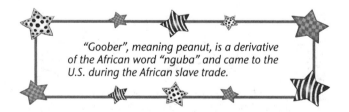

"Goober", meaning peanut, is a derivative of the African word "nguba" and came to the U.S. during the African slave trade.

Peach Sauce

6 cups fresh peaches, peeled, sliced
¾ cup sugar
¼ teaspoon ground cinnamon
Pound cake or ice cream

★ Combine peaches and 1 cup water in large saucepan and cook over medium heat for 10 minutes. Reduce heat, cover and simmer for additional 10 minutes. Cool.

★ Combine peaches, sugar and cinnamon in blender and process until smooth and creamy. Pour mixture into pint jars and refrigerate. Serve over pound cake or ice cream. Yields 2 pints.

Butter Pecan Sauce

¾ cup pecan pieces
1 - 2 tablespoons butter
¾ cup pack brown sugar
¼ cup cornstarch
¾ cup whipping cream
Ice cream

★ Preheat oven to 300°. Place pecan pieces on baking pan and toast in oven for about 15 minutes. Remove, cool and process into small pieces, but not ground.

★ Melt butter in saucepan and add brown sugar, cornstarch and pecans. Stir constantly over medium heat and cook until mixtures starts to thicken.

★ Add whipping cream and continue to cook until it almost boils, reduce heat and stir until it reaches sauce consistency. Remove from heat, cool slightly and pour over ice cream. Yields 1 cup.

Peach or Apricot Fritters

1 cup flour
1½ teaspoons baking powder
2 tablespoons sugar
½ cup milk
1 egg, well beaten
5 - 6 tart peaches or apricots, pitted, quartered
Canola oil
Powdered sugar

★ Sift flour, baking powder, sugar and ½ teaspoon salt in bowl. Add milk and egg and mix well. Dip each piece of fruit in batter and fry in deep hot fat, 340° to 375°, until brown. Drain on paper towels and sprinkle with powdered sugar. Yields 20 to 24 fritters.

TIP: If you don't have a thermometer for your oil, just heat oil until a drop of water splatters if dropped in oil.

Sopapillas

Sopapillas are puffy, deep-fried, "pillows"
of dough, traditionally served with honey.

4 cups flour
1 tablespoon baking powder
1 tablespoon sugar
3 tablespoons shortening
Powdered sugar
Canola oil
Honey

★ Combine flour, baking powder, 2 teaspoons salt and sugar in large bowl. Cut in shortening, stir and add just enough water to make doughy. Let stand for 15 minutes.

★ Layout wax paper on counter, spread powdered sugar lightly on surface and roll out dough to about ¼ inch thickness. Cut into 3 inch squares.

★ Heat oil in deep-fryer, drop squares into oil and cook until golden brown. Drain on paper towels. Serve with honey.

TIP: *Sopapillas may also be rolled in mixture of ½ cup sugar mixed with 1 tablespoon ground cinnamon.*

Easy Cinnamon Crisps

Flour tortillas
Canola oil
Sugar
Ground cinnamon

★ Cut tortillas into wedges and carefully place in large skillet with hot oil. Fry until golden brown, remove from skillet and drain on paper towels. Sprinkle both sides of tortilla wedges heavily with sugar and cinnamon.

Fast food in American originated with small, cheap hamburgers called sliders sold at the White Castle in Wichita, Kansas in 1916. The hamburger place grew to encompass much of the Midwest and northeast. It wasn't until after World War II when people had shiny new cars that more fast food restaurants came on the scene. In 1948 the McDonald brothers started a hamburger joint without tables and chairs and people sat in their cars to eat their hamburgers. As McDonald's grew, more hamburger fast food restaurant popped up in chains across the country: Burger King, Jack-in-the-Box, Wendy's franchises led the way for Arby's, Church's and dozens more.

Funnel Cakes

Funnel cakes are one of the most popular treats at fairs and festivals.

1⅔ cups flour
¾ teaspoon baking soda
½ teaspoon cream of tartar
2 tablespoons sugar
1 cup milk
1 egg
Canola oil
¼ cup powdered sugar

★ Mix flour, baking soda, cream of tartar, sugar and ¼ teaspoon salt in large bowl. In separate bowl, beat milk and egg. Pour into dry mixture and beat until smooth and creamy.

★ Heat several inches of oil in large skillet. Pour ¾ cup batter into funnel while holding funnel closed. When oil is hot enough, remove finger from hole and let batter stream through funnel. Make circular motions with funnel so batter crosses and overlaps itself forming a lattice pattern.

★ Fry until golden brown, flip and brown other side. Drain on paper towels and sprinkle with powdered sugar. Eat immediately. Serves about 8.

Crullers

The Dutch brought us cookies and crullers, a form of doughnut,
very popular in the North, Northeast and California.

¼ cup (½ stick) butter, softened
1 cup sugar
2 eggs, beaten
1 cup milk
3½ teaspoons baking powder
1 teaspoon nutmeg
Flour
Canola oil
Powdered sugar

★ Cream butter, sugar and eggs. Sift baking powder, nutmeg, and ½ teaspoon salt with 1 cup flour and add alternatively with milk to first mixture. Add additional flour to make dough stiff.

★ On floured board, roll dough ½-inch thick and cut into strips. Twist strips and place in sizzling hot oil until golden. Drain on paper towels. When cool, roll in powdered sugar. Yields 3 dozen.

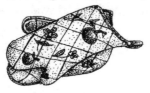

Sweets – Candies

Peanut Butter Haystacks

1 cup sugar
¾ cup light corn syrup
1 (16 ounce) jar crunchy peanut butter
4½ cups chow mein noodles

★ In saucepan over medium heat, bring sugar and corn syrup to boil and stir in peanut butter. Remove from heat and stir in noodles. Drop by spoonfuls onto wax paper and allow to cool. Yields about 2 dozen.

Tumbleweeds

1 (12 ounce) package butterscotch chips
¼ cup peanut butter
1 (12 ounce) can peanuts
1 (4 ounce) can shoe-string potatoes

★ Melt butterscotch chips with peanut butter in saucepan over low heat and mix well. Stir in peanuts and shoe-string potatoes. Drop tablespoonfuls of mixture onto wax paper. Store in airtight container. Yields about 2 dozen.

Peanut Krispies

½ cup (1 stick) butter
2 cups peanut butter
1 (1 pound) box powdered sugar
3½ cups rice crispy cereal
¾ cup chopped peanuts

★ Melt butter in large saucepan. Add peanut butter and powdered sugar and mix well. Add cereal and peanuts and mix well. Drop teaspoonfuls of mixture onto wax paper. Yields 2 to 3 dozen.

Orange Coconut Stacks

1 (1 pound) package orange slices
2 cups flaked coconut
1 cup chopped pecans
1 (14 ounce) can sweetened condensed milk
2 cups powdered sugar

★ Preheat oven to 350°. Cut orange slices into small pieces and put in baking dish with coconut, pecans and sweetened condensed milk.

★ Bake for 10 to 15 minutes or until bubbly. Add powdered sugar and mix well. Drop teaspoonfuls of mixture onto wax paper. Yields 3 dozen.

Crunchy Peanut Brittle

2 cups sugar
½ cup light corn syrup
2 cups dry-roasted peanuts
1 tablespoon butter
1 teaspoon baking soda

★ Combine sugar and corn syrup in saucepan. Cook over low heat and stir constantly until sugar dissolves. Cover and cook over medium heat for additional 2 minutes.

★ Add peanuts and cook uncovered, stirring occasionally, to hard-crack stage (300°). Stir in butter and baking soda. Pour into sprayed jellyroll pan and spread thinly. Cool and break into pieces. Yields 3 dozen pieces.

Candied Pecans

1 (16 ounce) box light brown sugar
2 teaspoons ground cinnamon
1 teaspoon vanilla
4 cups pecan halves

★ Combine brown sugar and cinnamon in medium saucepan and add ½ cup water. Cook until mixture reaches soft-ball stage (234-243°) when dropped into cold water.

★ Cook for 15 minutes and add vanilla and pecan halves. Stir until pecans coat well and syrup is thick. Pour immediately onto wax paper and separate halves immediately. Store in airtight container. Yields 4 cups.

No-Fail Fudge

1⅓ cups sugar
⅔ cup evaporated milk
¼ cup (½ stick) butter
1 (7 ounce) jar marshmallow creme
1 (12 ounce) package semi-sweet chocolate pieces
1 teaspoon vanilla
1 cup chopped walnuts

★ Combine sugar, evaporated milk, butter, marshmallow creme and ¼ teaspoon salt in large saucepan over medium-high heat. Stir constantly while fudge cooks on a low boil for exactly 5 minutes.

★ Remove from heat, add chocolate pieces and vanilla. Stir until chocolate melts. Stir in walnuts. Pour into buttered 8-inch square pan. Cool and cut into squares. Yields 2 pounds.

White Chocolate Fudge

1 (8 ounce) package cream cheese, softened
4 cups powdered sugar
1½ teaspoons vanilla
12 ounces almond bark, melted
¾ cup chopped pecans

★ Beat cream cheese in bowl on medium speed until smooth, gradually add powdered sugar and vanilla and beat well to mix. Stir in melted almond bark and pecans. Spread into sprayed 8-inch square pan. Refrigerate until firm. Yields 12 squares.

Chocolate Leaves

4 ounces semi-sweet chocolate pieces
Non-poisonous leaves with well-defined veins and at least ¼-inch stems

★ Melt chocolate. Wash leaves and dry. Brush melted chocolate on backs of leaves with clean ½-inch artist's brush. Put in freezer for 2 to 3 minutes or until hard enough to peel leaf from chocolate.

★ Place chocolate leaves in plastic bag with air in it to cushion leaves. Keep refrigerated until needed. To keep leaves for longer time, use 6 ounces melted semi-sweet chocolate combined with block of melted paraffin and follow preceding directions.

TIP: A camellia leaf is a good choice because of its size. Rose, lemon, orange, bay, ficus and holly leaves are also good.

Date-Nut Loaf Candy

6 cups sugar
1 (12 ounce) can evaporated milk
½ cup light corn syrup
1 cup (2 sticks) butter
2 (8 ounce) boxes chopped dates
3 cups chopped pecans or walnuts
1 tablespoon vanilla

★ Cook sugar, evaporated milk, corn syrup and butter in saucepan for 5 minutes or until it boils. Stir constantly with wooden or plastic spoon so mixture will not scorch.

★ Add dates and cook until it forms soft-ball stage in cup of cold water (234°). Remove from heat and beat until thick. Add pecans and vanilla and stir until very thick.

★ Spoon out mixture onto damp cup towel to make roll. Keep wrapped until it is firm enough to slice.

Sugar Plum Candy

1¼ pounds almond bark, chopped
1½ cups red and green miniature marshmallows
1½ cups peanut butter cereal
1½ cups rice crispy cereal
1½ cups mixed nuts

★ Melt almond bark in double boiler over low heat. Place marshmallows, cereals and nuts in large bowl. Pour melted bark over mixture and stir to coat.

★ Drop teaspoonfuls of mixture onto wax paper-lined cookie sheet. Let stand until set and store in airtight container. Yields 3 dozen.

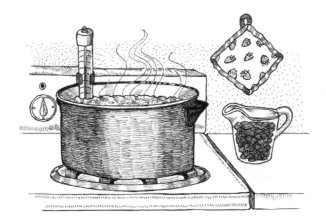

Index

G

O

Q

R

W

Y

Z

Cookbooks Published by Cookbook Resources, LLC
Bringing Family and Friends to the Table

The Best 1001 Short, Easy Recipes
1001 Slow Cooker Recipes
1001 Short, Easy, Inexpensive Recipes
1001 Fast Easy Recipes
1001 America's Favorite Recipes
Easy Slow Cooker Cookbook
Busy Woman's Slow Cooker Recipes
Busy Woman's Quick & Easy Recipes
365 Easy Soups and Stews
365 Easy Chicken Recipes
365 Easy One-Dish Recipes
365 Easy Soup Recipes
365 Easy Vegetarian Recipes
365 Easy Casserole Recipes
365 Easy Pasta Recipes
365 Easy Slow Cooker Recipes
Super Simple Cupcake Recipes
Leaving Home Cookbook
and Survival Guide
Essential 3-4-5 Ingredient Recipes
Ultimate 4 Ingredient Cookbook
Easy Cooking with 5 Ingredients
The Best of Cooking with 3 Ingredients
Easy Diabetic Recipes
Ultimate 4 Ingredient
Diabetic Cookbook
4-Ingredient Recipes
for 30-Minute Meals
Cooking with Beer
The Washington Cookbook
The Pennsylvania Cookbook
The California Cookbook
Best-Loved New England Recipes
Best-Loved Canadian Recipes
Best-Loved Recipes
from the Pacific Northwest

Easy Slow Cooker Recipes
(Handbook with Photos)
Cool Smoothies (Handbook with Photos)
Easy Cupcake Recipes
(Handbook with Photos)
Easy Soup Recipes
(Handbook with Photos)
Classic Tex-Mex and Texas Cooking
Best-Loved Southern Recipes
Classic Southwest Cooking
Miss Sadie's Southern Cooking
Classic Pennsylvania Dutch Cooking
The Quilters' Cookbook
Healthy Cooking with 4 Ingredients
Trophy Hunter's Wild Game Cookbook
Recipe Keeper
Simple Old-Fashioned Baking
Quick Fixes with Cake Mixes
Kitchen Keepsakes
& More Kitchen Keepsakes
Cookbook 25 Years
Texas Longhorn Cookbook
Gifts for the Cookie Jar
All New Gifts for the Cookie Jar
The Big Bake Sale Cookbook
Easy One-Dish Meals
Easy Potluck Recipes
Easy Casseroles Cookbook
Easy Desserts
Sunday Night Suppers
Easy Church Suppers
365 Easy Meals
Gourmet Cooking with 5 Ingredients
Muffins In A Jar
A Little Taste of Texas
A Little Taste of Texas II
Ultimate Gifts for the Cookie Jar

cookbook
resources LLC

www.cookbookresources.com
Toll-Free 866-229-2665
Your Ultimate Source for Easy Cookbooks

1001 AMERICA'S FAVORITE RECIPES

Easy Time-Tested Family Recipes

cookbook resources LLC

www.cookbookresources.com

Toll-Free 866-229-2665

Your Ultimate Source for Easy Cookbooks